Focus on GRAMMAR 5

FOURTH EDITION

Jay Maurer

ALWAYS LEARNING

PEARSON

Focus on Grammar 5: An Integrated Skills Approach, Fourth Edition

Pearson Education, 10 Bank Street, White Plains, NY 10606

Staff credits: The people who made up the ***Focus on Grammar 5, Fourth Edition*** team, representing editorial, production, design, and manufacturing, are John Barnes, Andrea Bryant, Elizabeth Carlson, Tracey Cataldo, Aerin Csigay, Dave Dickey, Christine Edmonds, Nancy Flaggman, Ann France, Shelley Gazes, Lise Minovitz, Barbara Perez, Robert Ruvo, and Debbie Sistino.

Cover image: Shutterstock.com
Text composition: ElectraGraphics, Inc.
Text font: New Aster

Library of Congress Cataloging-in-Publication Data

Schoenberg, Irene, 1946–
Focus on grammar. 1: an integrated skills approach / Irene E. Schoenberg, Jay Maurer. -- 3rd ed.
p. cm.
Includes index.
ISBN 0-13-245591-9 — ISBN 0-13-254647-7 — ISBN 0-13-254648-5 — ISBN 0-13-254649-3 — ISBN 0-13-254650-7 1. English language—Textbooks for foreign speakers. 2. English language—Grammar—Problems, exercises, etc. I. Maurer, Jay. II. Title.
PE1128.S3456824 2011
428.2'4—dc22

2011014126

Printed in the United States of America

ISBN 10: 0-13-254650-7
ISBN 13: 978-0-13-254650-8

6 7 8 9 10—V082—16 15 14

ISBN 10: 0-13-216980-0 (with MyLab)
ISBN 13: 978-0-13-216980-6 (with MyLab)

1 2 3 4 5 6 7 8 9 10—V082—16 15 14 13 12 11

CONTENTS

WELCOME TO *FOCUS ON GRAMMAR*

Now in a new edition, the popular five-level ***Focus on Grammar*** course continues to provide an integrated-skills approach to help students understand and practice English grammar. Centered on thematic instruction, ***Focus on Grammar*** combines controlled and communicative practice with critical thinking skills and ongoing assessment. Students gain the confidence they need to speak and write English accurately and fluently.

NEW for the FOURTH EDITION

VOCABULARY

Key vocabulary is highlighted, practiced, and recycled throughout the unit.

PRONUNCIATION

Now, in every unit, pronunciation points and activities help students improve spoken accuracy and fluency.

LISTENING

Expanded listening tasks allow students to develop a range of listening skills.

UPDATED CHARTS and NOTES

Target structures are presented in a clear, easy-to-read format.

NEW READINGS

High-interest readings, updated or completely new, in a variety of genres integrate grammar and vocabulary in natural contexts.

NEW UNIT REVIEWS

Students can check their understanding and monitor their progress after completing each unit.

MyFocusOnGrammarLab

An easy-to-use online learning and assessment program offers online homework and individualized instruction anywhere, anytime.

Teacher's Resource Pack

One compact resource includes:

THE TEACHER'S MANUAL: General Teaching Notes, Unit Teaching Notes, the Student Book Audioscript, and the Student Book Answer Key.

TEACHER'S RESOURCE DISC: Bound into the Resource Pack, this CD-ROM contains reproducible Placement, Part, and Unit Tests, as well as customizable Test-Generating Software. It also includes reproducible Internet Activities and PowerPoint® Grammar Presentations.

THE *FOCUS ON GRAMMAR* APPROACH

The new edition follows the same successful four-step approach of previous editions. The books provide an abundance of both controlled and communicative exercises so that students can bridge the gap between identifying grammatical structures and using them. The many communicative activities in each Student Book provide opportunities for critical thinking while enabling students to personalize what they have learned.

- **Step 1: Grammar in Context** highlights the target structures in realistic contexts, such as conversations, magazine articles, and blog posts.
- **Step 2: Grammar Presentation** presents the structures in clear and accessible grammar charts and notes with multiple examples of form and usage.
- **Step 3: Focused Practice** provides numerous and varied controlled exercises for both the form and meaning of the new structures.
- **Step 4: Communication Practice** includes listening and pronunciation and allows students to use the new structures freely and creatively in motivating, open-ended speaking and writing activities.

Recycling

Underpinning the scope and sequence of the ***Focus on Grammar*** series is the belief that students need to use target structures and vocabulary many times, in different contexts. New grammar and vocabulary are recycled throughout the book. Students have maximum exposure and become confident using the language in speech and in writing.

Assessment

Extensive testing informs instruction and allows teachers and students to measure progress.

- **Unit Reviews** at the end of every Student Book unit assess students' understanding of the grammar and allow students to monitor their own progress.
- Easy to administer and score, **Part and Unit Tests** provide teachers with a valid and reliable means to determine how well students know the material they are about to study and to assess students' mastery after they complete the material. These tests can be found on MyFocusOnGrammarLab, where they include immediate feedback and remediation, and as reproducible tests on the Teacher's Resource Disc.
- **Test-Generating Software** on the Teacher's Resource Disc includes a bank of *additional* test items teachers can use to create customized tests.
- A reproducible **Placement Test** on the Teacher's Resource Disc is designed to help teachers place students into one of the five levels of the ***Focus on Grammar*** course.

COMPONENTS

In addition to the Student Books, Teacher's Resource Packs, and MyLabs, the complete ***Focus on Grammar*** course includes:

Workbooks Contain additional contextualized exercises appropriate for self-study.

Audio Program Includes all of the listening and pronunciation exercises and opening passages from the Student Book. Some Student Books are packaged with the complete audio program (mp3 files). Alternatively, the audio program is available on a classroom set of CDs and on the MyLab.

THE *FOCUS ON GRAMMAR* UNIT

Focus on Grammar introduces grammar structures in the context of unified themes. All units follow a **four-step approach**, taking learners from grammar in context to communicative practice.

STEP 1 GRAMMAR IN CONTEXT

This section presents the target structure(s) in a natural context. As students read the **high-interest texts**, they encounter the form, meaning, and use of the grammar. **Before You Read** activities create interest and elicit students' knowledge about the topic. **After You Read** activities build students' reading vocabulary and comprehension.

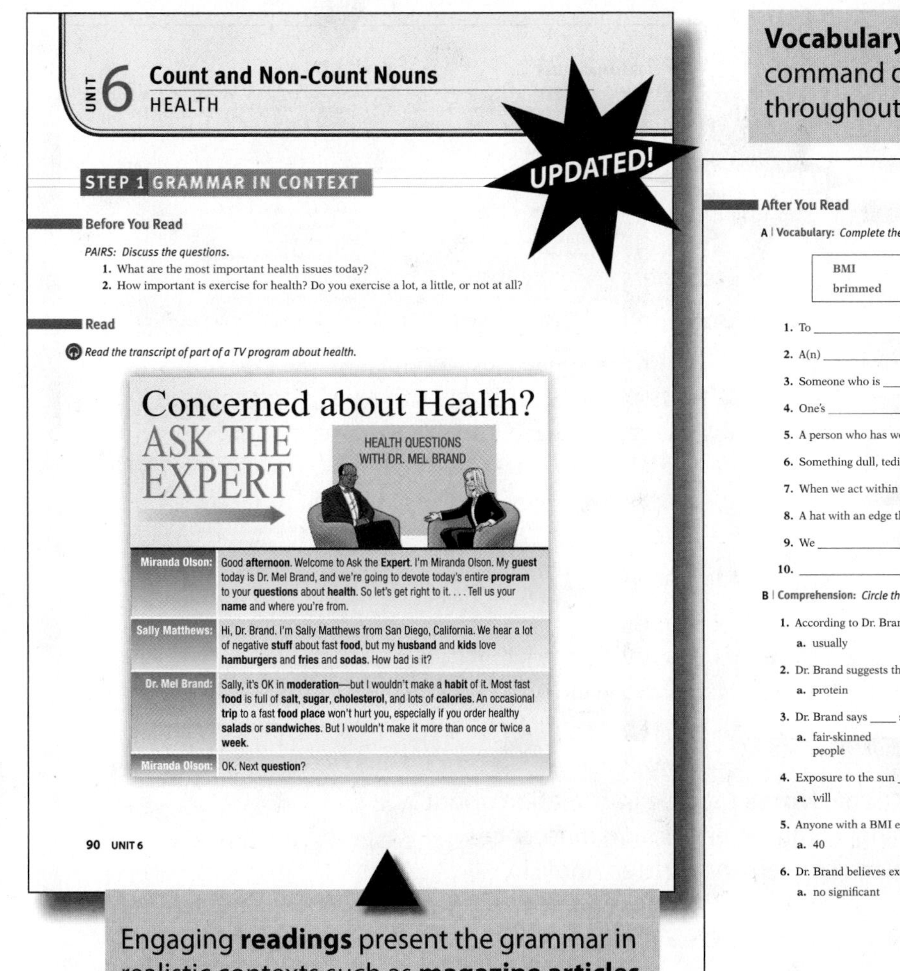

UNIT 6 Count and Non-Count Nouns
HEALTH

UPDATED!

STEP 1 GRAMMAR IN CONTEXT

Before You Read

PAIRS: Discuss the questions.

1. What are the most important health issues today?
2. How important is exercise for health? Do you exercise a lot, a little, or not at all?

Read

Read the transcript of part of a TV program about health.

Concerned about Health?
ASK THE EXPERT
HEALTH QUESTIONS WITH DR. MEL BRAND

Miranda Olson: Good **afternoon**. Welcome to Ask the **Expert**. I'm Miranda Olson. My **guest** today is Dr. Mel Brand, and we're going to devote today's entire **program** to your **questions** about **health**. So let's get right to it. . . . Tell us your **name** and where you're from.

Sally Matthews: Hi, Dr. Brand. I'm Sally Matthews from San Diego, California. We hear a lot of negative **stuff** about fast **food**, but my **husband** and **kids** love **hamburgers** and **fries** and **sodas**. How bad is it?

Dr. Mel Brand: Sally, it's OK in **moderation**—but I wouldn't make a **habit** of it. Most fast **food** is full of **salt**, **sugar**, **cholesterol**, and lots of **calories**. An occasional **trip** to a fast **food place** won't hurt you, especially if you order healthy **salads** or **sandwiches**. But I wouldn't make it more than once or twice a **week**.

Miranda Olson: OK. Next **question**?

90 UNIT 6

Engaging **readings** present the grammar in realistic contexts such as **magazine articles** and **blog posts**.

Vocabulary exercises improve students' command of English. Vocabulary is **recycled** throughout the unit.

NEW!

After You Read

A | Vocabulary: *Complete the definitions with the correct word or phrase from the box.*

BMI	champ	drag	obese	sunblock
brimmed	devote	in moderation	side with	telling

1. To _______________ someone is to agree with that person.
2. A(n) _______________ example or argument is one that is very effective.
3. Someone who is _______________ is very much overweight.
4. One's _______________ is a numerical measurement of body fat.
5. A person who has won competitions is a(n) _______________.
6. Something dull, tedious, or uninteresting is called a(n) _______________.
7. When we act within reasonable limits we do things _______________.
8. A hat with an edge that gives protection or shade is said to be _______________.
9. We _______________ our time or attention to an activity when we focus on it completely.
10. _______________ is a cream or oil for your skin that prevents sunburn.

B | Comprehension: *Circle the letter of the correct answer.*

1. According to Dr. Brand, consuming fast food is ____ OK.
   a. usually b. occasionally c. never d. always
2. Dr. Brand suggests that too much ____ in food is not beneficial.
   a. protein b. calcium c. fiber d. cholesterol
3. Dr. Brand says ____ should wear sunblock if they spend time in the sun.
   a. fair-skinned people b. dark- skinned people c. people over 40 d. everyone
4. Exposure to the sun ____ cause skin cancer.
   a. will b. shouldn't c. can d. won't usually
5. Anyone with a BMI exceeding ____ is considered overweight.
   a. 40 b. 35 c. 25 d. 20
6. Dr. Brand believes exercise is of ____ importance to someone overweight.
   a. no significant b. great c. some d. minimal

92 UNIT 6

Reading comprehension tasks focus on the meaning of the text and draw students' attention to the target structure.

STEP 2 GRAMMAR PRESENTATION

This section gives students a comprehensive and explicit overview of the grammar with detailed **Grammar Charts** and **Grammar Notes** that present the form, meaning, and use of the structure(s).

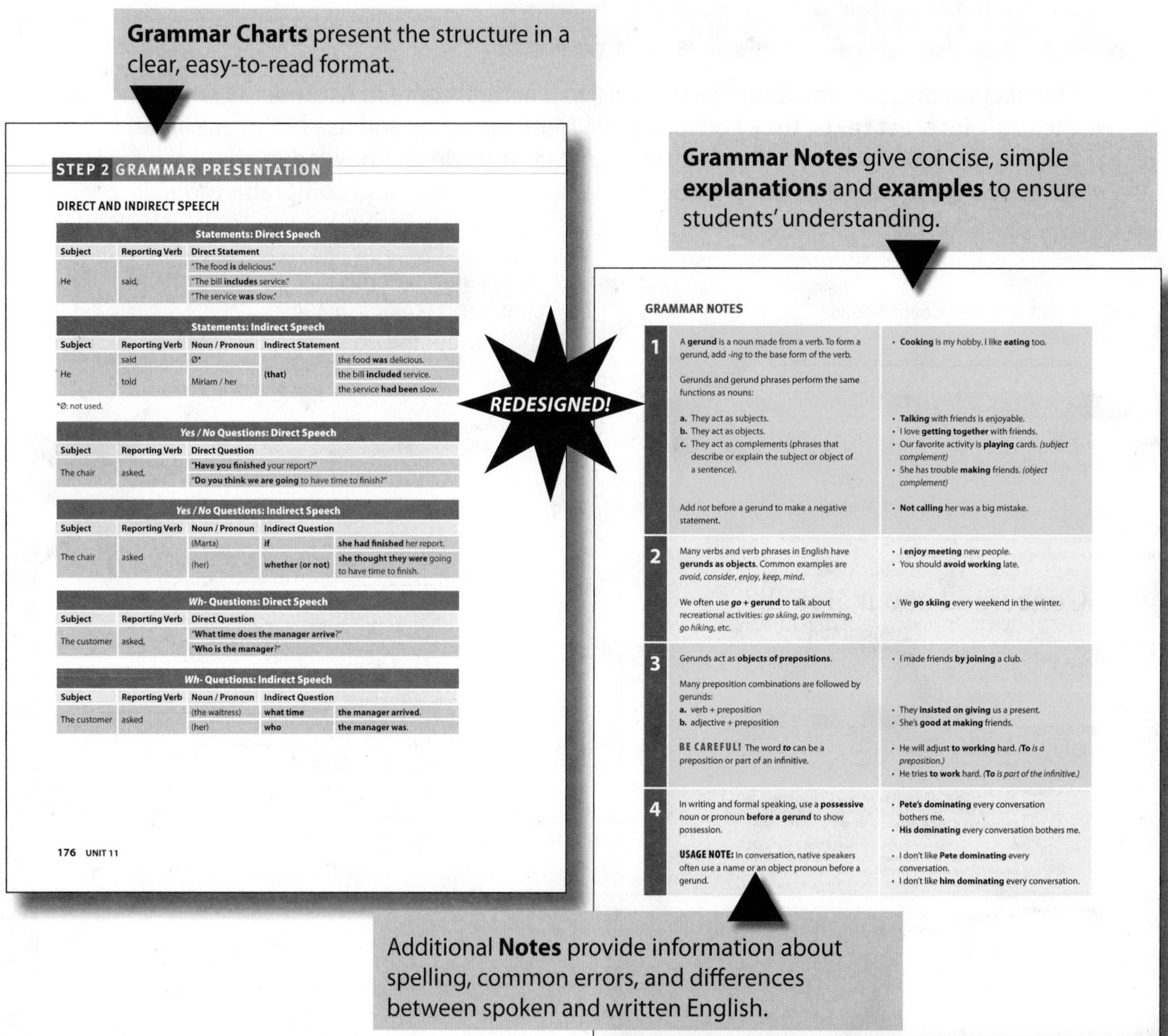

Grammar Charts present the structure in a clear, easy-to-read format.
Grammar Notes give concise, simple **explanations** and **examples** to ensure students' understanding.
REDESIGNED!
Additional **Notes** provide information about spelling, common errors, and differences between spoken and written English.

STEP 2 GRAMMAR PRESENTATION

DIRECT AND INDIRECT SPEECH

Statements: Direct Speech		
Subject	**Reporting Verb**	**Direct Statement**
He	said,	"The food **is** delicious."
		"The bill **includes** service."
		"The service **was** slow."

Statements: Indirect Speech				
Subject	**Reporting Verb**	**Noun / Pronoun**	**Indirect Statement**	
He	said	Ø*	(that)	the food **was** delicious.
	told	Miriam / her		the bill **included** service.
				the service **had been** slow.

*Ø: not used.

Yes / No Questions: Direct Speech		
Subject	**Reporting Verb**	**Direct Question**
The chair	asked,	"**Have you finished** your report?"
		"**Do you think we are going** to have time to finish?"

Yes / No Questions: Indirect Speech				
Subject	**Reporting Verb**	**Noun / Pronoun**	**Indirect Question**	
The chair	asked	(Marta)	if	**she had finished** her report.
		(her)	whether (or not)	**she thought they were** going to have time to finish.

Wh- Questions: Direct Speech		
Subject	**Reporting Verb**	**Direct Question**
The customer	asked,	"**What time does the manager arrive?**"
		"**Who is the manager?**"

Wh- Questions: Indirect Speech				
Subject	**Reporting Verb**	**Noun / Pronoun**	**Indirect Question**	
The customer	asked	(the waitress)	what time	**the manager arrived.**
		(her)	who	**the manager was.**

176 UNIT 11

GRAMMAR NOTES

1	A **gerund** is a noun made from a verb. To form a gerund, add *-ing* to the base form of the verb.	• **Cooking** is my hobby. I like **eating** too.
	Gerunds and gerund phrases perform the same functions as nouns:	
	a. They act as subjects. **b.** They act as objects. **c.** They act as complements (phrases that describe or explain the subject or object of a sentence).	• **Talking** with friends is enjoyable. • I love **getting together** with friends. • Our favorite activity is **playing** cards. *(subject complement)* • She has trouble **making** friends. *(object complement)*
	Add *not* before a gerund to make a negative statement.	• **Not calling** her was a big mistake.
2	Many verbs and verb phrases in English have **gerunds as objects.** Common examples are *avoid, consider, enjoy, keep, mind.*	• I **enjoy meeting** new people. • You should **avoid working** late.
	We often use ***go* + gerund** to talk about recreational activities: *go skiing, go swimming, go hiking,* etc.	• We **go skiing** every weekend in the winter.
3	Gerunds act as **objects of prepositions.**	• I made friends **by joining** a club.
	Many preposition combinations are followed by gerunds: **a.** verb + preposition **b.** adjective + preposition	• They **insisted on giving** us a present. • She's **good at making** friends.
	BE CAREFUL! The word ***to*** can be a preposition or part of an infinitive.	• He will adjust **to working** hard. *(**To** is a preposition.)* • He tries **to work** hard. *(**To** is part of the infinitive.)*
4	In writing and formal speaking, use a **possessive** noun or pronoun **before a gerund** to show possession.	• **Pete's dominating** every conversation bothers me. • **His dominating** every conversation bothers me.
	USAGE NOTE: In conversation, native speakers often use a name or an object pronoun before a gerund.	• I don't like **Pete dominating** every conversation. • I don't like **him dominating** every conversation.

STEP 3 FOCUSED PRACTICE

Controlled practice activities in this section lead students to master form, meaning, and use of the target grammar.

STEP 3 FOCUSED PRACTICE

EXERCISE 1: Discover the Grammar

A | *Read the sentences. Underline each noun clause and identify it as* **S** *(used as a subject),* **O** *(used as an object), or* **C** *(used as a complement).*

____ **1.** Moe was sure that the mansion would be her favorite gift.

____ **2.** What wasn't so admirable was their rivalry.

____ **3.** All I know is that the chicken you gave me was delicious.

____ **4.** Their mother said there was nothing she needed.

B | *Look at the sentences. Underline the embedded question in each. For each embedded question, write the direct question it was derived from.*

1. Each brother constantly tried to figure out how he could outdo the other two.

How can I outdo the other two?

2. Curly was wondering what he could do to top his brothers.

____

3. At first he wondered if he could afford it.

____

4. I don't know if you believed me.

____

5. I don't know what you mean.

____

EXERCISE 2: Embedded Questions *(Grammar Notes 4–7)*

Based on the exchanges in the chart, complete the story with embedded **yes / no** *and* **wh-***questions. Put the verbs in the simple past or the past perfect.*

1. A: Excuse me. How far is the nearest town? **B:** I don't know.
2. A: Well, what's the name of the nearest town? **B:** I'm not sure.
3. A: Can I borrow your cell phone? **B:** What's a cell phone?

162 UNIT 10

Discover the Grammar activities develop students' recognition and understanding of the target structure before they are asked to produce it.

A **variety of exercise types** engage students and guide them from recognition and understanding to accurate production of the grammar structures.

An **Editing** exercise ends every Focused Practice section and teaches students to find and correct typical mistakes.

EXERCISE 5: Editing

Read the letter. It has eight mistakes in the use of direct and indirect speech. The first mistake is already corrected. Find and correct seven more.

November 20

Dear Emily,

I just wanted to fill you in on Tim's school adventures. About two months ago Melanie said she ~~feels~~ felt we should switch Tim to the public school. He'd been in a private school for several months, as you know. I asked her why did she think that, and she said, "He's miserable where he is, and the quality of education is poor. He says he doesn't really have any friends." I couldn't help but agree. She said she thought we can move him to the local high school, which has a good academic reputation. I told that I agreed but that we should ask Tim. The next morning we asked Tim if he wanted to stay at the private school. I was surprised at how strong his response was. He said me that he hated the school and didn't want to go there any longer. So we changed him. He's been at the new school for a month now, and he's doing well. Whenever I ask him does he have his homework done, he says, "Dad, I've already finished it." He's made several new friends. Every now and then he asks us why didn't we let him change sooner. He says people are treating him as an individual now. I'm just glad we moved him when we did.

Not much else is new. Oh, yes—I do need to ask are you coming for the holidays. Write soon and let us know. Or call.

Love,

Charles

Direct and Indirect Speech **185**

STEP 4 COMMUNICATION PRACTICE

This section provides practice with the structure in **listening** and **pronunciation** exercises as well as in communicative, open-ended **speaking** and **writing** activities that move students toward fluency.

Listening activities allow students to hear the grammar in natural contexts and to practice a range of listening skills.

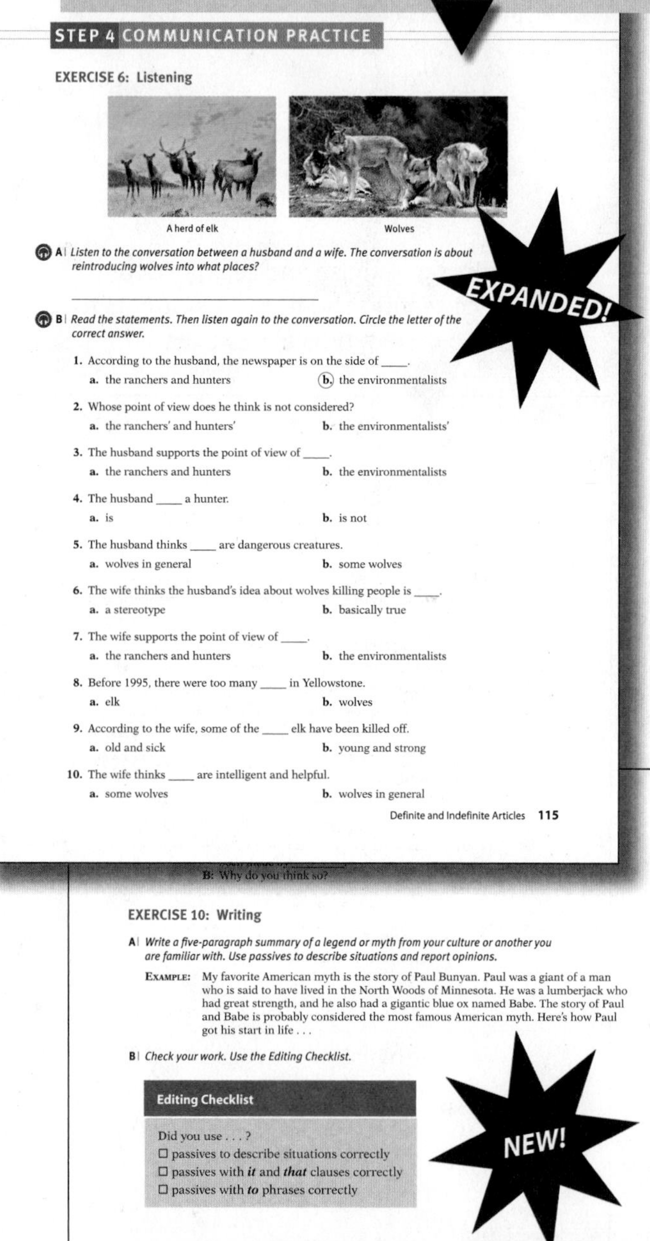

STEP 4 COMMUNICATION PRACTICE

EXERCISE 6: Listening

A herd of elk

Wolves

A | *Listen to the conversation between a husband and a wife. The conversation is about reintroducing wolves into what places?*

B | *Read the statements. Then listen again to the conversation. Circle the letter of the correct answer.*

1. According to the husband, the newspaper is on the side of ____.
   a. the ranchers and hunters (b.) the environmentalists
2. Whose point of view does he think is not considered?
   a. the ranchers' and hunters' b. the environmentalists'
3. The husband supports the point of view of ____.
   a. the ranchers and hunters b. the environmentalists
4. The husband ____ a hunter.
   a. is b. is not
5. The husband thinks ____ are dangerous creatures.
   a. wolves in general b. some wolves
6. The wife thinks the husband's idea about wolves killing people is ____.
   a. a stereotype b. basically true
7. The wife supports the point of view of ____.
   a. the ranchers and hunters b. the environmentalists
8. Before 1995, there were too many ____ in Yellowstone.
   a. elk b. wolves
9. According to the wife, some of the ____ elk have been killed off.
   a. old and sick b. young and strong
10. The wife thinks ____ are intelligent and helpful.
    a. some wolves b. wolves in general

Definite and Indefinite Articles 115

B: Why do you think so?

EXERCISE 10: Writing

A | *Write a five-paragraph summary of a legend or myth from your culture or another you are familiar with. Use passives to describe situations and report opinions.*

EXAMPLE: My favorite American myth is the story of Paul Bunyan. Paul was a giant of a man who is said to have lived in the North Woods of Minnesota. He was a lumberjack who had great strength, and he also had a gigantic blue ox named Babe. The story of Paul and Babe is probably considered the most famous American myth. Here's how Paul got his start in life . . .

B | *Check your work. Use the Editing Checklist.*

Editing Checklist

Did you use . . . ?
☐ passives to describe situations correctly
☐ passives with *it* and *that* clauses correctly
☐ passives with *to* phrases correctly

Pronunciation Notes and **exercises** improve students' spoken fluency and accuracy.

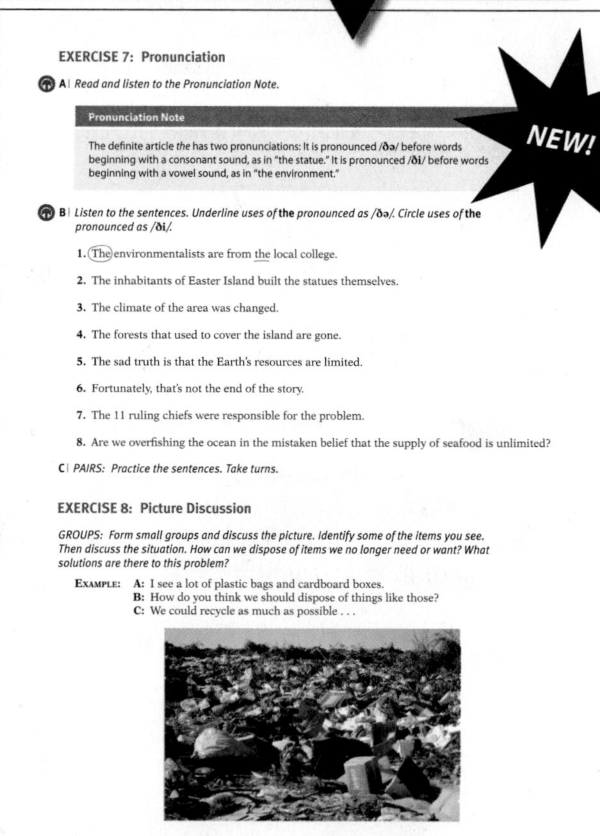

EXERCISE 7: Pronunciation

A | *Read and listen to the Pronunciation Note.*

Pronunciation Note

The definite article *the* has two pronunciations: It is pronounced /ðə/ before words beginning with a consonant sound, as in "the statue." It is pronounced /ði/ before words beginning with a vowel sound, as in "the environment."

B | *Listen to the sentences. Underline uses of* **the** *pronounced as /ðə/. Circle uses of* **the** *pronounced as /ði/.*

1. (The) environmentalists are from the local college.
2. The inhabitants of Easter Island built the statues themselves.
3. The climate of the area was changed.
4. The forests that used to cover the island are gone.
5. The sad truth is that the Earth's resources are limited.
6. Fortunately, that's not the end of the story.
7. The 11 ruling chiefs were responsible for the problem.
8. Are we overfishing the ocean in the mistaken belief that the supply of seafood is unlimited?

C | *PAIRS: Practice the sentences. Take turns.*

EXERCISE 8: Picture Discussion

GROUPS: Form small groups and discuss the picture. Identify some of the items you see. Then discuss the situation. How can we dispose of items we no longer need or want? What solutions are there to this problem?

EXAMPLE: A: I see a lot of plastic bags and cardboard boxes.
B: How do you think we should dispose of things like those?
C: We could recycle as much as possible . . .

116 UNIT 7

Writing activities encourage students to produce meaningful writing that integrates the grammar structure.

An **Editing Checklist** teaches students to correct their mistakes and revise their work.

Speaking activities help students synthesize the grammar through discussions, debates, games, and problem-solving tasks, developing their fluency.

Unit Reviews give students the opportunity to check their understanding of the target structure. **Answers** at the back of the book allow students to monitor their own progress.

UNIT 5 **Review**

Check your answers on page UR-1.
Do you need to review anything?

A | *Circle the correct word or phrase to complete each sentence.*

1. That must / may be the answer to the mystery. All evidence points to it.
2. Ellen might / will be here later, but I don't know for sure.
3. A monk must / might have made the trip, but the evidence isn't conclusive.
4. It couldn't / shouldn't have been Newfoundland, which is too far north.
5. We should / may find out what really happened later today. Louis says he knows.
6. You may not / ought not to have trouble solving the problem—you're good at math.
7. They had to / might have been home—I heard their music.
8. She might be / 's got to be the one who took it. No one else had access to it.
9. They had to be / must have been away last week. Their car was gone.
10. There must / might be a key around here somewhere. Dad said he had one.

B | *In the blank after each sentence, write a modal or modal-like expression of certainty with a meaning similar to the underlined phrase.*

1. It's possible that Jeremy had to work late. ______
2. It's very likely that Mari missed her flight. ______
3. It's impossible that they heard the news. ______
4. It's likely that we'll know the answer soon. ______
5. You had the opportunity to get a scholarship. ______

C | *Circle the letter of the one underlined word or phrase in each sentence that is not correct.*

1. Might (A) she have forgotten (B), or could she had (C) had to (D) work? A B C D
2. I think (A) Ed isn't (B) here because he should (C) be (D) sick.
3. Al can't (A) get (B) here by 7:00, but he shouldn't (C) make (D) it b
4. I suppose they couldn't (A) be working (B) late at the office didn't mention (C) it, and neither did (D) Mary.
5. I'm sorry; I could (A) had (B) called to say I'd be (C) late, but I

84 Unit 5 Review: Modals to Express Degrees of Certainty

Extended writing tasks help students integrate the grammar structure as they follow the steps of the **writing process**.

PART II

From Grammar to Writing
TOPIC SENTENCES

An important way to strengthen your writing is to provide a **topic sentence** for each paragraph. A topic sentence is a general sentence that covers the paragraph's content. All the supporting examples and details of the paragraph must fit logically under this sentence, which usually comes first.

EXAMPLE: **For me, a dog is a better pet than a cat.** When I come home from work, for example, my dog comes to meet me at the door. He is always glad to see me. My cat, on the other hand, couldn't care less whether I'm at home or not, as long as I keep filling her food dish. Another good thing about a dog is that you can teach him tricks. Cats, however, can't be bothered to learn anything new. The best thing about a dog, though, is that he's a great companion. I can take my dog on hikes and walks. He goes everywhere with me. As we all know, you can't take a cat for a walk.

The topic sentence for this paragraph tells the reader what to expect in the paragraph: some reasons why the writer considers a dog a superior pet.

1 | *Each of the word groups is a fragment but is also a potential topic sentence. Make necessary additions to each.*

EXAMPLE: Reasons why the legal driving age should be raised. (not an independent clause)
Correction: There are several reasons why the legal driving age should be raised.

1. A city where exciting and mysterious things happen.
______
2. Reasons why college isn't for everybody.
______
3. Wild animals not making good pets.
______
4. Regular exercise and its benefits.
______

2 | *Look at the following paragraphs containing supporting details but no topic sentences. For each set of details, write an appropriate topic sentence.*

1. ______
   a. For one thing, there's almost always a traffic jam I get stuck in, and I'm often late to work.
   b. Also, there's not always a parking place when I do get to work.
   c. Worst of all, I'm spending more money on gas and car maintenance than I would if I took public transportation.

(continued on next page)

From Grammar to Writing **85**

Scope and Sequence

UNIT	READING	WRITING	LISTENING
1 page 2 **Grammar:** Present Time **Theme:** The Digital World	An article: *Connected!*	Two or three paragraphs about electronic devices in your life	A conversation about identity theft
2 page 15 **Grammar:** Past Time **Theme:** Marriage	An article: *A Marriage Made on the Internet?*	Two or three paragraphs about a situation that turned out unexpectedly	A broadcast about an unusual wedding
3 page 32 **Grammar:** Future Time **Theme:** Travel	An article: *Getting the Most Out of It!*	Two or three paragraphs about a world traveler's opinions or on your dream vacation	A family conversation about what to do on a trip
PART I **From Grammar to Writing,** page 45 **The Sentence: Avoiding Sentence Fragments:** Write a composition about a travel experience.			
4 page 50 **Grammar:** Modals to Express Degrees of Necessity **Theme:** Cultural Differences	An article: *What We Should and Shouldn't Have Done*	Two or three paragraphs about a situation you should have handled differently	A conversation about a gift for a surprise party
5 page 69 **Grammar:** Modals to Express Degrees of Certainty **Theme:** Puzzles	An article: *Who Really Discovered America?*	Three or four paragraphs about a world mystery	A discussion about hearing one's recorded voice
PART II **From Grammar to Writing,** page 85 **Topic Sentences:** Write a composition about a cross-cultural experience.			
6 page 90 **Grammar:** Count and Non-Count Nouns **Theme:** Health	A transcript of a TV program: *Concerned about Health? Ask the Expert*	Three or four paragraphs about health issues	A conversation between a doctor and a patient about health needs

SPEAKING	PRONUNCIATION	VOCABULARY	
Group Discussion: Electronic devices which are important in your life *Class Discussion:* The dangers of texting while driving	Two pronunciations of the letters *ng*	24/7 contemplating digitally do without	profile staying on top of telecommute tends
Information Gap: A married couple who took risks and made changes *Picture Discussion:* A married couple's relationship *Group Discussion:* Changes in one another's lives	Contracting auxiliary verbs in past forms	came up with out of the blue pondered tie the knot	turned in turned out ultimately*
Picture Discussion: What you think will happen in the future *Group Discussion:* Opinions of a world traveler	Contracting auxiliary verbs in future forms	chart your own course excruciatingly hectic landmarks	maximize* mindset out of whack scrapbook
Information Gap: Cultural differences and travel problems *Discussion:* Correct behavior in your culture	Reduction of modals and modal-like auxiliaries	chuckle decline* gracious have someone over	perplexed pointer praise rectify
Pair Discussion: Possible solutions to various puzzling events *Group Discussion:* Explanations to the mystery of Atlantis	Reductions of *to* and *have* in modal constructions	artifacts cohorts contenders debris	monasteries monks potential* stems from
Discussion: Statements about personal experiences *Personal Inventory:* Responses to a survey about health	Reduction of *of*	BMI brimmed champ devote* drag	in moderation obese side with sunblock telling

* = AWL (Academic Word List) items

UNIT	READING	WRITING	LISTENING
7 page 105 **Grammar:** Definite and Indefinite Articles **Theme:** Environmental Concerns	An article: *The Real Mystery of Easter Island*	Three or four paragraphs about your opinions on an environmental issue	A conversation about wolves
8 page 120 **Grammar:** Quantifiers **Theme:** Money	An article: *What's Happening to Cash?*	Three or four paragraphs about an interesting experience with money	A conversation between diners about how to pay for their meal
9 page 134 **Grammar:** Modification of Nouns **Theme:** Expectations	An article: *The Expectation Syndrome: I Hope for It, but I Don't Expect It*	Three or four paragraphs about an unexpected outcome	A conversation on anxieties about public speaking
PART III From Grammar to Writing, page 150 **Agreement:** Write a composition about societal issues.			
10 page 156 **Grammar:** Noun Clauses: Subjects, Objects, and Complements **Theme:** Humor	A humorous story: *The Three Brothers*	Three to five paragraphs about a humorous incident	A conversation about a humorous incident
11 page 173 **Grammar:** Direct and Indirect Speech **Theme:** Communication and Misunderstanding	An interview: *Understanding Misunderstandings*	Three to five paragraphs about a news story that interested you	A presentation about avoiding verbal conflict
PART IV From Grammar to Writing, page 191 **Direct and Indirect Speech:** Write a composition about a humorous incident.			
12 page 196 **Grammar:** Adjective Clauses: Review and Expansion **Theme:** Personality Types	An article: *What Type Are You?*	Five or more paragraphs about the personality type that fits you	A telephone conversation between a college student and his parents

SPEAKING	PRONUNCIATION	VOCABULARY	
Picture Discussion: Solutions to the problem of disposing of unwanted items *Game:* Asking *who* and *what* questions	Two pronunciations of *the*	bark desolate drastically hauling	ostrich-like rivalry toppled over trunk
Game: World facts *Personal Inventory:* Your life now compared to your life five years ago	Unstressed vowels	correspondingly* crisp e.g. fiat i.e.	the jury is still out live beyond our means succeeding take plastic
Story Discussion: A famous Arabic story *Picture Discussion:* A famous disaster at sea	Pausing between modifiers in the same category	buff exploit* irony live up to marathon	otherworldly relinquish surge syndrome tedious
Pair Discussion: Airline humor *Class Discussion:* Presenting a joke or amusing story	Intonation in *wh-*, *yes/no*, and embedded questions	ecstatic exemplary in a dilemma inclination* on call	one-upmanship outdo supplant uniqueness*
Group Reporting: Game about miscommunication *Picture Discussion:* An auto accident	Blending of /t/ or /d/ plus /y/	bottom line chair civility distressed glared	minimize* rancor short-handed spin sugarcoat
Pair Discussion: Dealing with conflict *Class Activity:* Identifying classmates based on descriptions given by others	Pauses in identifying and nonidentifying adjective clauses	charismatic correlation embrace entrepreneurs	gravitate toward insight* spotlight without mincing words

* = AWL (Academic Word List) items

UNIT	READING	WRITING	LISTENING
13 page 211 **Grammar:** Adjective Clauses with Prepositions; Adjective Phrases **Theme:** Movies	Movie reviews: *Five to Revisit*	A movie review of three or more paragraphs	Weekly movie reviews by a TV film reviewer
PART V	**From Grammar to Writing**, page 229 **Punctuating Adjective Clauses and Phrases:** Write a composition about a photograph.		
14 page 234 **Grammar:** The Passive: Review and Expansion **Theme:** Unsolved Mysteries	An article: *Did He Get Away with It?*	Five or more paragraphs about an unsolved mystery	A news bulletin about an accident
15 page 250 **Grammar:** The Passive to Describe Situations and to Report Opinions **Theme:** Legends and Myths	An article: *The Strangest of Peoples*	A five-paragraph summary of a legend or myth	A news bulletin about a natural disaster
PART VI	**From Grammar to Writing**, page 266 **Parallel Structure: Nouns, Articles, and Voice:** Write a composition about an unsolved mystery or unusual experience.		
16 page 270 **Grammar:** Gerunds **Theme:** Friendship	An article: *Friends*	Five or more paragraphs about a friend who fits a particular category	A telephone conversation about a club
17 page 285 **Grammar:** Infinitives **Theme:** Procrastination	An article: *Seize the Day*	Three or more paragraphs about a time you put off doing something that needed to be done	A news bulletin about a prison escape
PART VII	**From Grammar to Writing**, page 303 **Parallel Structure: Gerunds and Infinitives:** Write a composition about a task you have difficulty accomplishing.		
18 page 308 **Grammar:** Adverbs: Sentence, Focus, and Negative **Theme:** Controversial Issues	A transcript of a radio call-in show: *Time to Sound Off*	Five paragraphs on a controversial topic	A radio call-in show about military service

SPEAKING	PRONUNCIATION	VOCABULARY	
Information Gap: Movie review: *A Beautiful Mind* *Group Discussion:* The current movie rating system *Picture Discussion:* The behavior of moviegoers	Vowel sound changes in words with the same spellings but different meanings	compilation* engrossing estranged incumbent on me	polarized spice up transcend vanquishing
Information Gap: Guessing a mystery object based on clues *Survey and Discussion:* Crime and punishment	*Has been* and *is being* in passive constructions	accomplice alias divulged gear get away with	hijacked inadvertently remains rotting
Game: People and places *Picture Discussion:* Famous people	The vowel sounds /ei/ and /ɛ/	bewitch font lacerates potions	repulsive rituals shrine supernatural
Personal Inventory: Life events *Group Discussion:* What you value in friendships	Pronunciation of nouns and verbs with the same spellings	catching up on coincide* context* counterpart	meander naive spare your feelings vulnerable
Personal Inventory: Personal beliefs and experiences *Group Discussion:* Famous sayings	The vowel sounds /æ/, /ɑ/, and /ʌ/	connotation flunk learned longhand	ring a bell scenario* tough nut to crack wretched
Personal Inventory: Personal beliefs and experiences *Pros and Cons:* Brainstorming ideas about controversial topics *Debate:* Debating a controversial topic	Sentence stress and meaning	compulsory controversial* fuzzy shed some light on	spirited stereotype uncensored willingly

* = AWL (Academic Word List) items

UNIT	READING	WRITING	LISTENING
19 page 323 **Grammar:** Adverb Clauses **Theme:** Sports	An editorial: *Are Sports Still Sporting?*	Three or four paragraphs about a sports topic	An interview with a sports star
20 page 340 **Grammar:** Adverb and Adverbial Phrases **Theme:** Compassion	An article: *Compassion*	Three or four paragraphs about a compassionate act you have witnessed	A news broadcast on world events
21 page 358 **Grammar:** Connectors **Theme:** Memory	An article: *Try to Remember*	Three or four paragraphs about a significant memory you have	An excerpt from a memory-training workshop
PART VIII	**From Grammar to Writing,** page 374 **Using Transitions:** Write a composition that expresses a strong opinion.		
22 page 378 **Grammar:** Conditionals; Other Ways to Express Unreality **Theme:** Intuition	A story: *Intuition*	Four or five paragraphs about a time when you ignored your intuition	A conversation about a student's moral quandary
23 page 396 **Grammar:** More Conditions; The Subjunctive **Theme:** Advice	Letters to an advice columnist and responses: *Ask Rosa*	Four or five paragraphs about a time when you took good advice and another when you took bad advice	A conversation advising a friend about her daughter's demands
PART IX	**From Grammar to Writing,** page 414 **Avoiding Run-On Sentences and Comma Splices:** Write a composition about an intuitive experience.		

SPEAKING	PRONUNCIATION	VOCABULARY	
Personal Inventory: Future possibilities *Picture Discussion:* Sports and violence	Placement of dependent adverb clauses and pauses in speaking	also-ran awry inevitable* lurking	partisanship prevalence stamina venues
Personal Inventory: Personal beliefs and expressions *Group Discussion:* Animal emotions	Vowel changes and stress shift in words of the same family	bandanna a blow was struck corneas dawned on decrepit	elude floored oozing petty weighed
Game: Connecting ideas *Picture Discussion:* A famous painting about memory	Pronunciation of clauses connected by conjunctions and those connected by transitions	core* glucose lobes mitigate	peg recollect tap vivid
Conditional Game: People and things *Personal Inventory:* Personal hopes and wishes *Group Discussion:* Story outcome	Contractions of the auxiliaries *would* and *had*	beastly bureau fluttered hailing inkling	mutilated sweltering token weirdo
Personal Inventory: Personal beliefs and experiences *Group Discussion:* Moral and political issues *Picture Discussion:* Advice about visiting another country	Silent consonants that are sometimes pronounced	at the end of my rope doormat intransigent lighten up neatnik	overbearing pigsty right the ship semblance slob

* = AWL (Academic Word List) items

About the Author / Acknowledgments

Jay Maurer has taught English in binational centers, colleges, and universities in Spain, Portugal, Mexico, the Somali Republic, and the United States; and intensive English at Columbia University's American Language Program. In addition, he has been a teacher of college composition, literature, and speech at Santa Fe Community College and Northern New Mexico Community College. He is the co-author with Penny LaPorte of the three-level *Structure Practice in Context* series; co-author with Irene Schoenberg of the five-level *True Colors* series and the *True Voices* video series; co-author with Irene Schoenberg of *Focus on Grammar 1*; and author of *Focus on Grammar 5*, editions 1 through 4. Currently he lives and writes in Arizona and Washington State. *Focus on Grammar 5: An Integrated Skills Approach*, Fourth Edition, has grown out of the author's experiences as a practicing teacher of both ESL and college writing.

Writing the fourth edition of *Focus on Grammar 5* has been even more interesting and rewarding than doing the first three editions. I'm indebted to many people who helped me in different ways. Specifically, though, I want to express my appreciation and gratitude to:

- My students over the years.
- **Marjorie Fuchs**, **Margaret Bonner**, and **Irene Schoenberg**—the other members of the FOG author team—for their support and encouragement.
- That genius, whoever he or she is, who created the joke about the parrot that has been floating around in cyberspace for a considerable time now. The same to the unknown authors of the bumper stickers.
- **Lise Minovitz** for her many well-taken comments about the manuscript, particularly in the early stages of the revision.
- **Amy Shearon** of Rice University for her careful review of the third edition and her many perceptive suggestions for improvement.
- **Debbie Sistino** for her vision and her excellent direction of the entire project. Thank you very much.

Above all I am grateful to:

- **John Barnes**, my editor, for his patience, his excellent eye for detail, his perceptive understanding of what works well in the classroom, and his overall vision. He has been instrumental in making this a better book.
- My wife **Priscilla** for her love, wonderful support, and assistance with the manuscript.
- My best friend.

Reviewers

We are grateful to the following reviewers for their many helpful comments:

Aida Aganagic, Seneca College, Toronto, Canada; **Aftab Ahmed**, American University of Sharjah, Sharjah, United Arab Emirates; **Todd Allen**, English Language Institute, Gainesville, FL; **Anthony Anderson**, University of Texas, Austin, TX; **Anna K. Andrade**, ASA Institute, New York, NY; **Bayda Asbridge**, Worcester State College, Worcester, MA; **Raquel Ashkenasi**, American Language Institute, La Jolla, CA; **James Bakker**, Mt. San Antonio College, Walnut, CA; **Kate Baldrige-Hale**, Harper College, Palatine, IL; **Leticia S. Banks**, ALCI-SDUSM, San Marcos, CA; **Aegina Barnes**, York College CUNY, Forest Hills, NY; **Sarah Barnhardt**, Community College of Baltimore County, Reisterstown, MD; **Kimberly Becker**, Nashville State Community College, Nashville, TN; **Holly Bell**, California State University, San Marcos, CA; **Anne Bliss**, University of Colorado, Boulder, CO; **Diana Booth**, Elgin Community College, Elgin, IL; **Barbara Boyer**, South Plainfield High School, South Plainfield, NJ; **Janna Brink**, Mt. San Antonio College, Walnut, CA; **AJ Brown**, Portland State University, Portland, OR; **Amanda Burgoyne**, Worcester State College, Worcester, MA; **Brenda Burlingame**, Independence High School, Charlotte, NC; **Sandra Byrd**, Shelby County High School and Kentucky State University, Shelbyville, KY; **Edward Carlstedt**, American University of Sharjah, Sharjah, United Arab Emirates; **Sean Cochran**, American Language Institute, Fullerton, CA; **Yanely Cordero**, Miami Dade College, Miami, FL; **Lin Cui**, William Rainey Harper College, Palatine, IL; **Sheila Detweiler**, College Lake County, Libertyville, IL; **Ann Duncan**, University of Texas, Austin, TX; **Debra Edell**, Merrill Middle School, Denver, CO; **Virginia Edwards**, Chandler-Gilbert Community College, Chandler, AZ; **Kenneth Fackler**, University of Tennessee, Martin, TN; **Jennifer Farnell**, American Language Program, Stamford, CT; **Allen P. Feiste**, Suwon University, Hwaseong, South Korea; **Mina Fowler**, Mt. San Antonio Community College, Rancho Cucamonga, CA; **Rosemary Franklin**, University of Cincinnati, Cincinnati, OH; **Christiane Galvani**, Texas Southern University, Sugar Land, TX; **Chester Gates**, Community College of Baltimore County, Baltimore, MD; **Luka Gavrilovic**, Quest Language Studies, Toronto, Canada; **Sally Gearhart**, Santa Rosa Community College, Santa Rosa, CA; **Shannon Gerrity**, James Lick Middle School, San Francisco, CA; **Jeanette Gerrity Gomez**, Prince George's Community College, Largo, MD; **Carlos Gonzalez**, Miami Dade College, Miami, FL; **Therese Gormley Hirmer**, University of Guelph, Guelph, Canada; **Sudeepa Gulati**, Long Beach City College, Long Beach, CA; **Anthony Halderman**, Cuesta College, San Luis Obispo, CA; **Ann A. Hall**, University of Texas, Austin, TX; **Cora Higgins**, Boston Academy of English, Boston, MA; **Michelle Hilton**, South Lane School District, Cottage Grove, OR; **Nicole Hines**, Troy University, Atlanta, GA; **Rosemary Hiruma**, American Language Institute, Long Beach, CA; **Harriet Hoffman**, University of Texas, Austin, TX; **Leah Holck**, Michigan State University, East Lansing, MI; **Christy Hunt**, English for Internationals, Roswell, GA; **Osmany Hurtado**, Miami Dade College, Miami, FL; **Isabel Innocenti**, Miami Dade College, Miami, FL; **Donna Janian**, Oxford Intensive School of English, Medford, MA; **Scott Jenison**, Antelope Valley College, Lancaster, CA; **Grace Kim**, Mt. San Antonio College, Diamond Bar, CA; **Brian King**, ELS Language Center, Chicago, IL; **Pam Kopitzke**, Modesto Junior College, Modesto, CA; **Elena Lattarulo**, American Language Institute, San Diego, CA; **Karen Lavaty**, Mt. San Antonio College, Glendora, CA; **JJ Lee-Gilbert**, Menlo-Atherton High School, Foster City, CA; **Ruth Luman**, Modesto Junior College, Modesto, CA; **Yvette Lyons**, Tarrant County College, Fort Worth, TX; **Janet Magnoni**, Diablo Valley College, Pleasant Hill, CA; **Meg Maher**, YWCA Princeton, Princeton, NJ; **Carmen Marquez-Rivera**, Curie Metropolitan High School, Chicago, IL; **Meredith Massey**, Prince George's Community College, Hyattsville, MD; **Linda Maynard**, Coastline Community College, Westminster, CA; **Eve Mazereeuw**, University of Guelph, Guelph, Canada; **Susanne McLaughlin**, Roosevelt University, Chicago, IL; **Madeline Medeiros**, Cuesta College, San Luis Obispo, CA; **Gioconda Melendez**, Miami Dade College, Miami, FL; **Marcia Menaker**, Passaic County Community College, Morris Plains, NJ; **Seabrook Mendoza**, Cal State San Marcos University, Wildomar, CA; **Anadalia Mendoza**, Felix Varela Senior High School, Miami, FL; **Charmaine Mergulhao**, Quest Language Studies, Toronto, Canada; **Dana Miho**, Mt. San Antonio College, San Jacinto, CA; **Sonia Nelson**, Centennial Middle School, Portland, OR; **Manuel Niebla**, Miami Dade College, Miami, FL; **Alice Nitta**, Leeward Community College, Pearl City, HI; **Gabriela Oliva**, Quest Language Studies, Toronto, Canada; **Sara Packer**, Portland State University, Portland, OR; **Lesley Painter**, New School, New York, NY; **Carlos Paz-Perez**, Miami Dade College, Miami, FL; **Ileana Perez**, Miami Dade College, Miami, FL; **Barbara Pogue**, Essex County College, Newark, NJ; **Phillips Potash**, University of Texas, Austin, TX; **Jada Pothina**, University of Texas, Austin, TX; **Ewa Pratt**, Des Moines Area Community College, Des Moines, IA; **Pedro Prentt**, Hudson County Community College, Jersey City, NJ; **Maida Purdy**, Miami Dade College, Miami, FL; **Dolores Quiles**, SUNY Ulster, Stone Ridge, NY; **Mark Rau**, American River College, Sacramento, CA; **Lynne Raxlen**, Seneca College, Toronto, Canada; **Lauren Rein**, English for Internationals, Sandy Springs, GA; **Diana Rivers**, NOCCCD, Cypress, CA; **Silvia Rodriguez**, Santa Ana College, Mission Viejo, CA; **Rolando Romero**, Miami Dade College, Miami, FL; **Pedro Rosabal**, Miami Dade College, Miami, FL; **Natalie Rublik**, University of Quebec, Chicoutimi, Quebec, Canada; **Matilde Sanchez**, Oxnard College, Oxnard, CA; **Therese Sarkis-Kruse**, Wilson Commencement, Rochester, NY; **Mike Sfiropoulos**, Palm Beach Community College, Boynton Beach, FL; **Amy Shearon**, Rice University, Houston, TX; **Sara Shore**, Modesto Junior College, Modesto, CA; **Patricia Silva**, Richard Daley College, Chicago, IL; **Stephanie Solomon**, Seattle Central Community College, Vashon, WA; **Roberta Steinberg**, Mount Ida College, Newton, MA; **Teresa Szymula**, Curie Metropolitan High School, Chicago, IL; **Hui-Lien Tang**, Jasper High School, Plano, TX; **Christine Tierney**, Houston Community College, Sugar Land, TX; **Ileana Torres**, Miami Dade College, Miami, FL; **Michelle Van Slyke**, Western Washington University, Bellingham, WA; **Melissa Villamil**, Houston Community College, Sugar Land, TX; **Elizabeth Wagenheim**, Prince George's Community College, Lago, MD; **Mark Wagner**, Worcester State College, Worcester, MA; **Angela Waigand**, American University of Sharjah, Sharjah, United Arab Emirates; **Merari Weber**, Metropolitan Skills Center, Los Angeles, CA; **Sonia Wei**, Seneca College, Toronto, Canada; and **Vicki Woodward**, Indiana University, Bloomington, IN.

Present, Past, and Future

UNIT	GRAMMAR FOCUS	THEME
1	Present Time	The Digital World
2	Past Time	Marriage
3	Future Time	Travel

UNIT 1 Present Time

THE DIGITAL WORLD

STEP 1 GRAMMAR IN CONTEXT

Before You Read

PAIRS: Discuss the questions.

1. What electronic devices do you use for communication with others? How often do you use them?
2. Do you think digital advances have changed our world for the better or for the worse?

Read

Read the article about staying in close connection with other people.

CONNECTED!

by James Marx

Most of us hardly **go** anywhere today without a cell phone or iPhone, an iPod, or a laptop —or so it **seems**. We**'re trying** to stay in 24/7 communication with each other. We **want** to be "connected." How **do** we **accomplish** this? We **use** the Internet to contact friends on MySpace or Facebook. We **send** and **receive** emails, **write** and **read** blogs, **call** others and **text** them on our cell phones. We**'re** "available" most of the time. **Is** this constant communication good? I **think** it**'s** positive overall, though there **is** a downside to living digitally.

My daughter, Allison, **is** an excellent example. Consider the social networking sites MySpace and Facebook. MySpace **has been** around since 2003 and Facebook since 2005. When you **join** one of them, you **develop** your own web page where you **present** your personal profile, **post** pictures, and **write** on your friends' "walls." Allison **has** a page on both of them and **spends** a lot of time keeping in touch with her friends. This evening Allison **is sitting** in front of the computer, **reading** posts on her wall, and **writing** responses. At the moment, she**'s laughing**, probably at a picture or amusing comment.

Then there**'s** my 15-year-old son, Nick, who **appears** addicted to his cell phone, which he**'s had** since his birthday four months ago. Right now Nick **is texting** friends—he**'s been doing** that for the last half hour—and **shows** no signs of stopping. I**'ve had** conversations with Nick's teachers, who **say** Nick **isn't doing** well, that they**'ve been having** difficulty getting his attention. Most of them **have outlawed** the use of cell phones in class. They **feel** bad about this but **believe** education **comes** first.

Then there**'s** my wife Elena, who **loves** email. After dinner every night Elena **gets** out her laptop, **logs** on to the Internet, and **reads** and **answers** her messages. That**'s** what Elena **is**

CONNECTED!

doing right now. She **says** she**'s getting** about 100 email messages daily and **is having** trouble staying on top of them.

And then there**'s** yours truly. As a writer for *In Touch Magazine*, I **go** to the office three days a week and **telecommute** the other two. When I**'m working** at home, I **write** a blog. By the way, **do** you **know** the origin of the word "blog"? It**'s** a contraction of "web log," which **is** a type of website. On my blog I **write** and **read** regular entries, **describe** events, and **comment** on what others **say**. There**'s** a blog on the Internet for just about everything. **Do** you **remember** the movie *Julie and Julia*? It**'s** about a young woman who, bored with her day job, **decides** to cook all of TV chef Julia Child's famous recipes and then **writes** a blog about each day's meal.

The downside I mentioned above **is** simply this: Staying in near-constant communication with others often **leads** to stress. It **takes** our time and **tends** to prevent us from spending quiet time alone, from reading, from contemplating things, from enjoying nature. We **hear** people saying things such as, "I just couldn't do without my BlackBerry." So would I give it all up? Not on your life! Through the Internet I **stay** in touch with friends I seldom **see**. But as with so many other things in our lives, we **need** to put things in balance.

After You Read

A | Vocabulary: *Match the blue words and phrases on the left with their meanings on the right.*

_____ **1.** We're trying to stay in **24/7** communication with each other.

_____ **2.** There is a downside to living **digitally**.

_____ **3.** You present your personal **profile** online.

_____ **4.** She's having trouble **staying on top of** her email.

_____ **5.** I **telecommute** two days a week.

_____ **6.** It **tends** to prevent us from spending quiet time alone.

_____ **7.** It also prevents us from **contemplating** things.

_____ **8.** Some say they couldn't **do without** their cell phone.

a. thinking about with attention

b. short description

c. continue to live minus (something)

d. is likely

e. managing

f. with electronic devices

g. constant

h. work from home

B | Comprehension: *Circle* **T (True)** *or* **F (False)**. *Correct the false statements.*

1. According to the author, most people today want to be in frequent communication with others. **T** **F**

2. The author thinks digital living is positive overall. **T** **F**

3. MySpace and Facebook are computer search engines. **T** **F**

4. Facebook became available before MySpace. **T** **F**

(continued on next page)

5. The author says most teachers have outlawed computers in class. T F

6. The word "blog" is a short form of "web log." T F

7. The film *Julie and Julia* is about a woman who writes a blog. T F

8. The author thinks staying in near-constant communication with others is always stressful. T F

STEP 2 GRAMMAR PRESENTATION

PRESENT TIME

Present Time: In General or Now

Simple Present	Present Progressive
	Be **+ Base Form + *-ing***
Today we **spend** a lot of money on electronic devices.	Jack **is looking** for a new iPod.

Present Time: From a Time in the Past Until Now

Present Perfect	Present Perfect Progressive
Have **+ Past Participle**	***Have been*** **+ Base Form + *-ing***
We **have had** email for 12 years.	He**'s been texting** his friends for the last half hour.

Action and Non-Action Verbs

Action Verbs		Most Non-Action Verbs
Simple Form	**Progressive Form**	**Simple Form**
They normally **drive** to work.	Today they**'re taking** the bus.	Teachers **know** he is a good student. They **want** to understand his problem.

Some Non-Action Verbs	
Simple Form (Stative Use)	**Progressive Form (Active Use)**
I **have** a new iPhone.	I**'m having** problems with it.
They **think** they need a better computer.	Please don't bother me; I**'m thinking**.
Our laptop **is** a great computer.	It**'s being** difficult today, though.

Action Verbs	Some Non-Action Verbs	
+ Adverb	**+ Adjective (Stative Use)**	**+ Adverb (Active Use)**
She **works constantly**. He**'s doing badly** in class.	Your car **looks good**. The soup **tastes delicious**. She **feels bad** about what she said.	He **looked thoughtfully** at the text message. You should **taste** that **carefully**—it's hot! The doctor **felt** the bruise **gently**.

GRAMMAR NOTES

1	Use the **simple present** to show actions, events, or states that are true in general or happen habitually.	• We **use** the Internet to stay in touch with friends. *(true in general)* • After dinner every night, Elena **gets out** her laptop. *(habitual)*
	We also use the simple present to narrate events in sequence.	• Elena **logs** on to the Internet, **reads** her email, and **starts** responding.
2	Use the **present progressive** to show actions or events in progress at the moment (not finished).	• Allison **is sitting** in front of the computer.
	BE CAREFUL! We generally don't use the progressive with non-action verbs.	• We **need** to put things in balance. NOT: We~~'re needing~~ to put things in balance.
3	The **present perfect** and the **present perfect progressive** connect the past with the present. Use them to show actions and states that began in the past and continue until now.	• **I've had** my iPod for six months. • He**'s been writing** a blog since 2008.
	They are often used with *for* + a length of time and *since* + a starting point.	
	Use the **present perfect**, not the present perfect progressive, to describe completed actions with a connection to the present.	• **I've bought** four cell phones in the last two years. NOT: I~~'ve been buying~~ four cell phones in the last two years.
4	**Action** verbs (also called **active**) describe actions.	• Computers **perform** tasks quickly. *(action)*
	Use **simple** verb forms (without *-ing*) to describe all of an action—the action in general.	• I **write** articles for a psychology magazine. *(in general)*
	Use **progressive** verb forms (with *-ing*) to describe part of an action—in progress at a specific time.	• Right now **I'm writing** my blog. *(in progress at the moment)*

(continued on next page)

5	**Non-action** verbs (also called **stative**) describe states such as appearance (*seem*), emotions (*love*), mental states (*know*), perceptions (*hear*), possession (*own*), and wants (*need*).	• You **seem** stressed. • Elena **loves** email. • We **hear** that all the time. • They **own** four computers. • I **need** a new phone.
	We most often use non-action verbs in the simple form and not in the progressive.	• I **know** my coworker well. NOT: ~~I'm knowing~~ . . .
	Some non-action verbs can be used to describe either states or actions. When they are used to describe actions, they usually have different meanings.	• We **have** a new laptop. *(possess)* • We**'re having** trouble with it. *(experiencing)* • He **is** a nice fellow. *(a state)* • Today he**'s not being** nice. *(behaving)*
6	We normally use **adverbs** with **action verbs**.	• She always **listens carefully**. • She **works hard** at her job.
	We normally use the verbs ***look***, ***sound***, ***feel***, ***smell***, and ***taste*** to show states, in which case they are used with **adjectives**, not adverbs.	• You **sound** really **excited**! NOT: You sound really ~~excitedly~~! • She **feels bad** about what she said. NOT: She feels ~~badly~~ . . .
	BE CAREFUL! The sense verbs are sometimes used to show actions, in which case they are used with adverbs.	• I don't **hear well** when other people are talking. *(an action—using one's ears)* • The fire alarm **sounded** a warning **loudly**. *(an action—making a noise)*

REFERENCE NOTES

For definitions and examples of **grammar terms**, see Glossary on page G-1.
For a list of **non-action verbs**, see Appendix 2 on page A-2.
For a list of **non-action verbs sometimes used in the progressive**, see Appendix 3 on page A-3.

STEP 3 FOCUSED PRACTICE

EXERCISE 1: Discover the Grammar

A | *Look at the sentences. Do the underlined verbs show habitual action* (**HA**) *or action in progress* (**AP**)*?*

HA **1.** Most of us hardly <u>go</u> anywhere today without an electronic device.

____ **2.** We<u>'re trying</u> to stay connected.

____ **3.** We <u>use</u> the Internet to contact friends.

____ **4.** Allison <u>is sitting</u> in front of the computer.

____ **5.** At the moment, she<u>'s laughing</u>.

____ **6.** Nick's teachers say he <u>isn't doing</u> well.

_____ **7.** Elena is having trouble staying on top of her email.

_____ **8.** When I'm working at home I write a blog.

_____ **9.** When I'm working at home I write a blog.

_____ **10.** Through the Internet I stay in touch with friends.

B | *Look at the sentences. Decide whether the underlined verbs describe actions (**A**) or states (**S**).*

1. Most people today hardly go anywhere without an electronic device. (A) S

2. At least it seems that way. A S

3. We want to be connected 24/7. A S

4. We text people on our cell phones. A S

5. Nick appears to be addicted to his cell phone. A S

6. On MySpace and Facebook you develop your own page. A S

7. Teachers feel bad about outlawing cell phones in class. A S

8. Elena loves her email. A S

9. I telecommute two days a week. A S

10. We need to put things in balance. A S

EXERCISE 2: Simple Present / Present Progressive

(Grammar Notes 1, 2)

Complete the account of a day in the life of James Marx, magazine writer and Internet blogger. Circle the correct forms of the underlined verbs.

Today is Monday, one of the two days a week that I (telecommute) / 'm telecommuting (1.). On these days, I walk / 'm walking (2.) about 50 steps to my home office, turn on / am turning on (3.) the computer, and start / am starting (4.) writing. For some reason, my computer printer gives / is giving (5.) me problems today, so at the moment I try / 'm trying (6.) to fix it. Ah, here we go. It works / 's working (7.) again.

This week I write / 'm writing (8.) on my blog about the dangers of text messaging. Currently our state legislature considers / is considering (9.) a law that would prohibit texting while driving or operating machinery. I think / 'm thinking (10.) it would be a good idea to pass it.

It's now 12:30 P.M., time for lunch. On these home days, I make / 'm making (11.) my own lunch. On the other three days, I have / 'm having (12.) lunch in the company cafeteria.

It's 3:30 P.M. I finished my blog an hour ago, and now I do / 'm doing (13.) some Internet research for an article I'm going to write in a few days. I love / 'm loving (14.) these quiet days at home.

EXERCISE 3: Present Perfect / Present Perfect Progressive

(Grammar Note 3)

Complete the sentences with present perfect or present perfect progressive forms of the verbs in parentheses. Use the progressive form if possible.

James and Elena Marx ___have known___ (1. know) each other for 20 years and __________ (2. be) married for 18. They __________ (3. live) in their current house for three years.

James __________ (4. be) a writer for 10 years. He __________ (5. work) for *In Touch Magazine* for eight years and __________ (6. write) an Internet blog for six. He __________ (7. also write) four books on popular culture.

Elena __________ (8. be) a high school English teacher for the last 12 years. During that time she __________ (9. teach) at six different schools. She __________ (10. teach) at her current school for five years now.

The Marxes are a "wired" family. They __________ (11. have) at least one home computer for 15 years. Over the years they __________ (12. own) six computers. James, Elena, Allison, and Nick __________ (13. communicate) with friends and relatives online for almost as long as they can remember.

EXERCISE 4: Action / Non-Action Verbs; Adverbs / Adjectives

(Grammar Notes 4–6)

Complete the statements with the correct verb from the box. Use each verb once in the simple present and once in the present progressive. Also choose the correct adverb or adjective.

be	feel	have	look	think

1. Your new iPhone ___looks___ (similar) / similarly to mine.
2. Our computer crashed, so we __________ frantic / frantically for a new one.
3. If your day is going bad / badly, you __________ a bad day.
4. Cell phone use has grown so rapid / rapidly that more people __________ cell phones today than land lines.
5. A person who __________ bad / badly about saying something should apologize.
6. I was fine yesterday, but today I __________ terrible / terribly.
7. When a person __________ clear / clearly, that person is using his or her brain.

8. Many people today ________________ a home computer is essential / essentially.

9. That child ________________ normal / normally a well-behaved student.

10. Today, however, she ________________ obnoxious / obnoxiously.

EXERCISE 5: Editing

Read the student essay. There are eleven mistakes in the use of present-time verbs, adjectives, and adverbs. The first mistake is already corrected. Find and correct ten more.

No Cell Phone Restrictions!

~~It's seeming~~ It seems that I constantly hear the same thing: "Cell phones are dangerous. We're needing to restrict them. People are dying because of cell phones." Well, I'm thinking cell phones themselves aren't the problem. I'm completely opposed to restrictions on them, and here's why:

First, people say cell phones are dangerous to health, so they should be limited. Supporters of this idea say there are studies showing that cell phones produce harmful radiation and can even cause cancer. I think this is nonsense. There hasn't been any real proof. It's sounding like just another study that ultimately isn't meaning anything.

Second, teachers say we shouldn't allow cell phones in classes because they're a distraction. I feel pretty angrily about this. Here's an example: Two weeks ago in my history class, a student had her cell phone on because her mother was really sick and might need a ride to the hospital. The student's mother couldn't contact anyone else. Actually, the mother did call, and the student called someone to help her mother. What if the phone hadn't been on? The teacher would feel pretty badly.

Third, people argue that using a cell phone while driving is dangerous. I disagree. It's no more dangerous than turning on the car radio or eating a sandwich. People do those things when they drive. The law says you have to have one hand on the steering wheel at all times. It's possible to use a cell phone correct with one hand. I use my cell phone careful; I always keep one hand on the wheel. Maybe there should be training in ways to use a cell phone good, but we shouldn't prohibit using handheld phones in cars.

This has always been a free country. I hope it stays that way.

STEP 4 COMMUNICATION PRACTICE

EXERCISE 6: Listening

A | *Listen to the conversation. Check (✓) the topic that is not mentioned.*

- ☐ credit cards
- ☐ cell phones
- ☐ identity theft
- ☐ the Internet

B | *Read the questions. Listen to the conversation. Then listen again and answer the questions in complete sentences.*

1. How are things going for Mary?

   Things aren't going well for her.

2. What kind of problem is Mary having?

   ____

3. What is wrong?

   ____

4. What is this a good example of?

   ____

5. What has the person who got the number been doing?

   ____

6. How much money is involved?

   ____

7. Does Mary have to pay back the money?

   ____

8. When are people supposed to report problems like this?

   ____

9. What does Mary say about the Internet?

   ____

10. According to Jim, what is the downside of the Internet?

    ____

EXERCISE 7: Pronunciation

A | *Read and listen to the Pronunciation Note.*

Pronunciation Note

The letters ***ng*** have two pronunciations: with the /g/ sound, /ŋg/, as in the word *English*, and without it, /ŋ/, as in the word *sing*. Note that the /g/ sound is never pronounced when a word ends in ***ng***.

B | *Listen to the sentences. Circle the letters* **ng** *when the* **g** *is pronounced (/ŋg/). Underline the letters* **ng** *when the* **g** *is not pronounced (/ŋ/).*

1. Elena has been teaching English for a long time.
2. A lot of new things are happening in the digital world.
3. James has been writing for a magazine and blogging on the Internet for years.
4. The longer he spoke, the angrier we got.
5. Bill is strong, but Bob is stronger.
6. My fingers are sore because I've been working in the yard.
7. He's been single for years, but now he's going to get married.

C | *PAIRS: Practice the sentences.*

EXERCISE 8: Group Discussion

A | *Fill out the chart on page 12 for yourself.*

Electronic Device or System	Have It	Don't Have It	Works Well	Often Use It	Seldom or Never Use It	Comments
Home computer	✓		✓	✓		*Spend several hours a day on it. Use it for writing, research, entertainment. Couldn't do without it.*
Laptop computer						
Email						
Cell phone or iPhone						
iPod or MP3 player						

B | *GROUPS: Discuss your answers. Talk about which electronic devices are important in your life and which are not.*

EXAMPLE: **A:** I have a home computer and love using it. I couldn't do without it.
B: Why?
A: I use it for a lot of things—for writing, doing research, watching things for entertainment.
C: Do you think you spend too much time on the computer?
A: Well . . .

C | *Report your answers to the class.*

EXERCISE 9: Class Discussion

A | *Read the excerpt from an Internet article on the dangers of texting while driving.*

According to a poll given Tuesday, August 7, 2007, 91 percent of Americans agree that text messaging while driving is just as dangerous as driving after having a few alcoholic beverages, but 57 percent admit that they do it.

The Harris Interactive survey, given by the cell phone messaging service Pinger Inc., found that 89 percent of respondents believe that messaging while driving should be banned because the act is very dangerous.

Of those polled, 66 percent said they had read text messages and emails while driving, and another 57 percent said they have sent them while driving. In May, Wisconsin was the first state to ban text messaging while driving, and now six other states are considering the same law. The poll included 2,049 people from the United States and took place from June 29 to July 3.

The majority of people that text message while they drive are young people, many of whom have only been driving a few years. Having these inexperienced drivers texting on the road is a very dangerous combination. Text messaging while driving significantly slows your reaction time. . . .

B | *CLASS: Discuss the following questions related to the article:*

1. Do you agree that text messaging while driving should be banned?
2. Do you agree that the majority of people who text message while they drive are young people?
3. What is the best way to solve this problem? Make several suggestions.

EXERCISE 10: Writing

A | *Write two or three paragraphs on the following topic, using present-time verbs.*

Of all the electronic devices mentioned in this unit—home computer, cell phone, iPod, MP3 player, laptop—which is the most beneficial to you? Which would be hard for you to do without? Give several reasons for your opinion.

Example: My cell phone is the electronic device that is most beneficial to me. There are several reasons why. The first is convenience: I carry my phone with me wherever I go. I have it whenever I need it. Also, it's light and fits easily into my pocket or book bag . . .

B | *Check your work. Use the Editing Checklist.*

Editing Checklist

Did you use . . . ?

- ☐ simple present correctly
- ☐ present progressive correctly
- ☐ action verbs correctly
- ☐ non-action verbs correctly

UNIT 1 Review

Check your answers on page UR-1.
Do you need to review anything?

A | *Complete the letter by circling the correct verb form.*

Dear Amy,

Just a note to tell you how we do / are doing (1.). Tim loves / is loving (2.) his job. Our house is on a bus line, so he takes / is taking (3.) the bus to work. I get / 'm getting (4.) to know our neighbors, who seem / are seeming (5.) friendly. Nancy attends / is attending (6.) kindergarten four days a week, but today is a holiday, so she plays / is playing (7.) outside. We really like / are liking (8.) Phoenix.

Love,
Martha

B | *Complete the paragraph with correct forms of the verbs in parentheses. Use the present perfect progressive if possible.*

Tim and Martha Baldwin ______ (1. live) in Phoenix since last March. Tim is a film director. He ______ (2. direct) five movies in his career and ______ (3. work) on a sixth since they moved to Phoenix. They ______ (4. own) their own house for six months and ______ (5. remodel) it since they bought it. Martha is a language teacher and ______ (6. run) an online tutoring service for three months.

C | *Circle the letter of the one underlined word or phrase in each sentence that is not correct.*

1. Frank <u>feels</u> (A) <u>badly</u> (B) that he <u>got</u> (C) <u>angry</u> (D) at the staff meeting. **A B C D**
2. Helen <u>sounded</u> (A) <u>tremendously</u> (B) <u>excitedly</u> (C) when she <u>called</u> (D). **A B C D**
3. The food <u>didn't smell</u> (A) <u>good</u> (B), but it <u>certainly</u> (C) tasted <u>well</u> (D). **A B C D**
4. Melanie <u>looked</u> (A) <u>angry</u> (B) at the person who <u>suddenly</u> (C) <u>cut</u> (D) in front of her in line. **A B C D**
5. The teacher <u>feels</u> (A) <u>bad</u> (B) yesterday when her students <u>behaved</u> (C) <u>badly</u> (D) in front of the school principal. **A B C D**
6. The situations <u>looked</u> (A) <u>similar</u> (B) at first, but they <u>were</u> (C) really <u>differently</u> (D). **A B C D**

UNIT 2 Past Time
MARRIAGE

STEP 1 GRAMMAR IN CONTEXT

Before You Read

PAIRS: Discuss the questions.

1. What do you think the term "arranged marriage" means?
2. Would you rather find your own person to marry or have someone else select that person for you?
3. Do you think an arranged marriage is likely to be a happy marriage?

Read

Read the article about an unusual marriage.

LIFESTYLES

A *Marriage* Made on the **Internet?**

How many Americans **have** ever **considered** asking friends or relatives to select their spouse for them? Not many. Yet this is exactly what David Weinlick **did**. He **had** long **been pondering** marriage and **had known** for some time that he **was going to get** married in June of 1998. When the wedding **would take place** and who **would be invited** he already **knew**. He just **didn't know** whom he **would be marrying**. You see, he **hadn't met** his bride yet.

It **started** some years ago. Friends **would ask** Weinlick, an anthropology student at the University of Minnesota, when he **was going to tie** the knot. He **would say** he **didn't know**. Eventually he **got** tired of these questions, so he **picked** a date out of the blue: June 13, 1998. As this date **was getting** closer, Weinlick, who **was** 28 at the time, **knew** he **had** to do something. His friend Steve Fletcher **came up with** the idea of a democratic selection process. Weinlick **liked** the idea, so he **advertised** for a bride on the Internet on a Bridal Nomination Committee website.

He **created** an application form and **asked** friends and relatives to interview the candidates and select the winner. They **did** this at a party before the ceremony on the day of the wedding.

Weinlick's friends and relatives **took** the request seriously. Though Weinlick **wasn't** sure who his bride **would be**, he **did want** to get married. He **said** he thinks commitment is important and that people have to work at relationships to make them successful.

(continued on next page)

Internet Marriage

Weinlick's sister **said** she **thought** all of the candidates **were** nice, but she **was looking** for someone really special—a person who **would fit** into family celebrations.

So who **won** the election? It **was** Elizabeth Runze, a pharmacy student at the University of Minnesota. She **hadn't met** Weinlick before she **picked up** a candidate survey on the Monday before the wedding. They **talked** briefly on that day and again on Tuesday when Runze **turned in** the completed survey. However, neither Weinlick nor Runze **knew** who **would** ultimately **be chosen** by Weinlick's friends and family on Saturday, the day of the wedding. After her Saturday selection by the committee, Runze **said** the day **was** the most incredible she **had** ever **experienced**.

Weinlick **was** happy too. After the selection, the groom **said** the plan **had turned out** almost exactly as he **had hoped**. By the time the wedding day **arrived**, Weinlick **had prepared** everything. The two **took** their vows at the Mall of America in Minneapolis while about 2,000 shoppers **looked on**.

Probably few Americans would do what Weinlick and Runze **did**. Their union qualifies as an "arranged marriage," a phenomenon that **has not been** popular in America. Arranged marriages are common in many other parts of the world, though, or at least they **used to be**. Maybe they're not such a bad idea.

After You Read

A | Vocabulary: *Match the blue words and phrases on the left with their meanings on the right.*

_____ **1.** Weinlick had **pondered** marriage for quite some time.

_____ **2.** Friends would ask Weinlick when he was going to **tie the knot**.

_____ **3.** Weinlick picked a date **out of the blue**.

_____ **4.** A friend of Weinlick **came up with** the idea of a democratic selection process.

_____ **5.** Weinlick and Runze talked briefly when she **turned in** her application.

_____ **6.** No one knew who would **ultimately** be chosen.

_____ **7.** Weinlick said the plan had **turned out** almost exactly as he'd hoped.

a. at random
b. had a particular result
c. considered
d. in the end
e. wed
f. submitted
g. originated, produced

B | Comprehension: *Circle* **T (True)** *or* **F (False).** *Correct the false statements.*

1. Weinlick had considered marriage for a long time before his wedding. **T F**

2. Weinlick had met his bride before the planning of his wedding. **T F**

3. He didn't know whom he would marry until shortly before the wedding. **T F**

4. He advertised for a bride in a newspaper. **T F**

5. The selection of Weinlick's bride was a democratic process. **T F**

6. Arranged marriages have traditionally been common in America. **T F**

STEP 2 GRAMMAR PRESENTATION

PAST TIME

Past Time: General or Specific (Definite)

Simple Past	Past Progressive
	Was / Were **+ Base Form + *-ing***
Weinlick **needed** to find a bride.	He **was looking** for someone special.
He **advertised** on the Internet.	

Past Time: Not Specific (Indefinite)

Present Perfect
Has / Have **+ Past Participle**
The couple **has** already **sent** the invitations.
They **have chosen** the date for the party.

Past Time: Habitual or Repeated

Used to **+ Base Form**	***Would*** **+ Base Form**
She **used to be** a pharmacist.	Some days she **would work** 12 hours.

Past Time: Before a Time in the Past

Past Perfect	Past Perfect Progressive
Had **+ Past Participle**	***Had been*** **+ Base Form + *-ing***
He **had met** her before the wedding.	He **had been planning** the wedding for months.

Past Time: After a Time in the Past But Before Now ("Future in the Past")

Was / Were going to **+ Base Form**	***Would*** **+ Base Form**
He knew he **was going to marry** soon.	He knew when the wedding **would be**.

GRAMMAR NOTES

1	Use the **simple past** to express an action, event, or state occurring at a general or specific time in the past.	• Runze **wanted** to get married. *(general)* • She **filled out** an application form several days before the wedding. *(specific)*
2	Use the **past progressive** to express an action that was in progress (not finished) at a time in the past.	• Runze **was studying** pharmacy at the University when she decided to get married.
3	Use the **present perfect** to express an action, event, or state occurring at an **indefinite** time in the past.	• How many Americans **have** ever **considered** an arranged marriage?
	BE CAREFUL! Don't use the present perfect with a past-time expression.	• Weinlick **got married a few years ago.** NOT: Weinlick ~~has gotten~~ married a few years ago.
	NOTE: The simple past is the definite past. The present perfect is the indefinite past.	• The two **met** on June 8, 1998. • They **have** already **met**.
	Remember that the present perfect also connects the past and the present. (See Unit 1.)	• I **have attended** many weddings since then.
4	Use ***used to*** + base form to show a habitual action, event, or state that was true in the past but is no longer true.	• Kayoko **used to play** tennis a lot.
	You can also use ***would*** + base form to express actions or events that occurred regularly during a period in the past.	• When we were children, we **would spend** every summer in Maine.
	BE CAREFUL! *Used to* and *would* are similar in meaning when they express past actions. However, only *used to* can show past location, state of being, or possession.	• I **used to live** in Chicago. *(location)* • Mia **used to be** a nurse. *(state of being)* • We **used to have** a summer home. *(possession)* NOT: I ~~would live~~ in Chicago. Mia ~~would be~~ a nurse. We ~~would have~~ a summer home.
5	Use the **past perfect** to show an action, event, or state of being that happened **before** a certain time in the past.	• By June 13, the family **had interviewed** dozens of candidates.
	Use the past perfect with the simple past to show which of two past actions, events, or states happened first.	• Weinlick and Runze **had known** each other for five days **when** they got married.
	The past perfect is usually used when we talk about the first event second.	• By the time the wedding day arrived, Weinlick **had prepared** everything.
	The past perfect is not often used in sentences with *before* or *after*. The simple past is generally used to describe both events.	• Weinlick **started** advertising for a bride after he **graduated** from college.

6	Use the **past perfect progressive** to express an action that was in progress **before** another past event.	• She **had been working** when she got married.
7	Use ***was / were going to / would*** + base form to describe an action, event, or state that was planned or expected in the past (before now). Sentences with *was / were going to / would* are sometimes called **future in the past**.	• Weinlick knew that he **was going to get** married on June 13, 1998. • He knew where the wedding **would be**.

REFERENCE NOTE

For a list of **verbs with irregular past forms and past participles**, see Appendix 1 on page A-1.

STEP 3 FOCUSED PRACTICE

EXERCISE 1: Discover the Grammar

A | *Look at these sentences based on the reading. Write the earlier-occurring action or state on the left and the later-occurring action or state on the right.*

1. Weinlick had known for a long time that he was going to get married on June 13, 1998.

   Weinlick had known for a long time / he was going to get married on June 13, 1998.

2. He just didn't know who he would be marrying.

   ____

3. Friends would repeatedly ask Weinlick when he was going to tie the knot.

   ____

4. Runze hadn't met Weinlick when she picked up her candidate survey.

   ____

5. By the time the wedding day arrived, Weinlick had prepared everything.

   ____

B | *Look at these sentences containing* **would**. *Is* **would** *used for future in the past* **(F)** *or habitual action in the past* **(H)**?

__F__ **1.** He already knew when the wedding would be and who would be invited.

_____ **2.** He just didn't know who the bride would be.

_____ **3.** Friends would repeatedly ask Weinlick when he was going to tie the knot.

_____ **4.** He would say he didn't know.

_____ **5.** Weinlick's sister added that it was important for her brother to marry someone who would fit in at family celebrations.

_____ **6.** Neither Weinlick nor Runze knew who would be chosen by his friends and family.

EXERCISE 2: Simple Past / Present Perfect

(Grammar Notes 1, 3)

Complete the story by circling the correct verb forms.

Ellen Rosetti and Mark Stevens (got married) / have gotten married **1.** almost a year ago. Their marriage almost didn't happen / hasn't happened **2.**, though. They got / have gotten **3.** to know each other on a blind date. Then, a week later, Ellen's friend Alice came / has come **4.** up with two extra concert tickets.

Ellen says, "On that second date, I thought / 've thought **5.**, 'He's the most opinionated man I ever met / I've ever met **6.**.' Then, a couple of weeks after the concert, Mark called up / has called up **7.** and asked / has asked **8.** me out. I wanted / 've wanted **9.** to say no, but something made / has made **10.** me accept. After that, one thing led / has led **11.** to another." For his part, Mark says, "Ellen is unique. I never knew / 've never known **12.** anyone even remotely like her."

Ellen says, "At first glance you might have trouble seeing how Mark and I could be married. In certain ways, we're as different as night and day. I'm an early bird; he's a night owl. He's conservative; I'm liberal. He always loved / 's always loved **13.** sports, and I was never able / 've never been able **14.** to stand them. I guess you might say, ultimately, that we're a case of opposites being attracted to each other."

EXERCISE 3: *Used To / Would*

(Grammar Note 4)

Jim Garcia and Mark Stevens both got married fairly recently. Fill in the blanks in their conversation with the correct forms of **used to** *or* **would** *and the verbs in parentheses. Use* **would** *if possible. If* **would** *occurs with a pronoun subject, use a contraction.*

MARK: So, Jim, how does it feel to be an old married man? Been about six months, hasn't it?

JIM: Yep. It feels great. It's a lot different, though.

MARK: Yeah? How so?

JIM: Well, I guess I'd say I ___used to have___ (1. have) a lot more freedom. Like on Saturdays, for example. I ________________ (2. sleep) until 11:00 or even noon. Then, when I got up, my buddies and I ________________ (3. go) out for breakfast at a restaurant. Now Jennifer and I get up at 8:00 at the latest. She's really an early bird. And I either make her breakfast, or she makes it for me. And then on Saturday nights I ________________ (4. go) out with the guys and stay out till all hours of the night. Now it's just the two of us. Sometimes we go out on Saturday night, and sometimes we don't.

MARK: Does that bother you?

JIM: You know, it doesn't. Life actually ________________ (5. be) kind of lonely. It's not anymore. What about you? Have things really changed?

MARK: They sure have. For one thing, the neighborhood is totally different. Remember the apartment I ________________ (6. live) in, right north of downtown? Well, Ellen and I just bought a house in the suburbs. That's a trip, let me tell you.

JIM: I'll bet.

MARK: Yeah. My weekends ________________ (7. be) my own. I ________________ (8. spend) all day Saturday working on my car or going mountain biking. Now I have to cut the grass and take care of the yard.

JIM: So would you change anything?

MARK: Well, I've pondered that question. No, I sure wouldn't. You know how everyone says how great it is to be single? Well, I ________________ (9. think) so too. Not now. Now I'd say "been there, done that."

JIM: Me too. I wouldn't change a thing.

EXERCISE 4: Simple Past / Past Perfect

(Grammar Notes 1, 5)

Using the simple past and past perfect, complete the story of how Jim Garcia and Jennifer O'Leary got married. Combine each pair of sentences into one sentence. Begin the new sentence with the connecting word or phrase in parentheses. You can present the two clauses in either order.

1. Jim Garcia and Jennifer O'Leary graduated from high school. They knew each other for three years. (when)

   When they graduated from high school, Jim Garcia and Jennifer O'Leary had known each other for three years.

2. Jim completed four years of military service, and Jennifer graduated from college. They both returned to their hometown about a year ago. (by the time)

   ____

3. Jennifer started teaching, and Jim took a job as a computer programmer. They saw each other again. (by the time)

   ____

4. Neither went out on any dates. They ran into each other in a drugstore one morning. (when)

   ____

5. Jim drove to Olson's Drugstore. He woke up with a splitting headache. (because)

   ____

6. Jennifer's younger sister fell and hurt herself and needed medicine. Jennifer also went to Olson's. (because)

   ____

7. A week passed. Jim asked Jennifer out on a date. (when)

   ____

8. Jim and Jennifer dated for three months. They got married. (when)

   ____

EXERCISE 5: Weinlick / Runze Updated

(Grammar Notes 1–3, 7)

How are David and Elizabeth Weinlick doing some time after getting married? Read the update. Then answer the questions in complete sentences.

Eleven years after David Weinlick and Elizabeth Runze wed in a public ceremony at the Mall of America, their marriage was still going strong. As of May 31, 2009, David and Elizabeth are the parents of four children: daughter Emily, son Charlie, daughter Zoe, and son Zed.

David and Elizabeth Weinlick in 2009

David and Elizabeth say, "We've never regretted it. It sounds like a crazy thing to do, but there was instant chemistry—and we did our dating after we married." They have always stressed that commitment is the thing that makes a marriage work. The feelings came later, they say. "The day we got married we had no relationship. Zero. Nothing!" Elizabeth commented. Feelings of love developed after they got to know each other. Friends of the couple have noted that the Weinlicks are very much in love.

Interestingly, statistics show that "regular" marriages have approximately a 50 percent success rate, while about 85 percent of "arranged" marriages are said to succeed. There was no guarantee the Weinlicks' marriage would succeed, of course, but by all accounts it is doing well.

1. Where did the Weinlicks wed?

   They wed at the Mall of America.

2. What was the state of their marriage 11 years after the wedding?

   ____

3. How many children have they had in their 11 years of marriage?

   ____

4. What have they never regretted?

   ____

5. What have they always stressed about marriage?

   ____

6. What have friends noted about the Weinlicks?

   ____

7. There was no guarantee of what?

   ____

EXERCISE 6: Editing

Read Jennifer Garcia's journal entry. There are nine mistakes in the use of verb constructions. The first mistake is already corrected. Find and correct eight more.

May 20

I just had to write today. It's our six-month anniversary. Jim and I ~~are~~ have been married six months as of today. So maybe this is the time for me to take stock of my situation. The obvious question is whether I'm happy I got married. The answer is "Absolutely." When I remember what my life has been like before we were married, I realize now how lonely I've been before. Jim is a wonderful guy. Since we both work, we took turns doing the housework. He's really good about that. When we have been dating, I wasn't sure whether or not I'll have to do all the housework. But I wasn't having any reason to worry. Today we split everything 50 / 50. The only complaint I have is that Jim snored at night. When I tell him he does that, he only says, "Well, sweetie, you snore too." I don't believe it. But if this is our only problem, I guess we're pretty lucky.

Well, I'd had a long and tiring day, but it's almost over. It's time to go to sleep.

STEP 4 COMMUNICATION PRACTICE

EXERCISE 7: Listening

A | *Listen to the news broadcast. In what country did the wedding take place?*

____

B | *Read the questions. Listen again to the news broadcast. Answer each question in a complete sentence containing a past-time verb.*

1. What did Samantha Yang and Darrell Hammer hire Reverend Martinez to do?

   They hired him to marry them while they were parachute jumping from a plane.

2. To date, how many jumps have Samantha and Darrell each made?

   ______

3. How long have they been members of the jumping group?

   ______

4. How were they originally going to get married?

   ______

5. Why did they decide not to do this? (first reason)

   ______

6. Why did they decide not to do this? (second reason)

   ______

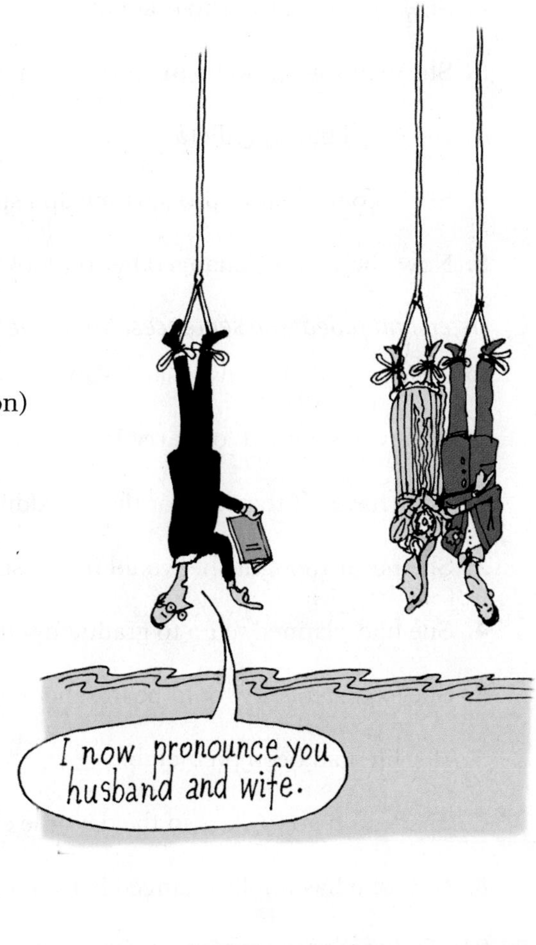

7. Had Reverend Martinez ever done this kind of wedding before?

   ______

8. Where did Reverend Martinez use to be a pastor?

   ______

Do you take this woman to be your lawfully wedded wife?

Unusual Weddings

I now pronounce you husband and wife.

EXERCISE 8: Pronunciation

A | *Read and listen to the Pronunciation Note.*

Pronunciation Note

In spoken English, auxiliary verbs in past verb forms are often contracted.

Examples: She**'s** recently been to see the doctor. (**'s** = **has**)
They**'ve** been to the theater several times. (**'ve** = **have**)
I**'d** been tired, so I took a nap. (**'d** = **had**)
In college, he**'d** spend hours studying. (**'d** = **would**)

B | *Listen and repeat the sentences. Underline the auxiliary in each sentence.*

Example: Jack's just asked Nancy to marry him.

1. Nancy's agreed to marry Jack.
2. They've set the date for their wedding.
3. She never thought she'd marry so soon.
4. She'd planned to go to graduate school.
5. She expected she'd be in school for a long time.
6. Her life'd been predictable.
7. She'd go to class in the daytime and study at night.
8. Now she's totally changed her outlook.

C | *Listen and repeat the sentences. Underline the auxiliary in each sentence.*

Example: Jack has just asked Nancy to marry him.

1. Nancy has agreed to marry Jack.
2. They have set the date for their wedding.
3. She never thought she would marry so soon.
4. She had planned to go to graduate school.
5. She expected she would be in school for a long time.
6. Her life had been predictable.
7. She would go to class in the daytime and study at night.
8. Now she has totally changed her outlook.

D | *PAIRS: Practice the sentences. One partner says a sentence with the contracted form. The other partner says the sentence with the full form.*

EXERCISE 9: Information Gap

A | *PAIRS: Complete the text. Each of you will read a version of the same story. Each version is missing some information. Take turns asking your partner questions to get the missing information.*

Student A, read the story about Jack Strait. Ask questions and fill in the missing information. Then answer Student B's questions.

Student B, turn to page 30 and follow the instructions there.

EXAMPLE: **A:** What kind of company did he use to work for?
B: He used to work for a company that . . . How long would he stay on the road?
A: He would stay on the road for . . .

Jack Strait's life is quite different now from the way it used to be. He used to work for a company that ____________________________. His job required him to do a lot of traveling. He would stay on the road for two or three weeks at a time. It was always the same: As soon as he pulled into a town, he would look for ____________________________.

The next morning he'd leave his business card at a lot of different establishments, hoping that someone would agree to see him. If he'd been lucky enough to arrange an appointment in advance, he'd show them ____________________________. Occasionally they would order a carpet or some linoleum; most often they wouldn't.

Jack's marriage began to suffer. He missed his wife a lot, but there wasn't much he could do about the situation. And when he was on the road, he hardly ever saw his children. He would try to ____________________________ if he had a spare moment. Usually, however, it was so late that they had already gone to bed. They were growing up without him.

Finally, his wife laid down the law, saying, "Why should we even be married if we're never going to see each other?" Jack decided she was right. He took a risk. He quit his job and started his own business. Things were difficult at first, but at least the family was together.

That was five years ago. Things have changed a lot since then. Jack and his family used to live in a small apartment. Now they own a house. Life is good.

B | *Compare your story with your partner's. Are they the same? Now discuss these questions: What did Jack's occupation use to be? Is it important to take risks in life as Jack did? Can you think of an example of a risk you have taken in your life?*

EXERCISE 10: Picture Discussion

PAIRS: Discuss the picture. Describe the situation. What is happening? Approximately how long do you think these people have been married? Do you think their relationship is less interesting or satisfactory than it used to be, or is it just different? Present your opinions to the class.

EXERCISE 11: Group Discussion

GROUPS: Talk about a significant change in each person's life. Each person says what has changed, what he or she was going to do, and what he or she is going to do now. Use the present perfect and future-in-the-past constructions. Choose from topics in the box or create your own topic. Report interesting examples to the class.

a move to another place	**education plans**	**marriage**	**career plans**

Example: My career plans have changed. I wasn't going to attend college. I was going to . . . Now I've decided to . . .

EXERCISE 12: Writing

A | *Write two or three paragraphs about the topic. Use the present perfect and future-in-the-past constructions.*

Describe a situation that has turned out differently from what you expected—for example, a marriage or other relationship, a job, college plans, a move, etc. First talk about what you thought would happen; then talk about what actually happened.

Example: I've been happily married for some time now, but when I was introduced to the man who is now my husband, it never occurred to me that we would end up husband and wife. In fact, when I met Dave, I thought he was the most arrogant man I had ever met. Here's how it happened . . .

B | *Check your work. Use the Editing Checklist.*

Editing Checklist

Did you use . . . ?
☐ simple present correctly
☐ past perfect correctly
☐ present perfect correctly
☐ future in the past correctly

INFORMATION GAP FOR STUDENT B

Student B, read the story about Jack Strait. Answer Student A's questions. Then ask your own questions and fill in the missing information.

EXAMPLE: **A:** What kind of company did he use to work for?
B: He used to work for a company that sold carpets and flooring. How long would he stay on the road?
A: He would stay on the road for . . .

Jack Strait's life is quite different now from the way it used to be. He used to work for a company that sold carpets and flooring. His job required him to do a lot of traveling. He would stay on the road for ____________________. It was always the same: As soon as he pulled into a town, he would look for a cheap motel to stay in.

The next morning he'd leave ____________________ at a lot of different establishments, hoping that someone would agree to see him. If he'd been lucky enough to arrange an appointment in advance, he'd show them his samples. Occasionally they would order ____________________; most often they wouldn't.

Jack's marriage began to suffer. He missed his wife a lot, but there wasn't much he could do about the situation. And when he was on the road, he hardly ever saw his children. He would try to call them in the evenings if he had a spare moment. Usually, however, it was so late that they had already gone to bed. They were growing up without him.

Finally, his wife laid down the law, saying, "Why should we even be married if we're never going to see each other?" Jack decided she was right. He took a risk. He quit his job and started his own business. Things were difficult at first, but at least the family was together.

That was five years ago. Things have changed a lot since then. Jack and his family used to live ____________________. Now they own a house. Life is good.

B | *Compare your story with your partner's. Are they the same? Now discuss these questions: What did Jack's occupation use to be? Is it important to take risks in life as Jack did? Can you think of an example of a risk you have taken in your life?*

UNIT **2** # Review

Check your answers on page UR-1.
Do you need to review anything?

A | *Complete the paragraph with simple past or present perfect forms of the verbs in parentheses.*

Ever since Julio and Darla ________ (1. get) married, they ________ (2. do) a lot of traveling. They ________ (3. be) to six countries and plan to see another two this summer. So far their favorite is Brazil, which they ________ (4. visit) twice. The first time ________ (5. be) in 2009. They ________ (6. go) again last year. Darla says, "When I was a girl, I always ________ (7. want) to marry a man who would take me to exotic places. Julio is that man. I ________ (8. never know) anyone so adventurous."

B | *Complete the paragraph with simple past and past perfect forms of the verbs from the box.*

attend	be	invite	know	meet	propose

Julio and Darla ________ (1.) at a Travel Club meeting, which Darla ________ (2.) because a friend ________ (3.) her. It ________ (4.) a classic case of love at first sight. They ________ (5.) each other for only two months by the time Julio ________ (6.).

C | *Circle the letter of the one underlined word or phrase in each sentence that is not correct.*

1. When I <u>talked</u> (A) to Jason, he <u>said</u> (B) he <u>didn't</u> (C) <u>used to be</u> (D) a serious student. **A B C D**
2. When we <u>lived</u> (A) in New York, we <u>would have</u> (B) a lot more friends than we <u>did</u> (C) when we <u>moved</u> (D) to Chicago. **A B C D**
3. I <u>am going to</u> (A) <u>write</u> (B) you as soon as I <u>got</u> (C) home, but it <u>slipped</u> (D) my mind. **A B C D**
4. Rosa and I <u>were going to</u> (A) <u>have</u> (B) dinner at a restaurant and then <u>go</u> (C) to a movie, but we <u>did</u> (D) after all. **A B C D**
5. We <u>went</u> (A) to the party, even though we <u>didn't know</u> (B) who else <u>will</u> (C) <u>be there</u> (D). **A B C D**
6. Mary and Carlos <u>called</u> (A) off their wedding, although they <u>had</u> (B) <u>been</u> (C) <u>planned</u> (D) it for months. **A B C D**

UNIT 3

Future Time
TRAVEL

STEP 1 GRAMMAR IN CONTEXT

Before You Read

PAIRS: Look at the pictures and discuss the questions.

1. How can you prevent this problem when you travel?
2. Where do you like to travel?
3. Is it important to learn some of the language and culture of a place you'll be visiting?

Read

Read the article about getting the most out of a trip.

Get the Most Out of It!

By Tammy Samuelson

So you**'re visiting** some new countries this year? You already have your tickets, and you **leave** in exactly four weeks. A month from now you**'ll be relaxing** in the sunshine or **visiting** famous landmarks. But are you prepared to maximize the enjoyment of your experience? In my capacity as *Times* travel editor, I've been journeying abroad since 1997, so I've learned a few things. In this week's column I**'m going to give** you suggestions in five areas that **will help** you get the most out of your trip.

FIRST TIP: Jetlag. If you've ever flown a significant distance away from your home time zone, you know lack of sleep is a problem. By the time you **arrive**, you**'ll have been flying** for eight to ten hours and **won't be able to keep** your eyes open. Then your entire body **will be** out of whack for days. Here's my suggestion: Take a late afternoon or evening flight, and make every effort to sleep on the plane, even if it's only for an hour or so. When you **land**, it **will** probably **be** late morning or early afternoon. Stay up until evening! Don't take a nap, no matter how excruciatingly tired and sleepy you feel. That way, you**'ll fall** into a new rhythm as naturally as possible. Your body **will adjust** much more quickly.

SECOND TIP: Tours. If you've been abroad before, I'd say go ahead and chart your own course. If you haven't, join a tour group. You can get excellent package deals that include

Get the Most Out of It!

accommodations and tours that hit the high points. Good tour leaders **will show** you the things you want to see. You'**ll make** new friends and **learn** a lot. Yes, it's true that tours can be hectic and intense. They're worth it, though.

THIRD TIP: Accommodations. Consider staying at bed and breakfasts. Package deals often don't allow you to choose your accommodations, but sometimes they set you up in B and B's. Bed and breakfasts are generally friendly places where small numbers of people stay, and they're often not that expensive. You'**ll meet** interesting people. The food is generally well prepared and nourishing.

FOURTH TIP: Money and valuables. Resist the temptation to carry your money, passport, or other valuables in a purse or wallet. Keep them in a money belt instead. Potential thieves **will be** out in force everywhere you go. They'**ll have** a lot more difficulty stealing from a money belt worn around your waist under your exterior clothing.

FIFTH TIP: Language and culture. Few things **will please** the inhabitants of the countries where you'**re going** more than your effort to learn something about them. Buy a phrasebook and start acquiring some of the basics of the language. Begin now and you'**ll have learned** enough to accomplish some basic communication by the time you **arrive**. Discover a bit of the history. Try to step out of your own mindset and put yourself into the shoes of the people who live there.

So there you have it. Take my advice. By the time you **get** home, you'**ll have acquired** some wonderful memories for your mental scrapbook. Make it the trip of a lifetime.

After You Read

A | **Vocabulary:** *Circle the letter of the best meaning for the* **blue** *words and phrases from the reading.*

1. You'll be relaxing or visiting famous **landmarks**.

a. cities **b.** famous objects or structures **c.** statues **d.** museums

2. Are you prepared to **maximize** the enjoyment of your experience?

a. make easy **b.** greatly decrease **c.** complicate **d.** greatly increase

3. Your entire body will be **out of whack** for days.

a. not working properly **b.** ill **c.** wounded **d.** semiconscious

4. Don't take a nap, no matter how **excruciatingly** tired and sleepy you feel.

a. pleasantly **b.** terribly **c.** interestingly **d.** boringly

5. Go ahead and **chart your own course**.

a. take a cruise **b.** plan an auto trip **c.** make individual arrangements **d.** ask for help

(continued on next page)

6. Tours can be **hectic** and intense.

a. full of hurried excitement **b.** full of pleasure **c.** full of danger **d.** full of expense

7. Try to step out of your own **mindset**.

a. culture **b.** opinion **c.** habitual mental attitude **d.** educational background

8. You'll have acquired some wonderful memories for your mental **scrapbook**.

a. photo album **b.** health **c.** allowance **d.** record

B | Comprehension: *Refer to the reading and complete each statement with a single word.*

1. Jetlag is strongly influenced by ________________ of sleep.
2. To avoid jetlag, you should stay up until ________________ of the day you arrive.
3. The author recommends taking ________________ if you haven't been abroad before.
4. Relatively small ________________ of people stay in bed and breakfasts at a given time.
5. You may be victimized by ________________ if you carry valuables in a wallet or purse.
6. To please the residents of countries you visit, you should buy and study a ________________.
7. You'll understand them better if you put ________________ in their shoes.

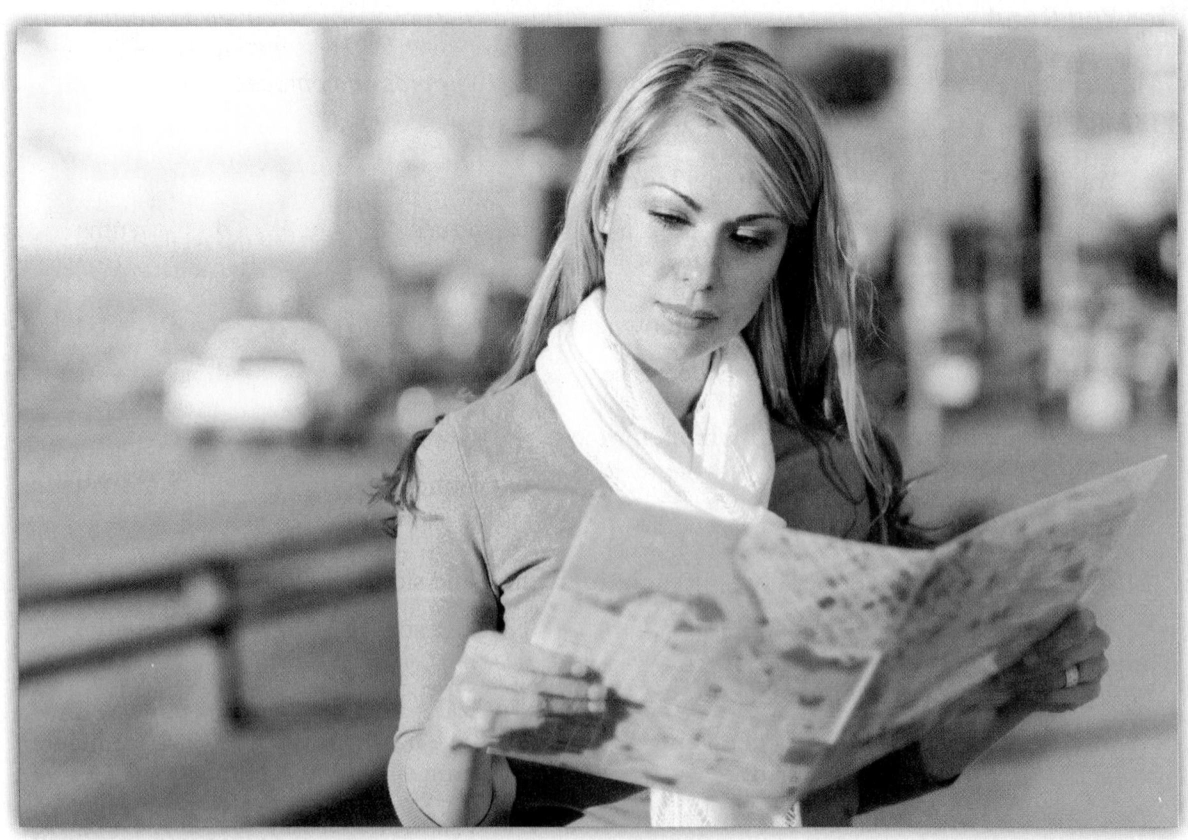

STEP 2 GRAMMAR PRESENTATION

FUTURE TIME

Future Time: A Time in the Future

Simple Future	Future Progressive
Will / Be going to **+ Base Form**	***Will be / Be going to*** **+** ***Be*** **+ Base Form +** ***-ing***
You**'ll like** the hotel. You**'re going to like** the hotel.	A week from now, you**'ll be relaxing** in the sun. A week from now, you**'re going to be relaxing** in the sun.

Simple Present	Present Progressive
	Be **+ Base Form +** ***-ing***
The tour **starts** tomorrow at 4:00 P.M.	We**'re visiting** our friends later this summer.

Two Actions in the Future
I**'ll call** you as soon as we **land**.

Future Perfect	Future Perfect Progressive
Will have **+ Past Participle**	***Will have been*** **+ Base Form +** ***-ing***
We**'ll have arrived** by 4:00 P.M.	We **will have been flying** for hours by then.

GRAMMAR NOTES

1

Use ***will*** or ***be going to*** to say what you think will happen in the future.

- I think I**'ll enjoy** the trip.

OR

- I think I**'m going to enjoy** the trip.

BE CAREFUL! Use *will*, not *be going to*, to express a future action decided on at the moment of speaking.

- Come by at noon. I**'ll change** my dentist's appointment.
  NOT: I~~'m going to~~ change my dentist's appointment.

NOTE: We most often use *be going to* to talk about a future situation that is planned or already developing.

- We**'re going to take** our vacation in June this year.
- Look at that sky! It**'s going to rain** for sure!

(continued on next page)

2	Use ***will be*** or ***be going to be*** + base form + *-ing* to describe an action that will be in progress at a certain time in the future. **USAGE NOTE:** We often use the **future progressive** informally to talk about a future intention.	• We**'ll be visiting** Florence on our Italy trip. • We**'re going to be spending** time in Rome too. • Next week at this time we**'ll be climbing** Kilimanjaro.
3	You can use the **simple present** to talk about a future action, state, or event that is part of a schedule or timetable.	• We **leave** on Saturday at 8:00 P.M. • The plane **arrives** in Rome at 8:30 A.M.
4	You can use the **present progressive** to talk about a future action or event that has already been arranged.	• We**'re traveling** to Japan in August. We already have our tickets.
5	To talk about two separate actions in the future, use ***will*** or ***be going to*** in the independent clause and the simple present in the dependent clause. **BE CAREFUL!** The verb in the dependent clause has the form of the simple present, but its meaning is future.	INDEPENDENT CLAUSE • We**'ll rent / 're going to rent** a car DEPENDENT CLAUSE when we **get** to Italy. NOT: We'll rent a car when we ~~will~~ get to Italy. • We'll leave for the airport as soon as the taxi **gets** here.
6	Use the **future perfect** to show an action, state, or event that will happen **before** a certain time in the future. You can also use the future perfect in the **progressive**. **NOTE:** We often use the future perfect with *by* and *by the time.*	• By the end of our trip, we**'ll have seen** a lot of wonderful things. • By the end of the summer, we**'ll have been traveling** for several weeks. • **By the time** we finish our trip, we**'ll have visited** 10 countries.

REFERENCE NOTE

For definitions and examples of **grammar terms**, see Glossary on page G-1.

STEP 3 FOCUSED PRACTICE

EXERCISE 1: Discover the Grammar

A | *These sentences from the reading express the future in several different ways. Underline the verbs showing future time and label the ways.*

1. So you're visiting some new countries this year? ___present progressive___
2. You leave in exactly four weeks. ________
3. A month from now you'll be relaxing in the sunshine. ________
4. I'm going to give you suggestions in five areas. ________
5. The suggestions will help you get the most out of your trip. ________
6. You'll have been flying for eight to ten hours. ________
7. When you land, it will probably be late morning. ________
8. By then you'll have acquired some wonderful memories. ________

B | *Look at the sentences. Does the underlined verb refer to present time* (**P**) *or future time* (**F**)*?*

__F__ 1. So you're visiting some new countries this year?

____ 2. You already have your tickets.

____ 3. You leave in exactly four weeks.

____ 4. When you land, it will probably be late morning or early afternoon.

____ 5. You can get package deals that include accommodations and tours.

____ 6. Package deals often don't allow you to choose your own accommodations.

____ 7. Few things will please the inhabitants of the countries where you're going more than learning something about them.

____ 8. You'll have learned enough to accomplish some basic communication by the time you arrive.

____ 9. Try to put yourself into the shoes of the people who live there.

____ 10. So there you have it.

EXERCISE 2: Present Progressive Future

(Grammar Notes 1, 3–4)

Nancy Osborne is traveling in Europe. Complete her letter to her friend Evelyn with the correct future forms of the verbs in the box. Use the present progressive if possible.

arrive	leave	move	see	take
go	mind	not be able to use	~~shine~~	write

London Towers Hotel

Sunday, July 19

Hi Evelyn,

Well, I've been in London for three days now, and it hasn't stopped raining. Fortunately, the Internet says the sun ___is going to shine___ (1.) tomorrow. Hallelujah! I went to the British Museum yesterday and had such a good time that I ______________ (2.) again this morning. In the afternoon I ______________ (3.) a tour of the Tower of London.

I've been staying at a bed and breakfast that's really nice, but it's also pretty expensive, so I ______________ (4.) to a hostel tonight. I don't think I ______________ (5.) staying there, since I don't need luxury.

I've met some really nice people at the B and B, including a lady who gave me a theater ticket she ______________ (6.). So I ______________ (7.) a play at a West End theater on Friday night. On Saturday I ______________ (8.) for France at 6 P.M. via the Chunnel train. I ______________ (9.) in Paris at 5:30 A.M. Can you believe that?

That's it for now. Hope things are OK with you. I ______________ (10.) again soon.

Best,
Nancy

EXERCISE 3: Two Actions in the Future

(Grammar Note 5)

Complete the sentences about the rest of Nancy's trip to Europe. Use the correct form of the verbs in parentheses. Each sentence will describe two actions or events in the future.

1. As soon as Nancy ___arrives___ (arrive) in Paris, she ___'ll find___ (find) an inexpensive place to stay.
2. She ________ (meet) her friend Carolyn the day after she ________ (arrive).
3. Nancy and Carolyn ________ (visit) the Eiffel Tower, the Louvre, and the Palace of Versailles before they ________ (leave) Paris.
4. When they ________ (finish) touring Paris, they ________ (take) a train to Rome.
5. They ________ (visit) Florence and Venice after they ________ (tour) Rome.
6. Before they ________ (fly) back to the U.S., they ________ (buy) souvenirs.

EXERCISE 4: Personal Inventory (Future)

(Grammar Notes 1–6)

Answer each question in a complete sentence, according to your own experience.

1. What do you think your life occupation will be?

   ____

2. Where do you think you'll be living in five years?

   ____

3. What are you going to do this evening after dinner?

   ____

4. Where are you going on your next vacation?

   ____

5. What are you going to do as soon as you leave English class today?

   ____

6. What time does your next English class begin?

   ____

7. By when will you have finished your studies?

   ____

8. In a year's time, how long will you have been studying English?

   ____

EXERCISE 5: Editing

Read the travel log. There are eleven mistakes in the use of future verbs. The first mistake is already corrected. Find and correct ten more.

Travel Log

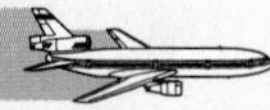

I am writing these words in English because I need the practice. At this moment I am on an airplane over the Pacific Ocean, on my way to a year of study at Columbia University in the United States. The plane left an hour ago. It's a 10-hour flight, so I hope I will have written a lot by the time we ~~will~~ land. I am looking forward to being there, but I am also a little afraid. What do I find when I will get to America? Will the Americans be arrogant and unfriendly? Will I make any friends? Am I happy? My best friend in Korea said, "You don't make any real friends when you'll be there." I am not so sure. I guess I find out.

* *

These were the words I wrote in my diary on the airplane last month. But I have been here for a month now, and I have found that things are a lot different from what I expected. The majority of people here are friendly. They go out of their way to help you if you need it, and my American friends invite me to go places. Soon I go hiking with a group from my dormitory.

Two of the ideas I had about the United States, however, seem to be true. One is that Americans don't pay much attention to rules. One of my best American friends says, in fact, "Rules are made to be broken." The other idea is about the American family. In Asia the family is very important, but some Asian people think the family means nothing in the United States. I don't know if this is true or not. But I think it might be true, since my American friends almost never mention their parents or their brothers and sisters. Anyway, I am going to have a chance to see a real American family. I go with my roommate Susan to spend Thanksgiving break with her family in Pennsylvania. When I will see her family, maybe I'm going to understand more.

STEP 4 COMMUNICATION PRACTICE

EXERCISE 6: Listening

A | *The Fosters are traveling in Canada. Listen to their conversation. What city are they visiting?*

____

B | *Read the sentences. Then listen again and write* **T (True)** *or* **F (False)**.

__T__ **1.** Tim is still in bed.

_____ **2.** The Fosters are going to the mall this morning.

_____ **3.** Amy and Tim want to go to the museum.

_____ **4.** Dad thinks the children can learn something at the museum.

_____ **5.** Tim thinks it's always important to learn new things.

_____ **6.** The Fosters are on the tour bus now.

_____ **7.** The Fosters will miss the bus if they don't hurry.

_____ **8.** Tim and Amy like tours.

_____ **9.** Amy and Tim would rather go to the museum by themselves than go on a tour.

_____ **10.** The Fosters are going to the mall before they go on the tour.

_____ **11.** The tour will end after 12:30.

EXERCISE 7: Pronunciation

A | *Read and listen to the Pronunciation Note.*

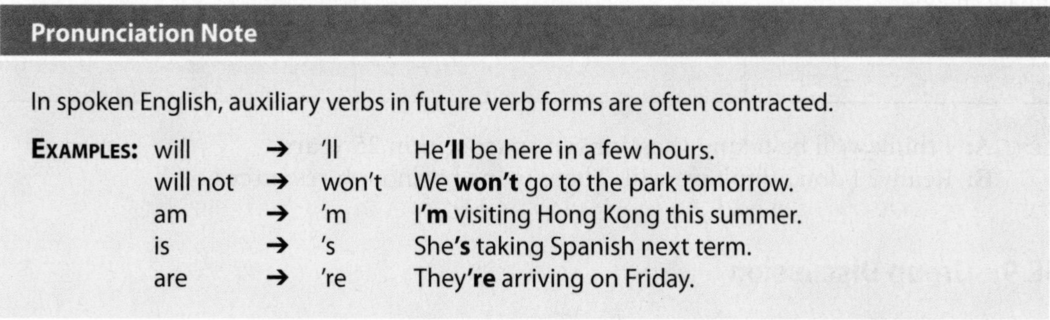

Pronunciation Note

In spoken English, auxiliary verbs in future verb forms are often contracted.

Examples:			
will	→	'll	He**'ll** be here in a few hours.
will not	→	won't	We **won't** go to the park tomorrow.
am	→	'm	I**'m** visiting Hong Kong this summer.
is	→	's	She**'s** taking Spanish next term.
are	→	're	They**'re** arriving on Friday.

B | *Listen to the sentences. Circle the future form you hear in each part of the sentences.*

1. I will not / won't be able to go with you tonight, but I will / I'll be able to go tomorrow night.

2. I'm / I am not going to attend college this fall, but I'm / I am going to attend in the spring.

3. I will / I'll be able to help you tomorrow; unfortunately, I will not / won't be able to help you today.

(continued on next page)

4. We <u>will not / won't</u> be traveling in Asia in July, but <u>we will / we'll</u> be there in August.

5. They <u>will not / won't</u> be moving to a new house in September, but <u>they will / they'll</u> be moving in November.

6. <u>We're not / We are not</u> leaving this weekend, but <u>we are / we're</u> leaving next weekend.

7. We <u>won't have / will not have</u> visited every South American country by the end of our trip, but we <u>will have / we'll have</u> seen most of them.

C | *PAIRS: Practice the sentences.*

EXERCISE 8: Pair Discussion

A | *Check (✓) the things that you believe will happen in the next 25 years. Add your own item in the last row.*

B | *Talk about each item with your partner.*

C | *Report your predictions to the class.*

Event	You	Your Partner
Take vacations in space		
Eliminate poverty		
End offshore oil drilling		
Stop climate change		

Example: **A:** I think we'll be taking vacations in space within 25 years.
B: Really? I don't think we will. There won't be enough resources.

EXERCISE 9: Group Discussion

A | *GROUPS: Read the short paragraph about world traveler John Clouse.*

Indiana attorney John Clouse was the first person to see all 317 of the world's officially recognized countries. Clouse, who died in June 2008, had the following comment about people around the world:

"I don't believe there are evil empires and evil people. Yes, there are some bad leaders in the world, but seeing people as individuals has taught me that they are all basically alike. You can be in some terrible places and someone will extend hospitality to you."

B | *Discuss the ideas in Clouse's statement, giving examples from your own experience to support your viewpoint. Touch on the following questions in your discussion:*

- Are there evil empires and evil people?
- Are people all basically alike?
- Will people always extend hospitality to you, wherever you are?

EXAMPLE: **A:** I disagree with Clouse. I believe there are evil empires and evil people. Maybe there aren't many, but there are some.
B: What's an example of an empire you think is evil?

C | *Report your group's conclusions to the class.*

EXERCISE 10: Writing

A | *Write two or three paragraphs on one of the following topics, making sure to use future constructions.*

- What is your response to the quote by Clouse in Exercise 9? Give examples from your own experience to support your viewpoint.
- Imagine you're going on your dream vacation next week. Describe the vacation.

EXAMPLE: For most of my life, my idea of a dream vacation has been to visit China. This dream is finally going to come true. I leave next Friday for a two-week trip to China with a group from work. We're going to visit Beijing, Shanghai, and the Great Wall. We're even going to . . .

B | *Check your work. Use the Editing Checklist.*

Editing Checklist

Did you use . . . ?
☐ future with ***will*** correctly
☐ future with ***be going to*** correctly
☐ simple present correctly
☐ present progressive correctly

UNIT 3 Review

Check your answers on page UR-1.

Do you need to review anything?

A | *Complete the telephone message with correct forms of the verbs from the box.*

be	call	get	have to	let	stop by

Hi, Mary. This is Bill. I ________ (1.) work late tonight, so I ________ (2.) late for dinner. I ________ (3.) you as soon as the boss ________ (4.) me leave. I ________ (5.) the store and pick up dessert before I ________ (6.) there. Bye. Love you.

B | *Complete the email with the correct forms of the verbs in parentheses. More than one answer is possible in some items.*

Dear Andy,

Sam and I are ________ (1. (take)) our vacation in Australia this year! Our plane ________ (2. (leave)) tonight and arrives in Tokyo tomorrow. Then there's a 10-hour flight to Sydney. By the time we ________ (3. (get)) there, we ________ (4. (fly)) for over 24 hours. We ________ (5. (be)) exhausted, but it will certainly be worth it. We ________ (6. (spend)) two and a half weeks in Australia. We ________ (7. (send)) you a postcard as soon as we ________ (8. (be)) settled in our bed and breakfast in Sydney. Stay tuned!

Martha

C | *Circle the letter of the one underlined word or phrase in each sentence that is not correct.*

1. <u>Call</u> (A) me when you <u>get</u> (B) to town; maybe <u>I'm going to</u> (C) <u>be</u> (D) free. **A B C D**
2. <u>As soon as</u> (A) <u>I'll hear</u> (B) from Mandy, <u>I'll let</u> (C) you know when <u>she's coming</u> (D). **A B C D**
3. I just <u>heard</u> (A) the weather report; <u>according to</u> (B) the forecast, <u>it's raining</u> (C) tonight, but tomorrow <u>it will be</u> (D) sunny and warm. **A B C D**
4. The boss <u>calls</u> (A) you <u>as soon as</u> (B) she <u>knows</u> (C) if there <u>will be</u> (D) a job. **A B C D**
5. <u>We'll</u> (A) <u>have been</u> (B) <u>traveled</u> (C) for over a month by the time we <u>return</u> (D). **A B C D**
6. <u>By the time</u> (A) the summer <u>is</u> (B) over, <u>I'll have</u> (C) <u>visiting</u> (D) 10 new countries. **A B C D**

From Grammar to Writing

THE SENTENCE: AVOIDING SENTENCE FRAGMENTS

You can strengthen your writing by writing complete sentences and avoiding sentence fragments. A complete sentence must have:

- a subject
- at least one verb that shows time
- at least one independent clause
- initial capitalization and end punctuation

These word groups are fragments, not sentences:

Sherry sitting and writing a letter. (no verb showing time)

Were taking the train to Barcelona. (no subject)

Such an exciting year. (no subject, no verb showing time)

As soon as they could. (not an independent clause)

We can change these fragments into sentences by doing the following:

Sherry was sitting and writing a letter. (adding a verb showing time)

The girls were taking the train to Barcelona. (adding a subject)

The year 2011 was such an exciting year. (adding a subject and a verb showing time)

They decided to return to Barcelona as soon as they could. (adding an independent clause)

1 | *Read the paragraph. There are eight sentences and eight fragments. The first sentence is already underlined. Find and underline seven more.*

In late December. Sherry, Akiko, and Lisa took a one-day trip to Barcelona. Not knowing anyone there. They stayed in a youth hostel for a very reasonable price. On their one day in the city. They visited the Sagrada Familia, Gaudí's famous church. All three girls were impressed by the church's beauty. And decided to climb to the top instead of taking the elevator. Nearing the top, Akiko began to feel dizzy and had to start down again. Sherry and Lisa continued climbing. However, even Sherry, who had done a great deal of mountain climbing in Canada. Felt nervous and unprotected at the summit. Both she and Lisa agreed that the view was magnificent. And the climb well worth it. The three decided to return to Barcelona. As soon as they could.

2 | *On your own paper, rewrite the paragraph, changing all the fragments to sentences by combining them appropriately.*

3 | *Read the paragraph. There are 16 sentences with mistakes in initial capitalization and end punctuation. The first mistake is already corrected. Find and correct 15 more. Do not add or eliminate any commas.*

last summer when my wife and I were traveling in Morocco, we had one of the most interesting bargaining experiences ever. we were in an open-air market in Rabat, and I really wanted to buy a Moroccan *jellaba,* a long, heavy, ankle-length garment there were several different shops where jellabas were sold, but Heather and I were drawn to one shop in particular I tried one jellaba on it fit perfectly, and I knew it was the one I wanted, so I asked the merchant how much it was he said it was $100 now I've always been uncomfortable about bargaining, so I was ready to pay his price Heather took me aside, however, and said that was too much and that he expected me to bargain when I said I couldn't bargain, she told me that bargaining was part of the game and that I should offer him less I sighed, tried to swallow the lump in my throat, and suggested $25 he smiled and asked for $75, whereupon I offered $35 he looked offended and shook his head Heather grabbed my hand, and we started walking away I thought that was going to be the end of the experience, but then the merchant came running after me, saying he'd accept $50 I ended up buying the jellaba for that amount, and I still have it since then I've developed courage and gained self-confidence, so, as they say, travel is indeed broadening.

4 | *Before you write . . .*

1. We often say, "Travel is broadening." Think of a time when you learned something significant during a travel experience. How did your behavior or thinking change because of your experience?
2. Describe the experience to a partner. Listen to your partner's experience.
3. Answer questions about your experience. Ask your partner about his or her experience. For example: *Where and when did it happen? Why did you . . . ? How did you feel? How has this experience changed you?*

5 | *Write a draft of a short composition (one or two paragraphs) about a travel experience in which you learned something significant. Follow the model. Include information that your partner asked about.*

I love to travel / often travel / recently traveled.

____

____

____

Several months ago, / A couple of years ago, / In 2011,

____

____

____

____

____

____

____

Now ____

____

____

____

____

____

____

6 | *Exchange compositions with a different partner. Complete the chart.*

1. The writer wrote complete sentences and avoided fragments. **Yes** ☐ **No** ☐

2. What I liked in the composition:

____

____

____

3. Questions I'd like the writer to answer about the composition:

Who ____?

What ____?

When ____?

Where ____?

Why ____?

How ____?

(Your own question) ______________________________________?

7 | *Work with your partner. Discuss each other's chart from Exercise 6. Then rewrite your own composition and make any necessary changes.*

MODALS AND OTHER AUXILIARIES

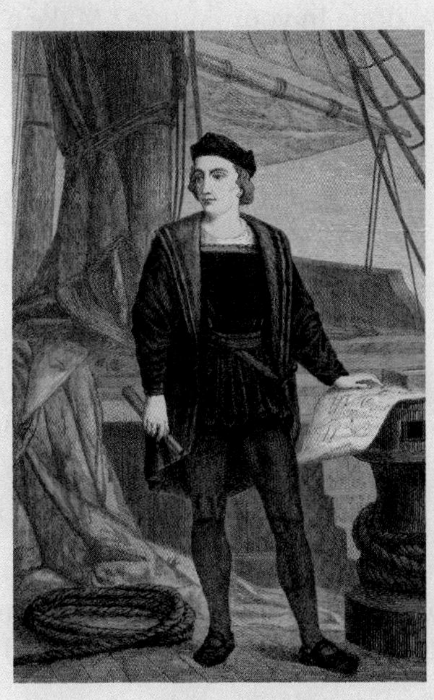

UNIT	GRAMMAR FOCUS	THEME
4	Modals to Express Degrees of Necessity	Cultural Differences
5	Modals to Express Degrees of Certainty	Puzzles

UNIT 4 Modals to Express Degrees of Necessity

CULTURAL DIFFERENCES

STEP 1 GRAMMAR IN CONTEXT

Before You Read

PAIRS: Look at the picture on page 51 and discuss the questions.

1. What are the people doing? Is this a practice in your culture?
2. What are some things that should and shouldn't be done in your culture? Make a short list.

Read

 *Read the article about cultural differences.*

What We Should and Shouldn't Have Done

Recently my wife and I had a cross-cultural experience that taught us about some things we **should have done** differently. My company sent me to work at our branch office in Japan. My Japanese co-workers have been friendly and gracious, and last week one of them invited us for dinner. We were honored, and the food was delicious. But though Masayuki and Yukiko, his wife, were most polite and friendly, we felt a bit uncomfortable about the evening. I asked my friend Junichi about it. He's lived in Japan and the United States, so he knows the cultural differences. He gave me several pointers. Now we know what we **should** and **shouldn't have done**.

The first tip was about shoes. We knew you**'re supposed to take** them **off** in a Japanese home. We didn't know you**'re supposed to arrange** them to point toward the door so when you leave you can put them on without turning around. But this wasn't a big mistake, Junichi said.

The second pointer was about gifts. We knew we **should take** a gift. Masayuki and Yukiko seemed a little shocked, though, when we pulled a CD out of a plastic bag and said, "We thought you'd like this rock and roll CD." Junichi chuckled and said, "Well, you **should have wrapped** the CD. It's OK to bring it in a plastic bag, but the gift **has to be wrapped**. And you **mustn't say** anything about it. Just give it to your hosts. The main problem, though, was the gift itself. A rock and roll CD isn't really appropriate."

What We **Should** and **Shouldn't** Have Done

"Well, what **should** we **have taken**?"

"A box of chocolates. Or you **could have taken** some flowers."

Then I told Junichi about what happened before dinner. Masayuki and Yukiko offered us some tea and snacks. The tea was delicious, but we had trouble finishing the raw sushi. Masayuki and Yukiko seemed perplexed. Junichi chuckled again and said, "In Japan it's considered impolite to leave half-eaten food on a plate."

"You mean you**'ve got to eat** everything that's offered?" I asked.

"You **don't have to**. But if you take something, you **must finish** it."

After dinner, Helen asked Yukiko if she **could help** in the kitchen. This is normal in the United States, but Junichi said you**'re not to do** this in Japan. Visitors **aren't allowed to go** into the kitchen.

Another thing you **shouldn't do**, he said, is praise an object in the house. If you do, your Japanese hosts might feel they **have to give** you the object. Fortunately, we didn't do that.

At evening's end, Masayuki offered us another drink. Not wanting to be impolite, we accepted. Finally we felt we absolutely **had to leave**, so when we were offered another drink, I said, "Thanks, we**'d better get going**; we **have to get up** early." Masayuki and Yukiko seemed relieved. Junichi said, "That's what you **should have done** in the first place. When you're offered a drink at the end of the evening, you **should decline** gently. Leaving earlier would have been fine."

I asked what we **might do** to rectify the situation. "**Shall** we **invite** them to our apartment?"

"Yes, I think you **ought to have** them **over**. But don't have an informal, Western-style party. Just make it a simple dinner for the four of you."

Good advice, I thought. What really struck me is how much we all have to learn about other cultures.

After You Read

A | Vocabulary: *Complete the definitions with the correct word or phrase from the box.*

chuckle	gracious	perplexed	praise
decline	have someone over	pointer	rectify

1. To be ________________ is to be polite, kind, and pleasant.
2. A ________________ is a suggestion, tip, or piece of advice.
3. To ________________ is to laugh quietly.
4. To feel ________________ is to be confused, puzzled, or troubled.
5. To ________________ something or someone is to express admiration.
6. To ________________ something is to refuse it.
7. To ________________ is to invite a person or persons to your home.
8. If you ________________ a situation, you improve or fix it.

B | Comprehension: *Circle the letter of the correct answer.*

1. The author and his wife _____.
   - **a.** followed exactly the Japanese custom of taking your shoes off
   - **b.** should have left their shoes pointing toward the door, but didn't
2. In Japan, it's a good idea to _____.
   - **a.** bring something like a rock and roll CD as a house gift
   - **b.** wrap a gift instead of just bringing it in the original bag
3. In Japan, it's wrong to _____.
   - **a.** talk about a gift when you give it to your host
   - **b.** bring a wrapped gift in a plastic bag
4. An appropriate gift to take to a Japanese home would be _____.
   - **a.** a CD
   - **b.** flowers
5. When you are offered something to eat in a Japanese home, you _____.
   - **a.** shouldn't take something unless you are sure you can finish it
   - **b.** don't have to worry about eating all of it
6. According to their Japanese friend, the author and his wife should _____.
   - **a.** ask Masayuki and Yukiko to join them for a quiet dinner party
   - **b.** ask Masayuki and Yukiko to a typical Western-style party

STEP 2 GRAMMAR PRESENTATION

MODALS TO EXPRESS DEGREES OF NECESSITY (RANGING FROM OBLIGATION TO NO OBLIGATION)

Necessity 100%

Obligation (Necessity)							
You	**must** **have to** **have got to**	**call**	them.	You	**must not** **can't** **are not allowed to**	**call**	them.
You	**had to**	**call**	them.	You	**weren't allowed to**	**call**	them.

Advice							
You	**had better** **should** **ought to**	**leave**	early.	You	**had better not** **shouldn't**	**leave**	early.
You	**should have** **ought to have**	**left**	early.	You	**shouldn't have**	**left**	early.

Expectation							
You	**are supposed to** **are to**	**take**	a gift.	You	**are not supposed to** **are not to**	**do**	this.
You	**were supposed to** **were to**	**take**	a gift.	You	**were not supposed to** **were not to**	**do**	this.

Suggestion			
You	**could** **might**	**give**	roses.
You	**could have** **might have**	**given**	roses.

No Obligation (No Necessity)			
You	**don't have to**	**call**	them.
You	**didn't have to**	**call**	them.

0%

GRAMMAR NOTES

1	**Modals** are auxiliary verbs. The modals are *can, could, may, might, shall, should, will, would, must, ought to*, and *had better*. Each modal has only one form for all persons.	• I / You / He / She / We / They **could take** some flowers.
	Use **simple modals** (modal + base form) to show degrees of necessity in the present and the future.	• We **should invite** Jim to the party tonight.
	Use **perfect modals** (modal + *have* + past participle) to show degrees of necessity in the past.	• We **should have invited** Jim to last week's party too.
	Modals show speakers' attitudes toward the actions they are describing. Modals are used to talk about obligations, advice, expectations, and suggestions.	• You **could invite** them **over**. • You **should leave** early.
2	Some **modal-like expressions** have meanings equivalent to or similar to meanings of modals: *must* — *have to, have got to* *should* — *ought to* *may* — *be allowed to*	• You **must / have to / have got to finish** everything on your plate. • You **should / ought to take** a gift. • Visitors **may not / are not allowed to help** in the kitchen.
3	Use ***must***, ***have to***, and ***have got to*** to show strong necessity. They are similar in meaning.	• You **must / have to / have got to arrive** on time.
	USAGE NOTES Use ***must*** in more formal English to show a very strong obligation that can't be escaped.	**A:** You mean you **must eat** everything they offer you?
	Use ***have to*** in all forms and situations, formal and informal.	**B:** No, you **don't have to**.
	Use ***have got to*** in conversation and informal writing. It is rarely used in the negative. Use ***don't have to*** instead.	• We**'ve got to get going**.
	Use ***will have to*** to show future necessity.	• We**'ll have to invite** them **over**.
	BE CAREFUL! Use *had to* + base form to show past necessity. Don't use *must have* + past participle.	• We **had to leave.** NOT: We ~~must have left~~.

4	Use ***must not*** to say that it is **necessary not** to do something (*that it is prohibited*). Use ***don't / doesn't have to*** + base form to say that something is **not necessary**. In the past, use ***didn't have to*** + base form to say that something **was not necessary**. **BE CAREFUL!** Although *must* and *have to* have similar meanings, *must not* and *don't have to* have very different meanings.	• You **must not smoke** here. • You **don't have to take** everything offered to you. • You **didn't have to bring** a gift. • We **mustn't miss** the flight. NOT: We ~~don't have to~~ miss the flight.
5	Use ***should*** or ***ought to*** to offer advice. They mean "it would be a good idea if . . ." or "it's the right thing to do" and are basically the same in most situations. We normally use *should*, not *ought to*, in questions and negatives. Use ***should have / ought to have*** + past participle to express advice about past situations. *Should have* and *ought to have* suggest that the action did not happen. *Shouldn't have* and *ought not to have* suggest that it did. **NOTE:** We sometimes use ***shall*** in questions to ask for advice or direction. In this meaning, *shall* is used only with *I* or *we*. When it is used with *we*, it is often followed by a sentence with *let's*. In this meaning, *shall* is similar to *should*.	• You **should / ought to decline** gently. **A: Should** I **invite** a guest? **B:** No, you **shouldn't**. • You **should / ought to have done** that the first time. • You **shouldn't / ought not to have mentioned** your gift. **A: Shall** we **get** them some flowers? **B:** Yes, **let's do** that.
6	***Had better*** is like *should* and *ought to* but stronger. Use ***had better*** to give a warning that something bad or negative will happen if advice isn't followed.	• We**'d better get going**, or we'll be late. • **Hadn't you better avoid** talking about politics during dinner?
7	Use ***be supposed to*** to show an expectation. Use it only in the present and the past. In the past, the affirmative suggests that the action didn't happen. The negative suggests that the action did happen. You can use ***be to*** + base form in more formal English to express a strong expectation.	• You**'re supposed to take off** your shoes when you enter a Japanese home. • We **were supposed to take** flowers. • We **weren't supposed to mention** the gift we'd brought. • All employees **are to attend** the company office party. • You**'re not to ask** any personal questions.

(continued on next page)

8	Use ***could*** or ***might*** + base form to make polite, not-too-strong suggestions about the present or future.	• You **could / might take** them some chocolates.
	Use ***could have / might have*** + past participle to make polite suggestions about a past opportunity. In this meaning, *might have* and *could have* mean that the action didn't happen.	• You **could have / might have taken** some flowers.

STEP 3 FOCUSED PRACTICE

EXERCISE 1: Discover the Grammar

Read the sentences. Circle the letter of the choice that best explains the meaning of the sentence.

1. We knew that you're supposed to take off your shoes when you enter a Japanese home, so we did.
   - (**a.**) Japanese people expect guests to remove their shoes.
   - **b.** It doesn't matter whether or not you wear your shoes in a Japanese home.
2. Well, you should have wrapped the CD.
   - **a.** You wrapped the CD, and that was the right thing to do.
   - **b.** You didn't wrap the CD, and that was a cultural mistake in Japan.
3. And you mustn't say anything about the gift.
   - **a.** It's not a good idea to say anything about the gift.
   - **b.** It's wrong to say anything about the gift.
4. Or you could have taken some flowers.
   - **a.** Flowers are an acceptable gift in Japan, but you didn't take any.
   - **b.** You made a cultural mistake by not taking flowers.
5. According to the rules of Japanese culture, visitors aren't allowed to go into the kitchen.
   - **a.** The Japanese expect visitors to stay out of the kitchen.
   - **b.** It's OK for visitors to go into a Japanese kitchen.

6. If you praise an object, your Japanese hosts might feel they have to give the object to you.
   - **a.** Japanese hosts might feel a strong obligation to give the object to you.
   - **b.** Japanese hosts might feel they can choose not to give the object to you.

7. When a Japanese host invites you to have a drink at the end of the evening, you should decline gently.
   - **a.** It's an obligation to decline gently.
   - **b.** It's a good idea to decline gently.

8. Yes, you ought to do that.
   - **a.** It doesn't matter whether you do that.
   - **b.** That would be the right thing to do.

9. Junichi says you are not to do this in Japan.
   - **a.** People won't care if you do this in Japan.
   - **b.** It's a cultural mistake to do this in Japan.

10. Shall we have them over?
    - **a.** Do you think they will come to our house?
    - **b.** Do you think we should ask them to come to our house?

EXERCISE 2: Modals

(Grammar Notes 3, 6–8)

Read the conversation between Fumiko, a visiting exchange student, and her American friend Jane. Complete the conversation with items from the box.

~~are you supposed to leave~~	ought to have given	supposed to do
could have left	should we have left	were supposed to leave
don't have to leave	should you leave	you're supposed to do
had to worry	should you tip	

JANE: Hi, Fumiko. How are things going?

FUMIKO: Really well. But I need some pointers about something.

JANE: Sure. What?

FUMIKO: Tipping. I just don't understand it. ___Are you supposed to leave___ (1.) a tip everywhere you eat? This is really bothering me. I've never ________________ (2.) about this before. We don't tip in Japan.

JANE: You don't?

FUMIKO: No. You're not really ________________ (3.) that. It's all included in the service charge.

JANE: Tell me more. Have you had a problem with this?

FUMIKO: Yeah. Last week a Chinese friend of mine and I had dinner at a restaurant. We knew we ________________ (4.) a tip, but we didn't know how much.

JANE: How much did you leave?

FUMIKO: About 25 percent. ________________ (5.) more?

JANE: Wow! Twenty-five percent. That's quite a bit. The service must have been really good.

FUMIKO: Actually, it wasn't. The waiter was pretty rude . . . and slow.

JANE: If you're not satisfied with the service, you ________________ (6.) anything.

FUMIKO: So how much ________________ (7.) the waiter if you're satisfied?

JANE: Between 15 and 20 percent. Fifteen is the usual.

FUMIKO: Hmmm. OK. Now here's another question. I'm confused about what ________________ (8.) if you're sitting at a lunch counter instead of at a table. ________________ (9.) anything for the person behind the counter?

JANE: It's a nice gesture. Why do you ask?

FUMIKO: Yesterday I had lunch at a cafeteria counter. The waitress was really nice and polite. I felt like I ______________________ her something.
10.

JANE: Did you?

FUMIKO: No.

JANE: Well, you ______________________ something. Maybe 5 to 10 percent.
11.

FUMIKO: Oh. OK. Next time I will.

EXERCISE 3: *Must / Have To / Should / Be Supposed To* *(Grammar Notes 3–4, 6–7)*

A | *Read the short essay about the treatment of babies in two different cultures.*

An American woman was spending a month teaching on the Indonesian island of Bali. She was staying at the home of a Balinese family, and late one afternoon the woman of the house was obliged to leave home for a time. When she came back, her eight-month-old son was lying on a large bed, crying loudly. "What is happening with my son?" asked the Balinese woman. "Oh," said the American teacher, "I don't think there's anything wrong with him. I just thought it would be good for him to crawl on the floor for a bit. I put him down to let him crawl, but he didn't seem to like it and started crying. I thought maybe it would be a good idea if he just cried to let his frustration out."

A discussion followed. The Balinese woman told the American that in Bali it is not considered a good thing to let babies cry. Since Balinese culture is characterized by the strength of the extended family, there is almost always someone available to pick children up if they start crying and carry them around. In fact, there is even a "putting down" ceremony that occurs when the child is ready to walk and may be put down on the ground for the first time. Further, the Balinese mother said, their children are not expected to crawl because that activity is seen as too much like what animals do.

The American was fascinated with what her Balinese host had told her. She pointed out that in the United States the extended family is not nearly as prevalent as in Bali, so there is often no one around to help with children. In many families, both mother and father work, so at the end of the day both are too tired to carry children around for long periods. Many also feel that it doesn't hurt babies to allow them to cry for a time. As for crawling, said the American woman, most American parents are delighted when their children learn to crawl, feeling that it is essential for them to develop that skill in order to gain muscular strength and prepare for walking.

Both women learned a great deal that day about the other's culture.

B | *Complete the sentences, using modals or modal-like expressions. Make some sentences negative if necessary.*

1. The incident happened because the Balinese woman ___had to___ leave home for a time.

2. The American woman thought the baby ________________ crawl around a bit on the floor.

3. In Bali, parents believe that babies ________________ be picked up and held most of the time, especially if they are crying.

4. The Balinese mother no doubt felt that her American guest ________________ put the baby down.

5. In Bali, children ________________ crawl since that is too much like what animals do.

6. Most American parents believe that their children ________________ crawl in order to develop muscular strength and prepare for walking.

EXERCISE 4: *Should Have / Could Have*

(Grammar Notes 6, 8)

Look again at the opening reading. Write six sentences about what the American couple should have done and shouldn't have done. Then write four sentences about what they could or might have done.

1. *They should have wrapped the CD.*
2. ________________
3. ________________
4. ________________
5. ________________
6. ________________
7. ________________
8. ________________
9. ________________
10. ________________

EXERCISE 5: Editing

Read the letter from Tong-Li, an international exchange student in Australia, to her friend Masako in Singapore. There are nine mistakes in the use of modals or modal-like expressions. The first mistake is already corrected. Find and correct eight more.

Dear Masako,

Sorry it's taken me so long to write. I ~~shouldn't~~ should have gotten to this weeks ago, but I've been so busy. I'm really looking forward to the holidays and seeing all you guys again. School is going well. It's tough but really interesting, and I'm sure I should be studying even more than I have been. Part of the problem is that I'm taking too many classes. You're only suppose to take five a term, but I'm taking six.

Anyway, I've gotten to know a lot of new people, including several Australians. I have this one really good friend, a girl named Jane. She invited me to her house last week for a party. Actually, it was my birthday, but I didn't know she knew that. I thought it was a party like any other. I figured I better take some kind of gift, but I couldn't decide what it should be. Finally, I came up with the idea of a bouquet of flowers. As soon as I got to the party, I gave it to Jane, and she was really happy to get it. But then the funniest thing happened. I guess I ought to expect something was up from the mysterious way Jane was acting, but I didn't. This was a surprise party—for me! As soon as I took off my coat and sat down, a lot of people jumped up from behind sofas and other places where they'd been hiding and shouted, "Surprise! Happy birthday!" I was embarrassed, but I must not have been because everyone was really friendly, and pretty soon I forgot about my embarrassment. Then they gave me presents. I was about to put them away, but Jane said, "Aren't you going to open them?" I was perplexed and didn't know what to do. In China you shouldn't have opened gifts right when you get them, but apparently you are supposed to in Australia. So I opened them. The nicest gift was a new blouse from Jane. She told me I must have gone and try it on immediately, so I did. It's beautiful. Anyway, what a party! I thought I knew all about Australian culture, but I guess I'm not as familiar with it as I thought. The custom of opening up presents in front of the gift giver is a strange one to me.

The weather is kind of chilly. How is it back in Singapore? Nice and warm? I shall bring you something special from Australia when I come?

Well, Masako, I'm running out of space, so I got to sign off. Write soon.

Best,

Tong-Li

STEP 4 COMMUNICATION PRACTICE

EXERCISE 6: Listening

A | *Listen to the telephone conversation. Where are Dad and Ray, and why?*

____

B | *Read the questions. Then listen again. Write complete answers, using modals or modal-like expressions.*

1. Why do Dad and Ray need to get home as soon as possible?

   Mom's surprise party is supposed to start in 15 minutes.

2. What is Bev's opinion about delaying Mom's present, and why?

   ____

3. What does Dad say when Bev reminds him about not putting things off till the last minute?

   ____

4. What is Dad's opinion about Bev's camera suggestion?

   ____

5. What is Bev's opinion about a dress?

   ____

6. What does Dad say about Bev's blouse suggestion?

   ____

7. What is Bev's scarf suggestion?

   ____

8. What does Bev say about getting home as soon as possible, and why?

   ____

EXERCISE 7: Pronunciation

A | *Read and listen to the Pronunciation Note.*

Pronunciation Note

In conversation and in rapid speech, modals and modal-like auxiliaries are often reduced.

EXAMPLES:

should / could / might + have	→	should've, could've, might've
have to	→	hafta
has to	→	hasta
supposed to	→	sposta
had better	→	'dbetter

B | *Listen and repeat the sentences with reduced forms of modals and modal-like auxiliaries.*

1. We have to take a gift to the party.
2. We should have had them over for dinner.
3. We're supposed to have dinner at their house on Monday.
4. You could have declined their offer to have a drink.
5. We had better leave now.
6. You might have gotten them some flowers.
7. He wasn't supposed to be here until Monday.
8. The gift has to be wrapped.

C | *PAIRS: Practice the sentences. One partner says a sentence with a full form. The other partner responds with the reduced form.*

EXERCISE 8: Information Gap

PAIRS: Complete the story. Each of you will read a version of the same story. Each version is missing some information. Take turns asking your partner questions to get the missing information.

Student A, read the story. Ask questions and fill in the missing information. Then answer Student B's questions.

Student B, turn to page 67 and follow the instructions there.

EXAMPLE: **A:** Where were they supposed to stay?
B: They were supposed to stay at . . . What should they have gotten?
A: They should have gotten . . .

A married couple was traveling in Europe and had just entered a new country. They had been having a wonderful time, but now everything was going wrong. The first problem was finding accommodations. They were supposed to stay at ____________________, but when they got to the hotel there was no record of their reservation. The wife said they should have gotten a confirmation number. They hadn't, unfortunately, so they had to spend the night ____________________. The next day they finally found a room at a hotel far from the center of town. There were two rooms available: a large one and a tiny one. Since they were on a tight budget, they decided they had better take the tiny one.

The second problem was communication. They were starving after spending hours looking for accommodations, so they went into a restaurant. A waiter brought them a menu, but they couldn't understand it. The husband said they should have ____________________. They hadn't done that, though, so they didn't know what to order.

Time passed. Other people were being served, but they weren't. Frustrated, they decided they had to do something. But what? They noticed that a boy about 11 years old seemed to be listening to their conversation. Soon the boy came over to their table. "Excuse me," he said. "You have to ____________________. Then they'll take your order." The husband and wife were both astonished but grateful. The wife said, "You speak our language very well. Did you study it somewhere?" The boy said, "I lived in Australia for three years. I learned English there." He asked, "Shall I help you order? I can translate the menu."

When the couple got back home, their friends asked them what they had liked best about the trip. The wife said, "Well, the best part was visiting that country where everything went wrong until that boy rectified the problem. At some point, everybody should ______________________________. You don't have to be miserable, but you need a challenge. That's when you learn things. Maybe that's what people mean when they say travel is broadening."

EXERCISE 9: Discussion

A | *SMALL GROUPS: Decide individually whether each of the behaviors in the chart is required, advised, allowed, or unimportant in your culture or another culture you are familiar with. Check (✓) the appropriate boxes. Then discuss the results with the other members of your group.*

B | *Report your results to the rest of the class.*

EXAMPLE: **A:** When you're invited to dinner in your culture, are you supposed to take a gift?
B: Absolutely. You must take a gift. And it has to be wrapped. What about in your culture?
A: It's pretty much optional. You should take a gift if it's a birthday party, but . . .

	Must	Should	Mustn't	Shouldn't	Don't Have To	Doesn't Matter
1. take a gift when invited somewhere						
2. ask how old someone is						
3. smoke without asking permission						
4. hug friends when you see them						
5. shake hands when you meet someone						
6. remove your shoes at someone's house						

(continued on next page)

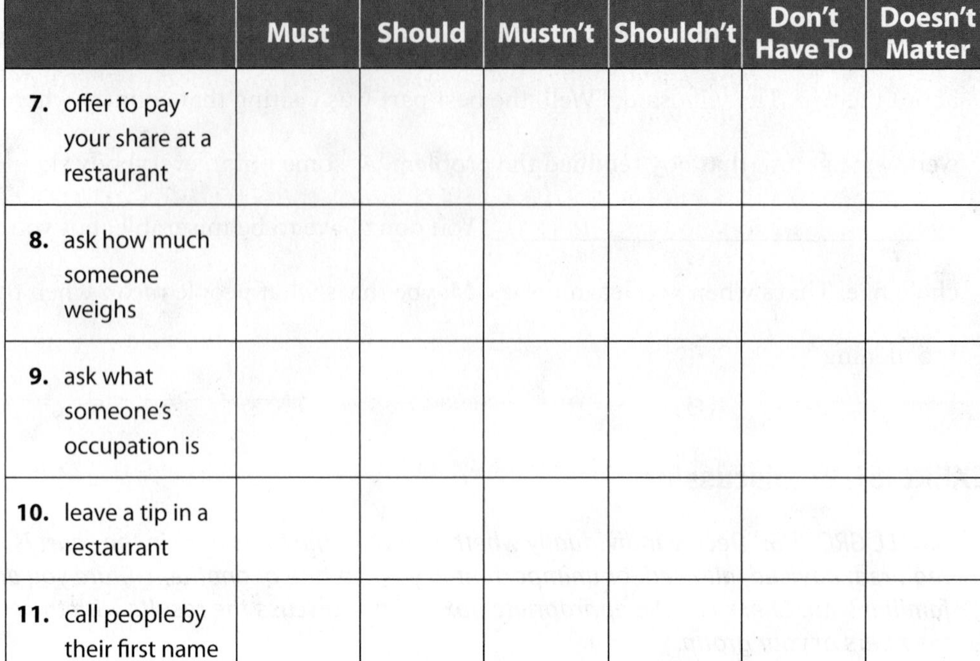

	Must	Should	Mustn't	Shouldn't	Don't Have To	Doesn't Matter
7. offer to pay your share at a restaurant						
8. ask how much someone weighs						
9. ask what someone's occupation is						
10. leave a tip in a restaurant						
11. call people by their first name						

EXERCISE 10: Writing

A | *Write two or three paragraphs about a past situation that you feel you should have handled differently. Tell what you should or could have done to rectify the situation (past) and what you should, could, or might do in a similar future situation.*

EXAMPLE: Two years ago my husband and I were traveling on a train in Europe. It was the middle of the night, and we were the only travelers in a sleeping car. We were both deeply asleep when suddenly our compartment door was loudly opened and several young people came in and began looking for their beds. They were talking very loudly and did not settle down and go to sleep. For a while we tolerated this and tried to go back to sleep but couldn't. Finally, my husband got very angry and started to yell at them. He shouldn't have done this, because they just laughed at him. Instead of this, he should have . . .

B | *Check your work. Use the Editing Checklist.*

Editing Checklist

Did you use . . . ?

☐ ***should***, ***could***, or ***might*** correctly

☐ ***should have*** correctly

☐ ***could have*** correctly

Information Gap for Student B

Student B, read the story. Answer Student A's questions. Then ask your own questions and fill in the missing information.

Example: **A:** Where were they supposed to stay?
B: They were supposed to stay at the Grand State Hotel. What should they have gotten?
A: They should have gotten . . .

A married couple was traveling in Europe and had just entered a new country. They had been having a wonderful time, but now everything was going wrong. The first problem was finding accommodations. They were supposed to stay at the Grand State Hotel, but when they got to the hotel there was no record of their reservation. The wife said they should have gotten ______________________________. They hadn't, unfortunately, so they had to spend the night at the train station. The next day they finally found a room at a hotel far from the center of town. There were two rooms available: a large one and a tiny one. Since they were on a tight budget, they decided they had better ______________________________.

The second problem was communication. They were starving after spending hours looking for accommodations, so they went into a restaurant. A waiter brought them a menu, but they couldn't understand it. The husband said they should have brought along a phrasebook. They hadn't done that, though, so they didn't know what to order.

Time passed. Other people were being served, but they weren't. Frustrated, they decided ______________________________. But what? They noticed that a boy about 11 years old seemed to be listening to their conversation. Soon the boy came over to their table. "Excuse me," he said. "You have to pay for your meal first. Then they'll take your order." The husband and wife were both astonished but grateful. The wife said, "You speak our language very well. Did you study it somewhere?" The boy said, "I lived in Australia for three years. I learned English there." He asked, "______________________________? I can translate the menu."

When the couple got back home, their friends asked them what they had liked best about the trip. The wife said, "Well, the best part was visiting that country where everything went wrong until that boy rectified the problem. At some point, everybody should experience difficulty. You don't have to ______________________________, but you need a challenge. That's when you learn things. Maybe that's what people mean when they say travel is broadening."

UNIT 4 Review

Check your answers on page UR-1.

Do you need to review anything?

A | *Circle the correct modal or modal-like expression to complete each sentence.*

1. You weren't supposed to / were supposed to mention the gift. Now it won't be a surprise!
2. She had to / didn't have to bring food. We have a lot left over from the party.
3. Bill might not have / shouldn't have told Ai about it! Now everyone will know.
4. You could / should take some flowers. Or a box of chocolates would be good.
5. We shouldn't / 'd better not discuss anything political. Sam loses his temper easily.
6. You must have / should have your passport with you. You'll be deported if you don't.
7. Chie should / 's got to pay her rent by Saturday. She'll be evicted if she doesn't.
8. You aren't allowed to / don't have to go into a Japanese kitchen. It's just not done.
9. Sami should have / could have given them a CD. They like flowers too.
10. Hadn't we better / Aren't we supposed to get going? The play starts in 20 minutes.

B | *In the blank after each sentence, write a single modal with a meaning similar to the underlined modal-like auxiliary.*

1. You have to be there by 10 A.M. sharp. ____________________
2. We ought to invite Hana over for dinner. ____________________
3. We aren't allowed to smoke in the office. ____________________
4. Ken has simply got to study harder. ____________________
5. Are you supposed to leave a tip here? ____________________

C | *Circle the letter of the one underlined word or phrase in each sentence that is not correct.*

1. We ought (A) look into (B) a tour if we can find (C) one that won't bankrupt (D) us. **A B C D**
2. All is to (A) attend (B) the party on Saturday and should (C) bring (D) a gift. **A B C D**
3. I ought to (A) take (B) extra cash along, and I don't have to (C) forget (D) my passport. **A B C D**
4. You had better (A) to set (B) your alarm, or you might not (C) wake up (D) on time. **A B C D**
5. I'd (A) invited (B) Bob to dinner Monday, but he must (C) decline (D) because he's sick. **A B C D**

UNIT 5

Modals to Express Degrees of Certainty

PUZZLES

STEP 1 GRAMMAR IN CONTEXT

Before You Read

PAIRS: Discuss the questions.

1. When people say, "Columbus discovered the New World," what do they mean?
2. What theories have you heard regarding who might have "discovered" the New World?

Read

Read the article about the discovery of America.

Who *Really* Discovered America?

A well-known school rhyme goes like this: "In fourteen hundred and ninety-two, Columbus sailed the ocean blue"—and then discovered America. However, Columbus **may not have been** the first non-Native American to visit the Western Hemisphere. So many other potential discoverers have been nominated that the question **might** almost **be rephrased** as "Who *didn't* discover America?" What does history show? Who *really* discovered the New World? Those suggested include the Vikings, the Japanese, the Chinese, the Egyptians, the Hebrews, the Portuguese, and some Irish monks.

The Vikings are the best-known contenders. Evidence suggests that Leif Erickson and cohorts visited the New World about the year 1000, almost 500 years before Columbus. Viking records and New World artifacts indicate they arrived at a place they named "Vinland the Good"—the land of grapes. Scholars originally thought Vinland **must have been** Newfoundland, but today it is believed Vinland **couldn't have been** that island since it is too far north for grapes to grow. **Could** the climate **have been** warmer in Erickson's day? Perhaps. However, current thought is that Vinland **may have been** the New England coast.

The Japanese are more recent candidates. Pottery fragments discovered in 1956 on the coast of Ecuador date back about 5,000 years. These fragments resemble Japanese pottery of the same era, but it has been established that there was no native pottery in Ecuador in 3000 B.C.E. **Could** the Japanese **have introduced** it? Smithsonian Institute scholars conclude that individuals **may have sailed** from Japan across

(continued on next page)

Christopher Columbus

Who *Really* Discovered America?

the Pacific to Ecuador, or Japanese fishermen **might have been swept** out to sea and **carried** 10,000 miles across the ocean. This theory **may sound** unlikely and **may** eventually **be disproved**, but the pottery evidence **must mean** something.

One interesting theory stems from the story of St. Brendan, a sixth-century Irish monk who made many voyages to establish monasteries. A sixth-century document suggests that Brendan made a journey far out into the Atlantic, reports of which **may have influenced** Columbus to believe that there really was a New World. Brendan and his fellow monks saw "sea monsters," "crystals rising up into the sky," and "a rain of bad-smelling rocks." In 1976, British navigation scholar Tim Severin decided to see if Brendan and his companions **could** really **have accomplished** this voyage. Using the specifications described in the St. Brendan text, they built a curragh, an Irish leather boat, and attempted the journey. On the way, they passed Greenland and wintered in Iceland, where they saw whales, a volcano, and icebergs. They theorized that Brendan's sea monsters **might have been** whales, the ice crystals icebergs, and the bad-smelling rocks volcanic debris. Severin's group did eventually get to Newfoundland, proving that a curragh **could have made** the journey to North America. Religious artifacts and stone carvings bearing vocabulary and grammatical constructions from Old Irish have been found in Virginia. This suggests that other missionaries **could have gone** to the New World after Brendan's return. Thus the story **may be** true.

But back to the original question: Who really "discovered" the New World? Future research **should get** us closer to an answer. Columbus did not, of course, really *discover* America. The real finders were the Native Americans who migrated across the Bering Strait more than 10,000 years ago.

The claim about Columbus really means that he started two-way communication between the Old World and the New. In that sense Columbus's reputation is still safe.

Could this boat have made it across the Atlantic?

After You Read

A | Vocabulary: *Match the* **blue** *words and phrases on the left with their meanings on the right.*

_____ **1.** So many other **potential** discoverers have been nominated . . .

_____ **2.** Those suggested include the Vikings, the Japanese, . . . and some Irish **monks**.

_____ **3.** The Vikings are the best-known **contenders**.

_____ **4.** Leif Erickson and **cohorts** visited the New World about the year 1000.

_____ **5.** New World **artifacts** indicate the Vikings arrived at a place they named Vinland the Good.

_____ **6.** One interesting theory **stems from** the story of St. Brendan.

_____ **7.** Brendan made many voyages to establish **monasteries**.

_____ **8.** The bad-smelling rocks may have been volcanic **debris**.

a. originates with

b. remains of an explosion

c. religious residences

d. possible

e. likely candidates

f. human-made objects

g. companions

h. members of an all-male religious group

B | Comprehension: *Circle* **T (True)** *or* **F (False)**. *Correct the false statements.*

1. Schoolchildren are often taught that Columbus discovered America. **T** **F**

2. Scholars originally theorized that Vinland was probably Newfoundland. **T** **F**

3. Scholars currently believe that Vinland couldn't have been Newfoundland because the island is too far south for grapes to grow. **T** **F**

4. Pottery fragments found in Ecuador date from the year 5000 B.C.E. **T** **F**

5. The story of St. Brendan almost certainly caused Columbus to believe that there was a New World. **T** **F**

6. St. Brendan and his companions could have gotten to America in a curragh. **T** **F**

7. The ice crystals seen by Brendan and his companions must have been icebergs. **T** **F**

8. Columbus didn't discover America, but he had a great deal to do with promoting contact between the Old World and the New. **T** **F**

STEP 2 GRAMMAR PRESENTATION

MODALS TO EXPRESS DEGREES OF CERTAINTY

Speculations about the Present							
It	**must** **has (got) to**	**be**	true.	It	**can't / couldn't** **must not**	**be**	true.
It	**may / might** **could**	**be**	true.	It	**may not** **might not**	**be**	true.

Speculations about the Past							
It	**must have** **had to have**	**been**	true.	It	**can't have** **couldn't have** **must not have**	**been**	true.
It	**may have** **might have** **could have**	**been**	true.	It	**may not have** **might not have**	**been**	true.

Speculations about the Future							
We	**should** **ought to**	**solve**	it soon.				
We	**may** **might** **could**	**solve**	it soon.	We	**may not** **might not**	**solve**	it soon.

GRAMMAR NOTES

1

We use **modals** and **modal-like expressions** to express different degrees of certainty. With these modals we speculate based on logic and facts.

- The story **must** be true. *(approximately 90% certain)*
- The story **might** be true. *(approximately 50% certain)*

Remember that we use modals with progressive as well as simple forms.

- He **may** be planning another trip.

When we want to state a fact we are absolutely—100%—sure of, we don't use modals.

- That story is true.
- He was planning another trip.

2	Use ***must / have to / have got to*** + base form when you are speculating about the present and are almost certain.	• The evidence **must / has to / has got to mean** something.
	To make a negative speculation, use ***can't / couldn't*** + base form.	• That theory **can't / couldn't be** right.
	Use ***must not*** + base form when you are slightly less certain.	• It **must not be** right. • The explorer **must not be** famous.
	NOTE: We normally don't contract *must not* in this meaning of *must*.	NOT: The explorer ~~mustn't~~ be famous.
	In questions, use ***could / couldn't*** + base form.	• **Could** that **be** the case? • **Couldn't** that **be** the explanation?
3	Use ***may / might / could*** + base form when you are speculating about the present and are less certain.	• We **may / might / could know** the answer soon.
	Use ***may not / might not*** + base form in the negative.	• They **may not / might not have** any evidence.
	BE CAREFUL! We usually do not contract *might not*, and we never contract *may not*.	NOT: They ~~mayn't~~ have any evidence.
	In questions, use ***could / might*** + base form.	• **Could / Might** that **be** correct?
4	Use ***must have / had to have*** + past participle when you are speculating about the past and are almost certain.	• They **must have / had to have visited** America.
	In the negative, use ***can't have / couldn't have*** + past participle to suggest impossibility.	• That **can't / couldn't have happened**.
	Use ***must not have*** + past participle when you are slightly less certain.	• He **must not have made** the trip.
	In questions, use ***can have / could have*** + past participle.	• **Can / Could** that **have been** the reason?

(continued on next page)

5	When you are speculating about the past and are less certain (about 50%), use ***may have / might have / could have*** + past participle.	• They **may / might / could have reached** the New World.
	BE CAREFUL! ***Could have*** + past participle has two meanings.	• He **could have gone**. I don't know for sure. *(It's a possibility—a degree of certainty)* • He **could have gone** but didn't. *(a missed opportunity)*
	In the negative, use ***may not have / might not have*** + past participle.	• They **may / might not have found** what they were looking for.
	In questions, use ***might have / could have*** + past participle.	• **Might / Could** they **have had** trouble?
6	Use ***should / ought to*** + base form when you are almost certain about a future action or event.	• Continued research **should / ought to get** us closer to an answer.
7	Use ***may / might / could*** + base form when you are less certain about a future action or event.	• We **may / might / could know** the answer soon.
	In the negative, use ***may / might + not / never*** + base form.	• However, we **may / might never know** the answer.

STEP 3 FOCUSED PRACTICE

EXERCISE 1: Discover the Grammar

Read the sentences. Circle the letter of the choice that best explains the meaning of the sentence.

1. Columbus may not have been the first to visit the Western Hemisphere.

(**a.**) He might not have been the first.

b. He could not have been the first.

2. It must have been about the year 1000 when Leif Erickson visited the New World.

a. I'm almost certain it was about the year 1000.

b. I think maybe it was about the year 1000.

3. The assumption is that Vinland couldn't have been Newfoundland.

a. It must not have been Newfoundland.

b. It can't have been Newfoundland.

4. How could the voyage have happened?

a. I'd like an explanation of how the voyage was impossible.

b. I'd like an explanation of how the voyage was possible.

5. Individuals may have sailed from Japan to Ecuador.

a. It's possible they did it.

b. It's almost certain they did it.

6. The pottery evidence must mean something.

a. I'm almost sure it means something.

b. I strongly doubt it means something.

7. Other missionaries could have gone to the New World after Brendan's return.

a. It's possible that they went.

b. They had the opportunity to go but didn't.

8. Continued research should get us closer to an answer.

a. It's possible that it will.

b. It's almost certain that it will.

EXERCISE 2: Affirmative Modals

(Grammar Notes 1–3, 6)

Read the conversation. Complete it with modal constructions from the box.

could be working	**might be**	**must have been visiting**
~~**could have gotten**~~	**might be meeting**	**should be**
may have had to	**must have**	

BLAKE: I wonder what's keeping Harry. He's usually on time for office parties. I suppose he ___could have gotten___ (1.) stuck in traffic.

SAMANTHA: Yeah, that's a possibility. Or he ______________ (2.) work late. I've never known him to be late for a party.

BLAKE: You know, I've always felt there's something a little puzzling—or even mysterious—about Harry.

SAMANTHA: What makes you say that?

BLAKE: Well, he never says much about his past. He's an interesting guy, but I don't know much about him. For all I know, he ______________ (3.) an international spy who works with mysterious cohorts.

(continued on next page)

SAMANTHA: I think I know what you mean. Or he ______________________ (4.) as a government agent.

BLAKE: This is potentially a case of *cherchez la femme.*

SAMANTHA: What does that mean?

BLAKE: It means "look for the woman." I figure he ______________________ (5.) a girlfriend that he doesn't want us to know about.

SAMANTHA: Yeah, maybe so. You know, now that I think of it, he always leaves work early on Friday afternoons. I see him go to the parking garage about 4:00, and it always seems like he's trying not to be seen. He ______________________ (6.) his secret love.

(The doorbell rings.)

BLAKE: Oh, wait a minute. There's the doorbell. Everyone else is here. That ______________________ (7.) him.

HARRY: Hi, folks. Sorry I'm late. Had some business to take care of.

SAMANTHA: Business, huh. You mean romantic business?

HARRY: Romantic business? What are you talking about?

BLAKE: We figure you ______________________ (8.) your lady love. After all, we see you leave early every Friday afternoon.

HARRY: Pretty funny. Well, there is a lady, and I love her. But it's not what you think.

SAMANTHA: What is it, then?

HARRY: My mother. She's 88 years old, and she lives in a retirement home. I go to see her every Friday.

EXERCISE 3: Affirmative / Interrogative Modals

(Grammar Notes 3–5)

Read the article about past cultures. Complete the sentences with past and present modal verbs, using the words in parentheses.

World Review

Where do we draw the line between myth or legend and reality? What happens to cultures when they disappear? We at *World Review* decided to explore these questions in this month's issue.

Let's first consider the ancient Pueblo people of the U.S. Southwest. Scholars think that these people, called the Anasazi or "ancient ones" by the Navajo, ___may have settled___ (1. may / settle) about 100 C.E. in the Four Corners area, where today the states of Arizona, Utah, Colorado, and New Mexico come together. We know from the evidence of artifacts and ruins that the Anasazi developed agriculture and built impressive cities and cliff dwellings. About the year 1300, however, something happened. The Anasazi abandoned their dwellings and migrated to the Rio Grande Valley in New Mexico and the White Mountains in Arizona. What ________________ (2. could / cause) this?

Today many anthropologists assume that today's Pueblo peoples in the Southwest ________________ (3. must / be) the descendants of the Anasazi. However, questions remain: What ________________ (4. might / bring) an end to their flourishing culture? Drought? Warfare? Are certain present-day Native Americans really descendants of the Anasazi? Or ________________ the Anasazi actually ________________ (5. could / disappear)?

Let's next turn our attention to Atlantis, the famed "lost continent" said to have existed in the Atlantic Ocean west of Gibraltar thousands of years ago. Is Atlantis a myth, or ________________ it ________________ (6. could / exist)? Plato wrote about Atlantis in two dialogues, describing it as a fabulous island, larger than Libya and Turkey. He believed that Atlantis

(*continued on next page*)

_______________ about 9,000 years before his time. The Atlanteans were reputed to
7. (had to / exist)

have conquered many lands around the Mediterranean and, he thought,

_______________ evil and greedy in the process. Their island or continent was
8. (must / become)

supposed to have sunk into the sea after being hit by earthquakes. _______________
9. (Could / there really / be)

an Atlantis? Certain writers think the present-day Basques _______________
10. (might / be)

descendants of survivors of the catastrophe, if there was one. Is the Atlantis story just an entertaining legend invented by Plato? Or, if Atlantis was real, is the problem simply that it existed so long ago that traces of its memory are all that remain? A contending theory is that reports of a disaster on the island of Thíra _______________ the Atlantis legend.
11. (may / influence)

Thíra, in the Mediterranean Sea north of Crete, was destroyed about 1500 B.C.E. by volcanic eruptions and earthquakes that covered the area with debris and devastated civilization on nearby Crete. Perhaps the Atlantis legend stems from the Thíra disaster. Perhaps the descendants of Atlanteans _______________ among us. At this point, we
12. (might / still / walk)

simply don't know.

EXERCISE 4: Personal Inventory (Future)

(Grammar Notes 6–7)

Write 10 sentences about things you might accomplish in the next 10 years. Write two sentences each with **should, ought to, may, might,** *and* **could.** *Then compare your sentences with a partner's.*

EXAMPLES: I **might get** married within 10 years.
I **should finish** my college education by 2015.

EXERCISE 5: Editing

Read the student essay. There are eight mistakes in the use of modals. The first mistake is already corrected. Find and correct seven more.

WHY WE ITCH

One ~~must~~ might think that with all the scientific progress made in the last century, researchers would be able by now to answer this very simple question: Why do we itch? Unfortunately, scientists can't answer this question with any certainty. They simply don't know.

There are some clear cases involving itching. If a patient goes to her doctor and complains of terrible itching, and the doctor finds hives or some other kind of rash, the doctor will probably say that she must eat something she was allergic to—or that she must not have been stung or bitten by some insect. Scientists can easily explain this kind of case. Most itching, however, does not have an obvious cause.

Here's what scientists do know: Right under the surface of the skin there are sensory receptors that register physical stimuli and carry messages to the brain. These receptors detect pain and let the brain know about it. If there is a high level of physical stimulation to the body, the sensory receptors might carried a message of pain to the brain. If the level of physical stimulation is low, the sensors might be report it as itchiness.

There has been a lot of speculation about the function of itching. Some researchers think the function of itching may to warn the body it is about to have a painful experience. Others theorize that early humans might developed itching as a way of knowing they needed to take insects out of their hair. Still others believe that itching could be a symptom of serious diseases such as diabetes and Hodgkin's disease.

One of the most interesting aspects of itching is that it may have be less tolerable than pain. Research has shown, in fact, that most of us tolerate pain better than itching. Many people will allow their skin to be painfully broken just so they can get rid of an itch.

STEP 4 COMMUNICATION PRACTICE

EXERCISE 6: Listening

A | *Listen to a discussion in a biology class. In what college class did the professor first hear a recording of his voice?*

____

B | *Now listen to statements made during the discussion. Then circle the letter of the sentence that gives the same information.*

1. **(a.)** It's almost impossible that it was me.
   b. It's possible that it was me.
2. **a.** There must be some mistake.
   b. There's possibly some mistake.
3. **a.** It's possible that all of you have had this experience before.
   b. It's almost certain that all of you have had this experience before.
4. **a.** You have probably figured out the answer.
   b. You will probably be able to figure out the answer.
5. **a.** It's got to be because we hear the sound in a different way.
   b. It's possibly because we hear the sound in a different way.
6. **a.** It's possibly because the sound travels through different substances.
   b. It's almost certainly because the sound travels through different substances.
7. **a.** It's certain that it's a combination of the two things.
   b. It's possible that it's a combination of the two things.
8. **a.** It's almost certain that the sound others hear is the real sound.
   b. It's unlikely that the sound others hear is the real sound.
9. **a.** The sound we heard was probably the real sound.
   b. The sound we hear is probably the real sound.
10. **a.** It's certain that internal hearing is more accurate than external hearing.
    b. It's almost certain that internal hearing is more accurate than external hearing.

EXERCISE 7: Pronunciation

A | *Read and listen to the Pronunciation Note.*

Pronunciation Note

In modal verb constructions, the word ***to*** is often reduced to /**tə**/. The word ***have*** is often reduced to /**əv**/.

B | *Listen to the conversations. In each conversation, a certain word is reduced in one sentence but not in the other. Circle the word that is reduced.*

1. **A:** Let's call Mary. She ought (to) be home by now.

   B: Yeah, she really ought to.

2. **A:** Bill should have gotten the package already.

   B: Yeah, he should definitely have it by now.

3. **A:** He's got to solve that problem before things get worse.

   B: You're right. He's got to.

4. **A:** We should have that job done professionally.

   B: Probably. Actually, I should have done it myself.

5. **A:** Do I have to finish this today?

   B: You don't have to, but it would be nice.

6. **A:** Nancy had to have her own way.

   B: Yes, but the situation had to have been tough on her.

C | *PAIRS: Practice the sentences. Take turns using unreduced and reduced forms.*

EXERCISE 8: Pair Discussion

A | *Work with a partner to solve the puzzles. Using modals of certainty, suggest several possible solutions to each puzzle, write them down—from most likely to least likely—and label them accordingly. Include a modal verb construction in each sentence.*

1. On November 22, 1978, an 18-year-old thief broke into a lady's house and demanded all her money. She gave him all she had: $11.50. The thief was so angry that he demanded she write him a check for $50. Two hours later, the police caught the thief. How?

   EXAMPLE: There **may have been** a security camera in the bank building.

2. A dog owner put some food in a pan for her cat. Then, because she didn't want her dog to eat the cat's food, she tied a six-foot rope around his neck. Then she left. When she came back, she discovered that the dog had eaten the cat's food. What happened?
3. Two monks decided to ride their bicycles from their monastery to another monastery in a town 6 miles away. They rode for a while and then reached a crossroads where they had to change direction. They discovered that the sign with arrows pointing to different towns in the area had blown down. They didn't know which road was the right one. Nevertheless, they were able to figure out which road to take. What do you think they did?
4. Roy Sullivan, a forest ranger in Virginia, had several experiences in his life in which he was struck by a powerful force. Two times his hair was set on fire. He had burns on his eyebrows, shoulder, stomach, chest, and ankle. Once he was driving when he was hit and was knocked 10 feet out of his car. What do you think happened to him?

B | *Report your answers to the class.*

EXERCISE 9: Group Discussion

A | *GROUPS: Look again at the story of Atlantis in Exercise 3. Which explanation do you think is the most likely? Which do you like best? Discuss your opinions with your partners.*

B | *Report your opinions to the class.*

EXAMPLE:
A: Which explanation do you like best about Atlantis?
B: Well, the one I like best is that the Basques are descendants of the Atlanteans. But I don't think it's the most likely explanation.
A: What is it, then?
B: I think it must have been . . .

EXERCISE 10: Writing

A | *Write three or four paragraphs about an interesting world mystery you have heard of. Using present and past modals of certainty, speculate on the causes and possible explanations. Use one of the following topics or choose your own:*

- How were the great pyramids in Egypt built?
- Are humans really to blame for the melting of the ice in Greenland and Antarctica?
- Does the Loch Ness monster really exist?
- How did the great statues get to Easter Island?

Example: Does the Loch Ness monster really exist? I've always wanted to believe it does, and for years I did believe that. Recently, however, I've come to a different conclusion. Reports of seeing the monster might be from people's imaginations. Or they could just be tricks. So the legend can't be true. Here's why I think this . . .

B | *Check your work. Use the Editing Checklist.*

Editing Checklist

Did you use . . . ?

☐ present modals of certainty correctly
☐ past modals of certainty correctly
☐ speculations about the future correctly

UNIT 5 Review

Check your answers on page UR-1.
Do you need to review anything?

A | *Circle the correct word or phrase to complete each sentence.*

1. That must / may be the answer to the mystery. All evidence points to it.
2. Ellen might / will be here later, but I don't know for sure.
3. A monk must / might have made the trip, but the evidence isn't conclusive.
4. It couldn't / shouldn't have been Newfoundland, which is too far north.
5. We should / may find out what really happened later today. Louis says he knows.
6. You may not / ought not to have trouble solving the problem—you're good at math.
7. They had to / might have been home—I heard their music.
8. She might be / 's got to be the one who took it. No one else had access to it.
9. They had to be / must have been away last week. Their car was gone.
10. There must / might be a key around here somewhere. Dad said he had one.

B | *In the blank after each sentence, write a modal or modal-like expression of certainty with a meaning similar to the underlined phrase.*

1. It's possible that Jeremy had to work late. ________________
2. It's very likely that Mari missed her flight. ________________
3. It's impossible that they heard the news. ________________
4. It's likely that we'll know the answer soon. ________________
5. You had the opportunity to get a scholarship. ________________

C | *Circle the letter of the one underlined word or phrase in each sentence that is not correct.*

1. Might (A) she have forgotten (B), or could she had (C) had to (D) work? **A B C D**
2. I think (A) Ed isn't (B) here because he should (C) be (D) sick. **A B C D**
3. Al can't (A) get (B) here by 7:00, but he shouldn't (C) make (D) it by 8:00. **A B C D**
4. I suppose they couldn't (A) be working (B) late at the office, but Amy didn't mention (C) it, and neither did (D) Mary. **A B C D**
5. I'm sorry; I could (A) had (B) called to say I'd be (C) late, but I forgot (D). **A B C D**

PART II

From Grammar to Writing

TOPIC SENTENCES

An important way to strengthen your writing is to provide a **topic sentence** for each paragraph. A topic sentence is a general sentence that covers the paragraph's content. All the supporting examples and details of the paragraph must fit logically under this sentence, which usually comes first.

EXAMPLE: **For me, a dog is a better pet than a cat.** When I come home from work, for example, my dog comes to meet me at the door. He is always glad to see me. My cat, on the other hand, couldn't care less whether I'm at home or not, as long as I keep filling her food dish. Another good thing about a dog is that you can teach him tricks. Cats, however, can't be bothered to learn anything new. The best thing about a dog, though, is that he's a great companion. I can take my dog on hikes and walks. He goes everywhere with me. As we all know, you can't take a cat for a walk.

The topic sentence for this paragraph tells the reader what to expect in the paragraph: some reasons why the writer considers a dog a superior pet.

1 | *Each of the word groups is a fragment but is also a potential topic sentence. Make necessary additions to each.*

EXAMPLE: Reasons why the legal driving age should be raised. (not an independent clause)
Correction: There are several reasons why the legal driving age should be raised.

1. A city where exciting and mysterious things happen.

____

2. Reasons why college isn't for everybody.

____

3. Wild animals not making good pets.

____

4. Regular exercise and its benefits.

____

2 | *Look at the following paragraphs containing supporting details but no topic sentences. For each set of details, write an appropriate topic sentence.*

1. ____

a. For one thing, there's almost always a traffic jam I get stuck in, and I'm often late to work.

b. Also, there's not always a parking place when I do get to work.

c. Worst of all, I'm spending more money on gas and car maintenance than I would if I took public transportation.

(continued on next page)

2. ____________________

   a. One is that I often fall asleep when watching the TV screen, no matter how interesting the video is.

   b. Another is that watching movies is basically a social experience, and I'm usually alone when I watch videos.

   c. The main reason is that the TV screen, no matter how large it is, diminishes the impact that you get when watching a movie on the big screen.

3. ____________________

   a. First, nothing spontaneous usually happens on a guided tour, but I've had lots of spontaneous experiences when I planned my own vacation.

   b. Second, tour guides present you with what *they* think is interesting, but when you are in charge of your own vacation, you do what *you* think is interesting.

   c. Most importantly, individually planned vacations can often be less expensive than guided tours.

4. ____________________

   a. First of all, cats don't bark and wake up the neighbors or bite the letter carrier.

   b. Second, dogs have to be walked at least two times a day, but cats handle their own exercise.

   c. Finally, cats eat a lot less than dogs.

3 | *Before you write . . .*

1. When we get to know people from other cultural backgrounds, we often learn a great deal about other cultures and about ourselves. Think about a significant experience you had involving someone from another culture. What did you learn? How did your behavior or thinking change because of your experience?
2. Describe the experience to a partner. Listen to your partner's experience.
3. Ask and answer questions about your experiences. For example: When did it happen? Why did you . . . ? Where were you when . . . ? How did you feel? What do you do or think now that is different from before?

4 | *Write a draft of a two- or three-paragraph composition about your cross-cultural experience. Follow the model. Include information that your partner asked about.*

Where, when, with whom the experience occurred . . .

____

____

____

The events that happened . . .

____

____

____

Changes in you and your behavior since the experience happened . . .

____

____

____

5 | *Exchange compositions with a different partner. Complete the chart.*

1. The writer provided an appropriate topic sentence for each paragraph. **Yes** ☐ **No** ☐

2. What I liked in the composition:

____

____

____

3. Questions I'd like the writer to answer about the composition:

Who ____?

What ____?

When ____?

Where ____?

Why ____?

How ____?

(Your own question) ____?

6 | *Work with your partner. Discuss each other's chart from Exercise 5. Then rewrite your own composition and make any necessary changes.*

PART III

NOUNS

UNIT	GRAMMAR FOCUS	THEME
6	Count and Non-Count Nouns	Health
7	Definite and Indefinite Articles	Environmental Concerns
8	Quantifiers	Money
9	Modification of Nouns	Expectations

UNIT 6 Count and Non-Count Nouns
HEALTH

STEP 1 GRAMMAR IN CONTEXT

Before You Read

PAIRS: Discuss the questions.

1. What are the most important health issues today?
2. How important is exercise for health? Do you exercise a lot, a little, or not at all?

Read

Read the transcript of part of a TV program about health.

Concerned about Health?
ASK THE EXPERT

HEALTH QUESTIONS WITH DR. MEL BRAND

Miranda Olson:	Good **afternoon**. Welcome to Ask the **Expert**. I'm Miranda Olson. My **guest** today is Dr. Mel Brand, and we're going to devote today's entire **program** to your **questions** about **health**. So let's get right to it. . . . Tell us your **name** and where you're from.
Sally Matthews:	Hi, Dr. Brand. I'm Sally Matthews from San Diego, California. We hear a lot of negative **stuff** about fast **food**, but my **husband** and **kids** love **hamburgers** and **fries** and **sodas**. How bad is it?
Dr. Mel Brand:	Sally, it's OK in **moderation**—but I wouldn't make a **habit** of it. Most fast **food** is full of **salt**, **sugar**, **cholesterol**, and lots of **calories**. An occasional **trip** to a fast **food place** won't hurt you, especially if you order healthy **salads** or **sandwiches**. But I wouldn't make it more than once or twice a **week**.
Miranda Olson:	OK. Next **question**?

Concerned about Health? ASK THE EXPERT

Bob Gonzales:	Dr. Brand, I'm Bob Gonzales from Tampa, Florida. I'm 25 years old, and my **question** is about **sun**. My lovely **wife** is a wonderful **woman**, but she's also a **member** of the **sunblock police**. She won't let me go out the **door** without putting **sunblock** on. I've always been able to get a good **tan**, so is this really necessary? It's a **drag**.
Dr. Brand:	Bob, I've got to side with your **wife**. The **sun** makes us feel wonderful, and we love its **warmth**, but it has its **dangers**. I've treated **patients** with **skin cancer**. The most telling **example** was an older **man** who hiked for 40 years and refused to wear a **hat**. He developed **skin cancer** and eventually died of it. I'm not trying to scare you, but you should wear **sunblock** if you're going out in the **sun** for more than a few **minutes**. And you should definitely wear a brimmed **hat** that protects your **face** and your **neck**. And that's all of us, not just fair-skinned **people**.
Miranda Olson:	OK. Next **question**?
Martina Smith:	Dr. Brand. I'm Martina Smith from Toronto, Ontario. My **question** is about **weight**. My **husband** is 5 **feet** 11 **inches** tall and weighs about 250. He used to be in good **shape** when he was a **tennis champ**, but now he doesn't get any **exercise**. When I try to get him to go to the **gym**, he either says he's too tired or he doesn't have **time**. Any **suggestions**?
Dr. Brand:	Martina, tell your **husband** he's way too heavy. Have you heard of **body mass index**? Anyone with a **BMI** more than 25 is considered overweight. Your **husband** would have a **BMI** of about 35, which puts him in the obese **category**. He's got to start exercising and taking off the **pounds**. Have him start slowly and build up to at least three **times** a **week**. Get him to play a **game** of **tennis** with you. But don't delay.
Miranda Olson:	All right. Another **question**?
Frank Lee:	Hi, Dr. Brand. I don't know if this is a **health question** or not, but is there a **cure** for **baldness**? I've been losing my **hair** since I was 35, and . . .

After You Read

A | Vocabulary: *Complete the definitions with the correct word or phrase from the box.*

BMI	champ	drag	obese	sunblock
brimmed	devote	in moderation	side with	telling

1. To ________________ someone is to agree with that person.
2. A(n) ________________ example or argument is one that is very effective.
3. Someone who is ________________ is very much overweight.
4. One's ________________ is a numerical measurement of body fat.
5. A person who has won competitions is a(n) ________________.
6. Something dull, tedious, or uninteresting is called a(n) ________________.
7. When we act within reasonable limits we do things ________________.
8. A hat with an edge that gives protection or shade is said to be ________________.
9. We ________________ our time or attention to an activity when we focus on it completely.
10. ________________ is a cream or oil for your skin that prevents sunburn.

B | Comprehension: *Circle the letter of the correct answer.*

1. According to Dr. Brand, consuming fast food is _____ OK.
   a. usually **b.** occasionally **c.** never **d.** always

2. Dr. Brand suggests that too much _____ in food is not beneficial.
   a. protein **b.** calcium **c.** fiber **d.** cholesterol

3. Dr. Brand says _____ should wear sunblock if they spend time in the sun.
   a. fair-skinned people **b.** dark- skinned people **c.** people over 40 **d.** everyone

4. Exposure to the sun _____ cause skin cancer.
   a. will **b.** shouldn't **c.** can **d.** won't usually

5. Anyone with a BMI exceeding _____ is considered overweight.
   a. 40 **b.** 35 **c.** 25 **d.** 20

6. Dr. Brand believes exercise is of _____ importance to someone overweight.
   a. no significant **b.** great **c.** some **d.** minimal

STEP 2 GRAMMAR PRESENTATION

NOUNS

Proper Nouns	Common Nouns
Mel Brand is a physician.	The **doctor** is an **expert**.

Count and Non-Count Nouns

Count Nouns			
Article or Number	**Noun**	**Verb**	
A One	**snack**	is	refreshing.
The Two	**snacks**	are	

Non-Count Nouns		
Noun	**Verb**	
Rice	is	nourishing.
Nutrition		important.

Nouns with Count and Non-Count Meanings

Count Meaning	Non-Count Meaning
There's **a hair** in my soup!	Sandra has black **hair**.
A chicken escaped from the henhouse.	We had **chicken** for dinner.
How many **times** did you eat out?	It takes **time** to prepare a good meal.
Please bring us **two coffees**.	I'd like some **coffee**.
Brie is **a** soft **cheese**.	**Cheese** is produced in France.
I see **a light** in the window.	The sun provides **light**.

Non-Count Nouns Made Countable

Non-Count Noun	Made Countable
You need **advice**.	Let me give you **a piece of advice**.
Let's play **tennis**.	Let's play **a game of tennis**.
There's not enough **salt** in the soup.	Add **one spoonful of salt**.
I like **bread** with my meal.	Please get **a loaf of bread** at the store.
It's unhealthy to eat **meat** every night.	The recipe takes **three pounds of meat**.
Please put more **paper** in the printer.	**Two packages of paper** are all we have.

GRAMMAR NOTES

1	**Nouns** name persons, places, and things. There are two types of nouns: **proper** nouns and **common** nouns.	
	Proper nouns name particular persons, places, or things. They are usually unique and are capitalized in writing.	• Dr. Brand, Ichiro Suzuki, São Paulo, China, the Empire State Building, Harrod's
	Common nouns refer to people, places, or things but are not the names of particular individuals.	• scientist, athlete, city, country, building, department store
2	There are two types of **common nouns**: count nouns and non-count nouns.	
	Count nouns refer to things that you can count separately. They can be singular or plural. You can use ***a*** or ***an*** before count nouns.	• one **woman**, eight **planets** • I'd like **a sandwich**. • Some **vegetables** are tasty. • That's **an** interesting **question**.
	Non-count nouns refer to things that you cannot count separately. They usually have no plural form. We usually do not use ***a*** or ***an*** with non-count nouns, though they are often preceded by *some* or *the*.	• You should avoid **cholesterol**. NOT: You should avoid ~~a cholesterol~~. • Let me give you **some advice**. NOT: Let me give you ~~an advice~~.
	We normally use a **singular verb** with a non-count noun. We use a **singular pronoun** to refer to the noun.	• **Rice feeds** millions. • **It** feeds millions.
3	Notice the following categories and examples of **non-count nouns**: Abstractions Diseases Food and Drink Natural phenomena Particles Others	 • chance, energy, honesty, love • AIDS, cancer, influenza, malaria • bread, coffee, fish, meat, tea, water • electricity, heat, lightning, rain, sun • dust, pepper, salt, sand, sugar • equipment, furniture, money, news, traffic

4	Many nouns have both a non-count and a count meaning.	• **Experience** is a great teacher. • College was **a** wonderful **experience**. • We eat **fish** twice a week. • My son caught **a fish** yesterday. • I want to be a professor of **history**. • I read **a history** of the Civil War. • Is **space** really the final frontier? • There's **an** empty **space** in that row. • People say **talk** is cheap. • We had **a** good **talk** last night. Other examples are *cuisine, film, rain, reading, work,* and *spice*.
5	We can **make certain non-count nouns countable** by adding a phrase that gives them a form, a limit, or a container. We use these phrases when we want to be more precise or emphatic.	**Non-Count Noun** — **Made Countable** furniture — a piece of furniture lightning — a flash / bolt of lightning meat — a piece of meat rice, sand — a grain of rice / sand tennis — a game of tennis water, rain — a drop of water / rain equipment — a piece of equipment
	NOTE: All of these nouns are commonly used with ***some*** or ***any***. Phrases such as *a piece of*, *a grain of*, and *a bolt of* sometimes sound more formal and are commonly found in writing.	• Can I give you **some advice**? *(more conversational)* • Can I give you **a piece of advice**? *(more formal)*
6	We can use many **non-count nouns** in a **countable sense** with *a / an* or in the plural to mean *kind / type / variety of*.	• In Italy, I tasted **a** new **pasta**. • That shop sells many different **teas**. • Many tasty **cheeses** are produced in France.
	A / an and plurals can also be used to indicate discrete amounts.	• I drank **a soda**. • Please bring us two **orange juices**.

(continued on next page)

7		
	Some nouns are irregular:	
	a. A few **non-count nouns** end in ***-s***.	• news, mathematics, economics, physics
	b. A few **count nouns** have **irregular plurals**. • *criterion, criteria* • *stimulus, stimuli* • *phenomenon, phenomena*	• Thunder is **an** atmospheric **phenomenon**. • Thunder and lightning are atmospheric **phenomena**.
	c. The count nouns ***people*** and ***police*** are plural, not singular. They take a plural verb.	• People are funny. NOT: ~~People is~~ funny. • The police are coming. NOT: The ~~police is~~ coming.
	In the singular, we generally use *person* and *police officer*.	• He's **an energetic person**. • She's **a police officer**.

REFERENCE NOTES

For a list of **non-count nouns**, see Appendix 5 on page A-4.
For a list of phrases for **counting non-count nouns**, see Appendix 6 on page A-5.
For a list of **irregular noun plurals**, see Appendix 4 on page A-3.

STEP 3 FOCUSED PRACTICE

EXERCISE 1: Discover the Grammar

Read the sentences based on the opening reading. Underline the count nouns. Circle the non-count nouns.

1. We're going to devote the entire program to your questions about health.
2. It's OK in moderation, but I wouldn't make a habit of it.
3. Most fast food is full of salt, sugar, cholesterol, and calories.
4. We love its warmth, but it has its dangers.
5. I've treated patients with skin cancer.
6. You should wear sunblock if you're going out in the sun for more than a few minutes.
7. He used to be in good shape when he was a tennis champ, but now he doesn't get any exercise.
8. Your husband would have a BMI of about 35, which puts him in the obese category.
9. Is there a cure for baldness?
10. I've been losing my hair for several years.

EXERCISE 2: Count / Non-Count Senses

(Grammar Notes 4, 6–7)

Interactive websites on the Internet give people information about entertainment, cultural events, and the weather. Fill in the blanks in the bulletin board messages, choosing the correct count or non-count form in parentheses.

Community Bulletin Board

[Follow-Ups] [Post a Reply] [Message Board Index]

Community Bulletin Board for August 26, 2012

Poet Jefferson Jung will give ___a reading___ (1. reading / a reading) of his poetry tonight in the Burlington Civic Center. He describes his latest book of poems as ________________ (2. work / a work) in progress.

Community Bulletin Board for August 27, 2012

On Monday afternoon at 4 P.M. at City Hall, Professor Helen Hammond, who has written ________________ (3. history / a history) of the space program, will give ________________ (4. talk / a talk) on the exploration of ________________ (5. space / a space) in the 21st century at ________________ (6. time / a time) when we seem to be running out of funds for the space program. Professor Hammond will focus on several of the government's ________________ (7. criterion / criteria) for suggesting budget cuts.

Community Bulletin Board for August 28, 2012

If you have not made reservations for the annual Labor Day picnic, ________________ (8. time / a time) is running short. ________________ (9. Work / A work) on the remodeling of Patton Pavilion, where the picnic will be held, is complete. All residents of Burlington are invited, but you must have a ticket, which will cover the price of dinner. The menu will include ________________ (10. fish / a fish), meat, and pasta as main courses. ________________ (11. Soda / A soda) and ________________ (12. milk / a milk) are free.

Community Bulletin Board for August 29, 2012

On Wednesday evening at 8:00 P.M. in the Civic Auditorium, Professor Mary Alice Waters will present a program on the Hmong, an ethnic group of China and Laos. Professor Waters, a professor of ________________ (13. history / a history) at the university, will show ________________ (14. film / a film) about marriage customs of the Hmong and other peoples of eastern Asia.

EXERCISE 3: Non-Count Nouns Made Countable

(Grammar Note 5)

Complete the pairs of sentences. In the sentences on the left, use **some** *or* **any**. *In the sentences on the right, use a phrase that makes the non-count noun countable.*

More Conversational	**More Formal**
1. a. When we moved to the new office, we lost _____*some*_____ equipment.	**b.** When we moved to the new office, we lost _____*a piece of*_____ equipment.
2. a. Look! I just saw ________________ lightning in the sky.	**b.** Look! I just saw ________________ lightning in the sky.
3. a. We didn't play ________________ tennis after all.	**b.** We didn't play ________________ tennis after all.
4. a. Let me give you ________________ advice: Don't buy that item.	**b.** Let me give you ________________ advice: Don't buy that item.
5. a. There hasn't been ________________ rain here for over a month.	**b.** There hasn't been ________________ rain here for over a month.
6. a. There wasn't ________________ rice left on the plate.	**b.** There wasn't ________________ rice left on the plate.
7. a. I had ________________ meat for dinner.	**b.** I had ________________ meat for dinner.
8. a. We bought ________________ furniture at the mall.	**b.** We bought ________________ furniture at the mall.

EXERCISE 4: Personal Inventory (Past)

(Grammar Notes 3–7)

Using your own personal experience, write a sentence for each of the prompts. Use the present perfect in each sentence.

EXAMPLE: best / time / had / in the last month
The best time I've had in the last month was my sister's wedding.

1. two best / films / seen / in the last year

____

2. two funniest people / ever met

____

3. best / advice / ever had

____

4. most enjoyable work / ever done

____

5. most beautiful work of art / ever seen

____

6. best / news / heard / this month

____

7. worst / traffic / ever seen

____

8. most interesting experience / had / in the last year

____

EXERCISE 5: Editing

Read the letter. There are nine mistakes in the use of count and non-count nouns. The first mistake is already corrected. Find and correct eight more.

Dear kids,

Your mom and I are having ‸a wonderful time in Brazil. We landed in Rio de Janeiro on Tuesday as scheduled and made it to our hotel without any problems. On Wednesday we walked and sunbathed on Copacabana and Ipanema beaches. The only problem was that I didn't put on any sunblock and got bad sunburn. There's a good news, though; it's better today. Actually, there's one other problem: We don't have enough furnitures in our hotel room. There's no place to put anything. But everything else has been great. We went to a samba show, and even though it was intended for tourists, it was a lot of fun.

The Brazilian people is very friendly and helpful. On Friday we had a flight to São Paulo scheduled for 9:00 A.M., and we missed the bus and couldn't get a taxi. But we were saved by one of the hotel employees, who gave us a ride to the airport. We got there just in time. Now we're in São Paulo. It's an exciting place, but I can't get over the traffic. It took two hours to get from our hotel to the downtown area. Yesterday we had lunch at a famous restaurant where they serve feijoada, a typical Brazilian food. It had so many spice in it that our mouths were on fire, but it was delicious. Tonight we're going to have dinner at a very famous restaurant where they serve every kind of meats you can think of.

(continued on next page)

The other thing about Brazil that's really interesting is the amount of coffees the Brazilians drink. They have little cups of coffee several times a day-called caffezinho. We tried it; it's very strong and sweet.

That's all for now. Your mom hasn't had a time to go shopping yet, which is good. You know how much I hate shopping.

Love,
Dad

STEP 4 COMMUNICATION PRACTICE

EXERCISE 6: Listening

A | ***Listen to the conversation. Why is Joe Smith at the doctor's office?***

____

B | ***Listen again. Answer each question with a complete sentence.***

1. What did the TV speaker say Joe needs to do?

   He said that he needs to lose weight.

2. What is his cholesterol level?

   ____

3. Which meal does Joe skip daily?

   ____

4. Why?

   ____

5. How much exercise does he get?

   ____

6. Where does he eat his midday meal?

   ____

7. What is Joe at high risk for?

   ____

8. Why isn't the doctor going to put Joe on a diet?

____

9. What will Joe still be able to eat?

____

10. How many times a week will Joe need to exercise at the beginning?

____

EXERCISE 7: Pronunciation

A | *Read and listen to the Pronunciation Note.*

Pronunciation Note

In fast speech, the word ***of*** in noun phrases is sometimes reduced to /ə/ before words beginning with a consonant. The pronunciation /**ə**v/ is maintained before words beginning with a vowel.

Examples: a lot **of** people = a lot**ə** people
a lot **of** advice = a lot**əv** advice

Note: This reduction sometimes happens in fast speech. It is perfectly correct to pronounce ***of*** as /**ə**v/ in all situations.

B | *Listen and repeat the sentences. Circle* **of** *where it is reduced to /ə/. Underline* **of** *where it maintains the pronunciation /***əv***/.*

1. I ate a lot (of) doughnuts for lunch.
2. Mary gave me an important piece <u>of</u> advice.
3. There were a lot of new people in class today.
4. We bought a new piece of furniture for the living room.
5. We lost a piece of equipment when we changed offices.
6. Can you pour me a glass of orange juice?
7. I had a delicious piece of meat for supper.
8. There was a large group of engineers at the convention.
9. I bought my fiancée a bouquet of flowers.
10. There was a basket of eggs on the kitchen table.

C | *PAIRS: Practice the sentences. Take turns.*

EXERCISE 8: Discussion

A | *Look again at the sentences you wrote in Exercise 4. Share your answers with the other members of your group.*

EXAMPLE: **A:** What's the best advice you've ever had?
B: The best advice I've ever had was to go to college.

B | *Report interesting examples to the entire class.*

EXERCISE 9: Personal Inventory

A | *Complete the survey by circling the answers that best apply to you.*

1. In general I'd say I'm _____.

a. in excellent health **b.** in good health **c.** in fair health **d.** not concerned about my health

2. The drink I like the best is _____.

a. water **b.** soda **c.** milk **d.** other

3. The best exercise for me is _____.

a. running **b.** swimming **c.** walking **d.** other

4. My absolute favorite food is _____.

a. meat **b.** pasta **c.** dessert **d.** other

5. I never miss _____.

a. a meal **b.** a social experience **c.** exercising **d.** watching my favorite TV show

6. My most challenging health issue is _____.

a. losing weight **b.** gaining weight **c.** avoiding stress **d.** other

7. I'm _____ ill.

a. often **b.** sometimes **c.** seldom **d.** never

B | *CLASS: Discuss your answers. What trends do you see?*

EXERCISE 10: Writing

A | *Write three or four paragraphs about one of these topics:*

- the single most important health issue in society today
- the single most important thing I can do to improve my health

Use both count and non-count nouns.

EXAMPLE: The single most important thing I can do to improve my health is to reduce my stress level. For several years now stress has been a problem in my life. I think the way to accomplish this is to do fewer things and do them better. I know I am involved in too many things, but somehow I can't help it. For example . . .

B | *Check your work. Use the Editing Checklist.*

Editing Checklist

Did you use . . . ?
- ☐ articles correctly
- ☐ count nouns correctly
- ☐ non-count nouns correctly

UNIT 6 Review

Check your answers on page UR-1.
Do you need to review anything?

A | *Identify the boldfaced word as a count noun* (**C**) *or a non-count noun* (**NC**).

1. Jack Sanderson describes his latest novel as a **work** in progress. ____
2. Let me give you some **advice**: Don't drop out of college. ____
3. My favorite dinner is fried **chicken** and mashed potatoes. ____
4. We saw an interesting new **film** at our local cinema last night. ____
5. I don't care much for potatoes, but I do like **rice**. ____
6. My favorite professor is giving a **talk** tonight. ____
7. In my view, **reading** is one of the most beneficial activities. ____

B | *Complete each sentence in two ways: first in a more conversational way and second in a more formal way.*

1. **a.** There hasn't been ________________ rain here for three months.
   b. There hasn't been ________________ rain here for three months.
2. **a.** We bought ________________ furniture at a discount store.
   b. We bought ________________ furniture at a discount store.
3. **a.** There wasn't ________________ rice left in the bowl.
   b. There wasn't ________________ rice left in the bowl.
4. **a.** We played ________________ tennis before dinner.
   b. We played ________________ tennis before dinner.

C | *Circle the letter of the underlined word or phrase in each sentence that is not correct.*

1. Ralph is in the intensive care unit (A) of the city hospital (B) after being struck by a lightning (C) on a camping trip (D). **A B C D**
2. Her son dislikes cauliflower (A), carrots (B), beans (C), and most other vegetable (D). **A B C D**
3. At the yard sale we bought some (A) garden equipment (B) and a (C) new furniture (D). **A B C D**
4. People (A) who lives (B) in glass houses (C) shouldn't throw stones (D). **A B C D**
5. It takes a (A) work (B) to prepare a (C) nutritious meal (D). **A B C D**

UNIT 7 Definite and Indefinite Articles

ENVIRONMENTAL CONCERNS

STEP 1 GRAMMAR IN CONTEXT

Before You Read

PAIRS: Discuss the questions.

1. What is an example of a serious environmental problem?
2. Do you think people exaggerate the seriousness of hazards to the environment? If so, what would be an example?
3. How can serious environmental problems be remedied?

Read

Read the article about an environmental disaster.

The Real Mystery of EASTER ISLAND

There are two mysteries about Easter Island. One is this: Who built its gigantic statues, and how were they moved? **The** other, greater **mystery** is what changed **the island** so drastically?

Easter Island, settled about **the year** 900 by Polynesians, lies in **the South Pacific** about 2,300 miles west of Chile, **the country** to which it belongs. If you go to Easter Island today, you'll see about 500 statues in various stages of disrepair—many toppled over. You'll also see more than 100 enormous platforms on which **the statues** stood.

This area was once a subtropical forest.

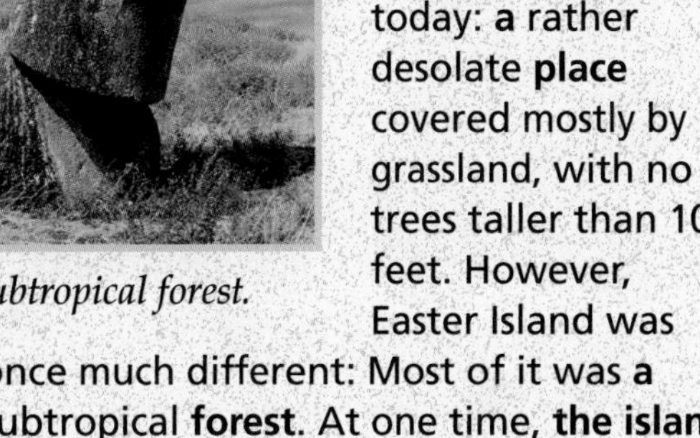

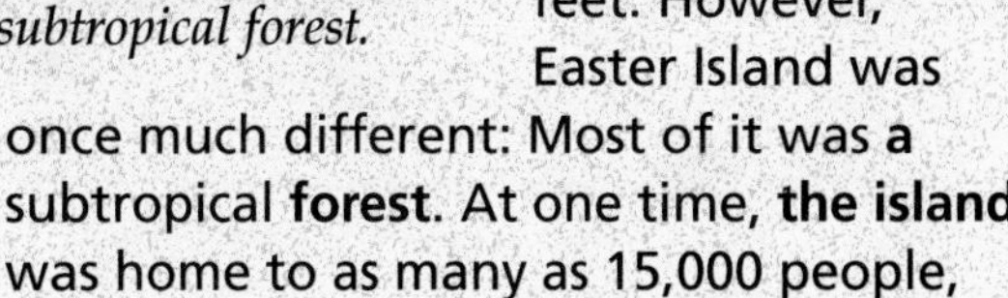

Easter Island was discovered by Dutch explorer Jacob Roggeveen on April 5, 1722— Easter Sunday. On landing, Roggeveen saw **the island** much as it is today: **a** rather desolate **place** covered mostly by grassland, with no trees taller than 10 feet. However, Easter Island was once much different: Most of it was **a** subtropical **forest**. At one time, **the island** was home to as many as 15,000 people,

(*continued on next page*)

while today there are only about 200. What occurred to cause such drastic changes?

The two **mysteries** are closely connected. It is believed today that **the Easter Islanders** built and moved **the statues** themselves. But how could they have done this? **The wheel** had been invented long before, but **the Easter Islanders** didn't have access to it, nor did they have cranes, metal tools, or large animals. **A** convincing **explanation** is that they devised canoe rails—ladders with parallel wooden logs connected by crosspieces—which they used to drag **the statues.** But large trees would have been required to build **the rails,** along with other kinds of trees to provide bark to make rope to pull **the statues**. Had such trees ever existed there?

Botanist John Flenly and anthropologist Paul Bahn believe they had. Studies have established that **the island** was once covered with forests. One of **the** principal **trees** was **the Chilean wine palm**, which grows as high as 65 feet and as wide as 3 feet. **The trunks** of **the wine palm** were presumably used to lift and move **the statues**, with **the bark** of other trees used to make rope for hauling. But what happened to **the trees**? Today **the deforestation** of Easter Island can be seen as one of **the** greatest environmental **disasters** of all time. No one knows for sure how or why it happened, but **the island** apparently experienced **a decline** several hundred years after being settled. It is thought that 11 ruling chiefs constructed **the statues** as competitive demonstrations of their power. As **the population** increased, **the rivalry** became fiercer. More land was cleared to grow crops, and more trees cut down for firewood and for moving **the statues.** This deforestation led to **the drying** of **the land, the loss** of nutrients in **the soil,** and eventually less and less rainfall. In effect, **the climate** was changed.

Why did **the Easter Islanders** allow **the disaster** to happen? Did they simply not recognize there was **a problem**, or was it too late to do anything when they figured it out? Perhaps more significantly, are there parallels for us today? Are we acting as **the Easter Islanders** did, but on a global **scale**? For example, does **the push** to cut down trees in **the name** of jobs and economic development make environmental sense? Are we overfishing **the ocean** in **an** ostrich-like **belief** that **the supply** of seafood is limitless? Are future catastrophes in **the works**? We mustn't shy away from these questions.

After You Read

A | Vocabulary: *Match the blue words and phrases on the left with their meanings on the right.*

_____ **1.** The greater mystery is what changed the island so **drastically**.

_____ **2.** You'll see about 500 statues in disrepair, many **toppled over**.

_____ **3.** The island today is a rather **desolate** place.

_____ **4.** The trees provided **bark** to make rope for pulling the statues.

_____ **5.** The **trunk** of the wine palm was used to lift and move the statues.

_____ **6.** The bark of other trees was used to make rope for **hauling**.

_____ **7.** As the population increased, the **rivalry** became fiercer.

_____ **8.** Do we have an **ostrich-like** belief that the supply of seafood is limitless?

a. pulling

b. competition

c. a tree's main stem

d. overturned

e. suddenly and severely

f. refusing to face reality

g. appearing deserted

h. a tree's outer covering

B | Comprehension: *Circle* **T (True)** *or* **F (False)**. *Correct the false statements.*

1. Easter Island was settled about the year 900 by Chileans. **T** **F**

2. When the island was settled, much of it was a subtropical forest. **T** **F**

3. The population of Easter Island today is much less than it once was. **T** **F**

4. The Easter Islanders used wheels to move their statues. **T** **F**

5. The island declined apparently because of political competition among chiefs. **T** **F**

6. The climate of Easter Island changed a great deal over the years. **T** **F**

7. Deforestation led to the island becoming wetter. **T** **F**

STEP 2 GRAMMAR PRESENTATION

INDEFINITE AND DEFINITE ARTICLES

***A / An*: Indefinite Article**		
	Non-Specific	**Generic**
Singular Count Nouns	He saw **a statue** at **an exhibition**.	**A statue** is **a** three-dimensional **figure**.

Zero Article (No Article)		
	Non-Specific	**Generic**
Plural Count Nouns	Easter Island has impressive **statues**.	**Statues** are made in all shapes and sizes.
Non-Count Nouns	The statues are made of **stone**.	**Stone** is an important building material.
Proper Nouns	**Ms. Johnson** spent a year on **Easter Island**. She worked in **Egypt** and **Hawaii**. She now lives in **New York City**.	

***The*: Definite Article**		
	Specific	**Generic**
Singular Count Nouns	He finally got a computer. **The computer** he got is good. It's **the best computer** in **the world**.	**The computer** is a great invention.
Plural Count Nouns	**The rain forests** in South America are being cut down.	**The rain forests** are in danger everywhere.
Non-Count Nouns	**The stone** from that quarry is very soft.	
Proper Nouns	She crossed **the Sahara**, visited **the Pyramids**, and sailed down **the Nile**.	

GRAMMAR NOTES

1	Speakers use **indefinite** (non-specific / generic) nouns when they do not have a particular person, place, or thing in mind. Use the indefinite article, ***a / an***, with indefinite **singular count nouns**.	• He wants to buy **a statue**. • She wants to be **an anthropologist**.
2	A noun is often **indefinite** the first time a speaker mentions it. It is usually **definite** after the first mention.	• I heard of **an** interesting **mystery**. • **The mystery** is about Easter Island.
3	Use **zero article** (no article) with indefinite plural count nouns, indefinite non-count nouns, names of people, names of most countries, and habitual locations.	• The island used to have tall **trees**. • **Platinum** and **gold** are valuable minerals. • **Mr. Flenly** is a botanist. • Many statues have been found in **Egypt**. • People spend most of their time at **work**, at **school**, or at **home**.

4	A noun is **generic** when it represents all members of a class or category of persons, places, or things—generic nouns talk about things in general.	
	Three common ways to use nouns generically are **a.** Indefinite article + count noun	• **A computer** is **a machine** that does calculations and processes information.
	b. Zero article + plural count noun	• **Computers** are **machines** that do calculations and process information.
	c. Zero article + non-count noun	• **Water** is essential for survival.
	NOTE: You can also make a generic statement with the definite article + adjective. A noun such as *people* is implied. The adjective is plural in meaning and takes a plural verb.	• **The rich are** fortunate. They need to help **the poor**, who **are** not so fortunate. *(= the rich people, the poor people)*
5	A noun is **definite** when the speaker and listener know which particular person, place, or thing is being talked about. Use the definite article, ***the***, with non-count nouns and singular and plural nouns that are definite for you and your listener.	• **The food** we had for lunch was terrible. • **The island** used to be covered by forests. • **The statues** were made by tribal chiefs.
	NOTE: A noun or noun phrase is normally definite if you can ask a *which* question about it. Nouns of this type are often followed by a phrase with *of*.	• **The population** of Easter Island has declined a great deal. • The population **of which island** has declined a great deal?
6	Use the **definite article** with nouns that describe something unique.	• **The sun** gives us light and heat.
	An adjective can often make a noun represent something unique. Examples are *first, last, only, right, wrong*, and the comparative and superlative forms of adjectives.	• It was **the worst disaster** in the country's history.
7	You can use the **definite article** generically to talk about inventions, musical instruments, living things, and parts of the body.	• **The wheel** was invented thousands of years ago. • She plays **the harp**. • **The wine palm** grew on Easter Island. • **The brain** is the seat of intelligence.

(continued on next page)

8 Note these other uses of the **definite article** with nouns:	
a. With public places	• the bank, the post office, the library
b. With the names of many geographical regions or features	• the Grand Canyon, the Colorado River, the Pacific Ocean, the Bahamas, the Gulf Coast
c. With the names of a few countries	• the Netherlands, the United States, the Dominican Republic
d. With the names of ships	• the *Titanic*, the *Queen Mary*

REFERENCE NOTE

For more complete lists of **nouns used with the definite article**, see Appendices 7–9 on pages A-5 and A-6.

STEP 3 FOCUSED PRACTICE

EXERCISE 1: Discover the Grammar

A | *Read the sentences based on the opening reading. For each sentence, identify the underlined word or phrase as non-specific* (**N**), *definite* (**D**), *or generic* (**G**).

N 1. We've become aware of an even greater mystery.

____ 2. Chile is the country to which Easter Island belongs.

____ 3. There are gigantic platforms all over the island.

____ 4. At one time the island was home to as many as 15,000 people.

____ 5. The wheel had been invented long before.

____ 6. Canoe rails are ladders with parallel wooden logs connected by crosspieces.

____ 7. The Chilean wine palm grows as high as 65 feet.

____ 8. Did they simply fail to recognize an eventual problem?

____ 9. Are we overfishing the ocean?

____ 10. Is the supply of seafood limitless?

B | *Read the sentences based on the reading. Then circle the letter of the choice that best explains the meaning of the sentence.*

1. Who built the statues there?

a. Who built some of the statues there?

(b.) Who built all of the statues there?

2. The island was settled by Polynesians.

a. Some of the Polynesians settled the island.

b. All of the Polynesians settled the island.

3. One of the principal trees in the forest was the Chilean wine palm.

a. There was one Chilean palm tree in the forest.

b. There were many Chilean palm trees in the forest.

4. But what happened to the trees on the island?
   a. What happened to all of the trees on the island?
   b. What happened to some of the trees on the island?

5. Trees were cut down to provide firewood.
   a. All of the trees were cut down.
   b. Some of the trees were cut down.

EXERCISE 2: Articles

(Grammar Notes 1–3, 5–6, 8)

Read the descriptions of two notable environmental disasters that have occurred in recent years. Fill in the blanks with the correct article in parentheses ("—" means no article is needed).

Hurricane Katrina: The Costliest Ever

On August 23, 2005, ____—____ (1. (— / The)) Hurricane Katrina formed over ________ (2. (— / the)) Bahamas and promptly moved westward along ________ (3. (a / the)) Gulf Coast of ________ (4. (— / the)) United States, causing very great destruction. At first ________ (5. (— / The)) Katrina was only ________ (6. (a / the)) Category 1 hurricane, but by the time it reached New Orleans it had become a Category 3. In terms of damage, it is considered one of ________ (7. (a / the)) five worst hurricanes in ________ (8. (— / the)) American history, largely because of ________ (9. (— / the)) failure of New Orleans's levee system. Eighty percent of ________ (10. (a / the)) city was flooded, and at least 1,836 people died. There was great criticism of ________ (11. (a / the)) way the government handled ________ (12. (— / the)) crisis.

Devastating Earthquake In Haiti

On ________ (13. (a / the)) afternoon of January 12, 2010, ________ (14. (— / the)) country of Haiti was struck by ________ (15. (a / the)) devastating earthquake that registered 7.0 on ________ (16. (a / the)) Richter Scale. ________ (17. (An / The)) epicenter of ________ (18. (— / the)) quake was near Leogane, ________ (19. (a / the)) town approximately 16 miles west of Port-au-Prince, ________ (20. (— / the)) country's capital. According to ________ (21. (a / the)) Haitian government, at least 230,000 people were killed, 300,000 injured, and 1,000,000 left homeless.

There was ________ (22. (— / an)) extremely severe damage to ________ (23. (an / the)) infrastructure of Port-au-Prince. Many nations responded with humanitarian aid.

EXERCISE 3: Articles

(Grammar Notes 1–2, 4–6, 8)

Read the two excerpts from the article "Earthweek: A Diary of the Planet." Fill in the blanks with the articles needed. Leave a blank if no article is necessary.

Permafrost Warning

___The___ (1.) melting of permafrost in Sweden's subarctic region due to global warming is believed to be releasing vast quantities of the greenhouse gas methane into __________ (2.) atmosphere. __________ (3.) research team, led by __________ (4.) GeoBiosphere Science Center at Lund University, said its research shows that __________ (5.) part of __________ (6.) soil that thaws during summer has become deeper since 1970, and the permafrost has disappeared entirely in some locations. "This has led to significant changes in the vegetation and to __________ (7.) subsequent increase in emission of the greenhouse gas methane," the team announced. The team added that methane is 25 times more damaging to __________ (8.) atmosphere than __________ (9.) carbon dioxide and often is overlooked in the discussion of greenhouse gases.

Plastic Pollution

__________ (10.) German magazine *Geo* published __________ (11.) report saying that __________ (12.) plastic trash has created __________ (13.) environmental hazard that stretches across __________ (14.) Pacific from California to Hawaii, resulting in more plastic than plankton on __________ (15.) water's surface. __________ (16.) March issue quotes biologist Charles Moore of the Algalita Marine Research Foundation as saying, "Most plastic floats near __________ (17.) sea surface where some is mistaken for __________ (18.) food by birds and fishes." The masses of plastic find their way into __________ (19.) Pacific from __________ (20.) western United States and __________ (21.) Canada after storms flush the debris downstream and ultimately into __________ (22.) ocean. Maritime observers have witnessed areas of floating plastic that stretch as far as the eye can see in __________ (23.) central Pacific.

EXERCISE 4: Generic Nouns

(Grammar Notes 4, 8)

Write two sentences about each invention or instrument. In the first sentence, write about the item's characteristics. In the second sentence, use the definite article to say when the item was invented.

Example: computer / electronic device / process information and perform high-speed calculations / 1944

A computer is an electronic device that processes information and performs high-speed calculations. / Computers are electronic devices that process information and perform high-speed calculations.

The computer was invented in 1944.

1. TV set / electronic device / receive electromagnetic waves, convert waves into images, display them on a screen / 1920s by Farnsworth and Zorinsky

____

____

2. wheel / circular device / turn around central point / 5,000 to 6,000 years ago

____

____

3. clarinet / woodwind instrument / use a reed / around 1700

____

____

4. guitars / stringed instruments / typically have six strings / in the 1400s in Spain

____

____

5. automobiles / self-powered traveling vehicles / 1874 by Siegfried Marcus in Vienna

____

____

6. telephones / communication devices / convert sound signals into waves and reconvert them into sounds / 1878 by Alexander Graham Bell

____

____

EXERCISE 5: Editing

Read the student composition about nuclear power. There are nine mistakes in the use of articles. The first mistake is already corrected. Find and correct eight more.

Nuclear Power

Many people today are against ~~the~~ nuclear power. I disagree with them for several reasons. First, we need the additional power sources. We are running out of the petroleum. Many environmentalists say we need to develop the use of geothermal and wind energy. I am certainly not against these sources, and we should work on developing them. But they can't do everything. Then there's the suggestion of hydroelectric power. Many say that even though there are the problems with it, it is better than going nuclear. I am big supporter of hydroelectric power, but it can't provide all the power we need either.

Second, many are against nuclear plants because they believe they are unsafe. They always mention the accidents at Chernobyl and Three-Mile Island as examples. Yes, these were serious problems, but we have learned from them. There haven't been the major problems with nuclear reactors for many years now. We can make nuclear power safe if we develop the strict controls and inspections. France produces about 77 percent of its power from nuclear energy. The French have had the issue of getting rid of nuclear waste, but they are working on it. If the French can do it, other countries can too.

Third, once a device is invented or a process is developed, it can't really be abandoned. Willy Brandt, a former German chancellor, said, "We cannot return to the age of nuclear innocence." We don't live in perfect world. There are potential dangers of using nuclear energy, but there are potential dangers in everything. As far as I am concerned, nuclear power will be necessity in the future.

STEP 4 COMMUNICATION PRACTICE

EXERCISE 6: Listening

A herd of elk

Wolves

A | *Listen to the conversation between a husband and a wife. The conversation is about reintroducing wolves into what places?*

____

B | *Read the statements. Then listen again to the conversation. Circle the letter of the correct answer.*

1. According to the husband, the newspaper is on the side of _____.

a. the ranchers and hunters **(b.)** the environmentalists

2. Whose point of view does he think is not considered?

a. the ranchers' and hunters' **b.** the environmentalists'

3. The husband supports the point of view of _____.

a. the ranchers and hunters **b.** the environmentalists

4. The husband _____ a hunter.

a. is **b.** is not

5. The husband thinks _____ are dangerous creatures.

a. wolves in general **b.** some wolves

6. The wife thinks the husband's idea about wolves killing people is _____.

a. a stereotype **b.** basically true

7. The wife supports the point of view of _____.

a. the ranchers and hunters **b.** the environmentalists

8. Before 1995, there were too many _____ in Yellowstone.

a. elk **b.** wolves

9. According to the wife, some of the _____ elk have been killed off.

a. old and sick **b.** young and strong

10. The wife thinks _____ are intelligent and helpful.

a. some wolves **b.** wolves in general

EXERCISE 7: Pronunciation

A | *Read and listen to the Pronunciation Note.*

Pronunciation Note

The definite article *the* has two pronunciations: It is pronounced /**ðə**/ before words beginning with a consonant sound, as in "the statue." It is pronounced /**ði**/ before words beginning with a vowel sound, as in "the environment."

B | *Listen to the sentences. Underline uses of* **the** *pronounced as /ðə/. Circle uses of* **the** *pronounced as /ði/.*

1. (The) environmentalists are from the local college.
2. The inhabitants of Easter Island built the statues themselves.
3. The climate of the area was changed.
4. The forests that used to cover the island are gone.
5. The sad truth is that the Earth's resources are limited.
6. Fortunately, that's not the end of the story.
7. The 11 ruling chiefs were responsible for the problem.
8. Are we overfishing the ocean in the mistaken belief that the supply of seafood is unlimited?

C | *PAIRS: Practice the sentences. Take turns.*

EXERCISE 8: Picture Discussion

GROUPS: Form small groups and discuss the picture. Identify some of the items you see. Then discuss the situation. How can we dispose of items we no longer need or want? What solutions are there to this problem?

EXAMPLE: **A:** I see a lot of plastic bags and cardboard boxes.
B: How do you think we should dispose of things like those?
C: We could recycle as much as possible . . .

EXERCISE 9: Game

TEAMS: Two teams take turns asking a **who** *or* **what** *question about each answer in the chart. Your teacher directs the game and awards points. Each question can earn two points, one for the correct question and one for correct use of the article.*

EXAMPLE: **A:** Answer: The country that owns Easter Island.
B: Question: What is Chile?

Answers				
The type of tree that used to grow on Easter Island	The ship that sank in the Atlantic in 1912 on its first voyage	The place in a city or town where one keeps one's money	The home country of the first European to see Easter Island	The name of the people who settled Easter Island
The animals that have been reintroduced in national parks	The circular object that was not used in moving the Easter Island statues	The outer covering of a tree	The body of water in which Easter Island is located	The people in a particular circumstance who have a great deal of money
The material from which the Easter Island statues are made	A form of precipitation that is necessary for crops to grow	A form of energy that involves the use of radioactive material	The device invented by Easter Islanders to move their statues	A liquid substance used to produce gasoline
The place in a city or town where one can mail letters	A type of natural phenomenon that devastated the country of Haiti in 2010	The part of the human body that is the seat of intelligence	The nation over which Hurricane Katrina formed	The electronic device invented in 1944 by Farnsworth and Zorinsky
A type of animal killed by wolves in Yellowstone National Park	A woodwind instrument that uses a reed and was invented about 1700	The people in a particular circumstance who are badly off economically	A polluting material in the ocean that birds and fish mistake for food	In the Arctic and subarctic region, the part of the soil that doesn't thaw in the summer

EXERCISE 10: Writing

A | *GROUPS: Choose an environmental issue from the list or develop your own idea. Write three to four paragraphs about the topic you select. Say why you think the issue is important and what should be done about it.*

Possible Issues

- saving endangered animals
- improving air quality
- building nuclear power plants
- disposing of garbage
- ensuring the supply of clean water

Example: Laws against air pollution have been in effect for decades now, but we haven't seen much progress in reducing air pollution. Actually, air pollution has gotten worse in many areas. If we want to make real progress, we need stricter laws, and we need to enforce them. There are three areas where we can improve: pollution from automobiles, factories, and the burning of forests. Let's look at each of these separately.

The automobile . . .

B | *Check your work. Use the Editing Checklist.*

Editing Checklist

Did you use . . . ?

☐ definite articles correctly

☐ indefinite articles correctly

☐ zero articles correctly

UNIT 7 Review

Check your answers on page UR-1.
Do you need to review anything?

A | *Identify each boldfaced word or phrase as non-specific* (**N**), *definite* (**D**), *or generic* (**G**).

1. **The clarinet** was invented around the year 1700. ____
2. My parents bought me **a trumpet** when I started band in middle school. ____
3. **The moon** is Earth's only satellite. ____
4. **Water** is an extremely valuable commodity in desert areas. ____
5. In my view, we need to help **the poor** in whatever way we can. ____
6. **The man** who is giving the lecture is my next-door neighbor. ____
7. The ship was hit by **an iceberg** on its maiden voyage. ____
8. There's **water** all over the kitchen floor. ____

B | *Fill in the blanks with* **a, an,** *or* **the** *where necessary. Leave a blank if no article is needed.*

Disaster at Sea: Many Lives Lost

April 16, 1912. ________ (1.) *Titanic,* ________ (2.) British steamer, sank in ________ (3.) North Atlantic last night after hitting ________ (4.) iceberg, disproving its builders' claims that it couldn't be sunk. ________ (5.) ship was on its maiden voyage from Southampton, England, to ________ (6.) New York City. More than 1,500 people perished, in large part because ________ (7.) lifeboats were felt to take up too much deck space, and there were only 20 of them.

C | *Circle the letter of the underlined word or phrase in each sentence that is not correct.*

1. One of the most famous inventions (A) in the (B) human history (C) is the wheel (D). **A B C D**
2. The CEO (A) of the company (B) lives in big house (C) in the suburbs (D). **A B C D**
3. Journey (A) is a three-hour trip (B) if the traffic (C) and the weather (D) are OK. **A B C D**
4. The plan (A) to build a (B) extensive monorail system (C) is a citizen-initiated proposal (D). **A B C D**
5. The extinction (A) of the dinosaurs (B) is still a matter of debate (C) in scientific community (D). **A B C D**

UNIT 8

Quantifiers
MONEY

STEP 1 GRAMMAR IN CONTEXT

Before You Read

PAIRS: Discuss the questions.

1. Do you pay for most things with cash, with credit cards, or by some other means?
2. What would be the advantages and disadvantages of living in a cashless society?

Read

 *Read the article about money.*

BUSINESS AND YOU | AUGUST 6, 2012 | BUSINESS TODAY

What's Happening to CA$H?

How did money originate, and where? The Babylonians were the first to develop actual "money" when they started to use gold and silver about 2500 B.C.E. In the succeeding centuries, **many** other **items** came to be used as currency, e.g., jewelry, land, and even cattle.

In the last **two centuries**, however, the movement has been away from the physical and toward the abstract. **One example** is fiat money, i.e., paper currency issued by a government. Fiat money isn't based on gold or silver; it has value only because the government says it does. Perhaps the most abstract type of money involves the electronic transfer of funds from **one** bank **account** to another. **No** actual **money** is transferred. The balance in **one account** is simply increased, and the balance in the other decreased correspondingly.

Does this mean that cash no longer has **any advantages**? Not at all. Suppose you're walking down a street and remember you need to buy **some flowers**. You see a vendor and decide this is the time to buy **a dozen roses**. Do you write a check or pull out your bank card? At this writing, **few** street **vendors** take checks, and even **fewer** take plastic. **Most of them** prefer cash. You

DO YOU TAKE ANY CREDIT CARDS?

What's Happening to CA$H?

simply hand the vendor **a few bills** and happily walk away with your flowers. Pretty easy, huh? It wouldn't be that easy without cash.

Or suppose you'd like to give **a little money** as a gift. It's a lot more personal and pleasing to receive **a few** crisp **bills** in a birthday card than a check. Suppose you're at a food fair and want **a couple of hot dogs**. It's much easier to pull out cash to pay for them. In restaurants these days, it's common to pay with a credit or debit card and include a tip. Sometimes, though, you might want to make a better emotional connection by leaving your server **some** actual **cash** in appreciation of good service.

So cash has its advantages. Of course, it has **a number of disadvantages** as well. You might be robbed. Carrying **a lot of coins** can make holes in your pockets. It's inconvenient to take **a great deal of money** with you to pay for large purchases; imagine trying to carry **enough cash** to pay for a house or a car—or even a sofa. Besides that, cash has been handled by **many** different **people** and is covered with germs.

Then there's the matter of paying bills. Traditionally, **most people** in North America have used checks, but the trend is to pay electronically. In Japan, payment for such things as heat, electricity, and water is handled by automatic deduction from a bank account. It's much easier than writing out **several checks** to different agencies. And since it's automatic, people don't have to worry about remembering to pay their bills.

There are **a number of disadvantages** to electronic money, however. Some people have **little use** for credit cards, saying that using them encourages us to live beyond our means. Others say using electronic money places too **much control** of our personal finances in the hands of strangers. Mistakes are easily made and hard to correct.

The jury is still out on whether the trend toward **less and less use** of cash is good or bad. What seems clear is that it's definitely growing.

After You Read

A | Vocabulary: *Match the blue words and phrases on the left with their meanings on the right.*

_____ **1.** In the **succeeding** centuries, many other items came to be used as currency.

_____ **2.** Many other items came to be used as currency, **e.g.**, jewelry, land, and cattle.

_____ **3.** **Fiat** money isn't based on gold or silver.

_____ **4.** The balance in the other account is **correspondingly** decreased.

_____ **5.** At this writing even fewer vendors **take plastic**.

_____ **6.** It's more personal to receive a few **crisp** bills than a check.

_____ **7.** Some say using credit cards encourages us to **live beyond our means**.

_____ **8.** **The jury is still out** on whether the trend toward less use of cash is good or bad.

_____ **9.** One example is fiat money, **i.e.**, paper currency issued by a government.

a. live a lifestyle we can't afford

b. the evidence isn't yet conclusive

c. in a parallel manner

d. specially authorized

e. following

f. firm or fresh

g. for example

h. that is

i. accept credit cards for payment

B | Comprehension: *Refer to the reading and complete each sentence with a single word.*

1. In recent years money has become less physical and more ________________.
2. Fiat money has value only because a ________________ says it has value.
3. Most street vendors would rather have ________________ than take a check or credit card.
4. We often leave a server a tip to show appreciation for good ________________.
5. It's inconvenient to use cash to pay for large ________________.
6. Since many people have used physical money, it may be covered with ________________.
7. The trend in bill paying is to pay ________________.
8. With electronic money, ________________ can exert control of our personal finances.

STEP 2 GRAMMAR PRESENTATION

QUANTIFIERS

Quantifiers	With Count Nouns	With Non-Count Nouns
One	**One store** is open.	Ø*
Each	**Each coin** is valuable.	Ø
Every	**Every bank** is closed.	Ø
Two	**Two stores** are open.	Ø
Both	**Both stores** are nearby.	Ø
A couple of	She bought **a couple of gifts**.	Ø
Several	She bought **several gifts**.	Ø
Few	They have **few investments**.	Ø
A few	She has **a few investments**.	Ø
Many	Does he own **many buildings**?	Ø
A great many	He owns **a great many buildings**.	Ø
A number of	He owns **a number of buildings**.	Ø
Little	Ø	They have **little money**.
A little	Ø	She has **a little money**.
Much	Ø	Does he have **much property**?
A great deal of	Ø	He owns **a great deal of property**.
No	They have **no bonds**.	They have **no insurance**.
Any	They don't have **any bonds**.	They don't have **any insurance**.
Some	They have **some stocks**.	They have **some cash**.
Enough	You have **enough stocks**.	You have **enough cash**.
A lot of / Lots of	He has **a lot of / lots of clients**.	He has **a lot of / lots of patience**.
Plenty of	He has **plenty of clients**.	He has **plenty of patience**.
Most	**Most banks** are safe.	**Most work** is useful.
All	**All banks** are insured.	**All work** is tiring.

*Ø: quantifier not used

GRAMMAR NOTES

1	**Quantifiers** state the number or amount of something. Quantifiers can be single words or phrases.	• I bought **a dozen tulips**. • There's **some money** in my account.
	Quantifiers are used with both nouns and pronouns.	• **A lot of people** vacation in the summer. • **Most of us** are going on the trip.
	Quantifiers are often used alone if the noun or pronoun has just been mentioned, as in a question.	**A:** Have you made **many friends** here? **B:** Yes, I've made **a lot**.
2	**Quantifiers** are used with different types of nouns: **a.** with singular count nouns: *one, each, every*, etc.	• I took **each item** back to the store. • We were able to solve **every problem**.
	b. with plural count nouns: *two, both, a couple of, a dozen, several, few, a few, many, a great many, a number of*, etc.	• We visited **a couple of countries**. • We bought **a few souvenirs**.
	c. with non-count nouns: *a little, little, much, a great deal of, a great amount of*, etc.	• I only make **a little money** at that job. • She earns **a great deal of money**.
	d. with both plural count nouns and non-count nouns: *no, any, some, enough, a lot of / lots of, plenty of, most, all*, etc.	• She has **no plans** to travel. • We took **no cash** on the trip.
3	Use ***a few / few*** with count nouns and ***a little / little*** with non-count nouns.	• Mary has **a few investments**. • She has saved **a little money**.
	Note the difference between *a few* and *few* and between *a little* and *little*. *A few* and *a little* are used to give a statement a positive sense. They mean "some—not a great number or amount but enough to be satisfactory."	• I have **a few** good **friends**. *(= some; enough to satisfy)* • We have **a little food** at home. *(= some; enough to satisfy)*
	Few and *little* are used to give a statement a negative sense. They mean "hardly any" or "not much at all—not enough to be satisfactory."	• Jerry has **few friends**. *(= not enough to be satisfactory)* • Mary has **little self-confidence**. *(= not enough to be satisfactory)*
	NOTE: If we add the word ***only*** to *a few* or *a little*, the positive sense disappears.	• I have **only a few** friends. *(= I would like more.)* • I have **only a little** money. *(= I would like more.)*
	BE CAREFUL! In comparison, use ***fewer*** with count nouns and ***less*** with non-count nouns. Use ***more*** with both count and non-count nouns.	• I have **fewer problems** than I used to. • I earn **less money**, though. • I have **more friends**. • I also have **more self-confidence**.

(continued on next page)

4	Use ***many*** with count nouns and ***much*** with non-count nouns.	• He doesn't have **many friends**. • I don't have **much trouble** getting to work.
	Use ***a great many*** with count nouns and ***a great deal of*** with non-count nouns. These quantifiers are rather formal and used more in writing than in speech.	• The government has **a great many responsibilities**. • Presidents are under **a great deal of stress**.
	BE CAREFUL! ***Much*** is not often used in affirmative sentences, especially in speech. It is usually replaced by ***a lot of*** or ***lots of***.	• We spend **a lot of money** on rent. • There's **lots of construction** going on.
	However, ***much*** is common in questions, negative statements, and in combination with the adverb ***too***.	• Did they spend **much money**? • She doesn't watch **much TV**. • I ate **too much** for dinner.
	Use ***number*** with count nouns and ***amount*** with non-count nouns.	• The **number of students** attending college has increased. • The **amount of stress** in people's lives seems to be increasing.
5	Use ***some*** and ***any*** with count nouns and non-count nouns.	• Did you make **some / any purchases**? • Do you have **some / any cash** with you?
	Use *some* in affirmative statements.	• Bill bought **some souvenirs**. • He borrowed **some money** from me.
	Use *any* in negative statements.	• Alice didn't take **any trips**. • She didn't have **any money**.
	Use both *some* and *any* in questions. In general, use *some* in offers and *any* in negative questions.	• Did you buy **some / any clothes**? • Would you like **some soda**? • Didn't you send **any postcards**?
	BE CAREFUL! Don't use two negatives in the same simple sentence.	• Jack **didn't** understand **anything**. NOT: Jack didn't understand ~~nothing~~.

6		
	Many **quantifiers** appear in phrases with the preposition ***of***. Use *of* + *the* or another determiner when you are specifying particular persons, places, things, or groups.	• **Most of the EU countries** are using the euro. • We saw **many of her films**.
	We generally use quantifiers without *of* when we have no particular person, place, thing, or group in mind.	• **Most people** don't understand the economy. • **Many restaurants** take credit cards.
	BE CAREFUL! Quantifiers with *of* can be used only with plural count nouns and non-count nouns.	• **Most of the coins** were very old. • **Most of the gold** was pure. NOT: ~~Most of~~ the coin was very old.
	NOTE: Quantifiers such as ***most of*** and ***many of*** can be followed by a singular or a plural verb, depending on the noun that follows *of*.	• Most of the **food has** been eaten *(non-count noun + singular verb)* • Most of the **people have** arrived. *(plural noun + plural verb)*

REFERENCE NOTE

For more information on **count and non-count nouns**, see Unit 7.

STEP 3 FOCUSED PRACTICE

EXERCISE 1: Discover the Grammar

Look at the sentences based on the opening reading. Could they be rewritten using the words in parentheses without changing the basic meaning or creating an incorrect sentence? Write **Y (Yes)** *or* **N (No)**.

__N__ **1.** This is a trend that has been developing for *many* years now. (much)

_____ **2.** Are there still *any* advantages to cash? (some)

_____ **3.** You suddenly remember you need to buy *some* flowers. (any)

_____ **4.** At this writing, *few* flower vendors take checks. (a few)

_____ **5.** *Few* vendors take plastic. (little)

_____ **6.** Suppose you'd like to give *a little* money as a gift. (little)

_____ **7.** It's *much* easier to pull out cash to pay for them. (a lot)

_____ **8.** Cash has *some* disadvantages as well. (any)

_____ **9.** Cash has been handled by *many* different people. (a lot of)

_____ **10.** *Most* people have paid their bills with checks. (a great deal of)

_____ **11.** It's easier than writing out *several* checks. (a little)

_____ **12.** Some people have *little* use for credit cards. (a little)

EXERCISE 2: Quantifiers

(Grammar Notes 2–5)

Complete the sentences by choosing the correct quantifier. The sentences are connected in a story.

1. We just got back from our second trip to Europe. This time we visited ___fewer___ countries. (less / fewer)
2. We didn't visit ________ of the Scandinavian countries this time. (some / any)
3. We spent ________ money this time too. (less / fewer)
4. We did buy ________ wonderful souvenirs, though. (some / any)
5. The last time we rented a car and were amazed by the ________ cars on the roads. (amount of / number of)
6. This time we traveled by train. We expected ________ people to be traveling that way. (much / a lot of)
7. However, there weren't very ________. (much / many)
8. We had ________ problems finding seats in the railroad cars. We never had to stand. (few / a few)
9. That's a good thing. My husband has ________ patience when it comes to competing with other passengers for places to sit. (little / a little)
10. The trip was so economical that we had ________ extra money at the end. (little / a little).

EXERCISE 3: Quantifiers

(Grammar Notes 2–6)

Ron and Ashley Lamont are trying to save money for a trip to South America. They are examining their budget. Complete their conversation with quantifiers from the box, using each expression once.

$50	**~~a lot of~~**	**every**	**less**	**much**
a couple of	**both of**	**few**	**more**	**one of**
a few	**enough**	**fewer**	**most of**	**some**

Ashley: Ron, we're still spending ___a lot of___ (1.) money on things we don't really need. After I pay the bills this month, we're going to have even ________ (2.) cash left over than we did last month. We're supposed to be saving for the trip to South America, remember? We're not saving ________ (3.) money. If we don't start saving ________ (4.), we won't be able to go.

Ron: What have we bought that we don't need?

Ashley: That exercise machine, for one thing. We've only used it ________________ times. We
5.
could get a year's membership at the gym for what it cost and still have something left over.

Ron: You mean ________________ us could get a membership, don't you?
6.

Ashley: No, ________________ us could. That's what I'm saying. The machine cost $500, and
7.
memberships are $200 each. Let's sell the thing and go to the gym.

Ron: Hmm. Maybe you're right. What else?

Ashley: Well, we're spending about ________________ extra a month on those premium cable
8.
channels. We'd have ________________ channels to choose from if we went back to the
9.
basic coverage, but we don't watch ________________ TV anyway.
10.

Ron: Yeah, you're right . . . And you know, I'd say we could get rid of call waiting on the phone. We've used it *very* ________________ times, and ________________ my friends say they
11. 12.
hate it when they call, and then another call comes in while we're talking.

Ashley: Uh-huh. Let's cancel it, then. And here's one more suggestion. We should start taking a bag lunch to work ________________ times a week instead of going out at noon. If we did
13.
these four things, we'd have ________________ money left ________________ month
14. 15.
that could go into our trip fund.

Ron: Oh no! Not my lunches with the boys! Lunchtime is when I get to see them.

Ashley: Invite them over to play volleyball. Then think of Rio de Janeiro.

EXERCISE 4: Numbers

(Grammar Notes 4–6)

Look at the chart. Then complete each sentence with the appropriate quantifier from the box. Use one quantifier twice.

Note: The figures are approximations.

	The World in 1960	The World in 2003–2009
Population	3,020,100,000	6, 829,360 (2009)
Birth rate per thousand people	31.2	19.86 (2009)
Death rate per thousand people	17.7	8.37 (2009)
Female life expectancy at birth	51.9 years	68.07 years (2009)
Male life expectancy at birth	48.6 years	64.29 years (2009)
Electricity use per person	1,445 kilowatt hours	2.596 kilowatt hours (2005)
TV sets per thousand people	112.8	215.5 (2003)
Gross domestic product per person	$2,607	$10,386 (2009)

a great deal of	**fewer**	**more**	**the number of**
~~**a great many**~~	**less**	**the amount of**	

1. ___A great many___ people were born between 1960 and 2009.
2. There were ________________ births per thousand people in 2009 than in 1960.
3. There were ________________ deaths per thousand people in 1960 than in 2009.
4. The life expectancy of men is ________________ than that of women.
5. On the average, ________________ females lived to be older than 52 or males older than 49 in 1960 than today.
6. There was ________________ growth in the use of electricity between 1960 and 2005.
7. There was a big increase in ________________ TV sets in the world between 1960 and 2003.
8. ________________ gross domestic product in 2009 was almost four times that of 1960.

EXERCISE 5: Editing

Read the excerpt from a president's speech. There are eight mistakes in the use of quantifiers. The first one is already corrected. Find and correct seven more.

My fellow citizens: We are at a time in our history when we need to make some real sacrifices. Recent presidents have made ~~a great deal of~~ a great many promises they didn't keep. Tonight you deserve to hear the truth. On the economy, we've made little progress, but we still have a great many work to do, so I'm proposing several measures. First, I want to raise taxes on the very wealthy because a few of them really pay their share. Second, many members of the middle class are carrying an unfair tax burden, so I'm asking for a tax cut for them. If I'm successful, most of you in the middle class will pay 10 percent less in taxes next year, though a few of you in the higher-income group may see your taxes rise little. Third, there are much loopholes in the current law that allow some people to avoid paying any taxes at all; I want to close these loopholes.

Further problems are that we have very few money available for health care reform, and we've made a little progress in reducing pollution and meeting clean air standards. Therefore, as my final measure, I am asking for a 50-cent-a-gallon tax on gasoline, which will result in many more people using public transportation and should create additional revenue. Thus, we will have enough money to finance our new health care program and will be helping the environment at the same time.

STEP 4 COMMUNICATION PRACTICE

EXERCISE 6: Listening

A | *Listen to the conversation in a restaurant. Who chose the restaurant?*

____

B | *Read the questions. Then listen again and circle the letter of the correct answer.*

1. Which restaurant has fewer menu choices?
   (**a.**) this restaurant **b.** the last restaurant
2. At which restaurant does the food cost less?
   a. this restaurant **b.** the last restaurant
3. How much money does Steve have?
   a. none at all **b.** a few dollars
4. Does Steve have enough money to pay the bill?
   a. yes **b.** no
5. How much is the bill?
   a. $75 **b.** $45
6. How many credit cards does Steve have?
   a. one **b.** none at all
7. Do Mary and Steve have enough money together to pay the bill?
   a. yes **b.** no
8. Are there any ATM machines nearby?
   a. Yes, there are. **b.** No, there aren't.

EXERCISE 7: Pronunciation

A | *Read and listen to the Pronunciation Note.*

Pronunciation Note

Remember that a vowel in an unstressed syllable normally takes **the schwa /ə/ sound**. Using the schwa sound correctly in unstressed syllables is important for being understood and for improving one's accent. For example, in the word *thousand,* the first vowel, represented by *ou,* is stressed. The second vowel, represented by *a,* is unstressed and has a schwa sound.

B | *Listen to the sentences. Then listen again and repeat. Circle the syllables that have no stress and in which the vowel assumes a schwa sound. The number in parentheses indicates the number of such syllables in the sentence.*

1. A lot of people vacation here. (4)
2. I have fewer problems than I used to. (2)
3. She doesn't watch much television. (3)
4. Presidents are under a great deal of stress. (4)
5. We are facing a great many challenges today. (4)
6. The amount of money I earn is minimal. (4)
7. The number of students in colleges is growing. (6)
8. I took each item back to the store. (3)

C | *PAIRS: Practice the sentences. Take turns.*

EXERCISE 8: Game

TEAMS: Form two teams. Each team uses its prompts to construct eight questions about world facts, using quantifiers. Then each team creates two questions of its own, for a total of 10 questions. The other team tries to answer each question correctly, using a complete sentence. For answers, see page G-AK2.

Example: country / more / people / China / India
A: Which country has more people, China or India?
B: China has more people.

Team A's Prompts

1. country / fewer / people / Canada / Mexico
2. country / more / land area / Canada / the United States
3. country / produce / less / oil / Venezuela / Mexico
4. country / no / snowfall / Somalia / Tanzania
5. country / fewer / rivers / Libya / Nigeria
6. country / smaller number / people / Monaco / Cyprus
7. country / produce / large amount / gold / Nigeria / South Africa
8. city / less / rainfall / Aswan, Egypt / Athens, Greece
9. ____________________
10. ____________________

(continued on next page)

Team B's Prompts

1. country / fewer / people / Great Britain / Spain
2. country / more / land area / Australia / Brazil
3. country / produce / less / oil / the United States / Saudi Arabia
4. country / no / military / Colombia / Costa Rica
5. country / fewer / rivers / Yemen / Turkey
6. country / smaller number / people / San Marino / Kuwait
7. country / use / larger amount / nuclear energy / the Netherlands / France
8. city / less / rainfall / Antofagasta, Chile / Nairobi, Kenya
9. ______________________________
10. ______________________________

EXERCISE 9: Personal Inventory

A | *Compare your life now to your life five years ago. Write eight sentences, using each of the quantifiers from the box.*

a few	a little	a lot	fewer	less	many	more	much

EXAMPLE: I have **more friends** now than I did five years ago.

B | *PAIRS: Discuss the changes in your life with your partner.*

C | *CLASS: Report interesting examples to the entire class.*

EXERCISE 10: Writing

A | *Write three or four paragraphs about an interesting experience you have had with money. Choose one of the topics or create your own topic. Use quantifiers where appropriate.*

- a time when you ran out of money
- a time when you tipped too much or too little
- a time when you lost your wallet or purse

EXAMPLE: The most interesting experience I've had with money was when I was visiting New York. I had gone to a restaurant and ordered an expensive meal. I thought I had enough money to pay for the meal, but I had a big surprise. Here's how it happened . . .

B | *Check your work. Use the Editing Checklist.*

Editing Checklist

Did you use . . . ?

☐ quantifiers with count nouns correctly

☐ quantifiers with non-count nouns correctly

UNIT 8 Review

Check your answers on page UR-1.
Do you need to review anything?

A | *Circle the correct word or phrase to complete each sentence.*

1. Most / Most of people enjoy eating a well-cooked meal.
2. The number of / amount of traffic on the freeway today is astounding.
3. I'd like to help you, but I don't have some / any time today.
4. My son Ali earned a lot of / much money at his part-time job.
5. Can you please get me a couple / a couple of candy bars at the store?
6. The number of / The amount of patients has increased.
7. About how much / many people live in your home town?
8. Bobby's problem is that he has little / a little motivation to get a job.
9. We have plenty / plenty of glasses and plates, so don't bring any.
10. We have any / no money left after our night on the town.

B | *In the blank after each sentence, write a quantifier with a meaning similar to the underlined word or phrase.*

1. We have made a lot of friends in our new neighborhood. ____________________
2. I don't have a lot of work to finish this afternoon. ____________________
3. He has a great deal of money in the bank. ____________________
4. Andrea has some problems in her new job. ____________________
5. We have many disagreements with your plan. ____________________
6. Each person in the class earned a good score. ____________________

C | *Circle the letter of the underlined word or phrase in each sentence that is not correct.*

1. There's just too much (A) traffic on the road today; the amount (B) of people driving is incredible, and I've never seen this many (C) cars in one (D) place. **A B C D**
2. I have less (A) money and fewer (B) friends, but a little (C) stress and no (D) complaints. **A B C D**
3. Many of (A) my co-workers (B) work hard, but a few (C) don't do nothing (D). **A B C D**
4. A great deal of (A) the people who work (B) in our office have a lot of (C) experience but less (D) training than I would expect. **A B C D**

UNIT 9
Modification of Nouns
EXPECTATIONS

STEP 1 GRAMMAR IN CONTEXT

Before You Read

PAIRS: Discuss the questions.

1. What is the difference between hoping for something to happen and expecting it to happen? Discuss this with your classmates.
2. In your experience, does what you expect to happen usually happen? Give an example.
3. How can expectations be a negative force? How can they be a positive force?

Read

Read the article about expectations.

POCKET DIGEST

THE EXPECTATION SYNDROME

I Hope for It, but I Don't Expect It

by Jessica Taylor

Picture the scene: It's the **29th Summer** Olympics in Beijing, China. The **Women's** Marathon is about at the **halfway** point when a **Romanian** runner, Constantina Dita, suddenly surges to the front of the pack. Most viewers probably expect her to hold the lead for a **short** time before relinquishing it to the favorites, who include **Kenyan** runner Catherine Ndereba and **Chinese** runner Zhou Chunxiu. Few if any expect Dita to win the **gold** medal—but win she does. As she enters the stadium, Dita begins to slow a bit, but the **roaring** crowd reenergizes her and enables her to win the race with a time of two hours, 26 minutes, a **22-second** lead over the **silver** medalist. The **38-year-old** Dita, who managed only a **20th-place** finish in the **2004 Athens** Olympics, becomes the **oldest women's marathon** champion.

Now picture another situation: Your **film-buff** friends have seen the **Academy Award-winning** *Avatar*. They rave about its **superb color** photography, its **fantastic computer-generated** scenes of **strange-looking, otherworldly** creatures, and its **awesome special 3-D** effects. They praise its **serious** but **heartwarming** treatment of the **age-old** conflict between exploiters and those they exploit. They say it's the **best English-language** movie in **recent** years. When you see it, though, you're disappointed. You don't find it as excellent as everyone has been saying. In fact, you feel it's a **predictable**, rather **tedious** movie—basically just another **special-effects fantasy** film.

The Expectation Syndrome

These situations illustrate what we might call "the **expectation** syndrome," a condition in which events do not turn out as we feel they will or should. Sometimes children do not meet their **parents' career** expectations of them; athletes do not win the contests people expect them to win; **great** literature doesn't live up to its reputation. I asked psychiatrist Robert Stevens whether expectations can actually make things turn out negatively, or whether we're merely talking about an **unpleasant**, **frustrating** irony of the **human** condition.

RS: Well, the mind has **immense** power to control outcomes. For example, there's a **medical** condition called "**focal** dystonia"—an **abnormal muscle** function caused by **extreme** concentration. Somehow, when athletes are concentrating too hard, **certain brain** functions are affected. They miss the basket, don't hit the ball, or lose the race. In effect, they're letting their expectations control them.

JT: Have you ever experienced this phenomenon in your **everyday** life?

RS: Yes. Here's a **personal** example from skiing that shows that the mind has **tremendous** power to control things. There are days when, as a **cautious intermediate** skier, I stand at the top of a **steep**, **icy** slope, plotting my **every** move down the course, fearing I'll fall. Sure enough, I do fall. Other days I feel different. My expectations are miles away. I forget about myself, ski well, and don't fall. When we focus excessively on goals, our expectations can take over and place us outside the process. On the other hand, when we concentrate on the process instead of the goal, we're usually more successful. Have you heard the phrase "trying too hard"? That's what people often do.

JT: Very interesting. What's your recommendation about expectations, then?

RS: Just that it's better to hope for things than to expect them.

After You Read

A | Vocabulary: *Match the* **blue** *words and phrases on the left with their meanings on the right.*

_____	**1.** We see the Romanian runner suddenly **surge** to the front of the pack.	**a.** boring, and continuing for a long time
_____	**2.** Most viewers probably think she will soon **relinquish** the lead in the race.	**b.** extraterrestrial
_____	**3.** Dita is the oldest women's **marathon** champion.	**c.** condition opposite to what is expected
_____	**4.** Your film-**buff** friends have seen *Avatar.*	**d.** set of physical or mental conditions that show you have a problem
_____	**5.** The film has many scenes of **otherworldly** creatures.	**e.** person interested in and knowledgeable about something
_____	**6.** The film is about people who **exploit** others.	**f.** move forward powerfully
_____	**7.** These situations illustrate "the expectation **syndrome**."	**g.** equal
_____	**8.** Great literature doesn't always **live up to** its reputation.	**h.** give up
_____	**9.** Are we talking about a frustrating **irony** of the human condition?	**i.** take unfair advantage of someone
_____	**10.** It's a predictable, rather **tedious** movie.	**j.** footrace of 26 miles, 385 yards (42.2 kilometers)

B | Comprehension: *Circle* **T (True)** *or* **F (False).** *Correct the false statements.*

1. Constantina Dita takes the lead about three-fourths of the way through the marathon. **T F**
2. Dita is the favorite to win the marathon. **T F**
3. Most spectators expect Dita to win the gold medal. **T F**
4. Dita is energized when she enters the stadium to complete the race. **T F**
5. Dita won a medal in the 2004 Athens Olympics. **T F**
6. To date, Dita is the oldest woman to win the marathon. **T F**
7. Among other things, *Avatar* is about people who take advantage of others unfairly. **T F**
8. The expectation syndrome occurs when events do not turn out as we want. **T F**
9. The human mind often controls outcomes of situations. **T F**
10. Expectations take over when we don't focus enough on goals. **T F**

STEP 2 GRAMMAR PRESENTATION

MODIFICATION OF NOUNS

	Adjective Modifier	Noun Modifier	Head Noun
I remember the		**Summer**	Olympics.
	wonderful		athletes.
	amazing	**volleyball**	games.
	unexpected	**Romanian**	victory.

Order of Adjective Modifiers								
	Opinion	**Size**	**Age**	**Shape**	**Color**	**Origin**	**Material**	
I saw a	**great**		**new**			**French**		movie.
I met its	**fascinating**		**young**			**Chinese**		director.
She had		**large**		**round**			**jade**	earrings.
She wore a		**long**			**red**		**silk**	dress.

Several Adjective Modifiers	
Different Modifier Categories	**Same Modifier Category**
A **great new epic** movie	A **serious, profound,** and **heartwarming** movie A **serious, profound, heartwarming** movie A **heartwarming, profound, serious** movie

Compound Modifiers		
The movie has lots of	**computer-generated** **strange-looking**	scenes. creatures.
The main character is a	**10-year-old** **long-haired, short-legged**	girl. boy.

GRAMMAR NOTES

1	Nouns can be modified both by adjectives and by other nouns. **Adjective** and **noun modifiers** usually come before the noun they modify. The noun that is modified is called the head noun.	ADJECTIVE MODIFIERS NOUN MODIFIER • Yao Ming is a **famous Chinese basketball** HEAD NOUN **player**.
2	**Noun modifiers** usually come directly before the nouns they modify. When there are both adjective and noun modifiers, the noun modifier comes closer to the head noun.	• **Milk chocolate** is chocolate made with milk. • **Chocolate milk** is milk with chocolate in it. ADJ. MOD. NOUN MOD. HEAD NOUN • Pelé is a **famous soccer player**.

(continued on next page)

3	Two common types of **adjective modifiers** are present participles and past participles (also called **participial adjectives**).	• It was a **boring** movie. • The **bored** viewers left.
	Remember that participial adjectives that end in ***-ing*** describe someone or something that causes a feeling.	• The result of the game was **shocking**. • The news is **exciting**.
	Participial adjectives that end in ***-ed*** describe someone who experiences a feeling.	• We were **shocked** by the result. • Everyone is **excited** by the news.
4	When there is **more than one modifier** of a noun, the modifiers generally occur in a **fixed order**. The following list shows the usual order of common adjective and noun modifiers. The order can be changed by the emphasis a speaker wants to give to a particular adjective. **NOTE:** Avoid using more than three adjective modifiers before a noun.	

Position	Category of Modifier	
1	Opinions	• ugly, beautiful, dull, interesting
2	Size	• big, tall, long, short
3	Age or temperature	• old, young, hot, cold
4	Shapes	• square, round, oval, diamond
5	Colors	• red, blue, pink, purple
6	Origins, nationalities, or social classes	• computer-generated, Brazilian, Chinese, middle-class
7	Materials	• wood, cotton, denim, silk, glass

5	When a noun has **two or more modifiers** in the **same category**, separate the adjectives with a comma. If the modifiers are in different categories, do not separate the adjectives with a comma.	• He is a **serious, hardworking** student. • I bought a **beautiful denim** shirt.
	NOTE: The order of adjectives in the same category can vary.	• He is a **serious, hardworking** student. • He is a **hardworking, serious** student.

6	**Compound modifiers** are constructed from more than one word. Here are four common kinds:	
	a. number + noun	• I work in a **10-story** building.
	b. noun + present participle	• It's a **prize-winning** film.
	c. noun + past participle	• It's a **crime-related** problem.
	d. adjective + past participle	• The actor plays a **long-haired, one-armed** pirate in the movie.
	When compound modifiers precede a noun, they are generally hyphenated.	
	BE CAREFUL! Plural nouns used as modifiers become singular when they come before the noun.	• Her daughter is 10 years old. • She has a **10-year-old** daughter. NOT: She has a ~~10-years-old~~ daughter.
7	**BE CAREFUL!** In written English, avoid having more than two noun modifiers together. Using too many noun modifiers in sequence can be confusing. Look at the example: Is Jerry a student who won an award for painting portraits? Is Jerry a painter who won an award for painting students? Is the award given by the students?	• Jerry Gonzales won the **student portrait painter** award.
	To avoid confusing sentences like this, break up the string of noun modifiers with prepositional phrases or rearrange the modifiers in some other way.	• Jerry Gonzales won the award for painting portraits of students. OR • Student Jerry Gonzales won the award for painting portraits.

STEP 3 FOCUSED PRACTICE

EXERCISE 1: Discover the Grammar

Read the sentences based on the opening article. Circle all head nouns that have noun or adjective modifiers before them. Underline adjective modifiers once and noun modifiers twice.

1. It's the 29th Summer (Olympics).
2. The Women's Marathon is about at the halfway point when a Romanian runner surges to the head of the pack.
3. Dita finishes the race with a 22-second lead over the silver medalist.
4. The 38-year-old Dita managed only a 20th-place finish in the 2004 Athens Olympics.

(continued on next page)

5. Your film-buff friends have seen the Academy Award–winning *Avatar.*

6. They love its strange-looking creatures and awesome special effects.

7. They admire its serious but heartwarming treatment of the age-old conflict between exploiters and those they exploit.

8. Children sometimes do not meet their parents' career expectations of them.

9. "Focal dystonia" is an abnormal muscle function caused by extreme concentration.

10. I stand at the top of a steep, icy slope, plotting my every move down the course.

EXERCISE 2: Multiple Modifiers

(Grammar Notes 4–5)

Bill and Nancy are dressing for a party being thrown by Nancy's new boss. Nancy isn't sure what is expected and is very worried about making a good impression. Unscramble the modifiers in their conversation. Place commas where they are needed.

Bill: This is a ___formal office___ **1. (office / formal)** party, isn't it? What if I wear my ____________ **2. (silk / new)** tie?

Nancy: That's fine, but don't wear that ____________ **3. (purple / denim / ugly)** shirt with it. People will think you don't have any ____________ **4. (suitable / dress-up)** clothes.

Bill: So what? Why should I pretend I like to dress up when I don't?

Nancy: Because there are going to be a lot of ____________ **5. (interesting / important)** businesspeople there, and I want to make a ____________ **6. (memorable / good)** impression. It's my job, remember? I don't want people to think I have a(n) ____________ **7. (unstylish / sloppy)** dresser for a husband, which of course you're not. Humor me just this once, OK, sweetie?

Hmm . . . I wonder if I should wear my ____________ **8. (round / sapphire / blue)** earrings or the ____________ **9. (green / oval / emerald)** ones.

(Later, at the party.)

Nancy: Hi, Paul. This is Bill, my husband.

Paul: Welcome. Bill, I'm glad to meet you. You two are our first guests to arrive. Help yourselves to snacks. There are some ____________ **10. (tomato-and-cheese / excellent)** sandwiches. You know, Nancy, I'm sorry I didn't make it clear this isn't a ____________ **11. (dress-up / fancy)** party. You two look great, but I hope you won't feel out of place.

Bill: Thanks. We'll be fine. By the way, Paul, I really like that ____________ **12. (beautiful / denim / purple)** shirt you're wearing. Where did you get it?

EXERCISE 3: Compound Modifiers

(Grammar Note 6)

Complete the sentences with compound modifiers. Add the indefinite article **a** / **an** *in all but Item 8.*

Pam and Allen Murray took their son Joshua to a reading specialist because Joshua could not read aloud in class. Dr. Tanaka, the specialist, asked Joshua a number of questions about his problems with reading. Joshua said that he got frustrated in his reading class, that even though it was only ______a 50-minute______ (**1. (lasting 50 minutes)**) period, it seemed to him like a year. During this particular semester, the teacher was giving the students oral reading assignments every day. At first the teacher had called on Joshua to read aloud, and Joshua would panic every time, even if it was only ____________________ (**2. (one paragraph in length)**) assignment. Now she was no longer calling on him.

Dr. Tanaka asked Joshua if he had any problems with silent reading. Joshua said he didn't, adding that he loved to read to himself and could finish ____________________ (**3. (300 pages in length)**) book in a day or two. Pam, Joshua's mother, noted that his reading comprehension was excellent.

Dr. Tanaka asked Pam and Allen how long this problem had been going on. Allen said it had begun when Joshua was in the first grade. Since Joshua was now 12, the situation had been ____________________ (**4. (lasting six years)**) ordeal. Dr. Tanaka wondered how the problem had started. Pam replied that she felt it was definitely ____________________ (**5. (related to stress)**) problem, for Joshua had lisped when he started school. Joshua added that he had felt bad when the other children would laugh at him when he pronounced his "s" sounds as "th" sounds. The problem simply got worse until Joshua was no longer able to read orally at all.

Dr. Tanaka agreed that teasing might have caused Joshua's problem but suggested another possibility—that Joshua's inability to read aloud could be ____________________ (**6. (related to eyesight)**) problem. He asked if it would be all right to test Joshua's vision. When the Murrays agreed, Dr. Tanaka asked Joshua to read two eye charts, which he was able to read perfectly. He then asked Joshua to read a short passage that he held at a distance. The passage went like this: "Night was falling in Dodge City. The gunfighter walked down the street wearing ____________________ (**7. (holding 10 gallons)**) hat."

Joshua read the passage with no difficulty at all, and Dr. Tanaka said he felt he now understood Joshua's problem well: He had ____________________ (**8. (induced by performance)**) anxiety.

(continued on next page)

He told the Murrays he had distracted Joshua by referring to his vision. He then said he had

______________________ program that would have Joshua reading aloud proficiently
9. (lasting two months)

if he was willing to try it. Joshua was more than willing, so the Murrays made arrangements to start

the program soon.

EXERCISE 4: Creative Sentences

(Grammar Notes 2–4, 6)

Write a sentence for each phrase, changing the phrase so that the modifier appears before the head noun. Use correct punctuation.

1. a flight that takes 10 hours

   Last month I was on a 10-hour flight from Bogotá to Buenos Aires.

2. a cat that has long hair

   ____

3. a jacket that is old and comfortable

   ____

4. an experience that amuses and interests you

   ____

5. a child who is 11 years old

   ____

6. a movie that wins an award

   ____

7. a table that has three legs

   ____

8. people who look unusual

   ____

9. a skirt that is made of cotton, is short, and is blue

   ____

10. a bowl originating in China and made of jade

____

11. a building that has 60 stories

____

12. a bag that weighs 90 pounds

____

EXERCISE 5: Editing

Read the entry from medical student Jennifer Yu's computer journal. There are eight mistakes in the use of modifiers. The first mistake is already corrected. Find and correct seven more.

medical school

FRIDAY: It's midnight, the end of a long day. My first week of ~~school medical~~ is over, and I'm exhausted but happy! I'm so glad I decided to go to the university. It was definitely a good decision. I'm not completely sure yet, but I think I want to go into psychiatry child because I love working with children—especially nine- and ten-years-old kids.

Yesterday our psychiatry class visited a large new hospital where many middle-class troubled children go for treatment. I expected to see a lot of boys and girls behaving badly, but most of them were pretty quiet and relaxed. They just looked like they needed some warm, personal attention.

Today in our surgery class we had a bright, hardworking teacher, a Brazilian young doctor who was substituting for our usual professor. We got a helpful foreign viewpoint on things.

The only thing I don't like about medical school is the cafeteria disgusting food. I'm going to have to start getting some hot tasty Chinese food from my local favorite place.

Well, it's time for me to get some sleep. I hope this computer new program works correctly.

STEP 4 COMMUNICATION PRACTICE

EXERCISE 6: Listening

A | *Joshua Murray is working on his reading program with Dr. Tanaka. Read the statements. Then listen to their conversation. Check (✓)* **True** *or* **False.**

	True	False
1. The first session will last only 30 minutes.	☑	☐
2. Joshua likes his own voice.	☐	☐
3. A rapid growth period occurs during adolescence.	☐	☐
4. Joshua is 13 years old.	☐	☐
5. Joshua is afraid of reading aloud.	☐	☐
6. The phrase that Joshua will say to distract himself will not be difficult to remember.	☐	☐
7. The people in the story have three dogs.	☐	☐
8. Large, warm, and furry dogs can keep you warm on a cold night.	☐	☐

B | *Complete selected sentences from the conversation. Include indefinite articles that you hear before the modifiers. Place commas between adjectives when the speaker pauses, and be sure to hyphenate compound modifiers.*

1. Our first meeting is only going to be ___a 30-minute session___.

2. I feel like ______________________.

3. And I feel like I have ______________________.

4. You're just going through ______________________.

5. Now, the key to getting you over this ______________________ is to distract you from thinking about how well you're doing.

6. Let's think of ______________________ that you can keep in the back of your mind.

7. "It was ______________________."

8. "It promised to be one of those ______________________."

9. It's a night that's so cold that you need ______________________ to sleep with to keep you warm.

EXERCISE 7: Pronunciation

A | *Read and listen to the Pronunciation Note.*

Pronunciation Note

When the modifiers of a noun are in the same category, we normally pause between them. In writing, we place a comma between the modifiers.

EXAMPLES: It was an **icy, dark, stormy** evening.
(All three modifiers are in the same category, so speakers pause between them.)

I'm going to wear my **round blue sapphire** earrings.
(The three modifiers are in different categories, so speakers do not pause between them.)

Note: If you can logically insert the word ***and*** between modifiers, the modifiers are in the same category and will be separated by commas in writing.

It was an icy **and** dark **and** stormy evening.

B | *Listen to the sentences. Place commas between modifiers in the same category.*

1. The film is a serious profound heartwarming treatment of an important issue.
2. We have some delicious cheese-and-pepperoni sandwiches.
3. That ugly grotesque decrepit building should be torn down.
4. The trip we took was an expensive silly miserable waste of time.
5. She's going to wear her new red silk dress.
6. We bought a beautiful new hybrid car.
7. My intelligent gracious 25-year-old daughter just got married.
8. Our little old fox terrier is a delight to have in the family.

C | *PAIRS: Practice the sentences. Take turns, making sure to pause between modifiers in the same category.*

EXERCISE 8: Story Discussion

A | *Read a famous Arabic story.*

Death Speaks

Long ago, a wealthy nobleman lived in Baghdad. One day, he sent a servant to the marketplace to buy food. Before long, the servant returned, terribly frightened. "Master," he said, "when I was in the marketplace just now I had a terrifying experience. I was about to pay for things when a woman bumped me, and I turned to see that it was Death. She waved her hands and put a spell on me. Master, may I please borrow your horse? It is not my time to die, so I will ride to Samarra to avoid my fate. Please let me have the horse; I must ride quickly." The nobleman gave the servant his horse, and the servant rode away as fast as he could.

Curious, the nobleman went to the marketplace and soon encountered me in the crowd. "Why did you wave your arms at my servant and cast a spell on him?" he asked me.

"I did not cast a spell on him," I answered. "When I saw him I waved my hands because I couldn't believe my eyes. You see, I was very surprised to see him in Baghdad since I am to meet him tonight in Samarra."

B | *PAIRS: Circle the letter of the correct answer. Then discuss your answers.*

1. In the story, Death is _____.

(**a.**) a personification — **b.** a normal human character

2. In the story, Death is _____.

a. male — **b.** female

3. In the last two paragraphs of the story, "I" and "me" refer to _____.

a. the merchant — **b.** Death

4. The servant expects to _____.

a. escape from Death — **b.** be captured by Death

5. The story suggests that _____.

a. it's possible to escape fate — **b.** it's not possible to escape fate

C | *Report your answers to the class. The class decides what the story shows about expectations.*

EXERCISE 9: Picture Discussion

A | *GROUPS: Look at the picture of the sinking of the* Titanic *in April 1912. Describe what you see, using as many modifiers as possible. Share your sentences with other groups.*

EXAMPLE: The ship was sinking into the dark, icy ocean waters.

B | *Discuss what the picture suggests about expectations with the other groups.*

EXAMPLE: The builders of the *Titanic* didn't expect it to sink.

EXERCISE 10: Writing

A | *Write three or four paragraphs about a situation that did not turn out as you expected it would. Did the situation have anything to do with the expectation syndrome? Pay special attention to the modification of nouns.*

Example: A year ago our school basketball team was having a great year. In the regular season, we had a 19-1 record: 19 wins and one loss, and that one loss was in our first game. It seemed like we couldn't lose. When we got to the playoffs, however, things didn't turn out as we expected they would. In our first playoff game . . .

B | *Check your work. Use the Editing Checklist.*

Editing Checklist

Did you use . . . ?

☐ adjectives correctly
☐ noun modifiers correctly
☐ modifiers in the correct order

UNIT 9 Review

Check your answers on page UR-2.
Do you need to review anything?

A | *Put the modifiers in the correct order.*

1. a (humid / summer / sweltering) ______________________ day
2. a (late / chilly / winter) ______________________ day
3. my (silk / pink / new) ______________________ tie
4. the (European / young / handsome) ______________________ actor
5. our (brick / new / beautiful) ______________________ house
6. the (little / dirty / old) ______________________ cabin

B | *Rewrite the phrases so that the modifiers come before the noun.*

1. a son who is eleven years old ______________________
2. a novel that has 900 pages ______________________
3. a bandit who had short hair ______________________
4. six periods of 55 minutes each ______________________
5. a proposal initiated by voters ______________________
6. people who look strange ______________________
7. a statue from China made of ivory ______________________
8. a cat that is gray and has short hair ______________________

C | *Circle the letter of the one underlined word or phrase in each sentence that is not correct.*

1. The two first films (A) in the film festival (B) were the most popular ones (C) in the current series (D). **A B C D**
2. A new skier (A) has a hard time (B) with steep dangerous slopes (C) on cold days (D). **A B C D**
3. My film-buff friends (A) praised the Academy Award-winning (B) *Avatar* for its awesome special effects (C) and strange looking creatures (D). **A B C D**
4. There's a medical condition (A) called "focal dystonia," (B) an abnormal, muscle function (C) caused by extreme concentration (D). **A B C D**
5. One of (A) my best bargains (B) was a silk blue shirt (C) from a street market (D). **A B C D**

From Grammar to Writing

AGREEMENT

A key aspect of clear and effective writing is **agreement** of verbs with their subjects and pronouns with their antecedents. Singular and plural nouns must combine with singular and plural verbs, respectively. Singular and plural pronouns must similarly link with singular and plural antecedents, and they must also agree in gender.

Examples of Subject-Verb Agreement:

Koalas live in Australia.
(The plural noun *koalas* must have a plural verb *live*.)

The **list** of students **was** posted on the bulletin board.
(The list was posted, not the students; *list* must have the singular verb *was*.)

There **are** 20 **students** in my English class.
(The plural subject *students* must have a plural verb *are*.)

Examples of Pronoun-Antecedent Agreement:

All the **students** brought **their** books to class on the first day.
(*Their* agrees in number with *students*.)

Jack ate **his** lunch quickly.
(*His* agrees in number and gender with *Jack*.)

Martha stopped by to see **her** mother after class.
(*Her* agrees in number and gender with *Martha*.)

Be Careful! In formal English, the pronouns *everyone / everybody, anyone / anybody, no one / nobody, someone / somebody* are considered grammatically singular. In conversation, however, they are often used in a plural sense.

Examples: **Everyone** brought **his / her / his or her** own lunch. (formal)
Everyone brought **their** own lunch. (conversational, informal)

In most writing it is best to use the forms *his, her,* or *his or her* with these pronouns.

1 | *In sentences 1–5, underline the subject and circle the correct verb to go with it.*

1. A list of available jobs was / were posted on the bulletin board.
2. One of my best friends has / have nine credit cards.
3. Mathematics is / are often considered a difficult subject.
4. Bipolar disorder and schizophrenia is / are two serious mental disorders.
5. The director and star of the film was / were Ben Affleck.

In sentences 6–10, circle the correct pronoun and underline its antecedent. Draw a line between the two. Use formal English.

6. All the students brought his / their books to class on the first day.

7. Each student must bring his or her / their own lunch to the picnic.

8. Frank drives his / her own car to school.

9. If any students come late, tell him / them where the picnic is.

10. Everybody may leave whenever he or she / they wishes.

2 | *Read the letter to the editor. In the blanks write the correct pronoun or correct form of the verb in parentheses. Use forms correct for formal English.*

Editor, The Times:

Many parts of our once-beautiful city __________ (be) starting to look like mini garbage dumps. You will recall that legislation requiring recycling within the city limits __________ (be) passed last year, and the mayor and other local politicians __________ (encourage) us to recycle, but in my apartment complex there __________ (be) no bins for recycling. The result is that people take no responsibility for __________ own actions, and everyone tosses __________ trash and recyclables—glass, plastic bottles, cans, etc.—right in with the food that is being thrown away. The manager of the complex and the owner of the building __________ (have) not bought any new containers for items that __________ (be) supposed to be recycled. So what else can residents do but mix __________ trash together? The owner __________ (be) responsible for breaking the law here. Not us! Meanwhile, trash cans in the downtown area __________ (be) overflowing with garbage, and vacant lots all around the city __________ (be) littered with soda cans, broken glass, and paper. The owner and publisher of your newspaper, Stanford Black, __________ (have) always been a supporter of a clean environment. I urge your paper to take leadership in solving this problem.

3 | *Before you write . . .*

1. Think about a significant environmental or societal issue that concerns you. State the problem as you see it. Why do you feel as you do?
2. Describe your issue to a partner. Listen to your partner's issue.
3. Ask and answer questions about your concerns. For example: What are the main reasons why you feel as you do? What examples can you give that support your experience? What do you think should be done about the problem?

4 | *Write a draft of a three-paragraph composition about your issue. Follow the model. Remember to include information that your partner asked about.*

The problem and reasons why I feel as I do:

____

____

____

____

Possible reasons people have the opposite point of view:

____

____

____

____

What I think should be done about the issue:

____

____

____

____

5 | *Exchange compositions with a different partner. Complete the chart.*

1. The writer used subjects, verbs, and pronouns correctly. **Yes** ☐ **No** ☐
2. What I liked in the composition:

   ____

   ____

   ____

3. Questions I'd like the writer to answer about the issue:

   Who ____?

   What ____?

   When ____?

   Where ____?

   Why ____?

   How ____?

   (Your own question) ________________________________?

6 | *Work with your partner. Discuss each other's chart from Exercise 5. Then rewrite your own composition and make any necessary changes.*

PART IV

NOUN CLAUSES

UNIT	GRAMMAR FOCUS	THEME
10	Noun Clauses: Subjects, Objects, and Complements	Humor
11	Direct and Indirect Speech	Communication and Misunderstanding

UNIT 10 Noun Clauses: Subjects, Objects, and Complements

HUMOR

STEP 1 GRAMMAR IN CONTEXT

Before You Read

PAIRS: Discuss the questions.

1. What kinds of things make you laugh?
2. What benefits do humor and laughter provide us?

Read

Read the story about brothers competing for their mother's love.

THE THREE BROTHERS

There once was a lady who had three sons. In many ways the relationship between the woman and her boys was exemplary. The sons were good citizens, well-off financially, and admirable persons overall. **What wasn't so admirable** was their rivalry, for a spirit of one-upmanship had always characterized their relationship. Each brother constantly tried to figure out **how he could outdo the other two. What the sons wanted** was a secure place in their mother's affections. They didn't understand **that their mother loved each boy for his own uniqueness. That the boys were intensely competitive** had always bothered the lady, but she didn't know what to do about it.

Time passed, and as the mother aged, she began to lose her sight. Before long, she was almost blind. The boys realized **that their mother's final days were approaching**, and, competitive to the end, each searched for a way to supplant the others. Each promised to buy her **whatever she wanted.** Their mother said **there was nothing she needed**, but the boys didn't believe her.

Moe, son number one, bought his mother a mansion. At first he wondered **whether he could afford it,** but money was no object **where his mother was concerned.** He was sure **that the mansion would be her favorite gift.**

Joe, son number two, felt **that he had to outdo Moe,** so he bought his mother a luxury car complete with a chauffeur on call 24 hours a day. Joe thought **that he would certainly win his mother's approval with this gift.**

Curly, son number three, was in a dilemma, wondering **what he could do to top his brothers.** While

THE THREE BROTHERS

The formula for the area of a circle is πr^2.

downtown one day, he happened to see a beautiful parrot in a pet store window. The store owner told him **that this specially trained parrot had memorized the entire *Encyclopedia Britannica*.** One could ask the parrot **whatever one wanted to know**, and the parrot would answer accurately. Curly was ecstatic and bought the parrot, convinced **this would make him number one in his mother's eyes.**

Soon the mother invited the boys over to her mansion. "Boys," she said, "I want to thank you all for your wonderful gifts. I don't know **if you believed me**, though, when I said **I didn't need anything.** Moe, this is a gorgeous house, but it's much too big for me. I live in only two rooms and don't have the energy or inclination to take care of the place. Please sell it.

"And Joe, that car you bought me is beautiful and luxurious, but I don't drive anymore. Plus, **the fact that the chauffeur doesn't speak English** is a problem. Please sell it."

Then she turned to Curly, saying, "But Curly, yours was the best gift of all. I just can't thank you enough."

Curly was pleased **that he was now number one in his mother's affections.** "That's great, Mom. Have you learned a lot from him?"

Puzzled, his mother said, "I don't know **what you mean**, son. All I know is **that the chicken you gave me was delicious.**"

After You Read

A | Vocabulary: *Circle the letter of the best meaning for the* **blue** *words and phrases from the reading.*

1. The relationship between the woman and her boys was **exemplary**.
   - a. predictable
   - b. admirable
   - c. formal
   - d. troubled
2. A spirit of **one-upmanship** had always characterized their relationship.
   - a. gaining an advantage
   - b. becoming wealthier
   - c. getting angry
   - d. achieving satisfaction
3. Each brother was constantly trying to figure out how he could **outdo** the others.
   - a. anger
   - b. do better than
   - c. tease
   - d. amuse
4. The mother loved each boy for his own **uniqueness**.
   - a. strangeness
   - b. unselfishness
   - c. individual qualities
   - d. energy
5. Each boy searched for a way to **supplant** the others.
   - a. take the place of
   - b. stimulate
   - c. anger
   - d. learn from
6. The car was accompanied by a chauffeur **on call** 24 hours a day.
   - a. in charge
   - b. on duty
   - c. present
   - d. available
7. Curly, son number three, was **in a dilemma**.
   - a. facing others' anger
   - b. facing a difficult choice
   - c. facing danger
   - d. facing financial problems
8. Curly was **ecstatic** and bought the parrot.
   - a. satisfied
   - b. amused
   - c. delighted
   - d. pleased with himself
9. I don't have the energy or **inclination** to take care of the place.
   - a. ability
   - b. desire
   - c. time
   - d. permission

B | Comprehension: *Circle* **T (True)** *or* **F (False)**. *Correct the false statements.*

1. A spirit of cooperation characterized the brothers' relationship. **T F**
2. Each son desired to be first in his mother's affections. **T F**
3. The boys' mother encouraged the spirit of competition between them. **T F**
4. The boys' mother told them she needed a lot of things. **T F**
5. All three brothers bought their mother things to earn her love. **T F**
6. The mother was pleased by the gifts of all three brothers. **T F**
7. The parrot knew a great deal. **T F**
8. The mother was aware of what the parrot could do. **T F**

STEP 2 GRAMMAR PRESENTATION

NOUN CLAUSES: SUBJECTS, OBJECTS, AND COMPLEMENTS

Noun Clauses Beginning with *That*

Subject	Object
That she loves them is obvious.	You can see **(that) she loves them.**
That they give gifts is unfortunate.	She knows **(that) they give gifts.**

Complement	
SUBJECT COMPLEMENT	The problem was **(that) the car was so expensive**.
ADJECTIVE COMPLEMENT	It is important **(that) people develop a sense of humor**.

Noun Clauses with Question Words

Subject	Object
What I should give her is obvious.	I wonder **what I should give her.**
Why he did that wasn't evident.	Can you explain **why he did that**?

Complement	
SUBJECT COMPLEMENT	The mystery is **how he could afford the car**.
ADJECTIVE COMPLEMENT	It's amusing **what she did with the bird**.

Noun Clauses with *Whether* or *If*

Subject	Object	
Whether she'll like it is hard to tell.	I wonder **whether / if she'll like it**.	
Whether it's useful or not matters to me.	I care about	**whether / if it's useful (or not).**
		whether (or not) it's useful.

Complement	
SUBJECT COMPLEMENT	The issue is **whether she needs such costly gifts**.
ADJECTIVE COMPLEMENT	He's uncertain **whether she'll like it**.

GRAMMAR NOTES

1

Noun clauses are dependent clauses that perform the same functions as regular nouns:

a. subjects

- **What I like** is a good joke.
- **What makes me laugh** is slapstick comedy.

b. objects

- I don't understand **why you find that funny**.
- You can see **that I am easily amused**.
- We're impressed by **what she's done**.

c. subject complements

- The question is **whether people will laugh**.

d. adjective complements

- It's clear **that laughter involves an emotion**.

Noun clauses begin with *that*, question words, words formed from *-ever* (*whatever, whoever, whomever, whichever*), or *whether* or *if*.

- We realize **that she was joking**.
- I don't understand **what it means**.
- **Whatever you decide** is fine with me.
- He doesn't know **if / whether it's true or not**.

2

We use the word ***that*** to introduce certain noun clauses. In such cases, *that* is a grammatical word that simply introduces a clause. It has no concrete meaning.

- **That she was a funny person** was apparent.

That can be omitted when it introduces an object noun clause or a complement noun clause, especially in speaking.

- I believe **(that) humor is healthy**.
- I told Sue **(that) she was a funny person**.
- It's odd **(that) you laugh so little**.

When *that* introduces a subject noun clause, it is **never omitted**.

- **That Joe has a good sense of humor** is obvious.
  NOT: ~~Joe has a good sense of humor is obvious.~~

Subject noun clauses beginning with *that* are formal.

BE CAREFUL! Do not confuse *that* and *what*. The word *that* simply introduces a noun clause. The word *what* refers to something definite. It serves as the object in the noun clause. It cannot be omitted.

- I know **(that) she is coming**.

O S V

- I don't know **what she is bringing**.

3

The fact that is sometimes used in place of *that* in subject noun clauses.

- **That you can laugh** is good.
- **The fact that you can laugh** is good.

The fact that **must** be used in place of *that* in noun clauses that are objects of prepositions.

- I'm impressed by **the fact that Bob is here**.
  NOT: I'm impressed ~~by that Bob is here~~.

It often functions as the subject of a sentence, with the noun clause coming at the end. Like the word *that*, *it*, when used with a noun clause, is a grammatical word with no concrete meaning.

- **It**'s funny **(that) you should say that**.

4	A **question** that is **changed to a noun clause** is called an **embedded question**. We use statement word order in embedded questions, not question word order.	• I don't even know **if she's from around here.** • I don't know **who she is.** NOT: I don't know ~~who is she.~~
	USAGE NOTE: An embedded question is more polite than a direct question.	• What time is it? *(direct)* • Do you know **what time it is**? *(more polite)*
	An embedded question can occur within a statement or within another question. An embedded question within a statement is followed by a period. An embedded question within another question is followed by a question mark.	• I'm not sure **what *incongruous* means.** • Do you know **how far it is to the nearest town**?
5	***Wh-* question words** introduce **embedded *wh-* questions.**	• Do you know **when she arrived**? • I'm not sure **how many children she has.**
	The subject of an embedded *wh-* question takes a singular verb.	• I'm not certain **who is going** with us.
	BE CAREFUL! Do not use *do*, *does*, or *did* in embedded questions.	• I have no idea **what she meant.** NOT: I have no idea ~~what did she mean.~~
6	We use ***if*** and ***whether (or not)*** to introduce **embedded *yes / no* questions.**	• Do you know **if she came to work today**? • Who knows **whether she's here**? • I have no idea **whether she came or not.**
	Note that *if* and *whether (or not)* are similar in meaning and can often be used interchangeably.	• We're not sure **if / whether (or not)** Bob is in town.
	BE CAREFUL! Do not use *if* to introduce a subject noun clause.	• **Whether (or not) she understood** is questionable. NOT: ~~If she understood is questionable.~~
	BE CAREFUL! Do not omit *if* or *whether (or not)* in embedded *yes / no* questions.	• It is difficult to say **if / whether (or not)** his plan will work. NOT: It is difficult to say ~~his plan will work.~~
7	***Whether . . . or not*** can replace ***whether*** in all noun clauses.	• We don't know **whether** she got the job. OR • We don't know **whether** she got the job **or not.**
	If . . . or not can replace ***whether*** in all but subject noun clauses.	• No one has told me **whether / if** she received the letter **or not.** • **Whether** she received it isn't known. NOT: ~~If she received it or not isn't known.~~

REFERENCE NOTES

For work on **noun clauses used to report speech**, see Unit 11.
For work on **noun clauses in conditional sentences**, see Unit 22.
For work on **noun clauses using the subjunctive**, see Unit 23.

STEP 3 FOCUSED PRACTICE

EXERCISE 1: Discover the Grammar

A | *Read the sentences. Underline each noun clause and identify it as* **S** *(used as a subject),* **O** *(used as an object), or* **C** *(used as a complement).*

_____ **1.** Moe was sure that the mansion would be her favorite gift.

_____ **2.** What wasn't so admirable was their rivalry.

_____ **3.** All I know is that the chicken you gave me was delicious.

_____ **4.** Their mother said there was nothing she needed.

B | *Look at the sentences. Underline the embedded question in each. For each embedded question, write the direct question it was derived from.*

1. Each brother constantly tried to figure out how he could outdo the other two.

How can I outdo the other two?

2. Curly was wondering what he could do to top his brothers.

____

3. At first he wondered if he could afford it.

____

4. I don't know if you believed me.

____

5. I don't know what you mean.

____

EXERCISE 2: Embedded Questions

(Grammar Notes 4–7)

Based on the exchanges in the chart, complete the story with embedded **yes** / **no** *and* **wh-***questions. Put the verbs in the simple past or the past perfect.*

1. A: Excuse me. How far is the nearest town? **B:** I don't know.
2. A: Well, what's the name of the nearest town? **B:** I'm not sure.
3. A: Can I borrow your cell phone? **B:** What's a cell phone?

4. A: Well, are there any towing companies nearby? **B:** I don't know that either.	
5. A: Do you know the people in that house there? **B:** No, I don't.	
6. A: How long have you lived around here? **B:** That's private information.	
7. A: What's your name? **B:** I'm not going to tell you.	
8. A: Do you know anything at all? **B:** Yes, I do. I'm smarter than you are. At least I know where I am, and you don't.	

My wife and I had an irritating experience a year ago when we were traveling in the Midwest. Our car broke down, and I saw a farmer working in a field. I was sure he could help me, so I went up to him. I asked him ___how far the nearest town was___ (1.). He said he didn't know. Then I asked him ______________________ (2.). He said he wasn't sure. I asked him ______________________ (3.). He asked me what a cell phone was. Then I asked him ______________________ (4.). He said he didn't know that either. I asked him ______________________ (5.) the people in a nearby house. He said he didn't.

I asked him ______________________ (6.) in the area. He said that was private information. Then I asked him ______________________ (7.). He said he wasn't going to tell me. I asked him ______________________ (8.). He said he did and that he was smarter than I was. He said he at least knew where he was, and I didn't.

EXERCISE 3: Embedded Questions

(Grammar Notes 4–5)

A | *Write negative answers to the direct questions. Use an embedded question inside a phrase, such as* **I don't know, I'm not entirely sure, I have no idea, I don't have a clue,** *and so on.*

Example: What happens to our diaphragm when we laugh?
I have no idea what happens to our diaphragm when we laugh.

1. What is a pun?

____

2. What does *hyperbole* mean?

____

3. What is the humor of the unexpected happening?

____

4. How does repetition work in humor?

____

5. What is the humor of the incongruous situation?

____

6. How does sarcasm differ from other humor?

____

7. What are endorphins?

____

B | *PAIRS: Read "A Thumbnail Sketch of Humor." Take turns asking and answering the questions from Part A.*

A Thumbnail Sketch of Humor

Pun

A pun is a kind of humor that depends on similarities in sound or meaning between two words. Example: A woman saw a bear a week before her baby was born. Frightened, she asked the doctor, "Will seeing that *bear* affect my baby?" The doctor said, "Yes. Your baby will have *bare* feet."

Hyperbole

Hyperbole, much used in humor, is exaggeration. Example: A: Why are you so tired? B: I got stuck in a traffic jam on the freeway. They've been working on that stupid freeway since about 1905!

Humor of the unexpected happening

A great deal of humor depends on what is called the humor of the unexpected happening. Example: In a movie, a woman in a restaurant opens her purse, and a bird flies out of it.

Repetition

Many humorous stories are structured on the basis of repetition of an element, most often three times. Example: A man can't find his car in a parking lot and tries to hitchhike. It is pouring rain. The first driver who drives along honks his horn and doesn't stop. The second car that comes by splashes water from a mud puddle all over him. Then another man comes out and unlocks the door of his parked car, next to the first man. Furious, the first man goes up to him, shakes him, and says, "I wouldn't accept a ride from you if you paid me."

Incongruous situation

The humor of the incongruous situation depends on normal things happening in unusual places. Example: No one thinks twice about seeing a dog in someone's yard, but if a dog enters an elevator in a downtown building, people will laugh.

Sarcasm

Sarcasm is a kind of irony. It can be mild and gentle, but it is more often biting and hurtful. Example: A: What do you think of Jones as a political candidate? B: Oh, he's sharp, all right. He's got a mind as good as any in the 12th century.

Physiological aspects of laughter

When we laugh, our diaphragm moves quickly up and down. Endorphins, hormones that are created in the brain when we laugh or exercise, are instrumental in lessening pain and contributing to a sense of well-being.

EXERCISE 4: Noun Clauses

(Grammar Notes 1–3)

PAIRS: Examine the bumper stickers and discuss the meaning of each one. On a separate piece of paper, write one or two sentences explaining the meaning of each, making sure to use a noun clause. Use phrases like those from the box.

the fact that	what this is about	what this means
what the humor depends on	what this is referring to	what's funny about this

EXAMPLE:

Is there life before coffee?

What this is referring to is the fact that many people cannot start the day without coffee. They act like they're dead.

1. HONK if you're illiterate

2. IF YOU DON'T LIKE THE WAY I DRIVE, STAY OFF THE SIDEWALK!

3. MISSING: HUSBAND AND DOG. ATTENTION: $100 Reward for Dog.

4. CHANGE IS INEVITABLE— EXCEPT FOR VENDING MACHINES.

5. I'm in no hurry. I'm on my way to work.

6. Everyone is entitled to my opinion.

7. FORGET ABOUT WORLD PEACE. VISUALIZE USING YOUR TURN SIGNAL.

8. ESCHEW OBFUSCATION.

EXERCISE 5: Editing

Read the following statements about the proper way to tell a joke. There are eight mistakes in the use of noun clauses. The first mistake is already corrected. Find and correct seven more.

Eight Pieces of Advice About Telling a Joke

1. Make sure ~~is~~ the joke you're telling ^is^ funny.
2. The best jokes are broad enough so that everyone can enjoy them. Be certain that no one will be embarrassed by that you tell.
3. Ask yourself is the joke you want to tell vulgar. If it is, don't tell it.
4. Before you begin, be certain you remember what are the key details. Run through them in your mind before you start speaking.
5. Make sure what you have everybody's attention when you're ready to start.

6. Be certain whether you remember what the punch line of the joke is. Nothing is worse than listening to a joke when the teller can't remember the punch line.
7. The fact can you remember a joke doesn't guarantee success. You have to make the experience a performance. Be animated and dramatic.
8. If to laugh at your own jokes is always a question. Many comedians are criticized because they laugh at their own jokes. Don't laugh at what you're saying. Let others do the laughing.

STEP 4 COMMUNICATION PRACTICE

EXERCISE 6: Listening

A | *Listen to the conversation. Where did the incident in Jean's story take place?*

____

B | *Read the questions. Listen to the conversation again. Write answers to the questions, using a noun clause in each case.*

1. What bothers Greg about jokes?

   What bothers Greg about jokes is that they're too programmed.

2. According to Greg, what is the expectation when someone tells a joke?

   ____

3. According to Greg, what does everyone think if you don't laugh?

   ____

4. What is Greg's basic problem about jokes?

   ____

5. What does he feel like in this situation?

   ____

6. What was the problem that some girls were causing?

   ____

7. What did the principal decide?

   ____

8. According to Jean, what did the principal want to show the girls?

   ____

EXERCISE 7: Pronunciation

A | *Read and listen to the Pronunciation Note.*

Pronunciation Note

Remember that in *wh-* questions, your voice goes up near the end of the sentence and then falls at the end. In *yes / no* questions, your voice gradually rises and is still rising at the end of the sentence. In embedded questions, your voice rises at the end whether or not the embedded question is a *wh-* question or a *yes / no* question.

EXAMPLES: Where did he go?

Do you know where he went?

Did he go?

Do you know if he went?

B | *Listen to the questions. Draw downward slanting or upward slanting arrows, depending on whether the voice drops at the end or continues to rise.*

1. Did she come?
2. When did she come?
3. How did they get here?
4. Did they get here?
5. Did he leave?
6. Why did he leave?
7. What does *ecstatic* mean?
8. Does *ecstatic* mean *happy*?

C | *PAIRS: Listen to the embedded questions. Then practice the questions, paying close attention to your intonation. Take turns.*

1. Do you know if she came?
2. Do you know when she came?
3. Do you know how they got here?
4. Do you know if they got here?
5. Do you know if he left?
6. Do you know why he left?
7. Do you know what *ecstatic* means?
8. Do you know if *ecstatic* means *happy*?

EXERCISE 8: Pair Discussion

A | *Read this article about airline humor.*

They *Do* Have a Sense of Humor

by David Field, *USA Today*

Airline crews may not seem like a humorous group as they walk through the airport terminal with that look of determination and dedication on their faces. But behind the serious behavior, they are a funny lot. Here are some classic airline jokes selected from the collective memory of aviation writers.

Flight Attendant Remarks

Before the no-smoking announcement: "This is a nonsmoking flight. If you must smoke, please ring your attendant call bell and one of us will escort you out to the wing."

After the no-smoking announcement: "Any passenger caught smoking in the lavatories will be asked to leave the plane immediately."

First-Time Fliers

Then there was the woman who, when asked if she wanted a window seat, responded, "No, not by the window. I've just had my hair done."

One passenger wanted to know how a plane could get from Chicago to Detroit, cities separated by a time zone, in just 15 minutes.

Although the flight time was 75 minutes, the time zone made their airline's scheduled departure seem like the flight took only 15 minutes. He was finally satisfied with the explanation that it was a *very* fast airplane.

Pilot Humor

When controllers are uncertain what a pilot plans or wants to do, they usually say, "Please state your intentions."

Few pilots are daring enough to respond literally. But one was once overheard: "I intend to retire to a small farm in Georgia and raise peaches."

Pet Stories

Two airline cargo handlers were removing a pet carrier from a plane's cargo hold and discovered the cat inside was dead.

Fearful of the saddened owner's anger, the two went to the nearest cat pound and found an animal of the same breed, size, and color, and proudly delivered it to its destination.

As the animal leaped out of the cage, the owner gasped in shock, turned to the cargo handlers, and exclaimed, "This is not my cat! My cat was dead when I shipped him! He was stuffed!"

Plane Humor

Pilots and maintenance crews usually communicate in writing. A pilot typically writes up an item to be repaired such as a cockpit gauge or switch.

An overnight maintenance crew responds in writing that the work was done or wasn't needed or couldn't be done.

A pilot once left a note complaining, "Dead bugs are on the cockpit windshield." When the pilot came back in the morning, maintenance had replied: "Sorry, live bugs not available."

B | *PAIRS: Tell your partner which jokes you find funny and which ones you don't. If you do find a particular joke humorous, explain what makes you laugh or smile about it. Explain to your partner what makes each joke a joke.*

Example: **A:** What I think is funny is the pilot's answer about retiring to Georgia to raise peaches.
B: Why?

EXERCISE 9: Class Discussion

A | *Prepare to present a joke or amusing story in class. Practice before you present it. Be prepared to explain what you find funny about it.*

B | *Present the joke or amusing story in class.*

C | *CLASS: Discuss whether or not you find the joke or story funny. Explain why or why not.*

EXERCISE 10: Writing

A | *Choose one of the activities for a writing assignment. Use noun clauses where appropriate.*

1. Write three to five paragraphs about a situation that you witnessed or participated in that you found humorous. Describe the situation fully, using a number of supporting details. Explain why the situation was funny for you.
2. If you know an extended joke (like the one in the opening reading of this unit), write it.

Example: One of the funniest situations I've ever been involved in happened in our office last year. It was April Fools' Day, and everyone in the office thought that we needed to play a practical joke on the office manager. She's always playing jokes on us, so we had to get back at her. Here's what we did . . .

B | *Check your work. Use the Editing Checklist.*

Editing Checklist

Did you use . . . ?
- ☐ subject noun clauses correctly
- ☐ object noun clauses correctly
- ☐ complement noun clauses correctly

UNIT 10 Review

Check your answers on page UR-2.
Do you need to review anything?

A | *Circle the correct noun clause to complete each sentence.*

1. I'm not sure what the punch line of the joke was / what was the punch line of the joke.
2. I don't know why does he always tell that joke / why he always tells that joke.
3. I'm not sure what time does the meeting start / what time the meeting starts.
4. I don't remember what *hyperbole* means / what means *hyperbole*.
5. I don't know whether Samira liked the party / Samira liked the party.
6. I have no idea that Mary does for a living / what Mary does for a living.
7. I'm not sure how long she's been a writer / how long has she been a writer.
8. We're not sure if or not / whether or not Danilo will be able to play.

B | *Correct the mistakes in the underlined phrases.*

1. Do you have any idea what did Mary mean? ______________________
2. We're not sure if or not Bob is coming. ______________________
3. However you want to do is fine with me. ______________________
4. Alison loves Kahlil is obvious. ______________________
5. I wonder that we should give Russell. ______________________
6. We're pleased by that Ben helped us. ______________________
7. Alice told Jim what she was delighted. ______________________

C | *Circle the letter of the choice that correctly completes each sentence. Note: Ø means no addition needed.*

1. A person who is telling a joke needs to remember _____ the key details are. **A B C D**
   (A) the fact that **(B)** that **(C)** why **(D)** what
2. I'm impressed by _____ Bill showed up to help. **A B C D**
   (A) that **(B)** the fact that **(C)** what **(D)** Ø
3. Most people don't think _____ airline pilots have a sense of humor. **A B C D**
   (A) Ø **(B)** what **(C)** the fact that **(D)** whether
4. _____ she understood the joke is questionable. **A B C D**
   (A) If **(B)** Whatever **(C)** Whether or not **(D)** Ø

UNIT 11

Direct and Indirect Speech

COMMUNICATION AND MISUNDERSTANDING

STEP 1 GRAMMAR IN CONTEXT

Before You Read

PAIRS: Discuss the questions.

1. In your experience, what are the most difficult kinds of misunderstandings to deal with? Give examples.
2. How can misunderstandings best be avoided?

Read

Read the interview with an expert on communication.

Understanding Misunderstandings

AN: Hello, everyone. I'm Ann Ness. Please welcome today's guest: communication expert Ellen Sands.

ES: Thanks for having me. You know, Ann, I think we're seeing a lot more verbal conflict these days than in the past. There seems to be a lot more rancor and a lot less civility. Today I want to talk about ways to avoid verbal conflict, or at least minimize it.

AN: Sounds good, Ellen. Let's roll.

ES: All right. First: People need to listen actively to each other. People hear things, but often they don't really listen. A couple of weeks ago I was at a restaurant in Los Angeles, sitting near a Japanese couple being served by an American waitress. The service was slow, and the couple seemed distressed. When the waitress brought the check, the man said, **"The bill seems very high. Did you include the service in it? How much is the service?"** The waitress said, **"You have to pay the tax."** The man said, **"The service was very slow. We have never waited so long to be served. We will pay the bill, but we won't pay for service."** Then they left angrily. The waitress just glared at them and didn't say anything. It wasn't a good situation, mainly because the waitress didn't listen actively.

(*continued on next page*)

Understanding Misunderstandings

AN: Let me see if I understand. When the waitress brought the check, the man said **the bill seemed very high**. He asked **how much the service was**. The waitress said **they had to pay the tax**. The man said **the service had been very slow** and **they had never waited so long to be served**. He said **they would pay the bill** but **they wouldn't pay for service**. Now what did the waitress do wrong?

ES: She didn't listen carefully. The man asked **if she had included the service in the bill**. Unfortunately, she never answered his question. That was the key thing he wanted to know.

AN: Did she do anything else wrong?

ES: She didn't address his concern about the slow service. She could have said, **"Yes, I'm really sorry about the service. We're short-handed today."**

AN: Very interesting. Now what's another way to avoid verbal conflict?

ES: One really good strategy is to state things positively instead of negatively. Recently I was sitting in as a consultant at a school board meeting. Right at the start the chair said, **"We're on a very tight schedule. Make your reports brief; no one will be allowed to take more than three minutes. And no one will be allowed to interrupt the person who's speaking. No one will ask any questions."** It wasn't a good meeting. You could have cut the silence with a knife.

AN: How could the chair have done better?

ES: He told them **to make their reports brief**, but he could have asked them **to try to limit their reports to three minutes**. He said **no one would be allowed to interrupt the person who was speaking**. He also said **no one would ask any questions**. He used a self-righteous tone and treated the attendees like schoolchildren. He could have asked them **to save questions until everyone had finished**. The bottom line is this: You don't have to sugarcoat your statements, but people will respond much better if you put a positive spin on things.

AN: All right. Thanks, Ellen. We'll be back shortly, after this commercial break.

After You Read

A | Vocabulary: *Match the blue words and phrases on the left with their meanings on the right.*

____ 1. There seems to be a lot more **rancor** and a lot less civility.

____ 2. There seems to be a lot more rancor and a lot less **civility**.

____ 3. I want to talk about ways to **minimize** verbal conflict.

____ 4. The couple seemed **distressed**.

____ 5. The waitress just **glared** at them and didn't say anything.

____ 6. We're **short-handed** today.

____ 7. How could the **chair** have done better?

____ 8. The **bottom line** is this: put a positive spin on things.

____ 9. You don't have to **sugarcoat** your statements.

____ 10. People will respond much better if you put a positive **spin** on things.

a. person in charge of a meeting

b. key point

c. courteous behavior

d. interpretation

e. bad or bitter feelings

f. looked angrily

g. make something appear to be nice

h. reduce to the smallest possible amount

i. without enough help

j. upset

B | Comprehension: *Refer to the reading and complete each statement with a single word.*

1. Ellen Sands is a(n) ________________ expert.
2. Sands believes there is ________________ rancor in communication today than in the past.
3. She also believes there is ________________ civility today than previously.
4. Sands says that a key aspect of good communication is ________________ listening.
5. In her first example, Sands talks of a couple from ________________.
6. The couple thought the service was too ________________.
7. The waitress never answered the man's question about whether the ________________ was included in the bill.
8. In her second example, Sands talks of the need to state things in a(n) ________________ manner.
9. The chair in her second example treated the attendees like ________________.

STEP 2 GRAMMAR PRESENTATION

DIRECT AND INDIRECT SPEECH

Statements: Direct Speech		
Subject	**Reporting Verb**	**Direct Statement**
He	said,	"The food **is** delicious."
		"The bill **includes** service."
		"The service **was** slow."

Statements: Indirect Speech				
Subject	**Reporting Verb**	**Noun / Pronoun**	**Indirect Statement**	
He	said	Ø*	**(that)**	the food **was** delicious.
	told	Miriam / her		the bill **included** service.
				the service **had been** slow.

*Ø: not used.

Yes / No Questions: Direct Speech		
Subject	**Reporting Verb**	**Direct Question**
The chair	asked,	"**Have you finished** your report?"
		"**Do you think we are going** to have time to finish?"

Yes / No Questions: Indirect Speech				
Subject	**Reporting Verb**	**Noun / Pronoun**	**Indirect Question**	
The chair	asked	(Marta)	**if**	**she had finished** her report.
		(her)	**whether (or not)**	**she thought they were** going to have time to finish.

Wh- Questions: Direct Speech		
Subject	**Reporting Verb**	**Direct Question**
The customer	asked,	"**What time does the manager arrive?**"
		"**Who is the manager?**"

Wh- Questions: Indirect Speech				
Subject	**Reporting Verb**	**Noun / Pronoun**	**Indirect Question**	
The customer	asked	(the waitress)	**what time**	**the manager arrived.**
		(her)	**who**	**the manager was.**

Verb Changes in Indirect Speech

Direct Speech				Indirect Speech			
		Verb				**Verb**	
He said,	"I	**report**	the news."	He said	(that) he	**reported**	the news.
		am reporting				**was reporting**	
		reported				**had reported**	
		have reported					
		had reported					
		will report				**would report**	
		can report				**could report**	
		should report				**should report**	

Other Changes in Indirect Speech

	Direct Speech	Indirect Speech
Pronouns	"Andy, are **you** listening?" Mary asked.	Mary asked Andy if **he** was listening.
Possessives	The boss said, "Sue, bring **your** camera."	The boss told Sue to bring **her** camera.
This	"Can I have **this** film?" Sam asked.	Sam asked if he could have **that** film.
Here	Mrs. Brown asked, "Will you be **here**?"	Mrs. Brown asked if I would be **there**.
Ago	"We came a year **ago**," Jim said.	Jim said (that) they had come a year **previously / before**.
Now	Bob asked, "Are you leaving **now**?"	Bob asked if I was leaving **then**.
Today	"I need to work **today**," Jack said.	Jack said (that) he needed to work **that day**.
Yesterday	The reporter asked, "Did you call **yesterday**?"	The reporter asked if I had called **the previous day / the day before**.
Tomorrow	"Are you arriving **tomorrow**?" Sarah asked.	Sarah asked if we were arriving **the next day**.

GRAMMAR NOTES

1	We can **report speech** in two ways: direct speech and indirect speech. **Direct speech** (also called **quoted speech**) is the exact words (or thoughts) of someone speaking (or thinking). It is enclosed in quotation marks and is often introduced by a reporting verb such as *asked*, *claimed*, *said*, *stated*, *told*, and *wondered*.	• She said, **"I want to talk about ways to avoid verbal conflict."** • The man asked, **"Does the bill include service?"**
	Indirect speech (also called **reported speech**) is someone's report of direct speech. It does not contain the exact words of a speaker and is not enclosed in quotation marks. Indirect speech reports what a speaker said in a **noun clause or phrase** introduced by a reporting verb.	NOUN CLAUSE • She said **(that) she wanted to talk about ways to avoid verbal conflict**. NOUN CLAUSE • The man asked **if the bill included service**.
	If a statement is reported, the noun clause can be introduced by *that*. If a question is reported, the noun clause is introduced by *if*, *whether (or not)*, or a *wh-* question word.	
	BE CAREFUL! Don't use quotation marks in indirect speech.	• John said **(that) he would be there**. NOT: John said ~~"he would be there."~~
2	The verbs ***say*** and ***tell*** are the most common **reporting verbs**. We usually use the simple past form of these verbs in both direct and indirect speech.	• Hal **said**, "Martha, we have to leave." • Hal **told** Martha they had to leave.
	BE CAREFUL! *Say* and *tell* have similar meanings, but they are used differently. We *say something* but *tell someone something*.	• Andy **told Freda** (that) she shouldn't worry. NOT: Andy ~~said~~ Freda that she shouldn't worry.
	USAGE NOTE: When the listener is mentioned, it is preferable to use *tell*.	• The chair **told us** to pay attention. • The chair **said** to pay attention.
	BE CAREFUL! Don't use *tell* when the listener is not mentioned.	• Ms. Sasser **said** (that) she was going to sit in on the meeting. NOT: Ms. Sasser ~~told~~ (that) she was going to sit in on the meeting.

" " Direct speech

3	To **report indirect questions**, we normally use *ask* in its simple past form.	• Mrs. Mason **asked** Mary if she was going to resign.
	BE CAREFUL! Indirect questions end with a period, not a question mark. Do not use *do*, *does*, or *did* in an indirect question.	• Sue asked Helen **if she had talked with her boss.** NOT: Sue asked Helen ~~did she talk~~ with her boss.
	Use ***if*** or ***whether (or not)***, not *that*, to introduce an **indirect *yes / no* question.** *If* and *whether (or not)* are similar in meaning and are often used interchangeably. We often use *whether (or not)* to emphasize alternatives or different possibilities.	• Bob asked, "Do you think she'll take the job?" • Bob asked **if / whether (or not)** I thought she would take the job.
	Use statement word order, not question word order, to report *yes / no* questions.	• I asked if **we would** know the answer soon. NOT: I asked ~~would we~~ know the answer soon.
4	Use **question words** to introduce **indirect *wh-* questions**.	• The man asked, "How much is the service?" • The man asked **how much the service was.** • "Which entrée do you prefer?" the waiter asked. • The waiter asked **which entrée I preferred.**
	Use statement word order to report indirect questions about the predicate.	• My daughter asked, "Why didn't he take our order?" • My daughter asked **why he hadn't taken our order**.
	Use question word order to report indirect questions about the subject.	• "Who is going to do the dishes?" Mom asked. • Mom asked **who was going to do the dishes.**
5	If the reporting verb is in the simple past, the **verb in the noun clause** often changes:	
	• imperative ➔ infinitive	• The teacher said, "**Open** your books." • The teacher told us **to open** our books.
	• simple present ➔ simple past	• Bill said, "I **invest** in the stock market." • Bill said (that) he **invested** in the stock market.
	• present progressive ➔ past progressive	• Mary asked, "John, **are** you **studying** political science?" • Mary asked John if he **was studying** political science.
	• simple past ➔ past perfect	• "Priscilla **prepared** a delicious meal," Mark said. • Mark said (that) Priscilla **had prepared** a delicious meal.
	• present perfect ➔ past perfect	• "Sam, **have** you ever **eaten** at that restaurant?" Jack asked. • Jack asked Sam if he **had** ever **eaten** at that restaurant.

(continued on next page)

6	In spoken English, we sometimes do not change verbs in a noun clause, especially if what we are reporting happened a short time ago.	• Yesterday Amy said, "Jack **didn't come to** work." • Yesterday Amy said Jack **didn't come to work.** OR • Yesterday Amy said Jack **hadn't come** to work.
	Even in formal English, we often do not change verbs to past forms if general truths are reported.	• "**Does it snow** here in the winter?" Kenny asked. • Kenny asked if it **snows** here in the winter. OR • Kenny asked if it **snowed** here in the winter.
	When the reporting verb is in the simple present, present progressive, present perfect, or future, the verb in the noun clause does not change.	• Betty says, "I'**m going to** buy a new car." • Betty says she'**s going to** buy a new car.
7	Certain **modals** often change in indirect speech. *Can, may, must,* and *will* ➔ *could, might, had to,* and *would,* respectively.	• "Sam, **can** you call me at 6:00 P.M.?" Ann asked. • Ann asked Sam if he **could** call her at 6:00 P.M. • "I **won't** be able to," replied Sam. • Sam replied that he **wouldn't** be able to.
	Could, might, ought to, should, and *would* do not change in indirect speech.	• I said, "Helen, I **might** attend the conference." • I told Helen (that) I **might** attend the conference. • "Sarah, you **should** be more careful," Dad said. • Dad told Sarah (that) she **should** be more careful.
8	In addition to verbs, certain **other words** change in indirect speech. To keep the speaker's original meaning, make these changes as well: • pronouns and possessive adjectives ➔ other forms	• Jeremy said, "**My** boss just promoted **me**." • Jeremy said **his** boss had just promoted **him.**
	• *this* ➔ *that* and *these* ➔ *those*	• Don asked, "Have you read **this** book?" • Don asked if I had read **that** book.
	• *here* ➔ *there*	• "Please be **here** for the meeting," Sally asked. • Sally asked me to be **there** for the meeting.
	• *now* ➔ *then*	• Mack said, "Alan's just arriving **now**." • Mack said Alan was just arriving **then.**
	• *ago* ➔ *before* or *previously*	• Julie said, "I got the job three years **ago**." • Julie said (that) she had gotten the job three years **previously / before**.
	• *yesterday* ➔ *the day before / the previous day* *today* ➔ *that day* *tomorrow* ➔ *the next day / the day after*	• "I can see you **tomorrow**," said Kayoko. • Kayoko said (that) she could see me **the next day**.

REFERENCE NOTES

For information and practice on **reporting statements and questions in conditional sentences**, see Unit 22.

For a list of **reporting verbs for reported speech**, see Appendix 23 on page A-10.

STEP 3 FOCUSED PRACTICE

EXERCISE 1: Discover the Grammar

A | *Look at these sentences from the opening reading. Match the sentences on the left with the description of the change to indirect speech on the right.*

h 1. He told them to make their reports brief.
____ 2. He said they wouldn't pay for service.
____ 3. The waitress said they had to pay the tax.
____ 4. He asked how much the service was.
____ 5. He said they had never waited so long to be served.
____ 6. He said the bill seemed very high.
____ 7. He said the service had been very slow.
____ 8. He asked if she had included the service in the bill.

a. present of *be* → past of *be*
b. simple present → simple past
c. present perfect → past perfect
d. simple past → past perfect
e. *will* → *would*
f. *have to* → *had to*
g. past of *be* → past perfect of *be*
h. imperative → infinitive

B | *Read each direct speech sentence. Is the change to indirect speech correct* (**C**) *or incorrect* (**I**)?

C 1. Direct: "We will pay the bill."
Indirect: He said we would pay the bill.

____ 2. Direct: "You have to pay the tax."
Indirect: She said they had to pay the tax.

____ 3. Direct: "We have never waited so long to be served."
Indirect: He said they'd never waited so long to be served.

____ 4. Direct: "Does the bill include service?"
Indirect: He asked does the bill include service.

____ 5. Direct: "How much is the service?"
Indirect: He asked how much was the service.

____ 6. Direct: "We're short of time."
Indirect: He said they had been short of time.

____ 7. Direct: "I'm really sorry about the service."
Indirect: She said she was really sorry about the service.

____ 8. Direct: "Make your reports brief."
Indirect: He said them to make their reports brief.

EXERCISE 2: Direct Speech to Indirect Speech

(Grammar Notes 5–7)

Both direct and indirect speech are used in headlines. Put the headlines into indirect speech.

1. ***SPACESHIP ONE*'S REPEAT TRIP EARNS $10 MILLION**
2. ***Scientist Linda Buck Has Unlocked the Secret of the Sense of Smell***
3. **MT. ST. ANDREA VOLCANO MAY ERUPT AGAIN**
4. *A NEW TAX CUT WILL BE PASSED SOON*
5. ***UNEMPLOYMENT IS INCREASING***
6. **Mercury-Contaminated Fish Is Dangerous to Eat**
7. **A FACE TRANSPLANT PROCEDURE HAS BEEN PERFECTED BY SPANISH SURGEONS**
8. **Three Local Schools Will Close Next Month**

1. *The headline said Spaceship One's repeat trip earned $10 million.*
2. The headline said Scientist Linda Buck had unlocked the Secret of the Sense
3. The headline said MT ST Andrea volcano might erupt again.
4. The headline said a new cut would be passed soon
5. The headline said unemployment was increasing.
6. The headline said Mercury-Contaminated fish was dangerous to eat.
7. The headline said a face transplant procedure had been perfected
8. The headline said three local schools would close next month

EXERCISE 3: Indirect Speech to Direct Speech

(Grammar Notes 3–4)

A substitute teacher came to a class and was asked many questions by the students. Read the teacher's answers to the students' questions. Write the questions in direct speech. Six of the questions will be **wh-** *questions and two will be* **yes / no** *questions.*

1. She told Mary that Leonardo da Vinci had painted the Mona Lisa.

   Mary asked, "Who painted the Mona Lisa?"

2. She told Sammi where the Rosetta Stone had been found.

   ____

3. She told Roberto how long World War II had lasted.

   ____

4. She told Mei-ling that Magellan had been from the country of Portugal.

   ____

5. She told William that a person born outside the United States couldn't become president.

   ____

6. She told Ewa in what century the modern Olympics had begun.

   ____

7. She told Amanda how many countries had joined the European Union.

   ____

8. She told Zelda that population growth was gradually increasing worldwide.

   ____

EXERCISE 4: Multiple Changes to Indirect Speech *(Grammar Notes 3–7)*

Read the conversation. Then complete the account with indirect speech forms. The number in parentheses indicates how many words are needed in each case.

SALLY: Dad, can you help me with my homework?

DAD: Yes, I can. What do you need?

SALLY: I have to write a report for my communications class. It's on a quotation.

DAD: OK. What's the quotation?

SALLY: It's by William Mizner, and it says, "A good listener is not only popular everywhere, but after a while he gets to know something."

DAD: What do you think it means?

SALLY: Well, maybe it's that people will like you if you're a good listener.

DAD: Good. That's part of it. Do you think it means anything else?

SALLY: Well, maybe that you can learn something if you listen.

DAD: Very good! You understand it really well.

My daughter Sally asked me *if I could help her with her* (1. (7)) homework. I told her ______________ (2. (2)) and asked her ______________ (3. (3)). She said ______________ (4. (4)) a report on a quotation for ______________ (5. (1)) communications class. I asked her ______________ (6. (4)). She said ______________ (7. (2)) by William Mizner and went like this: "A good listener is not only popular everywhere, but after a while he gets to know something." I asked her ______________ (8. (5)). She said she thought maybe ______________ (9. (2)) that people ______________ (10. (2)) you if you were a good listener. I told her that ______________ (11. (1)) part of it and asked ______________ (12. (5)) anything else. She said she thought maybe it meant you ______________ (13. (2)) something if you listened. I told her ______________ (14. (2)) it really well.

EXERCISE 5: Editing

Read the letter. It has eight mistakes in the use of direct and indirect speech. The first mistake is already corrected. Find and correct seven more.

November 20

Dear Emily,

I just wanted to fill you in on Tim's school adventures. About two months ago Melanie said she ~~feels~~ *felt* we should switch Tim to the public school. He'd been in a private school for several months, as you know. I asked her why did she think that, and she said, "He's miserable where he is, and the quality of education is poor. He says he doesn't really have any friends." I couldn't help but agree. She said she thought we can move him to the local high school, which has a good academic reputation. I told that I agreed but that we should ask Tim. The next morning we asked Tim if he wanted to stay at the private school. I was surprised at how strong his response was. He said me that he hated the school and didn't want to go there any longer. So we changed him. He's been at the new school for a month now, and he's doing well. Whenever I ask him does he have his homework done, he says, "Dad, I've already finished it." He's made several new friends. Every now and then he asks us why didn't we let him change sooner. He says people are treating him as an individual now. I'm just glad we moved him when we did.

Not much else is new. Oh, yes—I do need to ask are you coming for the holidays. Write soon and let us know. Or call.

Love,

Charles

STEP 4 COMMUNICATION PRACTICE

EXERCISE 6: Listening

A | *Listen to the next part of Ellen Sands's presentation. What are the two methods of minimizing verbal conflict that Sands has already mentioned?*

____

____

B | *Read the questions. Listen again. Then answer each question in a complete sentence.*

1. What is a third method of reducing verbal conflict?

   A third method is speaking about yourself instead of about the other person.

2. Does this method involve returning anger for anger?

   ____

3. Two sisters came to Sands for help with what kind of dispute?

   ____

4. What were they arguing about?

   ____

5. What did Rosa say about Alicia?

   ____

6. What did Alicia say in response to Rosa?

   ____

7. What is the first thing Alicia could have said?

   ____

8. What is the second thing Alicia could have said?

   ____

EXERCISE 7: Pronunciation

A | *Read and listen to the Pronunciation Note.*

Pronunciation Note

In English, consonant blending often occurs when a /**t**/ sound or a /**d**/ sound is followed by a /**y**/ sound. The combination /**t**/ + /**y**/ → /**tʃ**/ , and the combination /**d**/ + /**y**/→ /**dʒ**/. The letters following /**t**/ or /**d**/ that indicate this blending are most commonly ***u*** and ***y*** and sometimes ***i*** and ***e***.

Examples: The couple was from **Portugal**. /**portʃəgəl**/
Did you finish your homework? /**didʒu**/

B | *Listen to and repeat the sentences. Underline the word in which consonant blending occurs. Then write the letter that represents the /**y**/ sound.*

1. It wasn't a good situation. ___u___
2. We're on a very tight schedule. _____
3. The quality of education is poor at that school. _____
4. The chair used a self-righteous tone. _____
5. Unfortunately, she never answered him. _____
6. Tim will graduate in 2014. _____
7. No one will ask any questions. _____
8. The modern Olympics began in the 19th century. _____
9. Spanish surgeons recently perfected a face transplant procedure. _____
10. He says people are treating him as an individual. _____

C | *PAIRS: Practice the sentences. Take turns, making sure that the words with consonant blending are pronounced correctly.*

EXERCISE 8: Group Reporting

GROUPS: Form two large groups, with each group sitting in a circle. Each group appoints a director. The director writes down a sentence about a general truth and whispers it to another student, who then whispers what was heard to the next student. The last student to hear the sentence writes it on the board. The director says whether the sentence is accurate. If it is not, the director locates where the message changed. Make the sentence long enough to be challenging but short enough to be easily remembered.

Example: **A:** Water freezes at 0 degrees Celsius.
B: She said (that) water freezes at 0 degrees Celsius.

EXERCISE 9: Picture Discussion

A | *GROUPS: Discuss what happened to cause the accident. Invent conversations for the police officers, the drivers, and the bystander. Report them in indirect speech.*

EXAMPLE: The woman said that the driver of the other car had been speeding but that she hadn't been.

B | *CLASS: Discuss who is most likely to give the most objective report of what happened and why.*

EXAMPLE: Neither driver is likely to give an objective report. The bystander is likely to give a disinterested report because . . .

EXERCISE 10: Writing

A | *Write a few paragraphs about a recent news story that interested you. The news story should contain examples of direct speech. Then write a summary of the article, changing direct speech forms to indirect speech.*

Example: The headline said, "He gave her his heart, then got a new one." Here's what the story was about:

A few hours before his wedding, Steven Dulka went to a hospital in Detroit, Michigan, to get a new heart. Dulka, who is 51 years old, was scheduled to marry Deidre Jacobsen. Unfortunately, Dulka had a heart inflammation and needed a transplant. About two hours before the wedding was set to start, Dulka got a call from a hospital administrator telling him that a heart had become available. Dulka told the administrator that he was getting married at 2:00 P.M. that day . . .

B | *Check your work. Use the Editing Checklist.*

Editing Checklist

Did you . . . ?

- ☐ use direct speech correctly
- ☐ use indirect speech correctly
- ☐ make verb changes in indirect speech correctly
- ☐ make other changes in indirect speech correctly

UNIT 11 Review

Check your answers on page UR-2.

Do you need to review anything?

A | *Circle the correct word or phrase to complete each sentence.*

1. Min-Ji told Ho-Jin it's / it was time to get up.
2. Mom told Mary she hoped she had finished / have finished her homework.
3. Rob asked Marisol are you / if she was ready to leave.
4. Dad told Tadao to be sure / be sure to feed the pets.
5. Juan told Maria don't / not to forget to turn off the TV.
6. John asked Dad would he / if he would pick him up.
7. Sally said that "she would come by" / she would come by.
8. She assured us she could / can be there by 8:00.

B | *Correct the mistakes in the underlined words or phrases.*

1. Marta asked José would he be late for dinner. __________
2. José said Marta he wouldn't be late. __________
3. Emiko told her father "I don't feel well." __________
4. Emiko's father told her she need to take her medicine. __________
5. Ali asked him had he ever seen snow. __________
6. He said, "I had seen snow many times." __________
7. The teacher told the students don't write in ink. __________
8. The students said, We didn't. __________

C | *Circle the letter of the one incorrect word, expression, or punctuation mark in each sentence.*

1. Ben asked (A) Amanda how long (B) she had (C) lived there? (D) — A B C D
2. Amanda said (A) Bill she (B) had lived (C) there (D) for six months. — A B C D
3. Jim asked (A), "(B)Dad, what does mean (C) *insipid* ?" (D) — A B C D
4. Frank told (A), "(B)Sami, I won't (C) be able to give you a ride today." (D) — A B C D
5. Alice asked (A) her mother (B) could she spend (C) the night at her friend's house. (D) — A B C D

From Grammar to Writing

DIRECT AND INDIRECT SPEECH

A strong piece of writing will sometimes contain a balance between statements in indirect speech and in direct speech. It is important for establishing good control of your writing properly to incorporate direct speech within indirect speech, and vice versa.

Direct speech (also called quoted speech) states the exact words of a speaker. **Indirect speech** (also called reported speech) reports the utterances of a speaker but does not repeat all of the speaker's exact words.

In direct speech, quotation marks enclose the quotation. The reporting verb, such as *said* or *asked*, is followed by a comma if it introduces the quotation. Quotation marks come **after** a final period, question mark, or exclamation point.

EXAMPLES:
Direct: Mary said, "John, we need to talk about our problems."
Indirect: Mary told John they needed to talk about their problems.
Direct: John asked, "Mary, are you mad at me?"
Indirect: John asked Mary if she was mad at him.

If the quotation is divided by the reporting verb, each part of the quotation is enclosed in quotation marks. The part of the quotation after the reporting statement does not begin with a capital letter unless the remainder of the quotation is a new sentence.

EXAMPLES:
Direct: "Asha," Daud said, "what time shall I pick you up?"
Indirect: Daud asked Asha what time he should pick her up.

1 | *Punctuate the sentences in direct speech. Add capital letters if necessary.*

1. Dad, I want to quit school and go to work, Jim murmured.
2. Jim, how would you evaluate your education his father queried
3. I absolutely hate going to school Jim responded (exclamation)
4. Jim, Frank said, you're crazy if you think it's going to be easy to get a job
5. Frank said Jim, don't be a fool (exclamation)
6. Jim's parents asked, Frank, when are you going to start taking your future seriously

2 | *Read the narrative. Punctuate the sentences in direct speech.*

The other night my friend Linh and I had a fun conversation about our recent mishaps. Linh and I are both rather clumsy guys, which can lead us to some hilarious experiences. Linh told me about the time he'd been invited to a Thanksgiving dinner he'd just as soon forget.

So what happened I asked.

Well, Linh said, we were all seated around an enormous table. I guess there were about 12 people there. Several of them were high-society types.

What were you doing with a bunch of high-society people I asked.

Good question, Linh answered. Actually, I was visiting my cousin, and I was her guest.

So what did you do wrong I asked.

I was telling a joke and gesturing energetically with my hands, Linh said. I was sitting just in front of the door to the kitchen. Just as the maid was bringing in the turkey on a big platter, I made a big gesture and knocked the turkey off the platter. It fell on the floor.

Oh, no I said. Then what?

Well, Linh said, the hostess just started laughing. She said she was glad she wasn't the only person who had ever done something like that. Then she told the maid to take the turkey back into the kitchen and wash it off. The maid did and eventually brought it back, as good as new.

How did you feel about the whole thing I asked.

Mortified at first Linh answered. But it all turned out OK because of the hostess. It's great when people make you feel you're not the only person who can make a stupid mistake.

3 | *Before you write . . .*

1. Talk with a partner about a short, humorous incident that happened to each of you.
2. Ask and answer questions about the incidents. Why do you find the situation funny? What about it interests you?

4 | *Write a draft of a one- or two-paragraph composition about your own humorous situation in direct speech, paying particular attention to correct use of commas and quotation marks. Use* **asked, said, told,** *and any other appropriate verbs. Then rewrite your composition in indirect speech. Follow the model. Remember to include information that your partner asked about.*

The events of my humorous situation:

____

____

____

What I find interesting about it:

____

____

____

What I learned from the situation:

____

____

____

5 | *Exchange compositions with a different partner. Complete the chart.*

1. The writer used subjects, verbs, and pronouns correctly. **Yes** ☐ **No** ☐
2. What I liked in the composition:

   ____

   ____

   ____

3. Questions I'd like the writer to answer about the composition:

   Who __________________________________?

   What __________________________________?

   When __________________________________?

   Where __________________________________?

   Why __________________________________?

   How __________________________________?

   (Your own question) __________________________?

6 | *Work with your partner. Discuss each other's chart from Exercise 5. Then rewrite your own composition and make any necessary changes.*

PART V

ADJECTIVE CLAUSES

UNIT 12 Adjective Clauses: Review and Expansion
PERSONALITY TYPES

STEP 1 GRAMMAR IN CONTEXT

Before You Read

PAIRS: Discuss the questions.

1. Complete the sentence with the one adjective that best describes your personality: "I am a person who is ________________."
2. Is it helpful to classify people into personality types or to place yourself in a personality category? Why or why not?

Read

Read the article about personality types.

WHAT TYPE ARE YOU?

Stella

Imagine you're at a party **where you know several people well**. The hosts have a new party game **that involves comparing each person to a flower**. Which flower would you choose for each person and which flower for yourself? Are you the kind of person **who resembles a daisy**, open to the world most of the time? Or are you more like a morning glory, **which opens up only at special moments**?

This may sound like just an amusing activity, but there is a science of personality

WHAT TYPE ARE YOU?

Rick

identification. Many personality tests and categories have been devised in the last century. Take a look at the following descriptions. Try to place yourself and people **you know** into one or more of the categories. You may learn something about your co-workers, friends, loved ones, and yourself. Bear in mind, though, that these are only broad outlines. Most people don't fit perfectly into a single category.

Extrovert or introvert? This category concerns the way **that people are energized**. An extrovert is basically a person **whose energies are activated by being with others**. An introvert is essentially a person **who is energized by being alone**. Stella is a good example of an extrovert. She's the kind of person **whom others consider shy**, but there's no correlation between shyness and either introversion or extroversion. At a party, Stella starts to open up and get energized once she meets people **who make her feel comfortable**. Her friend Rick is the opposite. He isn't shy, but after he's been at a party for a while, he's tired and ready to go home. He finds the conversation interesting enough but is just as likely to be imagining a time **when he is hiking alone in the mountains**.

Type A? Type A's are "drivers," competitive individuals **who have a no-nonsense approach to life**. They're the kind of people **who tell you exactly what they think without mincing words**. They embrace risk and change and often turn out to be entrepreneurs. Nancy, **who started her own greeting card business three years ago**, is the perfect example. However, Nancy is impatient with detail and routine, **which is why she has hired Paul and Mandy to manage her business**.

Type B? Type B's are socializers. They're extroverts, the kind of people **who love the spotlight**. They love to entertain people. They often gravitate toward jobs in sales or marketing or as performers on radio and TV. Nancy's husband Jack, **whom most people consider a charismatic person**, is a good example. He's the host of a two-hour talk radio show.

Type C? Type C's are lovers of detail. They tend to be individuals **who become accountants, programmers, or engineers**. Type C's are sensitive, **which can translate into trouble communicating with others**. Paul, an accountant, is an example. He's the type of person **who loves the details that Nancy hates**.

Type D? Type D people are those **who like routine and tend not to enjoy adventure**. Not surprisingly, they usually resist change. They like to be told what to do. They're often compassionate. Mandy, **who loves her office job**, wouldn't be happy as the boss, but she appreciates working for Nancy.

In the end we're left with this question: What good is classifying people? It certainly doesn't give us any magical powers or tools for relationships. But it can give us insight. It can help us understand others better and perhaps minimize conflict. Best of all, it can help us understand ourselves.

After You Read

A | Vocabulary: *Match the blue words and phrases on the left with their meanings on the right.*

_____ **1.** There's no **correlation** between shyness and either introversion or extroversion.

_____ **2.** They tell you exactly what they think **without mincing words**.

_____ **3.** They **embrace** risk and change and often turn out to be entrepreneurs.

_____ **4.** They embrace risk and change and often turn out to be **entrepreneurs**.

_____ **5.** Type B's love the **spotlight**.

_____ **6.** They often **gravitate toward** jobs in sales or marketing.

_____ **7.** Most people consider Jack a **charismatic** person.

_____ **8.** Learning to classify people can give us **insight**.

a. move or are drawn to

b. center of attention

c. having special charm or personal qualities to attract people

d. deep understanding

e. shared relationship

f. eagerly accept

g. people who own and run a business

h. speaking plainly and honestly of something unpleasant

B | Comprehension: *Circle* **T (True)** *or* **F (False)**. *Correct the false statements.*

1. Most people fit perfectly into a personality category. **T** **F**

2. An extrovert is a person who is energized by others. **T** **F**

3. An introvert is a person who is energized by being alone. **T** **F**

4. There's a correlation between shyness and introversion. **T** **F**

5. A Type A person likes change. **T** **F**

6. A Type B person is an introvert. **T** **F**

7. A Type C person sometimes has trouble communicating with others. **T** **F**

8. A Type D person does not like to be told what to do. **T** **F**

STEP 2 GRAMMAR PRESENTATION

ADJECTIVE CLAUSES: REVIEW AND EXPANSION

Adjective Clauses: Placement

Main Clause		Adjective Clause	
	Noun / Pronoun	**Relative Pronoun**	
They met	a woman	**who**	**teaches psychology.**
I've read	everything	**that**	**discusses her work.**

Main . . .	Adjective Clause		. . . Clause
Noun / Pronoun	**Relative Pronoun**		
The woman	**who**	**teaches psychology**	is also a writer.
Everything	**that**	**discusses her work**	is very positive.

Relative Pronouns as Subjects: *Who, Which, That*

People			Things		
I have a friend	**who**	loves to talk.	This is a book	**which**	is useful.
I have friends	**that**	love to talk.	These are books	**that**	are useful.

Relative Pronouns as Objects: *Who(m), Which, That, Ø**

People			Things		
This is the doctor	**who(m)** **that** **Ø**	we consulted.	This is the test	**which** **that** **Ø**	he gave us.

*Ø = no pronoun

Whose + Noun to Indicate Possession

People	Things
She is the woman **whose son** is so famous.	It's the book **whose reviews** were so good.
She is the woman **whose son** I am tutoring.	It's the book **whose reviews** I have just read.

Where and *When* in Adjective Clauses

Where			*When*		
Place			**Time**		
I remember the café	**where**	we met.	I remember the day	**(when)** **(that)** **Ø**	we parted.

(continued on next page)

Adjective Clauses: Identifying or Nonidentifying

Adjective Clauses That Identify	Adjective Clauses That Do Not Identify
No Commas	**Commas**
The woman **who / that created the test** studied psychology. The test **which / that / Ø she created** describes personality types.	Sara Gomez, **who created the test**, studied psychology. The Gomez test, **which she created**, describes personality types.

GRAMMAR NOTES

1	A sentence with an **adjective clause** can be seen as a combination of two sentences.	*John is a man. + He works hard. =* • John is a man **who works hard**. *Mary is interesting. + I like her a lot. =* • Mary, **whom I like a lot**, is interesting.
2	An adjective clause is a **dependent clause**. It modifies a noun or a pronoun in a main clause.	• Frank, **who is an introvert**, spends a lot of time alone. • Let's do something **that is fun**.
	An adjective clause often begins with a **relative pronoun**: ***who***, ***whom***, ***which***, or ***that***. It can also begin with ***whose***, ***when***, or ***where***. The word that begins an adjective clause usually comes directly after the noun or pronoun that the clause modifies.	• Toronto, **which is the largest city in Canada**, is a beautiful place.
	An adjective clause can occur after a main clause or inside a main clause.	• Harriet is a woman **whom I respect**. • The house **that we bought** is in the suburbs.
3	To refer to people, use ***who*** and ***that*** as the subjects of verbs in adjective clauses.	• The Ings are the **people who** bought the house. • Sam is the **man that** lives next door to me.
	To refer to things, use ***which*** and ***that*** as the subjects of verbs in adjective clauses.	• Math is the **subject which** is the easiest for me.
	USAGE NOTE: *That* is less formal than *who* or *which*.	• This is the **car that** is the nicest.
	The verb in an adjective clause agrees with the noun or pronoun that the clause modifies.	• There are many **people who have taken** this personality test. • This test is the **one that is** the best known.
	BE CAREFUL! Do not use a double subject in an adjective clause.	• Extroverts are people **who like to be with others**. NOT: Extroverts are people who ~~they~~ like to be with others.

4	To refer to people, use ***whom***, ***who***, and ***that*** as the **objects** of verbs in adjective clauses. *Whom* is quite formal. *Who* and *that* are less formal and used in conversation and informal writing. *That* is the least formal.	• **Mr. Pitkin, whom** I mentioned yesterday, is my boss. • Mr. Pitkin was the **person who** I mentioned. • Mr. Pitkin was the **person that** I mentioned.
	To refer to things, use ***which*** and ***that*** as the **objects** of verbs in adjective clauses. *Which* is a bit more formal.	• The **test which** I took was difficult. • The **test that** I took was difficult.
	In conversation and informal writing, you can sometimes omit the relative pronoun if it is an object. This is the most common spoken form. *(See Note 8 for more information on omitting relative pronouns.)*	• Mr. Pitkin is the man **I mentioned**. • The test **I took** was difficult.
	The verb in an adjective clause agrees with the subject of the clause, not with the object.	• The Wangs are the people **that Sally sees frequently**. NOT: The Wangs are the people that Sally ~~see~~ frequently.
5	Use ***whose*** to introduce an adjective clause that indicates **possession**. We use *whose* to replace *his / her / its / their* + noun. An adjective clause with *whose* can modify people or things.	*Ken is the man + We met his wife. =* • Ken is the man **whose wife we met.** *It's a theory. + Its origins go back many years. =* • It's a theory **whose origins go back many years**.
	BE CAREFUL! *Whose* cannot be omitted.	• Harvey, **whose house we're renting**, is a lawyer. NOT: Harvey, ~~house we're renting~~, is a lawyer.
6	You can use ***where*** to introduce an adjective clause that modifies a noun of **place**. *Where* replaces the word *there*.	*This is the restaurant. + We ate there. =* • This is the restaurant **where we ate**.
	BE CAREFUL! Use an adjective clause with ***where*** only if you can restate the location with the word ***there***. Do not use an adjective clause with *where* if the location cannot be stated in this way.	• Chihuahua is the town **where I was born**. = Chihuahua is the town. I was born **there**. NOT: Rio de Janeiro is a city ~~where has beautiful scenery~~. • Rio de Janeiro is a city **that has beautiful scenery**.
	NOTE: *Where* can be replaced by *which* or *that* + a preposition, such as *in*, *at*, or *for*. In this type of adjective clause, *which / that* can be omitted.	• This is the building **where** she works. • This is the building **(that)** she works **in**.

(continued on next page)

7	You can use ***when*** or ***that*** to begin an adjective clause that modifies a noun of **time**. You can omit *when* and *that* in this type of adjective clause. A sentence without *when* or *that* is informal.	• I can't think of a time **when / that I wasn't happy**. • I can't think of a time **I wasn't happy**.
8	An adjective clause that distinguishes one person or thing from another is called **identifying** or essential. The clause is not enclosed in commas.	• The man **who delivers the mail** is friendly.
	An adjective clause that adds extra information but does not distinguish one person or thing from another is called **nonidentifying** or nonessential. The clause is enclosed in commas.	• The man, **who delivers the mail**, is friendly.
	BE CAREFUL! **a.** You can omit relative pronouns only in identifying adjective clauses. You cannot omit the relative pronoun in a nonidentifying adjective clause.	• The man **you met on Friday** is Tarik. • That's Tarik, **whom you met on Friday**. NOT: That's Tarik, ~~you met on Friday~~.
	b. Don't use ***that*** as a relative pronoun in a nonidentifying clause.	• The Gomez test, **which I took a long time ago**, has proved to be accurate. NOT: The Gomez test, ~~that I took a long time ago~~, has proved to be accurate.
	You can use ***which*** informally to refer to an entire previous idea.	• **Helen is hardworking, which** impresses me.
	In formal writing and speech, use a noun at the beginning of a ***that*** or ***which*** clause.	• **Helen is hardworking, a characteristic that / which** impresses me.

STEP 3 FOCUSED PRACTICE

EXERCISE 1: Discover the Grammar

A | *Read these sentences based on the opening reading. Could the relative pronoun be replaced by the relative pronoun in parentheses without creating a different meaning or making an incorrect sentence? Write* **Y (Yes)** *or* **N (No)**.

__Y__ **1.** Are you the kind of person **who** resembles a daisy? (that)

_____ **2.** Or are you more like a morning glory, **which** opens up only at special moments? (that)

_____ **3.** Stella gets energized once she meets people **who** make her feel comfortable. (whom)

_____ **4.** He is likely to be imagining a time **when** he was hiking alone in the mountains. (Ø)

_____ **5.** She's the kind of person **whom** others consider shy. (that)

_____ **6.** Nancy is impatient with detail and routine, **which** is why she has hired Paul and Mandy to manage her business. (that)

_____ **7.** Type B's are the kind of people **who** love the spotlight. (which)

_____ **8.** Mandy, **who** loves her office job, wouldn't be happy as the boss. (that)

B *Read the sentences based on the opening reading. Underline the adjective clause in each sentence. Then identify the clause as identifying* **(I)** *or nonidentifying* **(NI).**

__I__ **1.** Imagine you're at a party where you know several people well.

_____ **2.** Are you the kind of person who resembles a daisy?

_____ **3.** Try to place yourself and people you know into one or more categories.

_____ **4.** Nancy, who started her own greeting card business several years ago, is the perfect example.

_____ **5.** An introvert is a person whose energies are activated by being alone.

_____ **6.** Nancy is impatient with detail and routine, which is why she has hired Paul and Mandy to manage her business.

_____ **7.** Nancy's husband Jack, whom most people consider a charismatic person, is a good example.

_____ **8.** Type C's are sensitive, which can translate into trouble communicating with others.

_____ **9.** Type D people are those who like routine and tend not to enjoy adventure.

EXERCISE 2: Relative Pronouns

(Grammar Notes 3, 5–6, 8)

Circle the correct relative pronoun in each sentence. The sentences are connected together in a story.

1. I come from a family that / whom has eight members.

2. I have three sisters and two brothers, that / which made things pretty crowded when we were growing up.

3. Our house, which / that is four stories high, has eight bedrooms.

4. The members of my family, who / whom are all interesting, fit nicely into the Type A to D categories.

5. My mother and father, who / whom both like to be with people a great deal, are extroverts.

6. My favorite brother, with who / whom I still spend a lot of time, is an introvert.

7. My other brother, who / which is a Type A, is a great guy but always has to be right.

8. My favorite sister, who / whose fiancé is the same age as I am, is a Type A.

9. Of my other two sisters, the one Ø / which I am closer to is a Type C.

10. I'm less close to the sister who / Ø is much older than I am. She's a Type D.

EXERCISE 3: Identifying / Nonidentifying Clauses

(Grammar Notes 3–8)

Combine each pair of sentences into one sentence with an adjective clause, using the relative pronoun in parentheses. Use the first sentence in each pair as the main clause. Add commas where necessary. The sentences are connected as a story.

1. The company makes computers. I work for the company. (that)

   The company that I work for makes computers.

2. The company has existed for 15 years. It is named Excelsior Computer. (which)

   ____

3. The building is located downtown. We do most of our work in the building. (where)

   ____

4. The office has been remodeled. I work in the office. (that)

   ____

5. Darren Corgatelli is the boss. His wife is my aunt. (whose)

   ____

6. Darren is an excellent boss. I've known Darren since I was a child. (whom)

   ____

7. Sarah Corgatelli keeps the company running smoothly. She is Darren's wife. (who)

   ____

8. I joined the company in 1995. I graduated from college then. (when)

   ____

9. I really admire my colleagues. Their advice has been invaluable. (whose)

   ____

10. Part of my job is telemarketing. I like telemarketing the least. (which)

    ____

EXERCISE 4: Formal / Informal

(Grammar Notes 4, 6–8)

Read two reports by an attorney. Complete the spoken report with informal adjective clauses, omitting relative pronouns if possible and using contractions. Complete the written report with formal adjective clauses. Do not omit relative pronouns and do not use contractions. Put all verbs in the correct forms.

Spoken Report

Our client is a guy *who's been in trouble* (1. have / be / in trouble) for minor offenses, but I don't think he's a murderer, ________ (2. be / why) I feel comfortable defending him. He did time in the penitentiary from 2008 to 2010, and according to all the reports he was a person ________ (3. the other prisoners / respected). Since he got out of jail in 2010, he's had a good employment record with Textrix, an electronics company ________ (4. he / have / be working for). The psychological reports on him show that when he was in prison he was a person ________ (5. the psychiatrists / consider) well-balanced and even-tempered, ________ (6. be / the reason) I don't think he's guilty.

Eager, Barnes, and Kirby
Attorneys at Law
555 North Liberty
Boston MA 02110

Formal Written Report

Our client is a man ________ (7. have / be / in trouble) for minor offenses, but I do not believe that he is a murderer, ________ (8. an opinion / make me) comfortable defending him. He served time in the penitentiary from 2008 to 2010, and according to all the reports he was a person ________ (9. the other prisoners / respect). Since he was released from prison in 2010, he has had a good employment record with Textrix, an electronics company ________ (10. he / have / be working for). His psychological profile suggests that when he was in prison he was a person ________ (11. the psychiatrists / consider) well balanced and even-tempered, ________ (12. evidence / make me) believe that he is not guilty.

EXERCISE 5: Editing

Read the letter from a college student to her parents. There are eight mistakes in the use of adjective clauses. The first mistake is already corrected. Find and correct seven more.

September 28

Dear Mom and Dad,

Well, the first week of college has been tough, but it's turned out OK. My advisor, who ~~she~~ is also from Winnipeg, told me about growing up there, so we had something when we could talk about. Since I haven't decided on a major, she had me take one of those tests show you what you're most interested in. She also had me do one of those personality inventories that they tell you what kind of person you are. According to these tests, I'm a person whom is classified as an extrovert. I also found out that I'm most interested in things involve being on the stage and performing in some way, that doesn't surprise me a bit. I always liked being in school plays. Remember? I signed up for two drama courses. Classes start on Wednesday, and I'm getting to know the other people in the dormitory which I live. It's pretty exciting being here.

Not much else right now. I'll call in a week or so.

Love,

Alice

STEP 4 COMMUNICATION PRACTICE

EXERCISE 6: Listening

A | *Listen to a telephone conversation that Al, a new college student, had with his parents. What doesn't Al like about one of his roommates?*

____

B | *Read the pairs of sentences. Then listen again to the conversation. Circle the letter of the sentence that correctly describes what you heard.*

1. **(a.)** Al likes his dormitory.
   b. Al doesn't like his dormitory.

2. **a.** The dormitory has one supervisor.
   b. The dormitory has more than one supervisor.

3. **a.** Both of Al's roommates are from Minnesota.
   b. One of Al's roommates is from Minnesota.

4. **a.** Al has one English class.
   b. Al has more than one English class.

5. **a.** Al has one history class.
   b. Al has more than one history class.

6. **a.** Al's writing class is going to be easy.
   b. Al's math class is going to be easy.

7. **a.** There is one group of girls living in the dormitory.
   b. There is more than one group of girls living in the dormitory.

8. **a.** The girls live on the same side of the building as Al.
   b. The girls live on the other side of the building from Al.

9. **a.** Al has one advisor.
   b. Al has more than one advisor.

EXERCISE 7: Pronunciation

A | *Read and listen to the Pronunciation Note.*

Pronunciation Note

Notice the difference in pronunciation between sentences with identifying adjective clauses and those with nonidentifying adjective clauses. Identifying clauses have no pauses before and after them. Nonidentifying clauses *do* have pauses before and after them.

Examples: The woman **who is wearing a red skirt and a green blouse** is my friend's mother.
(no pauses—the clause is used to identify one particular woman)

The woman, **who is wearing a red skirt and a green blouse**, is my friend's mother.
(pauses—the clause does not identify one particular woman)

B | *Listen to the sentences. Place commas in sentences with nonidentifying clauses. Do not place commas in sentences with identifying clauses. Then circle the phrase that explains the meaning of the sentence.*

1. The man, who lives down the street from me, is a friend of my father.
   (one man) more than one man
2. The man who lives down the street from me is a friend of my father.
   one man more than one man
3. The tie which has a stain on it needs to be dry-cleaned.
   one tie more than one tie
4. The tie which has a stain on it needs to be dry-cleaned.
   one tie more than one tie
5. The teacher who handed out the awards is really a well-known scientist.
   one teacher more than one teacher
6. The teacher who handed out the awards is really a well-known scientist.
   one teacher more than one teacher
7. The student who lives close to the campus has low gasoline bills.
   one student more than one student
8. The student who lives close to the campus has low gasoline bills.
   one student more than one student
9. The garden which Mary planted is the most beautiful one of all.
   one garden more than one garden
10. The garden which Mary planted is the most beautiful one of all.
    one garden more than one garden

C | *PAIRS: Practice the sentences. Take turns. Your partner indicates which sentences you say.*

EXERCISE 8: Pair Discussion

A | *PAIRS: How can you deal with someone you are not getting along with? Describe a conflict situation that you have had. How did you handle it? Were you successful?*

B | *Share your conclusions with the class.*

Example: **A:** How do you deal with a person you don't get along with?
B: Well, when there's a problem with someone that I can't solve, I . . .

EXERCISE 9: Class Activity

A | *The instructor gives each student in the class the name of another student. Each student writes two sentences about his or her student. One sentence must contain an identifying adjective clause; the other must contain a nonidentifying adjective clause. Make the sentences challenging.*

Examples: The student **I am writing about** is sitting in the second row.
Mr. / Ms. X, **who is wearing blue**, works at a store.

B | *CLASS: Read each sentence aloud. The class tries to identify the student being talked about.*

EXERCISE 10: Writing

A | *Consider the personality categories that have been mentioned in this unit and choose the one that fits you best. Write five or more paragraphs explaining your choice. Include several examples from your experience. Use adjective clauses in your composition.*

Example: No single personality type applies perfectly to a person, but for me one comes closer than all the others. The personality category that fits me most closely is Type B. First, Type B's are social people who are basically extroverts. I think this category fits me quite well. Here's why . . .

B | *Check your work. Use the Editing Checklist.*

Editing Checklist

Did you use . . . ?

- ☐ adjective clauses correctly
- ☐ ***who(m), which***, and ***that*** correctly
- ☐ ***whose, where***, and ***when*** correctly

UNIT 12 Review

Check your answers on page UR-2.

Do you need to review anything?

A | *Circle the correct word or phrase to complete each sentence.*

1. The lady who / which is my teacher is the third from the right.
2. Hong Kong is the city that / where I was born.
3. Elena, that / whom you met at the conference, left you a phone message.
4. The man whose / which car we borrowed is my father's boss.
5. Franco Gomez is energetic, that / which is why we should hire him.
6. I can't remember a time where / when he wasn't helpful.
7. Lions are animals that Lea see / sees often at the zoo.
8. Chuy is a person who / who he prefers to be alone.

B | *Correct the mistakes in the underlined phrases.*

1. The man whom lives next door is wearing a coat. ____________________
2. The book, Sara bought, was written by Jorge Amado. ____________________
3. The woman who dog is barking is very wealthy. ____________________
4. The man we met him is in the second row. ____________________
5. Barranquilla is the city which I was born. ____________________
6. I'm thinking of the time which we spoke. ____________________
7. Ms. Voicu who is a student is from Romania. ____________________
8. Sally, who's parents work here, lives alone. ____________________

C | *Circle the letter of the one underlined word or phrase in each sentence that is not correct.*

1. Al, whom (A) is a freshman, likes the people (B) he (C) is rooming with (D). **A B C D**
2. Ari, an extrovert loves (A) working with others but who can (B) also work alone, shone in her last job, which (C) is why she's the one we should hire (D). **A B C D**
3. Jaime, who (A) is with a company that (B) stresses teamwork, is someone who (C) values the people with he works (D). **A B C D**
4. Police in Miami (A) are (B) investigating a crime (C) happened (D) last night. **A B C D**

UNIT 13 Adjective Clauses with Prepositions; Adjective Phrases

MOVIES

STEP 1 GRAMMAR IN CONTEXT

Before You Read

PAIRS: Discuss the questions.

1. Do you like movies? What do you look for in a movie? Do you see movies primarily for entertainment, or do you want a film to be something more?
2. Which kind of movie do you like better—one in which you already know what is going to happen or one in which you don't know what is going to happen?

Read

Read the movie reviews.

At the Movies

FIVE TO REVISIT

by Dartagnan Fletcher

Here we are at the end of another 10 years. I guess it's incumbent on me as a film critic to come up with a compilation of "The Best Movies of the Decade." The trouble is, I've seen a lot of movies since 2000, **many of which are outstanding in their own way**. To narrow down my list I'll start with five pictures **that anyone interested in cinema should revisit—or see for the first time**.

★ First: *Julie and Julia*. Anyone **having even the slightest interest in food** should see this one. Julie, a young woman **caught in a dead-end job**, decides to spice up her life by cooking all 524 recipes in a famous cookbook and writing a blog about it. That didn't sound like a very exciting plot, but I was astonished at how enjoyable and hilarious the movie turned out to be. This film, **starring Meryl Streep and Amy Adams**, is about finding what you really want to do in life.

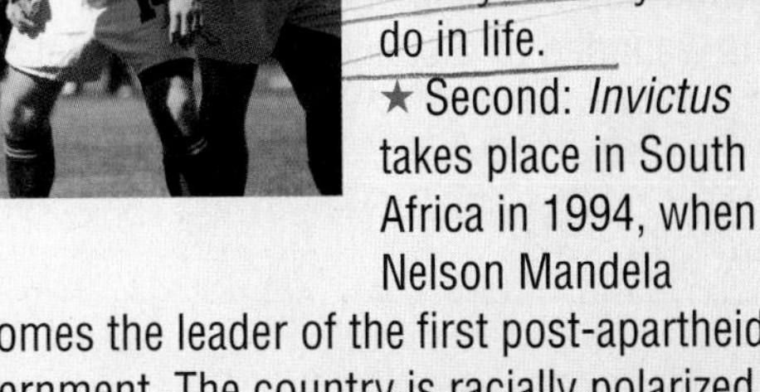

Invictus

★ Second: *Invictus* takes place in South Africa in 1994, when Nelson Mandela becomes the leader of the first post-apartheid government. The country is racially polarized, but Mandela insists that blacks and whites reconcile. Mandela reaches out to François Pienaar, the captain of the mostly-white national

(continued on next page)

FIVE TO REVISIT ▪ At the Movies

rugby team, **with whom he develops an enduring friendship**. **Criticized by some for his efforts**, Mandela persists in his vision of bringing blacks and whites together for the good of the nation. The picture stars Morgan Freeman and Matt Damon as Mandela and Pienaar, **both of whom play their roles to near perfection**. Clint Eastwood, **whose films I'm always impressed with**, directed with great skill.

Avatar

★ Third: Science fiction films, **a compelling example of which is *Avatar***, continue to be popular. The movie, **set on a planetary moon called Pandora**, is a good-guys-versus-bad-guys story **in which the inhabitants of Pandora end up vanquishing a band of exploiters from Earth**. *Avatar*, **directed by James Cameron of *Titanic* fame**, is one of the most beautiful pictures ever made, with special effects **rivaled by those of few other films**.

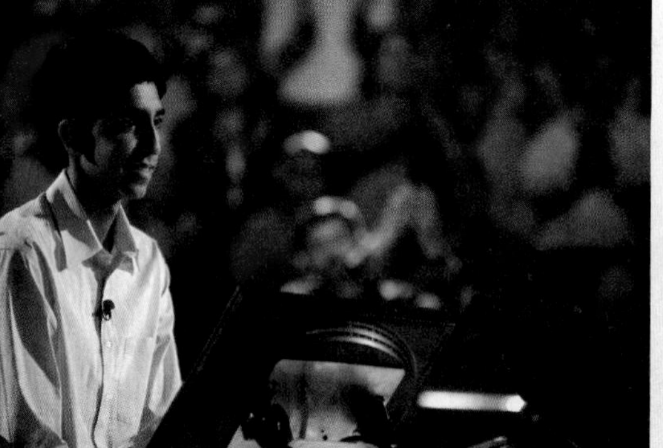

Slumdog Millionaire

★ Fourth: *Babel* is an engrossing story about the need for people to communicate. It shows the interconnectedness of events through three sets of characters **whose lives intersect**. An American couple, **played by Brad Pitt and Cate Blanchett**, are traveling in Morocco when the wife is wounded by a stray bullet. The bullet comes from a gun **left in Morocco** by a Japanese man **who'd been on safari**. The Japanese man has a daughter **he's estranged from**. Meanwhile, the American couple's Mexican housekeeper, **to whom they've entrusted their children**, takes the kids to her son's wedding in Mexico, where unfortunate events occur. This film is complicated but well worth your attention.

★ Fifth: *Slumdog Millionaire*, my favorite among favorites, is the story of Jamal, Salim, and Latika, three orphans from the slums of Mumbai **who manage to transcend their environment**. Jamal, **now 18**, is a contestant on India's version of *Who Wants to Be a Millionaire?* **About to answer the grand prize question**, Jamal is arrested and charged with cheating. After all, how could a "slumdog" really be this knowledgeable? In a series of flashbacks, Jamal recounts events in his life **illustrating how he knew the answers to the questions**. In the process he finds the lovely Latika, **from whom he's become separated**. The film, **featuring Dev Patel and Freida Pinto as hero and heroine**, is one of the most original pictures in a long time.

After You Read

A | Vocabulary: *Match the blue words and phrases on the left with their meanings on the right.*

____ **1.** It's **incumbent on me** to come up with a "best movie" compilation.

____ **2.** It's incumbent on me to come up with a "best movie" **compilation.**

____ **3.** Julie decides to **spice up** her life.

____ **4.** South Africa was racially **polarized**.

____ **5.** The inhabitants of Pandora end up **vanquishing** a group of exploiters.

____ **6.** *Babel* is an **engrossing** story about the need for people to communicate.

____ **7.** The Japanese man has a daughter he's **estranged** from.

____ **8.** The three orphans manage to **transcend** their environment.

a. divided into opposing groups
b. defeating
c. alienated
d. list
e. fascinating
f. make more interesting
g. my responsibility
h. rise above

B | Comprehension: *Refer to the reading and complete each sentence with a single word.*

1. The author of the article is a movie ________________.

2. *Julie and Julia* is about the activity of ________________.

3. Nelson Mandela was the leader of the first South African ________________ after the end of apartheid.

4. Mandela insisted that blacks and whites ________________.

5. In *Avatar,* the natives of Pandora defeat some ________________ from Earth.

6. The film *Babel* illustrates the ________________ of human events.

7. The action of *Slumdog Millionaire* takes place in the country of ________________.

8. The three main characters of *Slumdog Millionaire* are able to rise above the limitations of their ________________.

ADJECTIVE CLAUSES WITH PREPOSITIONS, QUANTIFIERS, OR NOUNS; ADJECTIVE PHRASES

Main Clause	Adjective Clause with Preposition			
People / Things	**Preposition**	**Relative Pronoun**		**Preposition**
He's the actor	**to**	**whom**	she was talking.	
		who(m) **that** **Ø***	she was talking	**to**.
It's the studio	**for**	**which**	he works.	
		which **that** **Ø**	he works	**for**.
That's the director		**whose**	movies I told you	**about**.
That's the movie			director I spoke	**of**.

*Ø = no pronoun

Main Clause	Adjective Clause with Quantifier			
People / Things	**Quantifier**	***Of***	**Relative Pronoun**	
I have many friends,	**all** **most** **a number**	**of**	**whom**	are actors.
I was in a lot of movies,	**some** **a few** **several**		**which**	were successes.
That's the director,	**a couple** **both** **two**		**whose**	movies are classics.
That's the movie,				actors got awards.

Main Clause	Adjective Clause with Noun		
Things	**Noun**	***Of Which***	
She makes comedies,	**an example**	**of which**	is *Julie and Julia*.
I love that series,	**an episode**		she directed.

Reducing Adjective Clauses to Adjective Phrases

	Adjective Clause
He's the actor	**who's from** the film school.
I saw the film	**which is based** on that book.
That's the man	**who was in charge** of lighting.
I read the scripts	**that are on my desk**.

	Adjective Phrase
He's the actor	**from** the film school.
I saw the film	**based** on that book.
That's the man	**in charge** of lighting.
I read the scripts	**on my desk**.

Changing Adjective Clauses to Adjective Phrases

	Adjective Clause
He's the actor	**who plays** the king.
Babel is a picture	**which stars** Brad Pitt.
It's a love story	**that takes** place in Rome.

	Adjective Phrase
He's the actor	**playing** the king.
Babel is a picture	**starring** Brad Pitt.
It's a love story	**taking** place in Rome.

GRAMMAR NOTES

1	The relative pronouns ***who(m)***, ***that***, ***which***, and ***whose*** after a noun can be used as **objects of prepositions** in adjective clauses.	• Bill is the man **to whom** I spoke. • That's the film **to which** he referred.
	Sentences with the preposition at the beginning of the clause are formal; sentences with the preposition at the end of the clause are informal.	• She's the director **to whom** I wrote. • She's the director **whom** I wrote **to**.
	NOTE: A preposition can come at the beginning of the clause before *who(m)*, *which*, and *whose*. It cannot come at the beginning in a clause with *that*.	• It is the studio **for which** he works. NOT: It is the studio ~~for that~~ he works.
	We can omit the relative pronouns *who(m)*, *that*, and *which* after a preposition. When we do this, the preposition moves to the end of the clause.	• He has a daughter **he's estranged from**. • That's the screenwriter **I read about**.
	BE CAREFUL! *Whose* cannot be omitted.	• He's the director **whose films I go to**. NOT: He's the director ~~films I go to~~.
	Remember that there are two types of adjective clauses: identifying (essential) and nonidentifying (nonessential).	• The film **to which I'm referring** is *Avatar. (identifying)* • *Avatar,* **to which I'm referring**, is exciting. *(nonidentifying)*
2	Some adjective clauses have the pattern **quantifier + *of* + relative pronoun**.	• The film has many stars, **few of whom** I recognized. • He made eight films, **all of which** I like.
	Quantifiers occur only in clauses with ***whom***, ***which***, and ***whose***. These clauses may refer to **people** or **things**. These clauses are formal.	
	If a clause with a quantifier occurs within the main clause, it is enclosed in commas. If it occurs **after** the main clause, a comma precedes it.	• Her books, **most of which I've read**, are popular. • I like her books, **most of which I've read**.

(continued on next page)

3	Some adjective clauses have the pattern **noun + *of which***. These clauses refer only to **things**. If a clause with a noun + *of which* occurs within the main clause, it is enclosed in commas. If it occurs **after** the main clause, a comma precedes it.	• Musicals, **an example of which** is *Mamma Mia*, are still popular. NOT: Actors, ~~an example of which is Johnny Depp,~~ earn a lot of money. • Strikes, **occurrences of which may delay filming**, are uncommon. • She has reviewed films, an **example of which is *Shrek***.
4	We sometimes **shorten adjective clauses** to **adjective phrases** with the same meaning. Remember that a clause is a group of words that has a subject and a verb. A phrase is a group of words that doesn't have both a subject and a verb.	• Anyone **who is interested in cinema** should see this film. *(adjective clause)* • Anyone **interested in cinema** should see this film. *(adjective phrase)*
5	To shorten an adjective clause with a ***be*** verb, **reduce** the clause to an adjective phrase by deleting the relative pronoun and the *be* verb. **BE CAREFUL!** Adjective clauses with *be* verbs can be reduced only when *who, which*, or *that* is the subject pronoun of the clause. If an adjective clause needs commas, the corresponding phrase also needs commas.	• *Slumdog Millionaire,* **which was directed by Danny Boyle**, won many awards. • *Slumdog Millionaire,* **directed by Danny Boyle**, won many awards. • I met George Clooney, **whose latest film is a hit**. NOT: I met George Clooney, ~~latest film is a hit~~. • Penélope Cruz starred in *Vicky Cristina Barcelona,* **which was released in 2008**. • Penélope Cruz starred in *Vicky Cristina Barcelona,* **released in 2008**.
6	If there is no *be* verb in the adjective clause, it is often possible to **change** the clause to an adjective phrase. Do this by deleting the relative pronoun and changing the verb to its *-ing* form. You can do this only when *who, which*, or *that* is the subject pronoun of the clause.	• *Avatar,* **which stars Sam Worthington**, is the top-earning film. • *Avatar,* **starring Sam Worthington**, is the top-earning film. • I like any movie **that features Helen Mirren**. • I like any movie **featuring Helen Mirren**.

STEP 3 FOCUSED PRACTICE

EXERCISE 1: Discover the Grammar

A | *Look at the sentences based on the opening reading. Underline the adjective clauses containing prepositions. Circle the noun(s) referred to in the adjective clause and draw a line between the noun(s) and the clause.*

1. I've seen a lot of movies since 2000, many of which are outstanding in their own way.
2. Mandela reaches out to François Pienaar, with whom he develops an enduring friendship.
3. The picture stars Morgan Freeman and Matt Damon, both of whom play their roles to near perfection.
4. Clint Eastwood, whose films I always go to, directed with great skill.
5. Science fiction films, a compelling example of which is *Avatar,* continue to be popular.
6. The movie is a story in which the Pandorans vanquish some exploiters from Earth.
7. The American couple's Mexican housekeeper, to whom they've entrusted their children, takes the kids to her son's wedding in Mexico.
8. In the process he finds the lovely Latika, from whom he's become separated.

B | *Look at the underlined adjective phrases. Make each phrase a clause by adding a relative pronoun and a verb or new verb form.*

1. Anyone interested in cinema should revisit these films.

   Anyone who is interested in cinema should revisit these films.

2. Julie is a young woman caught in a dead-end job.

   Julie who is caught in a dead-end job is a young woman.

3. This film, starring Meryl Streep and Amy Adams, is about finding what you really want to do in life.

   This film, which is starring Meryl Streep and Amy Adams, is about ——

4. The movie, set on a planetary moon called Pandora, is a good-guys-versus-bad-guys story.

   The movie, which is set on a planetary moon called Pandora, is a ——

5. *Avatar,* directed by James Cameron of *Titanic* fame, is one of the most beautiful pictures ever made.

   Avatar, which is directed by James Cameron of Titanic fame, is one of the most beautiful pictures ever made.

(continued on next page)

6. The movie has special effects rivaled by those of few other films.

____

7. The bullet comes from a gun left in Morocco by a Japanese man.

____

8. The film, featuring Dev Patel and Freida Pinto as hero and heroine, is one of the most original pictures in a long time.

____

EXERCISE 2: Adjective Clauses with Quantifiers

(Grammar Note 2)

Complete the following statements about movies using adjective clauses with the pattern quantifier + preposition + relative pronoun.

1. Animated productions, ___most of which are loved by children___, continue to increase in popularity.
   (most / be / loved by children)

2. *Titanic* and *Avatar*, ________________, are critical and commercial successes.
   (both / be / directed by James Cameron)

3. Roberto Benigni, Pedro Almodóvar, and Lina Wertmüller, ________________, are becoming better known in the United States.
   (all / be / highly regarded European directors)

4. *Star Wars, The Empire Strikes Back,* and *Return of the Jedi,* ________________, are the middle three films in a planned nine-part series.
   (all / have / earn a great deal of money)

5. Sean Connery, Roger Moore, and Daniel Craig, ________________, are from Great Britain, while Pierce Brosnan is from Ireland.
   (all / have / play the role of James Bond)

6. Nicole Kidman and Ewan McGregor, ________________, surprised everyone with their singing in *Moulin Rouge*.
   (neither / be / known as a singer)

EXERCISE 3: Adjective Phrases

(Grammar Notes 5–6)

Combine each pair of sentences into one sentence with an adjective phrase. The adjective phrase comes from the first sentence, except in item 4, where it comes from the second sentence.

1. *E.T.* was directed by Steven Spielberg. It was the top-earning film until it was passed by *Titanic*.

   E.T., *directed by Steven Spielberg, was the top-earning film until it was passed by* Titanic.

2. *Spider-Man* is based on the popular comic book. It is one of the highest-earning movies of all time.

3. *The Pirates of the Caribbean* films star Johnny Depp. They are all very popular.

4. Clint Eastwood has directed many big movies. These include *Million Dollar Baby, Gran Torino,* and *Invictus*.

5. The Harry Potter novels were written by J. K. Rowling. They have translated well to the screen.

EXERCISE 4: Clause to Sentence

(Grammar Notes 2–3, 5–6)

Each sentence is about types of films and contains an adjective clause or phrase. Imagine that each was formed from an original pair of sentences. Write the original pairs.

1. Comedies, examples of which are *Legally Blonde, Julie and Julia,* and *Marley and Me,* have continued to be popular and successful.

   Comedies have continued to be popular and successful. Examples of these are Legally Blonde, Julie and Julia, *and* Marley and Me.

2. Many science fiction films have been financially successful, including *Spider-Man, Jurassic Park,* and *Avatar.*

(continued on next page)

3. The top-earning animated films, both of which I've seen, are *Finding Nemo* and *Shrek 2*.

____

____

4. *The Hurt Locker,* featuring lesser-known actors, was the best picture of 2009.

____

____

5. *Beverly Hills Chihuahua* stars Drew Barrymore and Andy Garcia, both of whom I respect.

____

____

EXERCISE 5: Personal Inventory

(Grammar Notes 2–3, 5–6)

Use the items from the box to describe movies you have seen or that you know about. Write a sentence with each item.

directed by	**featuring**	**(*quantifier*) + of which**
examples of which	**including**	**starring**

Examples: I've seen a lot of Arnold Schwarzenegger's movies, **including** *Terminator I, II,* and *III;* and *True Lies.*

Dances with Wolves and *Unforgiven,* **both of which I've seen**, made westerns more popular.

1. ____

2. ____

3. ____

4. ____

5. ____

6. ____

EXERCISE 6: Editing

Read the letter. There are six mistakes in the use of adjective clauses and phrases. The first mistake is already corrected. Find and correct five more. Delete verbs or change pronouns where necessary, but do not change punctuation or add relative pronouns.

July 28

Dear Brent,

Sarah and I are having a great time in Los Angeles. We spent the first day at the beach in Venice and saw where The Sting was filmed—you know, that famous movie ~~starred~~ starring Paul Newman and Robert Redford? Yesterday we went to Universal Studios and learned about all the cinematic tricks, most of that I wasn't aware of. Amazing! The funny thing is that even though you know the illusion presented on the screen is just an illusion, you still believe it's real when you see the movie. Then we took the tram tour around the premises and saw several actors working, some of which I recognized. I felt like jumping off the tram and shouting, "Would everyone famous please give me your autograph?" In the evening we went to a party at the home of one of Sarah's friends, many of them are connected with the movie business. I had a really interesting conversation with a fellow working in the industry who claims that a lot of movies making these days are modeled conceptually after amusement park rides. Just like the rides, the movies start slowly and easily, then they have a lot of twists and turns are calculated to scare you to death, and they end happily. Maybe Pirates of the Caribbean is an example. Pretty fascinating, huh? What next?

Sorry to spend so much time talking about movies, but you know what an addict I am. Anyway, I'll let you know my arrival time, which I'm not sure of yet, so that you can pick me up at the airport.

Love you lots,

Amanda

STEP 4 COMMUNICATION PRACTICE

EXERCISE 7: Listening

A | *Listen to the film reviewer give her weekly review. Of the five movies, which is her all-time favorite?*

____

B | *Read the sentences. Then listen to excerpts from the review. Write* **T (True)** *or* **F (False)** *to indicate if each item correctly restates the sentence that you hear.*

__T__ **1.** The film festival can be seen this holiday weekend.
_____ **2.** None of these great movies has been shown in more than a decade.
_____ **3.** *A Beautiful Mind* is about a character created by director Ron Howard.
_____ **4.** Jennifer Connelly won an Oscar for her portrayal of Nash's wife.
_____ **5.** *Rashomon* is probably the most famous modern film from China.
_____ **6.** *Rashomon* is about the way people view truth.
_____ **7.** *Chicago* has only one main star.
_____ **8.** Michael J. Fox was responsible for launching *Back to the Future.*
_____ **9.** All who regard themselves as serious movie buffs must see *Casablanca.*
_____ **10.** The reviewer says black-and-white movies are not pretty.

EXERCISE 8: Pronunciation

A | *Read and listen to the Pronunciation Note.*

Pronunciation Note

A number of words in English change their vowel sound but not the spelling of that vowel when the word changes form or use. For sounds and examples, refer to Appendix 25 on page A-11.

Examples: I **read** the newspaper every day. (present form) /**i**/ vowel
I **read** the newspaper yesterday evening. (past form) /**ɛ**/ vowel
John is a great **athlete**. /**i**/ vowel
He's always participated in **athletics**. /**ɛ**/ vowel

B | *Listen to the sentences. Circle the pronunciation of the boldfaced vowel in each word.*

1. a. He is the h**e**ro. — /ɪ/ or /ɛ/ (circled: /ɪ/)

b. She is the h**e**roine. — /ɪ/ or /ɛ/ (circled: /ɛ/)

2. a. It's a n**a**tional problem. — /eɪ/ or /æ/

b. It's for the good of the n**a**tion. — /eɪ/ or /æ/

3. a. It's located in S**ou**th Africa. /aʊ/ or /ʌ/

b. It's in a s**ou**thern city. /aʊ/ or /ʌ/

4. a. Their actions were atr**o**cious. /oʊ/ or /ɑ/

b. They committed atr**o**cities. /oʊ/ or /ɑ/

5. a. The ch**i**ldren are safe. /aɪ/ or /ɪ/

b. A ch**i**ld must be protected. /aɪ/ or /ɪ/

C | *PAIRS: Practice the sentences.*

EXERCISE 9: Information Gap

PAIRS: Each of you will read a version of a review of the film A Beautiful Mind. *Each version is missing some information. Take turns asking your partner questions to get the missing information.*

Student A, read the review of A Beautiful Mind. *Ask questions and fill in the missing information. Then answer Student B's questions.*

Student B, turn to the Information Gap on page 227 and follow the instructions there.

EXAMPLE: **A:** What is the movie inspired by?
B: It is inspired by . . . What was Nash's occupation?
A: Nash was . . .

A Beautiful Mind
(2002) C-135 m.

Rating: ★★★ **Director:** Ron Howard
Starring: Russell Crowe, Jennifer Connelly, Ed Harris, Paul Bettany, Christopher Plummer, Adam Goldberg, Judd Hirsch, Josh Lucas, Anthony Rapp, Austin Pendleton

An unusual story inspired by ________________________ in the life of John Nash, a brilliant West Virginia mathematician who flowers at Princeton in the late 1940s and goes to work at ________________________. But his marriage and sanity are put to a painful test. ________________________ is amazing—and completely unexpected. Crowe is excellent as usual, and the film offers an overdue showcase for ________________________ as the student who becomes his wife. Oscar winner for Best Picture, Director, Supporting Actress (Connelly), and Adapted Screenplay (Akiva Goldsman). PG-13.

EXERCISE 10: Group Discussion

Look at the chart describing the current movie rating system. Then complete the questionnaire for yourself; circle **yes** *or* **no**. *Discuss your answers with a partner. Then discuss your answers with the class as a whole.*

Example: **A:** I think many movies are too violent today.
B: I disagree. Sometimes violence is necessary for the director to make the point.

Movie Ratings	Description
G	Suitable for general audiences, all ages.
PG	Parental guidance is suggested; some material may not be appropriate for children.
PG-13	Parents strongly cautioned; some material may not be appropriate for children under 13.
R	Restricted; anyone under 17 must be accompanied by a parent or adult guardian.
NC-17	No one under 17 is admitted.

Movies and Rating Systems		
Movie rating systems are a good idea.	yes	no
Rating systems are enforced in my area.	yes	no
If I want to see a movie, I don't pay attention to the rating.	yes	no
Many movies today are too violent.	yes	no
Movie rating systems should be made stronger.	yes	no

EXERCISE 11: Picture Discussion

A | *PAIRS: Discuss the picture, using adjective clauses or phrases whenever possible.*

Example: **A:** In the theater there are a lot of people trying to concentrate on the movie.
B: One man, annoying the people near him, is talking on his cell phone.

B | *CLASS: What is proper behavior at movie theaters? Discuss these points with the class as a whole:*

- Should cell phones be allowed in movie theaters?
- Should moviegoers have to pick up their own trash?
- Should small children be allowed at movies?
- Should people be allowed to talk during showings of movies?

Example: **A:** I don't think cell phones should be allowed in movie theaters.
B: Why not?
A: It's inconsiderate to other people because . . .

EXERCISE 12: Writing

A | *Write your own movie review in three or more paragraphs. Choose a film that you liked or disliked, but try to be objective in your review. Read your review to the class, and answer any questions your classmates might ask about the movie. Use adjective clauses with prepositions and adjective phrases as appropriate.*

EXAMPLE: One of the best movies I've seen recently is *Super Size Me,* directed by Morgan Spurlock. Spurlock, fascinated by the recent court case in which two American women sued McDonald's for serving food that was less than healthy, decided to find out whether or not fast food is really unhealthy. His plan was simple: eat nothing but McDonald's food for a month. The film is about his month-long adventure. It's humorous and interesting, and . . .

B | *Check your work. Use the Editing Checklist.*

Editing Checklist

Did you use . . . ?

- ☐ adjective clauses with prepositions correctly
- ☐ adjective clauses with quantifiers correctly
- ☐ adjective clauses with nouns correctly
- ☐ adjective phrases correctly

Information Gap for Student B

Student B, read the review of A Beautiful Mind. *Answer Student A's questions. Then ask your own questions and fill in the missing information.*

Example: **A:** What is the movie inspired by?
B: It is inspired by incidents in the life of John Nash. What was Nash's occupation?
A: Nash was . . .

A Beautiful Mind

(2002) C-135 m.

Rating: ★★★ **Director:** Ron Howard

Starring: Russell Crowe, Jennifer Connelly, Ed Harris, Paul Bettany, Christopher Plummer, Adam Goldberg, Judd Hirsch, Josh Lucas, Anthony Rapp, Austin Pendleton

An unusual story inspired by incidents in the life of John Nash, a brilliant West Virginia ________________________ who flowers at Princeton in the late 1940s and goes to work at M.I.T. But his ________________________ are put to a painful test. The central story twist is amazing—and completely unexpected. ___________________ is excellent as usual, and the film offers an overdue showcase for Connelly as the student who becomes ________________________. Oscar winner for Best Picture, Director, Supporting Actress (Connelly), and Adapted Screenplay (Akiva Goldsman). PG-13.

UNIT 13 Review

Check your answers on page UR-2.

Do you need to review anything?

A | *Circle the correct pronoun in each adjective clause.*

1. *The Wizard of Oz, Dumbo,* and *Fantasia,* all of whom / which I've seen, are classics.
2. Pedro Almodóvar, which / whose films I enjoy, is a well-known Spanish director.
3. Streep and Adams, both of who / whom are prominent actresses, star in *Julie and Julia.*
4. *Avatar* and *2012,* neither of them / which I've seen yet, are science fiction movies.
5. Cruz and Hayek, both of which / whom are Spanish-speaking, are prominent actresses.
6. Anyone interested / interesting in film history should attend the lecture.
7. *Invictus,* which was / that was directed by Clint Eastwood, is a powerful film.
8. I try to see any movie stars / starring Jackie Chan.

B | *Correct the mistakes in the underlined words or phrases.*

1. He has directed five films, all of them I like. ________________
2. I'm taking two new courses, neither of them is interesting. ________________
3. I made two friends, both of them are teachers, this week. ________________
4. We saw great films, examples of them are *Tron* and *Up.* ________________
5. Several actors, one of which I've met, are in town. ________________
6. The novel is about a young man which is caught in a dead-end job. ________________
7. Emiko was the employee whom was in charge of bookkeeping. ________________
8. Boyle has won many awards, one of that was an Oscar. ________________

C | *Circle the letter of the one underlined word or phrase in each sentence that is not correct.*

1. The films all starred Depp, that readily explains their success. **A B C D**
   (A all, B starred, C that, D readily)
2. Anyone interested in film must see *The Fighter,* that opens today. **A B C D**
   (A interested, B must, C that, D opens)
3. Strikes, occurrences of them can delay filming, are uncommon. **A B C D**
   (A occurrences, B of, C them, D filming)
4. The writer to whom I referred is Saki, most of which works I've read. **A B C D**
   (A to, B whom, C most, D which)

From Grammar to Writing

PUNCTUATING ADJECTIVE CLAUSES AND PHRASES

You can strengthen your writing by judiciously using adjective clauses and phrases and by punctuating them correctly. Remember that the two types of adjective clauses and phrases are **identifying** and **nonidentifying**. Identifiying adjective clauses give information essential for distinguishing one person or thing from another. Nonidentifying clauses give additional (= nonessential) information that doesn't identify. Only nonidentifying clauses are set off by commas.

Examples: I saw three movies last week. The movie **that I liked best** was *Salt. (essential—says which movie I'm commenting on)*
Salt, **which stars Angelina Jolie**, is a spy movie. *(nonessential—adds information)*

Adjective phrases perform the same identifying and nonidentifying functions. Only nonidentifying phrases are set off by commas.

Examples: A movie **directed by George Lucas** is likely to be a blockbuster. *(essential—says which type of movie is likely to be a blockbuster)*
Avatar, **directed by James Cameron**, has awesome special effects. *(nonessential—adds extra information about* Avatar.*)*

1 | *Punctuate the pairs of sentences containing adjective clauses and phrases. One sentence or phrase in each pair is identifying, and the other is nonidentifying.*

1. a. College students who live close to campuses spend less money on gas.
b. College students who are expected to study hard have to become responsible for themselves.

2. a. People who are the only animals with a capacity for creative language have highly developed brains.
b. People who live in glass houses shouldn't throw stones.

3. a. The car which was invented in the late 19th century has revolutionized modern life.
b. The car that I would really like to buy is the one in the far corner of the lot.

4. a. Science fiction movies which have become extremely popular in the last two decades often earn hundreds of millions of dollars for their studios.
b. The science fiction movies that have earned the most money collectively are the *Star Wars* films.

5. a. The panda that was given to the National Zoo died recently.
b. The panda which is native only to China is on the Endangered Species List.

(continued on next page)

6. a. A film directed by Steven Spielberg is likely to be a blockbuster.

   b. *A Beautiful Mind* directed by Ron Howard won the Academy Award for best picture.

7. a. Many Canadians including Donald Sutherland and Michael J. Fox are major international film stars.

   b. A film directed by Pedro Almodóvar is likely to be a financial success.

2 | *Complete the punctuation of this letter containing adjective clauses and phrases.*

September 30

Dear Mom and Dad,

Thanks again for bringing me down here to the university last weekend. Classes didn't start until Wednesday, so I had a few days to get adjusted. I'm signed up for five courses: zoology, calculus, English, and two history classes. It's a heavy load, but they're all courses that will count for my degree. The zoology class which meets at 8:00 every morning is going to be my hardest subject. The history class that I have in the morning is on Western civilization; the one that I have in the afternoon is on early U.S. history. Calculus which I have at noon every day looks like it's going to be relatively easy. Besides zoology, the other class that's going to be hard is English which we have to write one composition a week for.

I like all of my roommates but one. There are four of us in our suite including two girls from Texas and a girl from Manitoba. Here's a picture of us. Sally who is from San Antonio is great; I feel like I've known her all my life. She's the one on the left. I also really like Anne the girl from Manitoba. She's the one on the right. But Heather the other girl from Texas is kind of a pain. She's the one next to me in the middle. Heather is one of those people who never tell you what's bothering them and then get hostile. All in all, though, it looks like it's going to be a great year. I'll write again in a week or so.

Love,

Vicky

3 | *Before you write . . .*

1. A well-known proverb in English says, "A picture is worth a thousand words." While this may be an overstatement, we can learn a great deal from close examination of a picture, and we can use that information to make our writing interesting. Find a photograph (in a magazine, book, or your own personal collection) that interests you and bring it to class.
2. Describe your picture to a partner. Listen to your partner's description.
3. Ask and answer questions about your and your partner's picture. Why is the picture significant to you? What about it interests or touches you?

4 | *Write a draft of a two- or three-paragraph composition about your picture. Follow the model. Remember to include information that your partner asked about. Use identifying and nonidentifying adjective clauses and phrases in your composition.*

The people and things or places in the picture:

____

____

____

____

My experience with the people, things, or places in the picture:

____

____

____

____

What specifically interests or touches me about the picture:

____

____

____

____

5 | *Exchange compositions with a different partner. Complete the chart.*

1. The writer used identifying and nonidentifying adjective clauses and phrases. **Yes** ☐ **No** ☐

2. What I liked in the composition:

____

____

____

3. Questions I'd like the writer to answer about the composition:

Who ____?

What ____?

When ____?

Where ____?

Why ____?

How ____?

(Your own question) ____?

6 | *Work with your partner. Discuss each other's chart from Exercise 5. Then rewrite your own compositions and make any necessary changes.*

PART VI

PASSIVE VOICE

UNIT	GRAMMAR FOCUS	THEME
14	The Passive: Review and Expansion	Unsolved Mysteries
15	The Passive to Describe Situations and to Report Opinions	Legends and Myths

UNIT 14

The Passive: Review and Expansion

UNSOLVED MYSTERIES

STEP 1 GRAMMAR IN CONTEXT

Before You Read

PAIRS: Discuss the questions.

1. Many people find unsolved mysteries fascinating. Do you enjoy hearing about them? If so, why? Do you know of any unsolved mysteries?
2. Some people think there is a need for mystery in life, for things to remain unexplained. Do you agree or disagree?
3. Why do people sometimes sympathize with criminals and want them to get away with their crimes?

Read

Read the news article about an unsolved mystery.

Did He Get Away With It?

Some crimes never **get solved**, and the case of Dan Cooper is one that **hasn't been**. Late in November of 1971, on a short flight between Portland and Seattle, a flight attendant **was handed** a note by a mysterious middle-aged man dressed in a dark suit. Leaning close to her, he said, "Miss, you'd better look at that note. I have a bomb." He then opened his briefcase so that she could see several red cylinders and a lot of wires. The man, who used the alias "Dan Cooper," was demanding $200,000, four parachutes, and a plane to fly him to Mexico.

The plane proceeded to Seattle with none of the other passengers even aware it **was being hijacked**. They got off the plane, and "Cooper" got what he was demanding: $200,000, all in $20 bills that **had been photocopied** by FBI agents so they **could** easily **be identified**. Then the plane **was refueled** and took off for Mexico.

A few minutes later, Cooper ordered the flight attendant to go to the cockpit and stay there. As she was leaving, she noticed him trying to tie something around his waist—presumably the bag of money. Then he opened the plane's rear stairway and jumped out of the plane. The crew felt pressure bumps that **were** probably **caused** by Cooper's jump. The air temperature was seven degrees below zero. Cooper was wearing no survival gear and only light, casual shoes.

Did He Get Away With It?

Cooper **has not been seen** or **heard from** since that night. Who was he? Did he get away with his plan? Or **was** he **killed** trying to commit the perfect crime?

Authorities speculate that Cooper landed near Ariel, a small town near the Columbia River north of Portland. Only one real clue **has been discovered**. In 1980, an eight-year-old boy inadvertently dug up $5,880 of Cooper's money near a riverbank. It was only a few inches below the surface of the earth, but it had decayed so much that only the picture and the serial numbers on the bills were visible. Rotting rubber bands **were found** along with the money, indicating that the cash **must have been deposited** there before the bands fell apart. Since then, the area **has been searched** thoroughly, but no trace of Cooper **has been found**.

What really happened? Many investigators believe that Cooper **had to have been killed** by the combination of the weather conditions and the impact of his fall, but if so, why **have** none of his remains ever **been discovered**? **Is** more information **known** than **has been divulged**? Is Cooper's body in some remote part of the wilderness area into which he jumped, or is he living a luxurious life under an alias somewhere? Did he **have** the $5,880 **buried** by an accomplice to throw the authorities off the track? Or did he bury it himself?

Cooper has become a legend. His story **has been told** in books and articles and even a movie. In Ariel the hijacking **is** still **celebrated** every year. Bar owner Dona Elliot says, "He did get away with it . . . so far." Others don't think so. Jerry Thomas, a retired soldier who has been working independently on the case, thinks that Cooper didn't survive the fall and his body **will** eventually **be found**. "I know there is something out here," he says. "There has to be."

As of 2011, none of the missing money **had been recovered**. The mystery goes on.

After You Read

A | Vocabulary: *Circle the letter of the best meaning for the* **blue** *words and phrases from the reading.*

1. The man, who used the **alias** "Dan Cooper," was demanding $200,000.
   a. nickname **b.** false name **c.** surname **d.** title
2. None of the other passengers were aware that the plane was being **hijacked**.
   a. destroyed **b.** affected **c.** forcibly taken over **d.** terrorized
3. Cooper was wearing no survival **gear** and only light, casual shoes.
   a. equipment **b.** trousers **c.** mechanical device **d.** overcoat
4. An eight-year-old boy **inadvertently** dug up $5,880 of Cooper's money.
   a. by careful planning **b.** by luck **c.** by great effort **d.** by accident
5. **Rotting** rubber bands were found along with the money.
   a. Decaying **b.** Elastic **c.** Ancient **d.** Manufactured
6. Why have none of Cooper's **remains** ever been discovered?
   a. messages **b.** body parts **c.** DNA samples **d.** clothes
7. Is more information known than has been **divulged**?
   a. proved **b.** suggested **c.** revealed **d.** claimed
8. Did Cooper have the money buried by an **accomplice**?
   a. consultant **b.** gang member **c.** relative **d.** helper in wrongdoing
9. Bar owner Dona Elliot believes that Cooper did **get away with** the crime.
   a. escape capture for **b.** commit **c.** pay for **d.** plan

B | Comprehension: *Circle* **T (True)** *or* **F (False)**. *Correct the false statements.*

1. The flight Cooper hijacked originated in Seattle. **T** **F**
2. Dan Cooper claimed to have a bomb. **T** **F**
3. The money Cooper received was in bills of different denominations. **T** **F**
4. The passengers were aware of what Cooper was doing. **T** **F**
5. A portion of Cooper's money was discovered by authorities. **T** **F**
6. Cooper was killed by the combination of the impact of his fall and the weather conditions. **T** **F**
7. Cooper may have buried the money dug up by the boy. **T** **F**
8. Most people think Cooper got away with the crime. **T** **F**

STEP 2 GRAMMAR PRESENTATION

THE PASSIVE: REVIEW AND EXPANSION

Active Sentences			Passive Sentences		
Subject	**Verb**	**Object**	**Subject**	***Be* + Past Participle**	**(*By* + Agent)**
Cooper	**hijacked**	the plane.	The plane	**was hijacked**	by Cooper.
Someone	**found**	the bills.	The bills	**were found.**	

Passive Verb Forms

		Be (not)	**Past Participle**	
Simple Present	The crime	**is (not)**	**investigated**	(by the new team).
Present Progressive		**is (not) being**		
Simple Past		**was (not)**		
Past Progressive		**was (not) being**		
Future		**will (not) be** **is (not) going to be**		
Present Perfect		**has (not) been**		
Past Perfect		**had (not) been**		
Future Perfect		**will (not) have been**		

The Passive with Modals

	Modals	***Be / Have Been***	**Past Participle**	
The case	**can (not)** **may (not)** **might (not)** **should (not)** **ought (not) to** **must (not)** **had better (not)**	**be**	**reopened**	in the future.
	could (not) **might (not)** **must (not)** **should (not)** **ought (not) to**	**have been**		years ago.

The Passive Causative

Subject	***Have / Get***	**Object**	**Past Participle**	**(*By* + Agent)**
We	**had**	the evidence	**checked**	by experts.
She	**has had**	the note	**analyzed.**	
They	**got**	the report	**printed**	by professionals.
He	**is going to get**	a copy	**made.**	

GRAMMAR NOTES

1	A sentence in the **passive voice** has a corresponding sentence in the **active voice**. The object in the active sentence becomes the subject in the passive sentence. We can say that the subject of a passive sentence is acted upon.	• The police never **catch some criminals**. (OBJECT) • **Some criminals** are never caught. (SUBJECT)
	The subject of the active sentence becomes the agent (preceded by the preposition ***by***) in the passive sentence, or disappears.	• **Someone took** the money. (SUBJECT) • The money **was taken (by someone)**. (AGENT)
	BE CAREFUL! Only transitive verbs, those that can be followed by an object, can be made passive. Intransitive verbs (those that cannot be followed by an object) cannot be made passive.	• No one **has seen** Cooper since 1971. • Cooper **has not been seen** since 1971. • Several people **died** in the accident. NOT: Several people ~~were~~ died in the accident.
2	**Passive sentences** are formed with *be* + past participle. They occur in present, past, and future forms.	• Police officers **are** well **trained**. • The suspect **was arrested** yesterday. • He **will be held** in the local jail.
	To make a negative passive sentence, place *not* after the first verb.	• Cooper **has not been caught**.
	Use the present progressive and past progressive passives to describe actions in progress (= not finished) at a certain time.	• The suspect **is being held** in prison. • The robbery occurred while the money **was being taken** to a bank.
3	Use the **passive** voice **a.** when you don't know who performed the action or when it is not important to say who performed it	• The money **was stolen**. • The plane **was refueled**.
	b. when you want to avoid mentioning the agent	• A criminal **is** sometimes **regarded** as a hero. *(We don't want to say who regards him as a hero.)*
	c. when you want to focus on the receiver or the result of an action instead of the agent	• The thief **was caught** by the detective. (RECEIVER: The thief; RESULT: was caught; AGENT: the detective)
4	Use the **passive with a *by* phrase** **a.** to introduce new information about the agent	• The money was stolen **by a person who has a criminal record**.
	b. to credit someone who did something	• The bills were photocopied **by FBI agents**.
	c. when the agent is surprising	• The money was found **by a little boy**.
	You can omit the *by* phrase in passive sentences if you feel it is unnecessary or undesirable to mention the agent.	• Why **hasn't** this crime **been solved**?

5	Most commonly, the direct object of an active sentence is the subject of the corresponding passive sentence.	DIRECT OBJECT • The police **arrested** the suspect. SUBJECT • The suspect **was arrested** by the police.
	However, an indirect object is sometimes the subject of a passive sentence.	INDIRECT OBJECT • The F.B.I. **gave** Cooper the money. SUBJECT • **Cooper was given** the money by the F.B.I.
6	We often use **modals** and modal-like auxiliaries in the passive. To form the present passive with a modal, use the modal + *be* + past participle. To form the past passive with a modal, use the modal + *have been* + past participle.	• The criminal **should be arrested**. • He **could have been arrested** before this.
	Use *have (got) to*, *had better*, *had to*, *must*, *ought to*, and *should* in passive sentences to express advisability, obligation, and necessity.	• The charges **had to be dropped**. • Criminal suspects **must be charged**.
	Use *can* and *could* to express present and past ability.	• Suspects **can't be kept** in jail. • The thief **could have been caught**.
	Use *will* and *be going to* to talk about future events.	• This prisoner **will be tried**. • The suspects **are going to be released**.
	Use *can't*, *could*, *may*, and *might* to talk about future possibility and impossibility.	• The mystery **may** never **be solved**. • He **can't be released** from jail.
7	The **passive** can also be formed with ***get***. The passive with *get* is more informal than the passive with *be*. It is conversational and characteristic of informal writing.	• Will that criminal ever **get caught**? • Our team **got beaten** in the soccer game.
	BE CAREFUL! Although the *be* passive is used both with action and non-action verbs, the *get* passive is used only with action verbs.	• More research **is needed** about the causes of crime. NOT: More research ~~gets needed~~ about the causes of crime.
8	*Have* and *get* + object + past participle are used to form the **passive causative**. There is usually little difference in meaning between the causative with *have* and with *get*.	• You should **have** your car **serviced**. • I just **got** my best suit **dry-cleaned**.
	The passive causative is used in the past, present, and future and with modals.	• We **had** the windows **washed**. • I **get** my car **tuned up** twice a year. • She**'s going to get** her hair **cut**.

(continued on next page)

9	Use the **passive causative** to talk about services or activities that people arrange for someone else to do.	• The detective **had** the evidence **analyzed**. • Sometimes criminals **get** their hair **dyed** or **shaved**.
	The passive causative can occur with a *by* phrase, but this phrase is often omitted. Use the *by* phrase only when it is necessary to mention the agent.	• I **got** my photos **developed** at the drugstore. • We **had** our house **inspected by Jim**.
	BE CAREFUL! Don't confuse the simple past causative with the past perfect.	• They **had** the grass **cut**. *(simple past causative—someone else cut the grass)* • They **had cut** the grass. *(past perfect—they had done this before a specific time in the past)*
	BE CAREFUL! Don't confuse the passive causative with the expression *to get something done* meaning *to finish something*.	• I **got** the work **done** by a mechanic. *(passive causative)* • I **got** the work **done** by noon. *(I finished the work by 12 P.M.)*

REFERENCE NOTE

For the use of **modals**, see Units 4 and 5.

I had my hair cut

I had cut my hair

We get the cleaning done by Francisco.

STEP 3 FOCUSED PRACTICE

EXERCISE 1: Discover the Grammar

*Look at these sentences based on the opening reading. Underline the passive construction in each sentence. Then write **a**, **b**, or **c** above it to show why the passive is used.*

a = don't know who performed the action or not important to say

b = desire to avoid mentioning who performed the action

c = focus on the receiver or result of an action

1. Some crimes never get solved.
2. A flight attendant was handed a note by a mysterious middle-aged man.
3. None of the other passengers were even aware the plane was being hijacked.
4. The twenty-dollar bills had all been photocopied by FBI agents.
5. Only one real clue has been discovered.
6. Rotting rubber bands were found along with the money.
7. Many investigators believe Cooper had to have been killed in the jump.
8. Is there additional information that has not been divulged?

EXERCISE 2: Transitive / Intransitive

(Grammar Notes 1–2)

Complete the sentences with the active or passive form of the verb in parentheses. Then identify the verbs as **T (Transitive)** *or* **I (Intransitive)**.

__I__ **1.** Criminals often ___return___ to the scene of a crime. (return)

____ **2.** If they are not careful, they ________________ (catch) by the authorities.

____ **3.** Smart criminals ________________ (disappear) entirely from the scene.

____ **4.** They never ________________ (go) back to the locale.

____ **5.** Usually a smart criminal ________________ (help) by one or more accomplices.

____ **6.** The accomplices ________________ (reward) by the intelligent criminal.

____ **7.** Most criminals, however, aren't smart. They ________________ (not realize) how resourceful the police are.

____ **8.** Crime scenes ________________ (watch) very closely by the police, but most criminals don't believe this.

EXERCISE 3: Progressive Passives

(Grammar Note 2)

Complete the TV news bulletin with present progressive and past progressive passives.

Here is breaking news from KKBO News Channel 6. Two suspects ___are being held___ **(1. hold)** in the county jail where they ________________ **(2. question)** about their role in a bank robbery that took place this morning at the downtown branch of First International Bank. As the bank's vault ________________ **(3. open)**, the suspects, wearing masks and carrying guns, burst in and demanded that an undisclosed amount of money be placed in a paper bag. They escaped with the funds but were later caught after a customer who ________________ **(4. help)** noticed the license plate number of the vehicle the suspects were driving and notified bank authorities. The identities of the two suspects ________________ **(5. withhold)** until the initial investigation is completed. Other bank customers ________________ **(6. currently / interview)** for additional information. This is Ron Mason for KKBO News Channel 6. Stay tuned for further updates.

EXERCISE 4: Various Passives

(Grammar Notes 2, 6)

Fill in the blanks in the article with passive constructions with **be** *and the correct forms of the verbs in parentheses.*

Two Unsolved Mysteries Continue to Fascinate

So you think there are no more mysteries, that all mysteries ___are solved___ (1. (solve)) in time? Think again. The pages of history are full of mysteries that ________ (2. (not / crack)). Consider, for example, the case of the ship *Mary Celeste*. The ship had left New York for Italy in 1872. Later it ________ (3. (sight)) floating east of the Azores. No one ________ (4. (find)) on board, though everything ________ (5. (determine)) to be in order, and there was no indication why the *Mary Celeste* ________ (6. (abandon)). Apparently, in fact, tables ________ (7. (set)) for afternoon tea. One theory speculates that the ship ________ (8. (might / threaten)) by an explosion that ________ (9. (cause)) by fumes from its cargo of alcohol. That theory, however, ________ (10. (not prove)).

A second perplexing mystery is that of Amelia Earhart, the famous aviator who in the 1920s and 1930s ________ (11. (consider)) the best example of an adventurous woman. Earhart flew across the Atlantic with two men in 1928 and set a record for a cross-Atlantic flight in 1932. In 1937 she embarked on her most ambitious plan, a flight around the world. Earhart began her flight in Miami in June and ________ (12. (accompany)) only by Fred Noonan, her navigator. They reached New Guinea and left for Howland in the South Pacific on July 1. After that, no radio reports or messages of any kind ________ (13. (receive)). No remains of her plane ________ (14. (discover)) by naval investigators in the years since then. Did she simply attempt the impossible? ________ (15. (Could / she and Noonan / kill)) when her plane ran out of fuel and crashed? Or could something else have happened? No one really knows. For the time being, at least, the riddle of the *Mary Celeste* and the fate of Amelia Earhart will have to remain mysterious. Some may think they ________ (16. (should / not solve)) at all.

EXERCISE 5: Passive Causative

(Grammar Notes 8–9)

A | *Read the sentences. Then circle the letter of the choice that best explains the meaning of the sentence.*

Last week Detective Harry Sadler had an extremely busy schedule. . . .

1. On Monday morning, he had a tooth pulled before going to work.

a. He pulled the tooth himself. **(b.)** He arranged for someone to pull the tooth.

2. When he got to work, he had some crime notes typed up.

a. He typed them himself. **b.** Someone else typed them.

3. In the afternoon, he had to review another officer's report. He had finished it by 6:00 P.M.

a. He finished it himself. **b.** Someone else finished it.

4. On Tuesday and Wednesday, he had to write his own report on a case he had been working on. He got it done by the end of the day.

a. He did it himself. **b.** Someone else did it.

5. On Thursday, Harry got some crime pictures microfilmed.

a. He microfilmed them himself. **b.** Someone else microfilmed them.

6. On Friday, he worked until 5:30 P.M. and then went to an appointment. He'd had his income taxes done and needed to go over them.

a. He did the taxes himself. **b.** Someone else did the taxes.

B | *Complete the paragraph using the passive causative or active past perfect forms of the verbs in parentheses. Use verbs in the progressive where necessary.*

Yesterday was a typically unpredictable day in the life of detective Harry Sadler. Since Harry hadn't been able to eat at home, he got some breakfast brought (**1. (get / some breakfast / bring)**) to his office as soon as he arrived. After breakfast he emailed some photos of a crime scene to the lab to ______ (**2. (have / them / enlarge)**). He spent two hours going over files and then left for the garage where he was ______ (**3. (get / his car / tune up)**). The mechanic said that he should also ______ (**4. (have / a tail light / replace)**). Harry agreed and arranged to pick the car up later. At lunchtime he met with the members of his team. Time was short, so they ______ (**5. (get / lunch / deliver)**) from a restaurant. They studied evidence they had ______ (**6. (get / analyze)**) by the crime lab. By 2:00 they ______ (**7. (have / complete / the work)**). After the meeting Harry wrote a report by hand. He ______ (**8. (have / finish / the report)**) by 4:00; then he ______ (**9. (have / it / type)**) by his secretary. At 5:30 he left, picked up his car, and met his wife for dinner. They were ______ (**10. (have / their kitchen / remodel)**) and couldn't do any cooking. At 9:00 P.M. they got home. It's good that Harry loves his work because it was another long, tiring, but interesting day.

EXERCISE 6: Editing

Read this student essay about the crop circles in Great Britain and elsewhere. There are nine mistakes in the use of the passive. The first one is already corrected. Find and correct eight more.

The Crop Circles

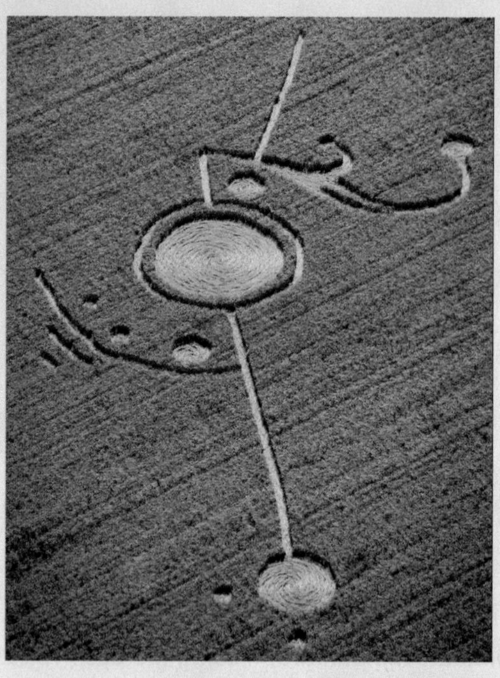

In our day we believe in science and have the feeling that every question can be ~~explain~~ explained and every problem can be solved. But some of us want the opposite. We don't want everything to be explained. We like puzzles. We feel that mystery is needed in our lives.

The mysterious crop circles that have been appeared around the world in the last 25 years or so are an example of this. These formations have reported in more than 20 countries, including the United States, Canada, and Australia. But most of them have been found in grain fields in southern England. These circles, which are large and flat, are caused by a force that flattens the grain but does not destroy it. They are still been made.

How have these circles been produced? By whom have they been made? Since the first discovery of the circles, many explanations have been proposed. According to some people, the circles have been made by spirit creatures such as fairies. Others say they have been caused by "Star Wars" experiments or are messages that have been leaving by extraterrestrials visiting our planet. Two British painters, David Chorley and Douglas Bower, say they were made the crop circles over a period of years as a joke. If this is true, however, how can we explain the crop circles in Australia and Canada and other places? They couldn't all have being made by Chorley and Bower, could they?

In 2002, director M. Night Shyamalan released his movie *Signs*, which is about the crop circle question. The movie shows clearly that the crop circles made by invading aliens from beyond our solar system. This is one interesting and enjoyable theory. More explanations like it get needed. What's fun is speculation. The mystery doesn't need to be solved.

STEP 4 COMMUNICATION PRACTICE

EXERCISE 7: Listening

A | *Listen to the news bulletin. What kind of accident occurred this evening?*

8Ave
Doutru

____

B | *Listen again. Answer each question with a complete sentence.*

1. What time did the accident occur?

   The accident occurred this evening at 8:45 P.M.

2. The boy was struck by what kind of car?

   The boy was struck by blue black Toyota Camry. black ca

3. What was the boy doing when he was struck?

   He was intertraction when he was struck

4. What happened to the car?

   The car was disappear 4446968

5. What kind of injuries did the boy sustain?

   The boy sustain massive injujuries

6. Where was the boy taken after the accident?

   The boy was taken after the accident at 4 Avenue

7. Where is the boy being cared for?

   Doutown hospital

   The boy is being cared fore Intensive Care Unit.

8. How is his condition described?

   His condition is described as critical

9. Anyone with information is asked to call what number?

   Anyone with information is asked to call 444 6968.

10. What is being offered?

    giving reward is being offered.

EXERCISE 8: Pronunciation

A | *Read and listen to the Pronunciation Note.*

Pronunciation Note

The phrase *has been* in a passive sentence means that the action has already been performed. The phrase *is being* in a passive sentence means that the action is happening now—still being performed.

EXAMPLES: The suspect **has been** questioned. *(has already happened)*
The suspect **is being** questioned. *(is happening now)*

B | *Listen to the sentences. Circle* **'s been (has been)** *or* **'s being (is being)** *depending on what you hear. Then circle* **already done** *or* **happening now.**

1. The prisoner 's been / 's being interrogated. already done / happening now
2. The issue 's been / 's being discussed. already done / happening now
3. Bob 's been / 's being promoted to police chief. already done / happening now
4. The investigation 's been / 's being completed. already done / happening now
5. The plane 's been / 's being hijacked. already done / happening now
6. The boy 's been / 's being treated for injuries. already done / happening now
7. The report 's been / 's being written. already done / happening now
8. The mystery 's been / 's being solved. already done / happening now

C | *PAIRS: Practice the sentences. Take turns.*

EXERCISE 9: Information Gap

PAIRS: Student A, read clues 1–4 to Student B. Student B will complete the clues. Switch roles after item 4. Then put the clues in the correct order and decide what the mystery object is.

Student B, turn to page 248 and follow the instructions there.

Student A's Clues

1. I was born, or maybe I should say I was created . . .
2. An all-night card game . . .
3. I was created by . . .
4. The "hero" type of me gets its name . . .

Student A's Completions

5. . . . have been known by my name since then.
6. . . . some slices of meat between two slices of bread.
7. . . . is shaped like a submarine.
8. . . . so he ordered a snack to be delivered to the gaming table.
9. . . . that I'm being eaten somewhere in the world this very minute.

EXERCISE 10: Survey and Discussion

A | *GROUPS: Within your group, conduct a survey of opinions on the questions. Write* **Y (Yes)** *or* **N (No)**. *Then discuss the responses.*

_____ Should juveniles indicted for crimes ever be tried as adults?

_____ Should juveniles be incarcerated with hardened criminals?

_____ In general, are criminals today punished sufficiently for the crimes they commit?

_____ In general, is the criminal justice system in your country being improved?

_____ Should hit-and-run drivers be jailed?

B | *CLASS: Discuss the conclusions of all the groups.*

EXERCISE 11: Picture Discussion

A | *GROUPS: Look at the photos of a UFO and "an alien from a UFO crash" near Roswell, New Mexico, in 1947. Discuss the pictures using passive verb constructions where appropriate.*

- What do the pictures represent?
- Was there really a UFO crash in 1947?
- Was the incident covered up by the government, as some people say?
- How can UFOs be explained?

EXAMPLE: **A:** Do you think the Roswell alien story was covered up by the government?
B: No, I don't.
C: How else can it be explained?
B: I think . . .

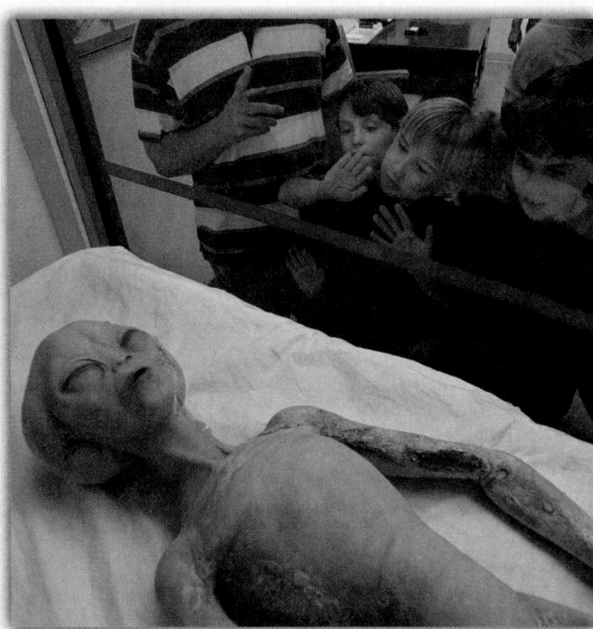

B | *CLASS: Share your conclusions with those of the other groups.*

EXERCISE 12: Writing

A | *Write a composition of five or more paragraphs describing an unsolved mystery. It could involve a crime, someone's disappearance, or some strange natural phenomenon. Describe what the mystery is and how it might have been caused. Offer some possible solutions to the mystery. Use passive constructions as appropriate.*

EXAMPLE: We've all heard about the Bermuda Triangle, an area in the Caribbean Sea where planes and ships supposedly get captured by unknown forces. One of the most famous mysteries of the Bermuda Triangle is the case of Flight 19, a U.S. military expedition that took off on December 5, 1945, to do navigational research. There were five planes, and all of them were piloted by skilled fliers . . .

B | *Check your work. Use the Editing Checklist.*

Editing Checklist

Did you use . . . ?

☐ passive verb forms correctly

☐ passives with modals correctly

☐ passive causatives correctly

INFORMATION GAP FOR STUDENT B

Choose one of phrases 1–4 to complete each clue that Student A reads. Switch roles after item 4. Then put the clues in the correct order and decide what the mystery object is.

Student B's Completions

1. . . . because of the hero-sized appetite that's needed to eat one.
2. . . . at 5:00 in the morning on August 6, 1762.
3. . . . was being played at a gaming table.
4. . . . an Englishman named John Montagu, the fourth earl of the place I was named after.

Student B's Clues

5. The snack ordered by my creator was composed of . . .
6. It's almost certain . . .
7. My creator was hungry but too busy to leave the game, . . .
8. Two slices of bread with a filling between them . . .
9. And the "submarine" type of me . . .

UNIT 14 Review

Check your answers on page UR-2.
Do you need to review anything?

A | *Circle the word or phrase that correctly completes each sentence.*

1. Right now a new hotel is constructed / is being constructed downtown.
2. Tadao had his car serviced / had serviced his car because he couldn't do it himself.
3. The thieves were caught / caught when they tried to spend stolen money.
4. The driver of the car died / was died in the accident.
5. Evidence shows that the theory has been / being disproved.
6. The children were been / being driven to school when the accident happened.
7. The work won't have been / been being finished by this weekend.
8. Without any help, I got the job done by noon / the job done by an assistant.

B | *Complete the sentences with the verb* report *in the indicated passive constructions.*

1. The news ________________ daily. (simple present)
2. The news ________________ right now. (present progressive)
3. The news ________________ twice today. (present perfect)
4. The news ________________ an hour ago. (simple past)
5. The news ________________ when the earthquake occurred. (past progressive)
6. The news ________________ an hour before the earthquake occurred. (past perfect)
7. The news ________________ at 5:00 P.M. (simple future)
8. The news ________________ by 3:30 P.M. (future perfect)

C | *Circle the letter of the one underlined word or phrase in each sentence that is not correct.*

1. The Turkish city of Trabzon has (A) just being (B) hit (C) by (D) a tsunami. **A B C D**
2. The tsunami got (A) caused (B) by (C) an earthquake centered (D) in the Black Sea. **A B C D**
3. Peace talks were (A) been (B) held (C) last week between (D) Tintoria and Illyria. **A B C D**
4. The United Nations had said (A), "We must (B) get (C) these talks start (D) again." **A B C D**

UNIT 15

The Passive to Describe Situations and to Report Opinions

LEGENDS AND MYTHS

STEP 1 GRAMMAR IN CONTEXT

Before You Read

PAIRS: Look at the picture on page 251 and discuss the questions.

1. What does the illustration show?
2. What is an aspect of your culture that might be hard for people of other cultures to understand? How would you explain it?

Read

Read the article about an unusual tribe of people.

THE STRANGEST OF PEOPLES

For decades anthropologists have studied strange and unusual peoples all over the world. One of the strangest is a group called the Nacirema, a prominent tribe living in North America.

The territory of the Nacirema **is located** between the Canadian Cree and the Tarahumara of Mexico. On the southeast their territory **is bordered** by the Caribbean. Relatively little **is known** of the origin of this people, though they **are said** to have come from somewhere in the East. In fact, the Nacirema **may be related** to certain European and African peoples.

Nacirema people spend a great deal of time on the appearance and health of their bodies. In Nacirema culture the body **is generally believed** to be ugly and likely to decay. The only way to prevent this decay is through participation in certain magical ceremonies. Every Nacirema house has a special shrine room dedicated to this purpose. Some Nacirema houses have more than one shrine room. In fact, it **is felt** in Nacirema culture that the more shrine rooms a family has, the richer it is.

What is in the shrine room? The focal point is a box built into the wall, inside which is a large collection of magical potions, medicines, and creams. Below the box is a small font from which water is obtained. Every day each member of the Nacirema family enters the shrine room, bows to the chest, and receives magic holy water from the fountain.

Several rituals in Nacirema culture are performed by one sex or the other, but not by both. Every morning, for example, a Nacirema man places a magic cream on his face and then scrapes and sometimes even lacerates his face with a sharp instrument. A similar ritual performed only by women involves the scraping of the legs and underarms.

THE STRANGEST OF PEOPLES

In Nacirema culture, the mouth **is regarded as** a highly significant part of the body. The Nacirema are fascinated by the mouth and believe its condition has an important and supernatural effect on all social relationships. The daily body ritual involves an activity which **would be considered** repulsive in some cultures. It **is reported** that the Nacirema actually insert into their mouths a stick on one end of which are plasticized hairs covered with a magical paste! They then move these sticks back and forth in their mouths in highly ritualized gestures.

Among the most important individuals in the culture are the "holy-mouth-people." Naciremans visit these practitioners once or twice a year. They possess excellent sharp instruments for performing their magic ceremonies. They place these instruments in the mouths of the Naciremans. If there are holes in the teeth, they are enlarged with these tools. Then a supernatural substance is placed in each hole. It **is said** that the purpose of this practice is to prevent decay in the teeth and to help Nacirema people to find spouses.

Another significant person in Nacirema culture is the "listener," a witch doctor who **is thought** to have the power to get rid of the devils in the heads of people who have been bewitched. Naciremans believe parents often bewitch their own children, especially while teaching the secret toilet rituals, and the listeners must "unbewitch" them. It is also **believed** that the secret to getting rid of these devils is simply to talk about them, usually while reclining on a sofa.

Clearly, the Nacirema are a magic-inspired tribe. Much more research is needed in order to understand this strange people.

After You Read

A | Vocabulary: *Circle the letter of the best meaning for the blue words from the reading.*

1. Every Nacirema house has a special **shrine** room dedicated to this purpose.
   a. work **b.** sleeping **c.** worship **d.** relaxation
2. Inside the box is a collection of **potions**, medicines, and creams.
   a. magical devices **b.** magical foods **c.** magical containers **d.** magical creams or liquids
3. Below the box is a small **font**.
   a. water source **b.** printing device **c.** door **d.** mirror
4. Several **rituals** in Nacirema culture are performed by one sex or the other.
   a. instructions **b.** greetings **c.** examinations **d.** ceremonial acts
5. A Nacirema man scrapes and sometimes even **lacerates** his face daily.
   a. washes **b.** cuts **c.** decorates **d.** takes care of
6. Then a **supernatural** substance is placed in each hole.
   a. having magical powers **b.** highly effective **c.** poisonous **d.** very expensive
7. The daily ritual involves a practice that would be considered **repulsive** in some cultures.
   a. dangerous **b.** barbaric **c.** attractive **d.** disgusting
8. Naciremans believe that parents often **bewitch** their own children.
   a. positively influence **b.** ignore totally **c.** magically control **d.** treat unkindly

B | Comprehension: *Complete each statement with a single word.*

1. In reality, the Nacirema people are the ______________
2. The shrine room is the ______________
3. The font in the shrine room is the ______________.
4. The activity of scraping the face, legs, or underarms is ______________
5. The stick that Naciremans insert in their mouths is a ______________
6. The holy-mouth-people are ______________
7. The listeners or witch doctors are in reality ______________
8. In reality, the devils in the heads of bewitched people are mental ______________.

STEP 2 GRAMMAR PRESENTATION

THE PASSIVE TO DESCRIBE SITUATIONS AND TO REPORT OPINIONS

Describing Situations or States (Stative Passive)

Active Sentences	Passive Sentences			
	Subject	*Be* + Past Participle	Prepositional Phrase	(*By* + Agent)
Ø*	The people	**are related**	(**to** each other).	Ø
	The country	**is composed**	**of** two regions.	
	The island	**is connected**	**to** the mainland.	
	The capital	**was located**	**in** the South.	

*Ø = These forms do not occur.

Reporting Opinions or Ideas

Active Sentences		
Subject	Verb	*That* Clause
Some anthropologists	**say** **think** **believe** **allege**	**(that)** the people came from the East.

Passive Sentences with *It* + *That* Clause			
It	*Be* + Past Participle	(*By* + Agent)	*That* Clause
It	**is said** **is thought** **is believed** **is alleged**	(by some anthropologists)	**(that)** the people came from the East.

Passive Sentences with *To* Phrase			
Subject	*Be* + Past Participle	(*By* + Agent)	*To* Phrase
The people	**are said** **are thought** **are believed** **are alleged**	(by some anthropologists)	**to** have come from the East.

GRAMMAR NOTES

1	Remember that the passive is used to describe situations in which the subject is acted upon. The passive is also used to describe situations or states. This use is called the **stative passive**.	• These peoples **are related** to each other. • St. Louis **is located** on the Missouri River.
	The stative passive is formed with *be* + past participle. Most stative passive sentences do not have a corresponding active sentence, and most do not contain a *by* phrase.	• Our two families **are related**. NOT: ~~Genealogists relate our two families.~~
	A few stative passives do have a corresponding active sentence. These include passives formed with *connect* and *surround*.	• England and France **are connected by** the Chunnel. • The Chunnel **connects** England and France.
2	We use the **stative passive** to describe situations or states. In stative passive sentences there is normally no action taking place.	• The United States **is composed** of 50 states.
	In stative passive constructions, the past participle functions as an adjective. It is often followed by a prepositional phrase.	• Cuba **is located** in the Caribbean.
	Stative passive sentences are often used in everyday English. Examples of stative passives: *be bordered by, be composed of, be connected to / with / by, be divided into / by, be found in, be located in / on, be made up of, be related to, be surrounded by.*	• Curitiba **is found** in southern Brazil. • A peninsula **is surrounded** by water on three sides.
3	**Passives** are commonly used to report ideas, beliefs, and opinions. They often occur in the form *it* + *be* + past participle + *that* clause. Common examples of verbs used to form this type of passive are *allege, assume, believe, claim, say*, and *think*.	• **It is assumed that** this culture is very old. • **It is said that** present-day Basques are descendants of Atlanteans.
	Passive sentences of this type have corresponding active sentences.	• Scholars **assume that** this culture is very old.
	BE CAREFUL! We use this structure only with verbs that can be followed by a *that* clause. *That* is optional and is frequently omitted in informal English. *Regard* cannot be followed by a *that* clause.	• It **is said (that)** these people came from Asia. NOT: ~~It is regarded (that) these people came from Asia.~~
	These passive structures may take an optional *by* phrase.	• It **is claimed (by some scholars) that** Shakespeare didn't write all his plays.

4	**Passives** that report ideas, beliefs, and opinions also commonly occur in the form subject + *be* + past participle + *to* phrase. This type of sentence can be converted from an equivalent active sentence with a *that* clause. A *by* phrase is optional.	• Scholars **assume that the culture dates** from 5000 B.C.E. • **The culture is assumed** (by scholars) **to date** from 5000 B.C.E. • Bigfoot **is thought** to live in the Pacific Northwest.
	The verb in the *to* phrase can be present or past.	• He is said **to be** the author. • The Japanese are thought **to have visited** the New World before Columbus.
	NOTE: *Consider* can take an infinitive but is often followed by just a noun phrase or an adjective. *Regard* is followed by *as* + a noun phrase.	• Native Americans **are considered (to be) the real discoverers**. • Columbus **is regarded as the discoverer of America**.
5	**Passive sentences** with *that* clauses or infinitive phrases are often used in academic discourse and in reporting the news. They create an objective impression by distancing the author from the idea.	• **It is believed that** the Abominable Snowman actually exists. • **The defendant is alleged to have committed** the crime.
	Authors can create the greatest distance between themselves and an idea by starting a passive sentence with *It* + *be* + past participle + *that* clause. This type of sentence is formal.	• **It is thought that** the Vikings explored the New World long ago.
	BE CAREFUL! This construction with *it* occurs only with verbs that can be followed by a clause beginning with *that*.	

REFERENCE NOTES

For use of ***that* clauses**, see Unit 10.
For use of **infinitive phrases**, see Unit 17.
For a list of **verbs used in the passive followed by a *that* clause**, see Appendix 10 on page A-6.
For a list of common **stative passive verbs + prepositions**, see Appendix 11 on page A-6.

STEP 3 FOCUSED PRACTICE

EXERCISE 1: Discover the Grammar

A | *Read the sentences based on the opening reading. Are the underlined passive structures stative passives* (**S**) *or opinion / belief passives* (**O**)?

__S__ **1.** The territory of the Nacirema is located roughly between that of the Tarahumara of Mexico and the Cree of Canada.

_____ **2.** On the southeast, their territory is bordered by the Caribbean.

_____ **3.** They are said to be from somewhere in the East.

_____ **4.** Actually, the Nacirema may be related to certain European and African peoples.

_____ **5.** In Nacirema culture, the body is generally considered ugly and likely to decay.

_____ **6.** It is felt that the more shrine rooms a family has, the higher its social status is.

_____ **7.** The mouth is regarded as a highly significant part of the body.

_____ **8.** The daily body ritual involves an activity which would be considered repulsive in some cultures.

_____ **9.** The "listener" is thought to have the power to get rid of the devils in the heads of bewitched people.

_____ **10.** In the shrine room, Naciremans are surrounded by a collection of potions, medications, and creams.

B | *Read the sentences from the opening reading. For each sentence, answer the questions* **yes** *or* **no**:

a. Could the sentence be rewritten with a *by* phrase?

b. Could the sentence be rewritten in the active voice?

1. The territory of the Nacirema is located roughly between that of the Tarahumara of Mexico and that of the Cree of Canada.

a. _________ **b.** _________

2. Actually, the Nacirema may be related to certain European and African peoples.

a. _________ **b.** _________

3. The mouth is regarded as a highly significant part of the body.

a. _________ **b.** _________

4. It is felt that the more shrine rooms a family has, the higher its social status is.

a. _________ **b.** _________

EXERCISE 2: Stative Passives

(Grammar Notes 1–2)

Look at the map. Complete the sentences by writing the stative passive forms of the verbs from the box. Some of the verbs may be used more than once.

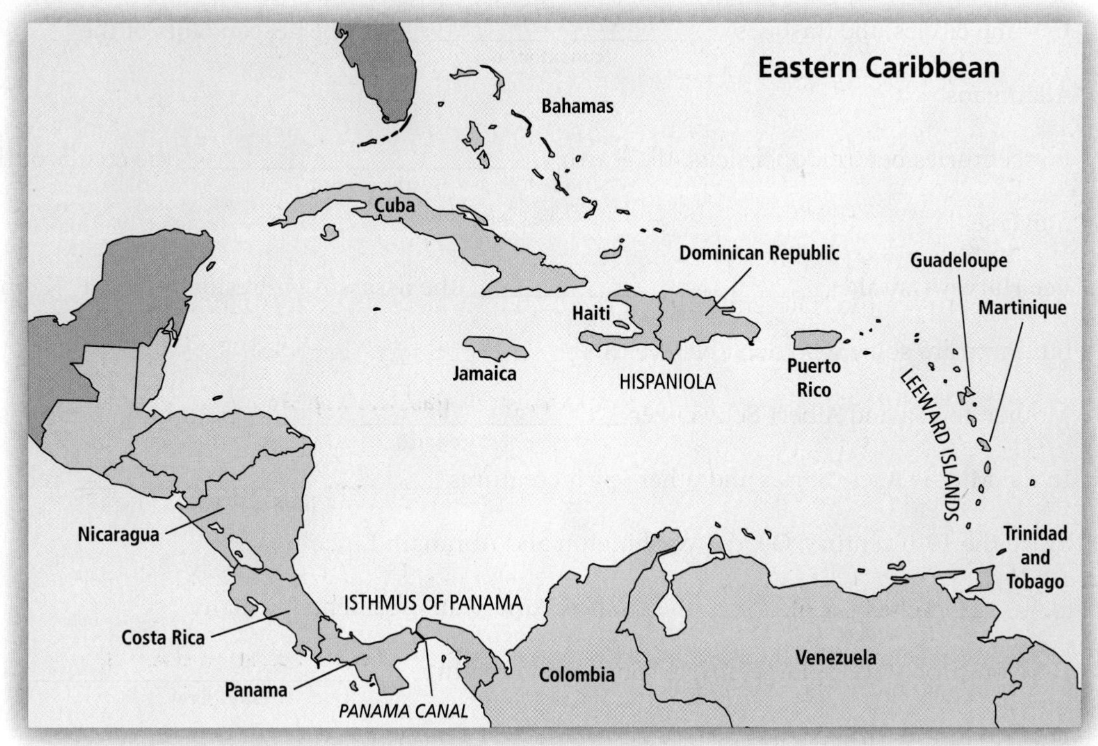

border by	**connect by**	**find (in)**	**make up of**
compose of	**divide into**	**locate (in)**	**surround by**

1. North and South America *are connected by* the Isthmus of Panama.
2. The island nations of the region, of course, are surrounded by the waters of the Caribbean.
3. The island of Hispaniola is divided into two nations: Haiti and the Dominican Republic.
4. Cuba is located about 90 miles south of Florida.
5. The nation of Trinidad and Tobago is composed of two separate islands: Trinidad and Tobago.
6. On the north, Costa Rica is bordered by Nicaragua and on the south by Panama.
7. The nation of The Bahamas is made up of many islands, some large and some small.
8. The nation of Panama is divided into two parts by the Panama Canal.
9. Jamaica and Puerto Rico are found west and east, respectively, of Hispaniola.
10. The French-speaking islands of Guadeloupe and Martinique are found in the eastern Caribbean, north of South America.

EXERCISE 3: Beliefs / Thoughts / Opinions *(Grammar Notes 4–5)*

A | *Complete the sentences with a present or past passive form of the verbs in parentheses. Add* **as** *or* **to** *as needed.*

1. In some circles, the Basques *are considered to be* **(consider / be)** the descendants of the Atlanteans.
2. For centuries before Copernicus, the Earth was thought to be **(think / be)** the center of the universe.
3. Lee Harvey Oswald is claimed to be **(claim / be)** the assassin of President John F. Kennedy, but there are some who don't believe this.
4. Mother Teresa and Albert Schweitzer are regarded as **(regard)** great humanitarians.
5. In the Middle Ages, fairies and other spirit creatures were believed to be **(believe / be)** real.
6. Since the 19th century, George Washington and Abraham Lincoln have been consided (to be) **(consider)** the greatest American presidents by many.
7. Bigfoot, supposedly a large, mysterious forest creature, is said to live **(say / live)** in the Pacific Northwest.
8. In the 15th century and afterwards, King Richard III of England was regarded as **(regard)** a monstrous king. Today he has a better reputation.
9. Today William Shakespeare is assumed to be **(assume / be)** the author of the plays credited to him, but some have suggested he couldn't have written them all.
10. From time to time, certain people are alleged to be **(allege / be)** criminals, but they are later proved innocent by DNA evidence.

HW Tues paper

B Rewrite sentences 2, 3, 5, 7, 9, and 10 using a passive sentence with **it** + **be** + past participle + **that** clause.

2. *For centuries before Copernicus, it was thought that the Earth was the center of the universe.*

3. It is claimed that Lee Harvey Oswald is the assassin of President John F. Kennedy, but there are some who don't believe this.

5. In the Middle Ages, it were believed that fairies & other spirit creatures were real.

7. It is said that Bigfoot, supposedly a large, mysterious forest creature lived in the

9. Today It is assumed that William Shakespeare was the author of the plays

10. From time to time, it is alleged that certain people are criminals, but they are later proved innocent by DNA evidence.

EXERCISE 4: Personal Inventory

(Grammar Note 4)

Use each of the items from the box to write passive sentences showing beliefs, opinions, or facts about people or things in your country.

allege to be	**believe to be**	**consider**	**say to be**
assume to be	**claim to be**	**regard as**	**think to be**

Example: Jorge Amado **is considered** one of the greatest Brazilian writers.

1.

2.

3.

4.

5.

6.

7.

8.

Wednesday
- Review Units 14 & 15 → quiz
- Read Unit 16

After Read (p. 272)

Grammar Notes (p. 274, 275)

EXERCISE 5: Editing

Read this student essay about a creature that may or may not be real. There are eight mistakes in passive constructions. The first one is already corrected. Find and correct seven more.

The Snowman

Every area of the world has its own legends, and Asia is no different. One of the most famous Asian legends is about the Abominable Snowman, also called the yeti, of the Himalayas. Is the yeti just a legend that is ~~believe~~ *believed* because people want things to be real, or does he really exist?

The yeti thought to be a huge creature—perhaps as tall as 8 feet. His body is supposed to be covered with long, brown hair. He says to have a pointed head and a hairless face that looks something like a man's. It is claimed that he lives near Mount Everest, the highest mountain in the world, which locates on the border of Nepal and Tibet.

Sightings of the yeti have been reported for centuries, but the yeti was made known to the rest of the world only in 1921. In that year, members of an expedition to climb Mount Everest saw very large tracks in the snow that looked like prints of human feet. No conclusive evidence of the yeti's existence was found during that expedition, but interest was stimulated. Other expeditions were undertaken. In 1951, explorer Eric Shipton led a search in which some gigantic, human-appearing tracks were found. Once again, the yeti himself was not seen. In 1969, Sir Edmund Hillary, who is regarded one of the greatest climbers ever, arranged another expedition, this time with the intention of not only seeing the yeti but also of capturing him. Once again, tracks were discovered, but that was all. Hillary eventually decided the footprints might simply considered normal animal tracks enlarged by the daytime melting of the snow. In 1964, Boris F. Porshev, a Russian scientist, said that he believed that the yeti actually existed. He theorized that the yeti is a surviving descendant of Neanderthal man, a creature who is believed to live from 200,000 to 25,000 years ago and is thought by some to be an ancestor of modern humans. Porshev has never actually been able to spot the yeti, however.

The mystery continues. Does the yeti really exist, or do people just want to believe he exists? It seems to me that there must be more to this mystery than just melted tracks. Centuries of reports by Himalayan trail guides must mean something. Besides, other yeti-type creatures have reported—most notably, Bigfoot in North America. Time will tell, but maybe we shouldn't be so quick to dismiss the Abominable Snowman as nothing more than an entertaining story.

STEP 4 COMMUNICATION PRACTICE

EXERCISE 6: Listening

A | *Listen to the news bulletin. What is the locale?*

____

B | *Listen again and check (✓)* **True** *or* **False.**

	True	**False**
1. The earthquakes are said to have registered a nine on the Richter scale.	☑	☐
2. The epicenter of the quakes was located in the Pacific Ocean.	☐	☐
3. The exact number of drowned people is known.	☐	☐
4. Coastal areas were hit by a tsunami.	☐	☐
5. It is thought that severe flooding has occurred inland.	☐	☐
6. The president was vacationing at his seaside retreat.	☐	☐
7. So far, no looting has been reported.	☐	☐
8. The president hopes citizens of the country will stay calm and law-abiding.	☐	☐
9. The citizens should go to low areas.	☐	☐

EXERCISE 7: Pronunciation

A | *Read and listen to the Pronunciation Note.*

Pronunciation Note

The vowel sound **/eɪ/** is a tense vowel in which the lips are spread wide.

The vowel sound **/ɛ/** is a lax vowel in which the lips are not spread wide.

EXAMPLES: Don't s**ay** that. **/eɪ/** *(tense)*
She s**ai**d that. **/ɛ/** *(lax)*
How do you spell ***mate***? *(tense)*
How do you spell ***met***? *(lax)*

B | *Listen to the sentences. Circle the /eɪ/ sounds. Underline the /ɛ/ sounds. Note: Consider only stressed syllables in the boldfaced words.*

1. She **said** a lot of **clever** things in the **paper** she wrote.
2. The people **spend** a **great** deal of time on the appearance and **health** of their bodies.
3. The **president says** that a **great** tragedy has struck the **nation**.
4. It is **alleged** that **they came** from the East.
5. It is **said** that **strange** creatures like the **yeti may** actually **exist**.
6. **Every day** each **member** of the family **enters** the room.
7. The countries of **Haiti** and the Dominican Republic are located on the **same** island.
8. **Betty's letter** arrived on **Wednesday** afternoon.

C | *PAIRS: Practice the sentences. Take turns.*

EXERCISE 8: Game

CLASS: Form two teams. Each team uses its prompts to construct six passive voice questions about people and places mentioned in this unit. Then each team creates two questions of its own, for a total of eight questions. The other team answers each question in a complete sentence. Add definite articles and put verbs in the past where necessary. For answers, see page G-AK3.

EXAMPLE: continents / connect by / Isthmus of Panama

A: Which continents are connected by the Isthmus of Panama?
B: North and South America are connected by the Isthmus of Panama.

Team A's Prompts

1. island / compose of / nations of Haiti, Dominican Republic
2. Central American country / border by / Panama, Nicaragua
3. people / consider by some / be / descendants of Atlanteans
4. legendary creature / think / live / Himalayas
5. individual / claim / be / assassin / U.S. President John F. Kennedy
6. individuals / regard / great humanitarians
7. ______________________________
8. ______________________________

Team B's Prompts

1. Caribbean nation / compose of / many islands
2. Caribbean nation / locate / about 90 miles south of Florida
3. forest creature / say / live / Pacific Northwest
4. lost continent / think / be located / Atlantic Ocean
5. planet / think / be / center of the universe / before Copernicus
6. presidents / regard by many / greatest American presidents
7. ______________________________
8. ______________________________

EXERCISE 9: Picture Discussion

A | *GROUPS: Look at the pictures. In small groups, talk about each of the people in the photos, using passive constructions.*

EXAMPLE: Albert Einstein is considered one of the greatest scientists of all time.

Albert Einstein

Mother Teresa

Queen Elizabeth I

Vincent van Gogh

B | *Discuss the quality of the individuals' contributions to culture. Who has made the most significant contributions? Share your conclusions with the class.*

Example: **A:** We believe the most significant contribution to world culture has been made by ________.

B: Why do you think so?

EXERCISE 10: Writing

A | *Write a five-paragraph summary of a legend or myth from your culture or another you are familiar with. Use passives to describe situations and report opinions.*

Example: My favorite American myth is the story of Paul Bunyan. Paul was a giant of a man who is said to have lived in the North Woods of Minnesota. He was a lumberjack who had great strength, and he also had a gigantic blue ox named Babe. The story of Paul and Babe is probably considered the most famous American myth. Here's how Paul got his start in life . . .

B | *Check your work. Use the Editing Checklist.*

Editing Checklist

Did you use . . . ?

- ☐ passives to describe situations correctly
- ☐ passives with ***it*** and ***that*** clauses correctly
- ☐ passives with ***to*** phrases correctly

UNIT 15 Review

Check your answers on page UR-2.
Do you need to review anything?

A | *Circle the word or phrase that correctly completes each sentence.*

1. Spain bordered by / is bordered by Portugal to the west and France to the north.
2. Europeans and Africans are regarded as / that the ancestors of the Nacirema.
3. It claims / is claimed that the nation of Atlantis actually existed.
4. The body is believed to be / is considered that it is ugly in Nacirema culture.
5. Gebru and I are related to / by marriage.
6. The capital locates in / is located in the center of the nation.
7. Bigfoot is thought to / thinks to live in the forests of the Pacific Northwest.
8. The Basques allege / are alleged to have come from Atlantis.

B | *Correct the mistakes in the underlined words.*

1. Denmark is bordered of Germany on the south. ____________
2. The yeti says to live in the Himalayas. ____________
3. An island is an area of land that surrounds on all sides by water. ____________
4. The Nacirema allege to be related to Europeans and Africans. ____________
5. Ilya and Irina believe to come from Ukraine. ____________
6. It is claiming by some that Homer was not one single person. ____________
7. Indonesia is composed from many islands, some large and some small. ____________
8. Mother Teresa regards as a great humanitarian. ____________

C | *Circle the letter of the one underlined word or phrase in each sentence that is not correct.*

1. It (A) is (B) regarded (C) that (D) Native Americans came originally from Asia. **A B C D**
2. It (A) says (B) by scholars (C) that Basque is unrelated (D) to other languages. **A B C D**
3. The yeti claimed (A) by witnesses (B) to be (C) covered (D) with long brown hair. **A B C D**
4. The culture is (A) assumed (B) by experts (C) date (D) from the year 3000 B.C.E. **A B C D**

From Grammar to Writing

PARALLEL STRUCTURE: NOUNS, ARTICLES, AND VOICE

Parallel structure (also called **parallelism**) is an important feature of English that makes our speaking, and especially our writing, easier to understand. You will strengthen your writing by making sure that appropriate items are in parallel structure. To do this, put all **items in a series** in the same grammatical form.

Examples: Over the weekend I **bought a new car**, **painted the living room**, and **planted a garden**. *(All three verbs in the predicate are in the simple past and in the active voice.)*

The prisoner was **arrested**, **taken** to the police station, **booked**, and **fingerprinted**. *(All four verbs are in the simple past and in the passive voice.)*

On her shopping trip, Mrs. Figueroa bought **a book**, **a dress**, and **a CD**. *(All three count nouns are preceded by the indefinite article.)*

We will concentrate in this Part on parallel structure with nouns and articles and with active or passive voice. See Part VII **From Grammar to Writing**, pages 303–306, for a discussion of parallel structure with gerunds and infinitives.

1 | *Read the text and correct the four mistakes in parallel structure with nouns and articles.*

Rolleen Laing poured herself a second cup of coffee as she ate her breakfast, which consisted of a fried egg, orange, and a piece of dry toast. She was 62 years old and had been successful as a university professor, writer of detective fiction, and an amateur detective. Just then the telephone rang. It was Harry Sadler, a local police detective. Ever since Rolleen had helped Harry crack a murder case several years previously, she had been called in as an unofficial consultant on several cases. She had helped Harry solve cases involving a hit-and-run victim, a murdered TV executive, and, most recently, koala stolen from the city zoo.

"Hi, Rolleen. This is Harry. You're needed on another case. It's a robbery this time. Some thieves broke into the art museum and stole a van Gogh, a Picasso, Gauguin, and a Matisse. Meet me at the museum at 10:00, OK?"

2 | *Read this paragraph about the Judge Crater mystery. Correct the five mistakes in parallel structure with the active or passive voice.*

On the evening of August 6, 1930, Judge Joseph Force Crater, a wealthy, successful, and good-looking New Yorker, disappeared without a trace. Earlier in the evening he had been seen with friends at a Manhattan restaurant, and they observed him departing. At 9:10 P.M. he walked out the door of the restaurant and hailed a taxi. He was soon driven away. No one ever saw or heard from him again. It was 10 days before he was even reported missing. On August 16, his wife called his courthouse, the secretary was asked of his whereabouts, and learned that he was probably off on political business. This news reassured Mrs. Crater somewhat, but when he still hadn't turned up by August 26, a group of his fellow judges started an investigation. A grand jury was convened, but its members could not come to any conclusion as to what had happened to Judge Crater. They theorized that the judge might have developed amnesia, might have run away voluntarily, or been a crime victim. His wife disagreed with the first two possibilities, holding that he had been murdered by someone in the Tammany Hall organization, the political machine that controlled New York City at the time. The mystery remains unsolved to this day. Crater could have been killed by a Tammany Hall agent, a girlfriend could have murdered him, or kidnapped by an organized crime group. He might, in fact, have suffered from amnesia, or his own disappearance might have been planned by him. Reports of Judge Crater sightings have continued to surface over the last several decades.

3 | *Before you write . . .*

1. Most of us are intrigued by unsolved mysteries and by unusual experiences. Think of an unsolved mystery that you are aware of or an unusual or mysterious experience that you have had.
2. Describe your mystery or unusual experience to a partner. Listen to your partner's description.
3. Ask and answer questions about your and your partner's topic. Why is the topic significant to you? What about it interests or touches you?

4 | *Write a draft of a composition about your unsolved mystery or unusual experience. Follow the model. Remember to include information that your partner asked about. Use at least one sentence containing passive voice verbs in parallel structure. Also include at least one sentence containing a series of nouns in parallel structure.*

The events of the mystery or unusual experience:

____

____

____

____

What specifically interests or touches me about the mystery or experience:

____

____

____

____

5 | *Exchange compositions with a different partner. Complete the chart.*

1. The writer used parallel series of passive voice verbs and of nouns and articles. **Yes** ☐ **No** ☐

2. What I liked in the composition:

____

____

____

3. Questions I'd like the writer to answer about the composition:

Who __________________________________?

What __________________________________?

When __________________________________?

Where __________________________________?

Why __________________________________?

How __________________________________?

(Your own question) __________________________?

6 | *Work with your partner. Discuss each other's chart from Exercise 5. Then rewrite your own composition and make any necessary changes.*

PART VII

GERUNDS AND INFINITIVES

UNIT	GRAMMAR FOCUS	THEME
16	Gerunds	Friendship
17	Infinitives	Procrastination

UNIT 16 Gerunds
FRIENDSHIP

STEP 1 GRAMMAR IN CONTEXT

Before You Read

PAIRS: Discuss the questions.

1. What do you value in friendships?
2. Are all of your friends the same type of friend (for example, long-term friends, special-interest friends), or are some different types of friends?

Read

Read the article about types of friends.

POPULAR PSYCHOLOGY

FRIENDS

by Jim Garcia

I was having difficulty **finding** a subject for this month's column until I remembered a childhood rhyme that went like this: "True friends are diamonds, precious and rare; false friends are oak leaves that fall anywhere." But are friendships really that black and white? This was my childhood concept, but I suspect my perception was pretty naive. I've long since stopped **thinking** in these terms. Some friends are true and others false, but there are many different types of "true" friends. In fact, I can recognize at least six types:

Type 1: Convenience Friends

These are the friends we make when our schedules and activities coincide. Years ago I played on a soccer team. I didn't have a way of **getting** to the practices and tried **taking** the bus, but it always got me there late. Then I learned that Andrés, a team member, lived near me. He had a car, and it was convenient for him to pick me up. We became friends by **riding** with each other and developed a good relationship. We didn't get together outside the soccer context, though.

Type 2: Special-interest friends

My brother, whose passion is **kayaking**, belongs to a kayaking club. He's made several good buddies at meetings and on river trips. They have great times, and **living** through dangerous experiences has made them close. Once the trips are over, though, they don't socialize with each other. Their special interest, kayaking, is the only thing that holds them together.

Type 3: Long-term friends

I have several of these, but my best long-time friend is a guy named Al. We've known each other since we were 12, and our friendship links our past to our present. We

FRIENDS

can go months without **contacting** each other, but whenever we do make contact it seems like we were together yesterday. We enjoy just **catching up on** each other's activities. We'd like to spend more time together, but it doesn't seem to matter if we don't.

Type 4: Cross-generational friends

We most often seek friends in our own age group, but cross-generational friendships are worth **pursuing**. My friend Bill is an example. He's about 25 years older than I am—a kind of father figure. He's more than that, though. Actually, Bill was my teacher in a university writing class. I was having trouble **figuring** out my career, but Bill supported my **becoming** a writer, and that's what I did. After the class was over, we became friends.

Type 5: Part-of-a-couple friends

My wife Amanda and Bill's wife Gretta are good examples of this common type of friendship. When our partner has a friend in another couple, we have to go through the often difficult process of **getting** to know the "other person" in that couple. People may feel they have little or nothing in common with their counterpart and may even rebel against **socializing** with a "friend" they didn't choose. Fortunately, Amanda and Gretta have become good friends on their own through their common interest in **collecting** rare books.

Type 6: "Best" friends

To me a best friend is a person with whom we don't have a problem **being** honest or vulnerable. It's someone who will never desert you, who keeps no record of wrongs, who doesn't spare your feelings or avoid **telling** you what you need to hear. I have two best friends. One is Ken, whom I met in the military. Our **having gone** through difficult experiences has bonded us for life. The other is Amanda. We love **having** long conversations that can meander everywhere and nowhere. Sometimes we talk for hours. We both love **being listened to**. Other times we like **being** together without **saying** much of anything. I would have a hard time **living** without my two "best" friends, but it's awfully important to have the others too.

After You Read

A | Vocabulary: *Match the blue words and phrases on the left with their meanings on the right.*

D 1. I now see that my perceiving friendship in this way was **naive**.

F 2. These are the friends we make when our schedules and activities **coincide**.

G 3. We didn't get together outside the soccer **context**, though.

E 4. We enjoy just **catching up on** each other's activities.

A 5. People may feel they have little or nothing in common with their **counterpart**.

C 6. A best friend is a person with whom we don't have a problem being honest or **vulnerable**.

H 7. It's someone who doesn't **spare your feelings**.

B 8. We love having conversations that can **meander** everywhere and nowhere.

a. person having a parallel position

b. move without a goal in mind

c. undefended

d. having or showing no experience

e. getting up to date with

f. happen at the same time

g. conditions in which something occurs

h. avoid hurting someone's ego

B | Comprehension: *Refer to the reading and complete each sentence with a single word.*

1. Convenience friends are those you make when your schedules and activities coincide.
2. The author's brother met a lot of friends through Kayaking, his special interest.
3. The author and his long-term friend Al can go months without contaching each other.
4. A cross-generational friend is someone from a different generation/age group.
5. The author's cross-generational friend Bill supported his becoming a writer.
6. A spouse may object to being with a friend he or she didn't choose.
7. A best friend is someone with whom you can easily be honest or vulnerable.
8. The author and his wife both place great importance on being listened to.

STEP 2 GRAMMAR PRESENTATION

GERUNDS

Gerund as Subject		
Gerund (Subject)	**Verb**	**Object**
Kayaking	involves	some risks.
Swimming	builds	endurance.
Not inviting him	will cause	resentment.

Gerund as Object		
Subject	**Verb**	**Gerund (Object)**
They	enjoy	**kayaking**.
I	went	**swimming**.
We	don't advise	**not inviting** him.

Gerund as Subject Complement		
Subject	**Verb**	**Gerund (Subject Complement)**
My sport	is	**skiing**.
His problem	is	**not exercising**.

Gerund as Object Complement			
Subject	**Verb**	**Object**	**Gerund (Object Complement)**
He	spends	time	**reading**.
She	found	him	**not working**.

Gerund as Object of a Preposition			
	Preposition	**Gerund**	
She insists	**on**	**going out**	every weekend.
He's accustomed	**to**	**giving**	parties.
They have a reason	**for**	**not inviting**	Michael.

Possessive + Gerund			
	Possessive	**Gerund**	
Bob and Helen worry about	**Emily's** **her** **the children's** **their**	**having**	so few friends.

Active and Passive Gerunds		
	Active Gerunds	**Passive Gerunds**
SIMPLE	**Inviting** them to her wedding was a nice gesture on her part.	**Being invited** to her wedding was a great surprise to them.
PAST	**Having invited** them to her wedding made her feel good.	**Having been invited** to her wedding is a fond memory for them.

GRAMMAR NOTES

go shopping

1	A **gerund** is a noun made from a verb. To form a gerund, add *-ing* to the base form of the verb. Gerunds and gerund phrases perform the same functions as nouns: **a.** They act as subjects. **b.** They act as objects. **c.** They act as complements (phrases that describe or explain the subject or object of a sentence). Add *not* before a gerund to make a negative statement.	• **Cooking** is my hobby. I like **eating** too. • **Talking** with friends is enjoyable. • I love **getting together** with friends. • Our favorite activity is **playing** cards. *(subject complement)* • She has trouble **making** friends. *(object complement)* • **Not calling** her was a big mistake.
2	Many verbs and verb phrases in English have **gerunds as objects**. Common examples are *avoid, consider, enjoy, keep, mind.* We often use ***go* + gerund** to talk about recreational activities: *go skiing, go swimming, go hiking,* etc.	• I **enjoy meeting** new people. • You should **avoid working** late. • We **go skiing** every weekend in the winter.
3	Gerunds act as **objects of prepositions**. Many preposition combinations are followed by gerunds: **a.** verb + preposition **b.** adjective + preposition **BE CAREFUL!** The word ***to*** can be a preposition or part of an infinitive.	• I made friends **by joining** a club. • They **insisted on giving** us a present. • She's **good at making** friends. • He will adjust **to working** hard. *(**To** is a preposition.)* • He tries **to work** hard. *(**To** is part of the infinitive.)*
4	In writing and formal speaking, use a **possessive** noun or pronoun **before a gerund** to show possession. **USAGE NOTE:** In conversation, native speakers often use a name or an object pronoun before a gerund.	• **Pete's dominating** every conversation bothers me. • **His dominating** every conversation bothers me. • I don't like **Pete dominating** every conversation. (Noun) • I don't like **him dominating** every conversation.

what do you look forward to doing?
- I look forward to enjoying my life.
I appreciate Pauline's giving me advice.
object

5	
Gerunds can occur in simple or past form. We can use a **simple gerund** (without a past participle) to make a generalization.	• **Making** friends is a natural thing to do.
We can use a **past gerund** (*having* + past participle) to show an action that occurred before the action of the main verb in the sentence.	• **Having met** Jane in my first week of college **helped** me throughout my college career.
NOTE: We use a past gerund to emphasize the difference in time between two actions. The simple gerund is also correct in many situations.	• **Having gone** to college is one of the best things **I've ever done.** OR • **Going** to college is one of the best things **I've ever done.**
Gerunds can occur in **passive** form. In the present, use *being* + past participle. In the past, use *having been* + past participle.	• She hates **being ignored**. • She's still angry at **having been ignored**.
BE CAREFUL! Many words in English end in *-ing*. Do not confuse gerunds with verbs in the progressive form or with present participles used as adjectives or in adverb phrases.	• I've been **making** friends at work. *(progressive form)* • Mary is enrolled in a **cooking** class. *(as adjective)* • **Walking** on the beach, I wondered why she was angry at me. *(adverb phrase)*

REFERENCE NOTES

For a list of common **verbs followed by gerunds**, see Appendix 12 on page A-6.
For a list of common **adjective + preposition combinations followed by gerunds**, see Appendix 16 on page A-8.

STEP 3 FOCUSED PRACTICE

EXERCISE 1: Discover the Grammar

A | *Read the sentences. Is the gerund used as a subject* (**S**), *an object* (**O**), *an object of a preposition* (**OP**), *or a subject or object complement* (**C**)?

____ **1.** I was having difficulty finding a subject.
____ **2.** I remembered learning a rhyme.
____ **3.** I didn't have a way of getting to the practices.
____ **4.** My brother's passion is kayaking.
____ **5.** We can go months without contacting each other.
____ **6.** I was having trouble figuring out my career.
____ **7.** Bill supported my becoming a writer.
____ **8.** I would have a hard time living without my two "best" friends.

B | *Are the* -ing *words in the sentences gerunds? Write* **Y (Yes)** *or* **N (No).**

___ **1.** I've long since stopped thinking of friendship in these terms.

___ **2.** These are the friends we make by engaging in some specific activity.

___ **3.** He belongs to a kayaking club.

___ **4.** We enjoy just catching up on each other's activities.

___ **5.** Cross-generational friendships are worth pursuing.

___ **6.** He was my teacher in a writing class.

___ **7.** They have become good friends on their own through their common interest in collecting rare books.

___ **8.** I would have a hard time being single again.

EXERCISE 2: Simple Gerunds

(Grammar Notes 1–4)

A | *Brian Hansen is constantly tired and dissatisfied. He has gone to a doctor to see if there is anything physically wrong with him. Complete the conversation with gerunds. Make the gerunds negative if necessary.*

Doctor: Well, Brian, what seems to be the problem?

Brian: I'm tired all the time. Some nights when I come home from work I'm so exhausted I don't feel like ___ (1. do) anything but collapsing on the sofa and ___ (2. vegetate) in front of the TV. Is there anything physically wrong with me?

Doctor: No, I've looked at your test results, and you're healthy. How long have you been feeling like this?

Brian: Oh, two or three months, I guess. Long enough so that I've begun ___ (3. worry) about ___ (4. have) any energy. Basically I'm not doing anything besides punching a time clock.

Doctor: How much are you working?

Brian: Well, I'm putting in a lot of overtime—all in all, at least 60 hours a week, I'd say.

Doctor: Why are you doing this? Are you trying to make yourself sick?

Brian: Well, at this point, ___ (5. work) overtime is out of the question. I've got a lot of bills to pay off. The other thing is that I only recently moved here, and I hardly know anyone, so my focus is on ___ (6. make) money for a while. I like ___ (7. socialize), and I really miss ___ (8. have) close friends, but I don't know quite how to go about ___ (9. meet) new people.

DOCTOR: You're not married, then?

BRIAN: No, not yet.

DOCTOR: Well, I think you need to stop __________ (10. work) so much and start __________ (11. play) a little—to put things in balance. I'd say you need a hobby—and some friends.

BRIAN: A hobby? You mean some boring thing like stamp __________ (12. collect)?

DOCTOR: No. That's an OK hobby if you like it, but there are more interesting ones.

BRIAN: Like what?

DOCTOR: Oh, maybe like karaoke. Do you like __________ (13. sing)?

BRIAN: I love music, but I don't have much of a voice. In my case, __________ (14. sing) is better than __________ (15. sing) off key.

DOCTOR: Well, have you ever gone __________ (16. orienteer)?

BRIAN: What's that?

DOCTOR: It's a contest. People use a map and a compass and try to be the first person to find locations of hidden clues.

BRIAN: Sounds interesting. Where can I find out more about it?

DOCTOR: I've got a friend who belongs to an orienteering club. I'll give you her number.

BRIAN: Super. Thanks.

B | *Complete the sentences with a possessive noun or pronoun and a gerund.*

1. I have two best friends, Bob and Mary. Bob is my co-worker. I'm grateful for ____*his giving*____ (he / give) me a ride to work every day.
2. I'm new to the firm, so I also appreciate __________ (Bob / help) me learn my job.
3. __________ (My boss / criticize) my work is hard to deal with, so Bob's encouragement is vital.
4. Mary is my neighbor. __________ (She / live) so close is wonderful.
5. I especially appreciate __________ (Mary / advise) me on tough issues.
6. She knows how to deal with __________ (I / become) discouraged.
7. I couldn't ask for two better friends than Bob and Mary. I'm thankful for __________ (they / be) there for me when I need them.
8. __________ (We / get) together frequently helps us stay close.

EXERCISE 3: Simple / Past Gerunds

(*Grammar Note 5*)

Complete the sentences with simple gerunds or past gerunds with **having** *+ past participle. Use a past gerund if it is possible to do so.*

Martha, who is 20 years older than I am, is my best cross-generational friend. ____________ **1. (meet)** her when I was an unhappy college sophomore is one of the best things that has ever happened to me. Martha and I have stayed friends. I look forward to ____________ **2. (see)** her whenever our schedules permit. Our relationship hasn't always been smooth, though. Martha and I were both in the same calculus class. I was having a lot of difficulty and was angry at myself for ____________ **3. (enroll)** in a class I didn't need for my degree. It was too late to drop the class, however, and since I was frustrated, I frequently got irritated with the teacher for ____________ **4. (assign)** so much difficult homework every day. Martha stopped me one day after class. She said she was tired of my continual ____________ **5. (argue)** with the teacher. "You need to grow up," she said. I was offended at first, but the older I get the clearer it is to me that her ____________ **6. (say)** that is one of the major events in my life. I had to change my negative attitude. I did need to grow up. A few days later I asked Martha if she would mind ____________ **7. (study)** with me and ____________ **8. (help)** me with the homework. She agreed. With a lot of patient work, I succeeded in ____________ **9. (pass)** the course. Eventually we became great friends. I suspect that most of us know someone whose ____________ **10. (tell)** us what we needed to hear when we needed to hear it has made a difference in our life. Martha has certainly made a difference in mine.

EXERCISE 4: Active / Passive Gerunds

(Grammar Notes 2, 4)

A | *Write a question using a passive gerund and an active gerund.*

Example: (like / awaken / by an alarm clock) (wake up / on your own)
Do you like **being awakened** by an alarm clock or **waking up** on your own?

passive active

1. (prefer / ask out on a date) (ask / someone / yourself)

   Do you prefere being asked out on a date or asking someone by yourself

2. (more interested in / entertain / yourself) (in / entertain / by others)

   Would it be more interested in entertaining yourself or in being entertained by others.

3. (prefer / prepare dinner / yourself) (invite / to dinner / by friends)

   Do you prefer preparing dinner yourself or being invited to dinner by friends?

4. (like / tell / what to do) (give / orders)

   Do you like being told what to do or giving orders.

5. (like / figure things out / yourself) (show / how to do things)

   Do you like figuring things out yourself or being shown how to do things?

6. (prefer / give / advice by friends) (give / your friends / advice)

   Do you prefer being given advice by friends or giving your friends advice ?

B | *PAIRS: Take turns asking and answering the questions.*

Example: **A:** Do you like being awakened by an alarm clock or waking up on your own?
B: I like waking up on my own. I hate being awakened by an alarm clock. What about you?

HW

EXERCISE 5: Editing

The letter has ten mistakes in the use of gerunds. The first mistake is already corrected. Find and correct nine more.

Dear Adam,

I've been here for three days and am having a great time, but I can't help ~~wish~~ wishing you were here too. Tell your boss I'm really angry at him. His not let you take any vacation time qualifies him for the Jerk-of-the-Year Award. (Just kidding. Don't say that!)

Believe it or not, the first night I missed hearing all the city noises, but I haven't really had any trouble to get used to the peace and quiet since then. Everything's so relaxed here—there's no rush around or write things down in your Daily Planner. Get out of New York City was definitely what I needed, even if it's only for two weeks. The ranch has lots of activities—horseback ride, river raft on the Rio Grande, hiking in the wilderness—you name it. The ranch employees do everything for you—being taken care of is nice for a change, and I love being chauffeured around Santa Fe in the ranch limousine. Tonight a group of us are going out to a country and western dance place called Rodeo Nites in Santa Fe, so having taken those two-step dance lessons last summer will come in handy. It's just too bad you couldn't come along so we could both have a good time. Tomorrow we're all going to Taos Pueblo to watch some weaving being done and to see some Native American dancing, which is great because I'm really interested in learn more about Native American culture. And I'm looking forward to see *Carmen* at the Santa Fe Opera on Saturday.

I'll write again in a day or two. Miss you lots.

Love,

Louise

STEP 4 COMMUNICATION PRACTICE

EXERCISE 6: Listening

A | *Brian Hansen and Jane Travanti are having a telephone conversation about the orienteering club Jane belongs to. Listen to the conversation. Answer both questions in a complete sentence.*

1. What is one requirement for participating in the club activities?

____

2. What will Brian use to find Darcy's Coffee Shop if he has trouble locating it?

____

B | *Listen again and check (✓)* **True** *or* **False.**

	True	False
1. Brian has tried orienteering before.	☐	☑
2. Dr. Stevens wants Brian to stop working.	☐	☐
3. Being experienced in orienteering is necessary to join Jane's club.	☐	☐
4. Jane's club tries to go orienteering at least twice a month.	☐	☐
5. In the summer, they get around by biking.	☐	☐
6. In the winter, they get around by cross-country skiing.	☐	☐
7. Brian has done cross-country skiing before.	☐	☐
8. Being single is a requirement for joining the club.	☐	☐
9. The club collects dues to pay for organizing their activities.	☐	☐
10. On the 15th, they'll get to the forest by carpooling.	☐	☐

EXERCISE 7: Pronunciation

A | *Read and listen to the Pronunciation Note.*

Pronunciation Note

We distinguish nouns and verbs that have the same spelling by modifying the stress. Nouns (and adjectives) have the stress on the first syllable. Verbs have it on the second syllable.

EXAMPLES: There are several interesting **ob**jects on the table. *(noun—stress on syllable 1)*
Mary ob**jects** to my working late hours. *(verb—stress on syllable 2)*

B | *Listen to the sentences. Circle the stressed syllable in each boldfaced word.*

1. I predict that the **rebel** will **rebel** against the plan.

2. The **suspect** I **suspect** is the one on the far left.

3. The band is going to **record** a new **record** for their album.

4. A **desert** is a place that people **desert**.

5. The dictator is going to **subject** the **subject** to difficult questioning.

6. The students are going to **present** their teacher with a wonderful **present**.

C | *PAIRS: Practice the sentences.*

EXERCISE 8: Personal Inventory

A | *Using events in your own life, complete the sentences with gerunds or gerund phrases.*

EXAMPLE: I especially enjoy **playing** board games with friends.

1. I especially enjoy ______________________________.
2. I have stopped ______________________________.
3. I've always avoided ______________________________.
4. I have trouble ______________________________.
5. I spend a lot of time ______________________________.
6. I'm looking forward to ______________________________.
7. I'm still not used to ______________________________.
8. I strongly dislike ______________________________.
9. On weekends I don't feel like ______________________________.
10. If you visit my country, I recommend ______________________________.

B | *PAIRS: Discuss your answers to the questions. Report interesting answers to the class.*

EXERCISE 9: Group Discussion

A | *What do you value in friendships? Add your own item to the chart. Then complete the chart for yourself by rating each item.*

3 = Very Important in a Friendship   2 = Somewhat Important in a Friendship   1 = Not Important in a Friendship

	Rating
Giving each other presents	
Always being honest with one another	
Not hurting each other's feelings	
Giving help whenever it is asked for	
Lending money if it is asked for	

B | *SMALL GROUPS: Discuss your answers with three classmates. Report your overall results to the class.*

EXERCISE 10: Writing

A | *Look at the categories of friendship in the opening reading. Choose one of the categories and write five or more paragraphs about a friend of yours who fits into it. Use gerunds and gerund phrases in your composition.*

Example: I have a friend named Sarah who perfectly fits the category of long-time friend. Sarah and I met when we were in the fifth grade, when I had just moved to a new town and didn't know anyone. Ever since Sarah and I became friends, we've enjoyed sharing all kinds of experiences and can't go more than a month or so without contacting each other. Making friends wasn't that easy at first, however . . .

B | *Check your work. Use the Editing Checklist.*

Editing Checklist

Did you use . . . ?

- ☐ gerunds as subjects correctly
- ☐ gerunds as objects correctly
- ☐ gerunds as complements correctly
- ☐ gerunds with prepositions correctly

UNIT 16 Review

Check your answers on page UR-3.
Do you need to review anything?

A | *Circle the word or phrase that correctly completes each sentence.*

1. Thank you very much for not to smoke / not smoking.
2. We go shopping / to have shopped every Saturday.
3. I'm bothered by Emiko's / Emiko is talking so loudly.
4. Me not giving / Not giving myself enough time to get to work was a mistake.
5. Carlos is used to have / to having his family near him.
6. People with glaucoma have difficulty to see / seeing.
7. Most people dislike being awakened / being awaken by an alarm clock.
8. Pavlina was annoyed at not having been invited / not to be invited.

B | *Correct the mistakes in the underlined words or phrases.*

1. Max has trouble to finish his work on time. ________
2. Missing my flight, I'll have to wait six hours for the next one. ________
3. We were bothered by his come in without asking permission. ________
4. Yoshi has stopped to drive to work and is now walking. ________
5. Li hates told what to do; he prefers making his own decisions. ________
6. Going to the movie was a good idea; it's definitely worth to see. ________
7. We're excited about Walid's having taking the job. ________
8. I suggest not to mention anything political to Dad. ________

C | *Circle the letter of the one underlined word or phrase in each sentence that is not correct.*

1. Mary's (A) invite (B) them (C) to the get-together was surprising (D) to us. **A B C D**
2. Be (A) invited (B) to (C) her get-together was astonishing (D) to them. **A B C D**
3. Bob is feeling (A) sad about not (B) have (C) called (D) you when he was in town. **A B C D**
4. Emiko is concerned about (A) her children's (B) not (C) have (D) any friends. **A B C D**

UNIT 17

Infinitives

PROCRASTINATION

STEP 1 GRAMMAR IN CONTEXT

Before You Read

PAIRS: Discuss the questions.

1. What is procrastination?
2. What are the dangers of procrastination?
3. Do you ever procrastinate? If so, in what situations?

Read

Read the article about procrastination.

SEIZE THE DAY

by Jessica Taylor

Picture this scenario: It's Sunday evening. Steve's sister Alice has a term paper due tomorrow. It's written in longhand, but it has **to be typed**. Alice doesn't type well.

ALICE: Steve, can you type my paper? It's due tomorrow.

STEVE: Alice, my friends are coming in half an hour, and I'm trying **to finish** something. I can't stop **to type** your paper now.

ALICE: But, Steve, you **have to**. I can't do it myself. It'll take me all night.

STEVE: Why didn't you ask me before now?

ALICE: I **forgot to**. I really did plan **to ask**. Steve, you've got to do it, or I'll flunk. Please?

STEVE: No, Alice, there's not enough time **to do** it now. You go start typing.

PROCRASTINATION
"Never put off until tomorrow what you can do the day after tomorrow."

(*continued on next page*)

SEIZE THE DAY

Does this situation ring a bell? It illustrates the problem of procrastination, which I asked psychiatrist Robert Stevens **to talk about**.

TAYLOR: I want **to ask** you if there's such a thing as a procrastination syndrome.

STEVENS: Well, I don't know if we can call it a syndrome, but for many people procrastination is a very serious problem.

TAYLOR: Can we start with a definition of procrastination?

STEVENS: Of course. **To procrastinate** is literally **to put** things **off** until tomorrow. It's a postponing of events until a later time. But unlike the word "postpone," which has a neutral sense, the word "procrastinate" has a negative connotation. There are sometimes good reasons **to postpone** things, but never **to procrastinate**. Procrastinating has the sense of avoidance.

TAYLOR: All right. Now what causes people **to procrastinate**? Supposedly it's laziness, isn't it?

STEVENS: That's a popular idea, but I'd have to say that laziness isn't the major cause. No, I think that fear is really the most important force that motivates people **to put** things **off**.

TAYLOR: Fear? Not laziness? Can you explain?

STEVENS: Well, it's like the expectation syndrome. People do what others expect in order **to live up to** their expectations. Procrastinators are afraid **to fail** or make mistakes, or maybe they don't want **to be rejected**. Interestingly, procrastination has nothing **to do** with education. Some of the most learned people are among the worst procrastinators.

TAYLOR: What would be an example of that?

STEVENS: Well, let's see . . . Suppose someone—a young woman we'll call Blanche—has been planning a party. She's mentioned the party to friends but has put off making any actual invitations. Either consciously or subconsciously, she expects **to fail**, so she delays calling people until the very last moment. Her friends expected her **to have called** them before now, and when she didn't they forgot about the event and made other plans. It's too short notice for most of them **to come**. Blanche's fear has caused things **to turn out** like this. She feels wretched about it, but she doesn't know how **to change**.

TAYLOR: Mmm-hmm. Well, what if a procrastinator would like **to change**? What would you advise that person **to do**?

STEVENS: Getting a procrastinator **to change** can be a tough nut **to crack**, but I recommend three principles for my clients. The first is never **to put off** until tomorrow what needs **to be done** today. **Not to avoid** painful or difficult things is the second. They're part of life. The third is contained in the Latin phrase *carpe diem*—"seize the day." I try **to consider** every experience an opportunity. I don't want people **to take** unnecessary or foolish risks, but I do advise them **not to put off** living. They may not get another chance.

TAYLOR: Well, Dr. Stevens, thanks for another stimulating discussion.

After You Read

A | Vocabulary: *Match the **blue** words and phrases on the left with their meanings on the right.*

____	**1.** Picture this **scenario**.	**a.** difficult problem to solve
____	**2.** The paper is written in **longhand**.	**b.** fail
____	**3.** Steve, you've got to do it, or I'll **flunk**.	**c.** educated
____	**4.** Does this situation **ring a bell**?	**d.** terrible
____	**5.** The word *procrastinate* has a negative **connotation**.	**e.** description of a possible situation
____	**6.** Some of the most **learned** people are among the worst procrastinators.	**f.** not in a machine-produced form
____	**7.** She feels **wretched** about her failure.	**g.** remind one of something
____	**8.** Getting a procrastinator to change can be a **tough nut to crack**.	**h.** meaning additional to the basic meaning

B | Comprehension: *Circle* **T (True)** *or* **F (False)**. *Correct the false statements.*

1. Steve is not going to type Alice's term paper. **T** **F**

2. The word *postpone* has a positive sense. **T** **F**

3. To procrastinate is literally to put things off until tomorrow. **T** **F**

4. Dr. Stevens believes it is sometimes appropriate to procrastinate. **T** **F**

5. Dr. Stevens believes that fear is the major cause of procrastination. **T** **F**

6. According to Dr. Stevens, procrastinators are afraid to fail. **T** **F**

7. Dr. Stevens believes it is sometimes permissible to avoid difficult or painful things. **T** **F**

8. Dr. Stevens thinks it is good to consider every experience an opportunity. **T** **F**

STEP 2 GRAMMAR PRESENTATION

INFINITIVES

Infinitive as Subject		
Infinitive (Subject)	**Verb**	**Object**
To procrastinate	causes	a lot of problems.
Not to go ahead	proved	a mistake.

Infinitive as Object		
Subject	**Verb**	**Infinitive (Object)**
Not everyone	wants	**to procrastinate**.
He	decided	**not to go ahead**.

Infinitive as Subject Complement			
Subject	**Verb**	**Infinitive (Subject Complement)**	
His job	is	**to motivate**	people.
Their real intention	is	**not to succeed**.	

It + Infinitive				
It	***Be***	**Adjective**	**(*For* / *Of* + Noun / Pronoun)**	**Infinitive**
It	is	foolish	(for Alice / her)	**to procrastinate**.
It	was	wrong	(of Hal / him)	**not to go ahead**.

Verbs Followed by Infinitives			
	Verb	**(Noun / Pronoun)**	**Infinitive**
They	**decided / hoped / neglected**, etc.	Ø*	**to call**.
	convinced / told / urged, etc.	Steve / him	
	expected / needed / wanted, etc.	(Steve / him)	

*Ø = not used

Adjectives Followed by Infinitives			
	Adjective	**Infinitive**	
Hal is	**reluctant**	**to complete**	his work on time.
He's	**careful**	**not to make**	mistakes.
They're	**happy**	**to hear**	the test has been postponed.

Nouns Followed by Infinitives			
	Noun	**Infinitive**	
He can always think of	**reasons**	**to put off**	studying.
It seems like	**the thing**	**to do**.	
She always shows	**reluctance**	**to finish**	a job.

Too / Enough with Infinitives			
	Too **+ Adjective / Adverb**	**Infinitive**	
The project is	**too** complicated	**to finish**	on time.
Alice types	**too** slowly	**to meet**	the deadline.
	Adjective / Adverb + ***Enough***	**Infinitive**	
Steve is	intelligent **enough**	**to understand**	the situation.
He didn't call	quickly **enough**	**to get**	the job.
	Enough **+ Noun**	**Infinitive**	
They have	**enough** intelligence	**to pass**	the test.
	intelligence **enough**		

Active and Passive Infinitives		
	Active Infinitives	**Passive Infinitives**
Simple Past	She plans **to invite** them.	They expect **to be invited**.
	She was glad **to have invited** them.	They were happy **to have been invited**.

GRAMMAR NOTES

1

An **infinitive** is *to* plus the base form of a verb. Infinitives and infinitive phrases often perform the same functions as nouns.

- **To graduate** from college is important. I want **to do** that.

a. They act as subjects.

- **To finish** what you started is advisable.

NOTE: Using an infinitive as a subject is formal. *It* + an infinitive phrase is more common. We often add *for* + a noun or pronoun to say who or what does the action.

- **It's** advisable **to finish** what you started.
- **It's** important **for a student to take** good notes in class.

b. They act as objects.

- I'd like **to invite** you to dinner.

c. They act as subject complements (phrases that describe or explain the subject of a sentence).

- A teacher's job is **to create** a desire to learn.

To make an infinitive negative, place *not* before *to*.

- I warned you **not to** put this off.

BE CAREFUL! Don't confuse *to* in an infinitive with *to* as a preposition. *To* in an infinitive is followed by the base form of the verb. *To* as a preposition is followed by a gerund, regular noun, or pronoun.

- I **plan to work** hard. *(infinitive)*
- **I'm used to working** hard. *(gerund)*

USAGE NOTE: To avoid repeating an infinitive just mentioned, replace the verb with *to*. This is called **ellipsis**.

- Steve knew he had to go to work, but he didn't want **to**.

(continued on next page)

2	Certain **verbs** are followed only by **infinitives**.	• She **offered to help** me. • He **learned to be** efficient.
	Other verbs are followed by a required noun or pronoun + an infinitive.	• I **warned Stan to make** the payments. Not: I warned ~~to make the payments~~.
	Still other verbs are followed by an optional noun or pronoun + an infinitive, depending on the meaning of the verb.	• We **expected to finish** on time. • We **expected Jim to finish** on time.
3	Certain **adjectives** can be followed by **infinitives**. These adjectives usually describe people, not things. They often express feelings about the action described in the infinitive. Common adjectives followed by infinitives: *afraid, amazed, excited, fortunate, glad, happy, important, likely, proud, reluctant, sorry,* and *willing*.	• George is **afraid to make** mistakes. • Mary is **not willing to help** us.
4	A **noun** is often followed by an **infinitive**. When this occurs, the infinitive gives information about the noun.	• Cozumel is a good **place to spend** a vacation. • Generosity is a good **trait to have**.
	A noun + infinitive often expresses advisability or necessity.	• Starting immediately is the **thing to do**.
5	**BE CAREFUL!** Remember that some verbs can be followed only by infinitives, others only by gerunds, and others by either infinitives or gerunds. These verbs fall into four patterns:	
	a. Examples of verbs and verb phrases followed only by infinitives: *appear, decide, expect, hope, manage, need, pretend, seem, want, would like*.	• They **managed to find** new jobs. • She **pretended to be** busy.
	b. Examples of verbs and verb phrases followed only by gerunds: *avoid, be worth, can't help, consider, enjoy, feel like, have trouble, keep, mind, miss, spend (time)*.	• We **considered hiring** him. • I don't **feel like working** today.
	c. Examples of verbs followed by infinitives or gerunds with no change in meaning: *begin, can't stand, continue, hate, like, love, prefer, start*.	• They **began to encourage** her. • They **began encouraging** her.
	d. Examples of verbs followed by infinitives or gerunds with a significant change in meaning: *forget, go on, quit, regret, remember, stop, try*.	• I **stopped / quit to go** to the movies. *(= I stopped / quit another activity in order to go to the movies.)* • I **stopped / quit going** to the movies. *(= I stopped / quit the activity of going to the movies.)*

6	The words ***too*** and ***enough*** are often used before infinitives. *Too* is used in the pattern *too* + adjective / adverb + infinitive. It implies a negative result.	• We're **too tired to do** any work today. • Sam started **too late to finish** on time.
	Enough + infinitive is used after an adjective / adverb.	• Ken is **strong enough to lift** 175 pounds. • Mia runs **fast enough to be** first.
	Enough can be used before a noun + infinitive.	• There's not **enough money to pay** for the repairs.
	Enough can also be used after a noun. This usage is formal.	• There is not **money enough to pay** for the repairs.
	NOTE: Add ***for*** **+ a noun or pronoun** to show who performs the action of the infinitive.	• There's not **enough money for Jane to pay** for the repairs.
7	Infinitives can occur in simple or past forms. We use a **simple infinitive** (without a past participle) to indicate an action in the same general time frame as the action in the main verb.	• I **expected** you **to call**.
	We use a **past infinitive** (*to* + *have* + past participle) to show an action that occurred before the action of the main verb in the sentence.	• You **seem to have forgotten** the report that was due today.
	Infinitives can occur in **passive** form. In the present, use *to* + *be* or *get* + past participle. In the past, use *to* + *have* + *been* + past participle. Use the past form to indicate an action that occurred before the action of the main verb.	• The work is supposed **to be finished** by tomorrow. • The work was **to have been done** before now.

REFERENCE NOTES

For a list of **verbs followed directly by infinitives**, see Appendix 13 on page A-7.
For **verbs followed by gerunds or infinitives**, see Unit 16 and Appendices 14 and 15 on page A-7.
For a list of **verbs followed by noun / pronoun + infinitives**, see Appendix 17 on page A-8.
For a list of **adjectives followed by infinitives**, see Appendix 18 on page A-8.

STEP 3 FOCUSED PRACTICE

EXERCISE 1: Discover the Grammar

A | *Read these sentences from the opening reading. Is each underlined infinitive or infinitive phrase used as a subject (**S**), an object (**O**), or a subject complement (**SC**)?*

O 1. I really did plan to ask.
O 2. I want to ask you if there's such a thing as . . .
S 3. To procrastinate is literally to put things off until tomorrow.
SC 4. To procrastinate is literally to put things off until tomorrow.
O 5. Maybe they don't want to be rejected.
O 6. She expects to fail.
SC 7. The first is never to put off until tomorrow what needs to be done today.
S 8. Not to avoid painful or difficult things is the second.
O 9. I try to consider every experience as an opportunity.

B | *Read the pairs of sentences. According to the first sentence in each pair, is the second sentence true (**T**) or false (**F**)?*

1. "I can't stop to type your paper now."
The speaker is not able to stop what he is doing for the purpose of typing the paper. **T** F
2. "I forgot to, Steve, but I really did plan to ask."
The speaker doesn't remember asking Steve. T **F**
3. "Maybe they don't want to be rejected."
Maybe they're worried about rejecting someone. T **F**
4. "Maybe they just don't want to be told *no*."
Maybe they always want to be given *yes* answers. **T** F
5. "Her friends no doubt expected her to have called them."
Her friends probably thought she was going to call them before now. **T** F
6. "The second piece of advice is not to avoid painful or difficult things."
The advice is to stay away from painful or difficult things. T **F**

EXERCISE 2: Verbs / Nouns / Infinitives

(Grammar Notes 2–3)

Complete the sentences with a verb + infinitive or verb + noun / pronoun + infinitive. Three constructions will contain adjectives as well. If necessary, refer to Appendices 13, 17, and 18 on pages A-7—A-8 for help in completing the exercise.

I'm basically a procrastinator. I've always wanted to stop (**1. (want / stop)**) procrastinating but never knew how. It started when I was a teenager and I had trouble getting my schoolwork done. My parents always warned me not to put off (**2. (warn / not / put off)**) doing my assignments, but they

__________ my own decisions. I guess they thought it __________ the consequences of one's actions, and they never __________ at any particular time, so I didn't. I guess I __________ from high school. When I got to college, I __________ my courses by doing things at the last minute or not doing them at all. However, things were different there. There were a hundred students in my history class, and the professor __________ a term paper. I put it off, of course, and didn't even start it until the day it was due. When I tried to turn it in a week late, the professor __________ it. That action __________ the course. I asked my counselor what to do, and she __________ the course and change my whole attitude toward finishing necessary tasks. She __________ my assignments without worrying about whether they were perfect. I took her advice and many painful months later, conquered the procrastination demon.

3. (want / make)
4. (be important / experience)
5. (force / study)
6. (be fortunate / graduate)
7. (expect / pass)
8. (require / write)
9. (refuse / accept)
10. (cause / fail)
11. (advise / retake)
12. (encourage / start)

EXERCISE 3: Past Infinitives

(Grammar Note 7)

Complete the account with past infinitives. One sentence will be in the passive.

My husband and I took a five-day trip out of town and left the kids in charge. On the morning we were returning, we called our son and daughter. We expected them ___to have cleaned___ (1. clean) the house because we were having dinner guests that evening. When I asked Jennifer about this, she at first seemed __________ (2. not / hear) me and quickly changed the subject. I persisted in the question, and this time Jennifer pretended __________ (3. not / understand) what I'd said. "You mean the house needs to be clean tonight?" she said. "Yes," I said. "Did you clean it?" "Well, sort of. Josh was supposed __________ (4. get) some cleaning supplies, but I can't find them anywhere. I did what I could, Mom." "Well, this is important, Jen. We expect you __________ (5. finish) the cleaning by the time we get home," I said in my firmest voice.

When we got home, the house appeared __________ (6. hit) by a tornado. The kids were nowhere to be found. Dirty dishes were everywhere. Jennifer and Josh appeared __________ (7. feed) the animals, but they seemed __________ (8. not / do) anything else. Next time we won't leave things to the kids.

EXERCISE 4: Passive Infinitives

(Grammar Note 8)

A | *For each item, complete the question with a passive infinitive.*

1. On your second day of a new job, you are an hour late to work. (fire / by the company)

   Would you expect *to be fired by the company*?

2. You have a flat tire on a busy freeway. (help / by a passing motorist)

   Would you expect ____________________?

3. You have put off paying your phone bill for more than two months. (your phone service / disconnect)

   Would you expect ____________________?

4. Your son or daughter has been stopped for speeding. (notify / by the police)

   Would you expect ____________________?

5. You are going 10 miles over the speed limit. (stop / by a police officer)

   Would you expect ____________________?

6. Your English term paper was due three days ago. (question / by your teacher)

   Would you expect ____________________?

B | *PAIRS: Take turns asking and answering the questions.*

EXAMPLE: **A:** On your second day of a new job, you are an hour late to work. Would you expect to be fired by the company?
B: No, I wouldn't expect to be fired by the company. How about you?

EXERCISE 5: *Too* / *Enough* / Infinitives

(Grammar Note 6)

For each situation, write a sentence with **too** *or* **enough** *and an infinitive.*

1. It's 5:15. Jill's flight leaves at 5:45, and it takes 45 minutes to get to the airport. (enough)

   Jill doesn't have enough time to get to the airport.

2. Jack's 10-page report is due in an hour. He types only 25 words a minute. (too)

   ____

3. Marcy wants to buy her friend's used car, which costs $5,000. She has $4,000 in the bank and is able to save $400 a month. Her friend must sell the car within three months. (enough)

   ____

4. Eve invited guests to dinner. She waited until 6:15 to start preparing the meal. The guests are expected by 7:00. (too)

   ____

5. Sally's doctor advised her to eat three meals a day to stay healthy. To lose weight, Sally ate only one small meal a day. She became quite sick. (enough)

____

6. Carlos is enrolled in an extremely difficult calculus class, but he is a very intelligent man and can pass the course if he applies himself. (enough)

____

EXERCISE 6: Editing

Read the entry from Alice's journal. There are ten mistakes in the use of infinitives. The first mistake is already corrected. Find and correct nine more.

I just had [to] write tonight. Until now I've never had the courage do this, but now I do. I've decided to have confronted Sarah about her irresponsibility. This is something that has been bothering me for some time now, but somehow I've always been reluctant force the issue. So here's the situation: Sarah invites people to do things, but she doesn't follow through. Last week she asked my fiancé, Al, and me have dinner, and she also invited our friends Mark and Debbie. The four of us made plans go to her house on Friday evening. Something told me I should call Sarah asking what we should bring, and it's a good thing I did. Sarah said, "Dinner? I'm not having dinner tonight. I know I mentioned it as a possibility, but I never settled it with you guys. You misunderstood me." Well, that's just silly. She told us planning on it for Friday evening at 7 P.M. When I told the others, they were furious. Al said, "I don't expect being treated like royalty. I do expect to be treated with consideration." So tomorrow I'm going to call Sarah up and make my point. I'm not going to allow her make my life miserable.

Enough for now. Time for bed.

STEP 4 COMMUNICATION PRACTICE

EXERCISE 7: Listening

A | *Listen to the news bulletin. How long a sentence did Charles Gallagher receive two years ago? Answer in a complete sentence.*

____

B | *Read the questions. Listen again. Answer each question in a complete sentence.*

1. How many prisoners are reported to have escaped?

   Three prisoners are reported to have escaped.

2. How are they believed to have escaped?

   ____

3. By whom are they believed to have been helped?

   ____

4. When was the new security system supposed to have been installed?

   ____

5. What are the prisoners thought to have?

   ____

6. In what direction are they believed to be heading?

   ____

7. What are listeners warned not to do?

   ____

8. What are they asked to do if they have any information?

   ____

EXERCISE 8: Pronunciation

A | *Read and listen to the Pronunciation Note.*

Pronunciation Note

Note the pronunciation of these three vowel sounds in English: /æ/ as in *cat*, /ɑ/ as in *cot*, /ʌ/ as in *cut*.

EXAMPLES: How do you spell *hat*? /æ/
How do you spell *hot*? /ɑ/
How do you spell *hut*? /ʌ/

B | *Listen to the sentences. Listen again and repeat. Then write the symbol for the boldfaced vowel in the underlined word: /æ/, /ɑ/, /ʌ/.*

1. I can't st**o**p to type your paper now. /ɑ/
2. There's not en**ou**gh time to do it now. _____
3. I'll fl**u**nk if you don't do it. _____
4. Steve, you h**a**ve to type my paper. _____
5. It illustrates the problem of procr**a**stination. _____
6. Some friends of mine are c**o**ming in half an hour. _____
7. I forg**o**t to ask you. _____
8. Procrastination is a very serious pr**o**blem. _____
9. Procrastination has n**o**thing to do with education. _____
10. The L**a**tin phrase *carpe diem* means "seize the day." _____
11. The word procrastinate has a negative c**o**nnotation. _____
12. Th**a**nks for another stimulating discussion. _____

C | *PAIRS: Practice the sentences.*

EXERCISE 9: Personal Inventory

A | *Write sentences on these topics, based on your own experience. Use infinitive or gerund structures.*

1. something you stopped doing

   I stopped taking a bus to school 2 months ago.

2. an activity you stopped in order to do something else

   I stopped

3. something you remember doing

   I remember calling my parents when I came home.

4. something you didn't remember to do

   I didn't remember to bring my keys last week

5. something you are reluctant to do

   I'm reluctant to go

6. something you have always been afraid to do

   I've always been afraid to talk with strangers.

7. something you feel is wrong for people to do

   I feel it's wrong for people to descriminate others by the third gender.

8. something you expected to have happened before now

   I expected

9. a quality that you feel is important to have

   I feel It's important for people to

10. something that you are happy to have experienced (use the past passive)

    I'm happy to have been

B | *SMALL GROUPS: Discuss your answers with others in your group. Report interesting examples to the class as a whole.*

EXERCISE 10: Group Discussion

A | *Put each saying in your own words, using infinitives.*

EXAMPLE: "It is better to light one candle than to curse the darkness."
—*The motto of the Christophers*

It's better **to do** one small, positive thing than **to complain** about a problem and **do** nothing.

1. "To be or not to be, that is the question."—*William Shakespeare*

____

2. "It is better to die on your feet than to live on your knees."—*attributed to Emiliano Zapata*

____

3. "To err is human, to forgive divine."—*Alexander Pope*

____

4. "It is better to seek than to find."—*source unknown*

____

5. "It is better to have loved and lost than never to have loved at all."—*Alfred, Lord Tennyson*

____

6. "It is better to arrive late than never to arrive at all."—*source unknown*

____

B | *SMALL GROUPS: Discuss with others in your group the extent to which you believe the sayings are true. Use infinitives. Report interesting conclusions to the class.*

EXAMPLE: I basically agree that it is better to light one candle than to curse the darkness. Complaining about a difficult situation doesn't help to solve it.

EXERCISE 11: Picture Discussion

SMALL GROUPS: Discuss the photo. What does it show about procrastination? Does it seem to say that procrastination is a bad thing, or perhaps partially a good thing? What would you advise the owner of this desk to do?

EXAMPLE: **A:** I would advise the owner of this desk to put the desk in order.
B: I disagree. I'd advise the owner to . . .

EXERCISE 12: Writing

A | *Most of us have procrastinated at one time or another. Write three or more paragraphs about a time when you put off doing something that needed to be done. Tell about the results. Speculate about the reasons for your procrastination and discuss the consequences. Use infinitives and infinitive phrases in your composition.*

Example: I've had lots of experiences with putting off things that needed to be done, but one that sticks in my mind is about getting my car tuned up. I was scheduled to go on a cross-country trip, and I knew I needed to take my car in for a tune-up. One thing led to another, though, and I continued to procrastinate. Finally, the day of my departure arrived, and I hadn't had the tune-up done. I said to myself . . .

B | *Check your work. Use the Editing Checklist.*

Editing Checklist

Did you use . . . ?

- ☐ infinitives as subjects correctly
- ☐ infinitives as objects correctly
- ☐ infinitives as subject complements correctly
- ☐ verbs followed by infinitives correctly

UNIT 17 Review

Check your answers on page UR-3.

Do you need to review anything?

A | *Circle the word or phrase that correctly completes each sentence.*

- **A:** What did Carlos decide to do / doing (1.) about his job?
  B: He quit accepting / to accept (2.) a position at Windale's.
- **A:** Did Ben ever manage giving up / to give up (3.) tobacco?
  B: Yes. He actually stopped to smoke / smoking (4.) two months ago.
- **A:** Did you remember to have locked / to lock (5.) the front door?
  B: I'm sure I locked / locking (6.) it when I left.
- **A:** Alicia is afraid to confront / confronting (7.) Jaime about the problem.
  B: That's because he hates to be criticized / to be criticizing (8.).

B | *Correct the mistakes in the underlined words or phrases.*

1. That child is not enough strong to lift the box. ____________
2. I warned not to procrastinate, but you did. ____________
3. There are occasionally good reasons postpone things. ____________
4. All term papers have to typed. ____________
5. I'm lucky to have Vijay as a friend many years ago. ____________
6. Jin-Su warned me to get involved in the argument. ____________
7. Said never came; he seems to forget the meeting. ____________
8. Berta was too tired finishing her assignment. ____________

C | *Circle the letter of the one underlined word or phrase that is not correct.*

1. You warned me (A) not to put off (B) doing (C) things, but I decided do (D) just that. **A B C D**
2. It was important (A) experience (B) freedom, so I was allowed (C) to choose (D). **A B C D**
3. The work was have (A) been done (B), but that seems not to (C) have happened (D). **A B C D**
4. We'd told you to clean up (A), but the place appeared (B) to be (C) hit (D) by a tornado. **A B C D**

From Grammar to Writing

PARALLEL STRUCTURE: GERUNDS AND INFINITIVES

Remember that in parallel structure, all items in a series are in the same grammatical form: singulars with singulars, plurals with plurals, actives with actives, passives with passives, and so forth. Parallelism makes our speaking and writing stronger and more communicative. Therefore, mixing gerunds and infinitives in the same series should always be avoided.

Examples: My summer hobbies are **hiking**, **boating**, and **swimming**. *(All three complements are gerunds.)*

I want to thank everyone for making this party a success. I especially appreciate **Sumi's inviting** the guests, **Rafal's cooking** the food, and **Jennifer's organizing** the whole thing. *(All three objects are gerund phrases.)*

When my friend Li started college, her goals were **to make** new friends and **to become** well educated. *(Both complements are infinitives.)*

A series of short infinitives or infinitive phrases may be presented with the word ***to*** before each item or before the first item only.

Example: Helen loves **to read**, **(to) write**, and **(to) attend** the opera.

If a sentence is long, it is often best to include the word ***to*** before each infinitive phrase.

Examples: In his sensitivity training at work, Dan learned **to listen** carefully to other people, **to consider** their feelings, and **to imagine** himself in their situations.

Applicants to the university are expected **to have completed** a college preparatory program, **to have graduated** in the upper third of their high school class, and **to have participated** in extracurricular activities.

1 | *Each of the sentences contains an error involving parallelism with gerunds or infinitives. Correct the nonparallel items.*

1. Ramiro loves camping, to collect stamps, and surfing the Internet.
2. Lately I've been trying to stop speeding in traffic, to schedule too many activities, and rushing through each day like a crazy person.
3. To have a happier family life, we should all focus on eating meals together, on airing our problems and concerns, and on take time to talk to one another.
4. I'm advising you not to sell your property, take out a loan, and not to buy a new house right now.

(continued on next page)

5. Most presidents want to be reelected to a second term, taken seriously by other world leaders, and to be remembered fondly after they leave office.
6. To be hired in this firm, you are expected to have earned a bachelor's degree and having worked in a bank for at least two years.

2 | *Read the paragraph about speech anxiety. Correct the 10 mistakes in parallelism with gerunds and infinitives.*

What are you most afraid of? Are you worried about being cheated, to lose your job, or contracting a deadly disease? Well, if you're like the vast majority of Americans, you fear standing up, to face an audience, and to deliver a speech more than anything else. Surveys have found that anxiety about public speaking terrifies Americans more than dying does. Somehow, people expect to be laughed at, ridiculed, or to be scorned by an audience. Many college students fear public speaking so much that they put off taking a speech class or even to think about it until their last term before graduation. Speech instructors and others familiar with the principles of public speaking stress that the technique of desensitization works best for overcoming speech anxiety. This idea holds that people can get over their fear of speaking in public by enrolling in a course, to attend the class faithfully, and to force themselves to perform the speech activities. Once they have discovered that it is rare for people to die, making fools of themselves, or to be laughed at while making a speech, they're on their way to success. Consequently, their anxiety becomes a little less each time they get up and talk in public. It may take a while, but eventually they find themselves able to stand up willingly, speaking comfortably, and expressing themselves clearly.

3 | *Before you write . . .*

1. Most of us have things that are easy for us to do, but we also have a number of things we have difficulty doing. Think of something that is particularly difficult for you to do.
2. Describe your difficult task to a partner. Listen to your partner's description.
3. Ask and answer questions about your and your partner's topic. Why do you think the task is hard for you? What could you do to make the task easier to accomplish?

4 | *Write a draft of a composition about the task you have difficulty accomplishing. Follow the model. Remember to include information that your partner asked about. Use examples of parallel structure with gerunds and with infinitives.*

Details about my difficult task:

____

____

____

____

Why I think the task is difficult for me:

____

____

____

____

What I could do to make the task easier to accomplish:

____

____

____

____

5 | *Exchange compositions with a different partner. Complete the chart.*

1. The writer used parallel structures with gerunds and infinitives. **Yes** ☐ **No** ☐

2. What I liked in the composition:

____

____

____

3. Questions I'd like the writer to answer about the composition:

Who ____?

What ____?

When ____?

Where ____?

Why ____?

How ____?

(Your own question) ____?

6 | *Work with your partner. Discuss each other's chart from Exercise 5. Then rewrite your own composition and make any necessary changes.*

PART VIII

ADVERBS

UNIT	GRAMMAR FOCUS	THEME
18	Adverbs: Sentence, Focus, and Negative	Controversial Issues
19	Adverb Clauses	Sports
20	Adverb and Adverbial Phrases	Compassion
21	Connectors	Memory

UNIT 18 Adverbs: Sentence, Focus, and Negative
CONTROVERSIAL ISSUES

STEP 1 GRAMMAR IN CONTEXT

Before You Read

PAIRS: Discuss the questions.

1. How do you feel about military service? Should it be required or voluntary?
2. What is your opinion of women in military service? Should women participate in combat?

Read

Read the transcript of a radio call-in show.

Time to Sound Off

Show #267

McGAFFEY: Good evening, and welcome to *Sound Off*, the international talk show where you express your uncensored opinions on today's controversial issues. I'm Mike McGaffey. Tonight's topics: Should military service be required or voluntary? Should women join the military, and if they do, should they fight in combat? Let's see if we can shed some light on these issues. Here's our first caller, Jerry Burns, from Kingston, Jamaica. Where do you stand, Jerry?

BURNS: Hi, Mike. **Basically**, I think military service should be voluntary. And I'm **definitely** against women in combat.

McGAFFEY: OK. Why should it be voluntary? Why shouldn't it be required of everyone?

BURNS: Because, **overall**, young people are not all the same. Some people have a military orientation. For them, military service is fine. Others aren't oriented that way. Compulsory military service interferes with their freedom, **essentially**.

Time to Sound Off

Show #267

McGAFFEY: But many argue that we all owe our country something. It protects us and gives us benefits. Shouldn't we give something in return?

BURNS: We should if we're motivated to. But it shouldn't be an obligation. And I'd go further: Military forces have done a lot of evil. Maybe we shouldn't **even** have them.

McGAFFEY: Hmm. I don't know, Jerry—I'm a pretty accepting guy, but **even** I find that suggestion extreme. But let's go to your second point. Why shouldn't women be in combat?

BURNS: Men and women are **clearly** different. Let's keep them that way. Women **just** aren't suited for combat. If women are in combat, they're **just** like men. **There** goes the difference.

McGAFFEY: Are you saying that **only** men are strong enough? That's an old stereotype, isn't it?

BURNS: I'm not saying that. I **just** don't think fighting is feminine.

McGAFFEY: Wow. All right, Jerry, very interesting. I expect we'll hear some pretty spirited responses to what you've said. Our next caller is Sarah Lopez from Toronto, Canada. Sarah, is Jerry on target, or is this just fuzzy thinking?

LOPEZ: Thanks, Mike. **Actually**, I couldn't disagree more with Jerry. It's not fuzzy thinking. He made his point clearly, but I **just** don't agree with him.

McGAFFEY: OK. So military service shouldn't be voluntary?

LOPEZ: No. If we're going to have it, it should be required.

McGAFFEY: Why?

LOPEZ: It's the only way to ensure fair treatment for all. People in the military make major sacrifices—sometimes they risk their lives. That kind of risk should be spread out evenly. **Actually**, I'd go further: I'd support required national service. It wouldn't have to be **only** military.

McGAFFEY: Expand a bit on that.

LOPEZ: There are lots of worthwhile things citizens can do for their country—like working in day-care centers, hospitals, or the Peace Corps. National service has been started in a few countries, and **hopefully** it will be adopted in a lot more.

McGAFFEY: All right. Now, Jerry opposes women in combat. What's your position? Should it be allowed?

LOPEZ: **Not only** should it be allowed, **but** it should **also** be promoted. I should know: I've been in the military for 18 months.

McGAFFEY: You have?

LOPEZ: Yes, and I totally disagree with the way Jerry characterizes women. **No way** is combat unfeminine!

McGAFFEY: Have you ever been in combat?

LOPEZ: No, but if I'm ever called to combat, I'll go willingly. Most women wouldn't agree with Jerry about maintaining the difference between the sexes. **Neither** do I.

McGAFFEY: OK, Sarah. Thanks. Let's see where we can go with this. Our next caller is from Singapore. **Here's** Lu Adijojo. Lu, what's your view?

After You Read

A | Vocabulary: *Circle the letter of the best meaning for the* **blue** *words and phrases from the reading.*

1. *Sound Off* is the international talk show where you express your **uncensored** opinions on today's controversial issues.

   a. unrestricted **b.** favorite **c.** emotional **d.** unpopular

2. *Sound Off* is the international talk show where you express your uncensored opinions on today's **controversial** issues.

   a. interesting **b.** exciting **c.** debatable **d.** terrible

3. Let's see if we can **shed some light on** these issues.

   a. criticize **b.** illuminate **c.** discuss **d.** disprove

4. **Compulsory** military service interferes with their freedom, essentially.

   a. Voluntary **b.** Required **c.** Difficult **d.** Unpleasant

5. That's an old **stereotype**, isn't it?

   a. standardized picture **b.** record **c.** first example **d.** lie

6. I expect we'll hear some pretty **spirited** responses to what you've said.

   a. angry **b.** thoughtful **c.** emotional **d.** religious

7. It's not **fuzzy** thinking.

   a. wrong **b.** unclear **c.** elementary **d.** ridiculous

8. And if I'm ever called to combat, I'll go **willingly**.

   a. without fear **b.** without pleasure **c.** without explanation **d.** without objection

B | Comprehension: *Refer to the reading and complete each statement with a single word.*

1. Jerry, the first caller, thinks military service should be ________________.
2. Jerry is ________________ women being in combat.
3. Jerry doesn't think fighting is ________________.
4. Sarah, the second caller, thinks military service should be ________________.
5. In her opinion, it's the only way to ensure ________________ treatment for everyone.
6. Sarah does not believe combat is ________________.

STEP 2 GRAMMAR PRESENTATION

ADVERBS: SENTENCE, FOCUS, AND NEGATIVE

Sentence Adverbs: Placement	
Beginning	**Clearly**, these are bitter controversies.
Middle	These are **clearly** bitter controversies.
End	These are bitter controversies, **clearly**.

Focus Adverbs: Placement and Meaning				
They	**just** don't	support what he says.		They think he's wrong.
	don't **just**			They agree with him 100 percent.
Even	he	can do	that.	Almost anyone can do that task.
She	can do	**even**	that.	It's amazing how many things she can do.
Only	men	can	attend.	Women can't.
Men	can	**only**		They can't do anything else.

Negative Adverbs: Placement and Inversion			
We	**rarely**	agree	on such things.
Rarely	do we		
I have	**seldom**	heard	that idea.
Seldom	have I		
They	**never**	disagreed	with him.
Never	did they	disagree	

GRAMMAR NOTES

1	Remember that adverbs modify verbs, adjectives, and other adverbs. Some adverbs also modify entire sentences. These are called **sentence adverbs** (also called viewpoint adverbs) because they express an opinion or view about an entire sentence. Common sentence adverbs are *actually, basically, certainly, clearly, definitely, essentially, fortunately, hopefully, obviously, overall, maybe, perhaps, possibly*, and *surely*.	• **Fortunately**, Bill's military service paid for his college education. *(= It is fortunate that Bill's military service paid for his college education.)*
	Some adverbs can function either as sentence adverbs or as simple adverbs.	• **Clearly**, he is a very good speaker. *(sentence adverb that modifies the entire idea—it is clear that he is a very good speaker)* • He speaks **clearly**. *(not a sentence adverb, but a simple adverb that modifies* speaks*)*
	You can use sentence adverbs in various places in a sentence. If the adverb comes first or last in a sentence, separate it from the rest of the sentence by a comma. If the adverb comes elsewhere in the sentence, it usually comes after the verb *be* and before other verbs. Where *be* follows a modal verb, the adverb comes after the modal. In these cases, *be* is usually not enclosed in commas.	• **Basically**, I'm in favor of that. • I'm in favor of that, **basically**. • I'm **basically** in favor of that. • I **basically** agree with the plan.
2	**Focus adverbs*** focus attention on a word or phrase. These adverbs usually precede the word or phrase focused on. Common focus adverbs are *even, just, only*, and *almost*.	• **Even I** believe that. *(focuses on* I*)* • I believe **even that**. *(focuses on* that*)*
	NOTE: Changing the position of a focus adverb often changes the meaning of the sentence.	• **Just teenagers** can attend the meetings. *(focuses on* teenagers*—they are the only ones allowed to attend)* • Teenagers can **just attend** the meetings. *(focuses on* attend*—they're not allowed to participate in the other club activities)*
	NOTE: In spoken English, the word you are focusing on is stressed.	• **Only** teenagers can attend. • Teenagers can **only** attend.

*The author wishes to acknowledge L. G. Alexander regarding the term ***focus adverb*** (*Longman Advanced Grammar, Reference and Practice,* New York: Longman Publishing, 1993).

3	**Negative adverbs** include *hardly*, *in no way* (informal *no way*), *little*, *neither*, *never*, *not only*, *only*, *rarely*, and *seldom*. In sentences or clauses beginning with a negative adverb, put the verb or auxiliary before the subject to emphasize the negative meaning.	• **Women are** required to serve in the military **only** in Israel. • **Only** in Israel **are women** drafted to serve in the military. • **He is seldom** on time. • **Seldom is he** on time.
	If the verb is in the simple present or simple past (except for the verb *be*), use *do*, *does*, or *did* after an initial negative adverb.	• **Rarely do** women **make** a career of the military.
	The negative adverb *not only* combines with *but also*.	• **Not only should we** allow that, **but** we should **also** encourage it.
	If the verb is in perfect form, place the auxiliary before the subject.	• **Never had I** heard such a strange idea.
	NOTE: Sentences beginning with *neither* are common in both formal and informal English. Sentences beginning with other negative adverbs usually sound more formal.	• My grandfather didn't join the military. **Neither** did my father. • **Seldom** have women served in combat. *(more formal)*
4	*Here* and *there* are other adverbs that force inversion when they come at the beginning of a sentence.	• **Here is your money**. • **There goes the bus**.
	BE CAREFUL! In a sentence beginning with *here* or *there*, invert the subject and verb if the subject is a noun. Don't invert them if it is a pronoun.	• **Here comes the bus.** • **Here it comes.** NOT: Here ~~the bus comes~~. NOT: Here ~~comes it~~.

REFERENCE NOTE

For a list of **sentence adverbs**, see Appendix 19 on page A-9.

1. Here is your money
2. There goes Sally
3. ~~Here your money is~~ Wrong
4. ~~There Sally goes~~ Wrong
5. Here it is
6. There She goes.

Subject pronouns.

STEP 3 FOCUSED PRACTICE

EXERCISE 1: Discover the Grammar

*Find and underline the adverb in each sentence. Then identify the adverbs as sentence adverbs (**S**), negative adverbs (**N**), or focus adverbs (**F**).*

F 1. Sarah doesn't just support the idea of women in combat.

____ 2. Basically, I think service should be voluntary.

____ 3. Young people aren't all the same, obviously.

____ 4. I'm a pretty accepting guy, but even I find that suggestion extreme.

____ 5. Men and women are clearly different.

____ 6. Little do many people realize how dangerous military service can be.

____ 7. I just don't agree with the basic idea.

____ 8. In some countries women are only allowed to perform medical duties in the military.

____ 9. Not only should it be allowed, but it should also be promoted.

____ 10. In Switzerland only men are allowed to serve in combat.

EXERCISE 2: Sentence Adverbs

(Grammar Note 1)

Combine each pair of statements into one statement. Use the adverb form of the underlined word.

1. National service is beneficial. This is obvious.

   Obviously, national service is beneficial. / National service is obviously beneficial. /
   National service is beneficial, obviously.

2. Military service can be dangerous. That's unfortunate.

   Unfortunately, Military service can be dangerous./ Military service can be unfortunalely dangerous. / Military service can be dangerous, unfortunately.

3. I'm against the death penalty. The essential reason for this is that I consider it cruel and unusual punishment.

   Essentially, I'm against the death penalty that I consider it cruel and unsual punish–
   I'm essentially against the death penalty that I consider it cruel and unsual punishment.
   I'm against the death penalty that I consider it cruel and unsual punishment, essentially

4. There's a lot more violence in movies than in the past. This is certain.

   Certainly, There's alot more violence in movies than in the past. / There's certainly a lot more violence in movie than in the past. / There's a lot more violence in movies than in the past, certainly.

5. Nuclear weapons can be eliminated. I'm hopeful this will be the case.

   Hopefully, nuclear weapons can be eliminated. / Nuclear weapons can be hopefully eliminated. / Nuclear weapons can be eliminated, hopefully.

6. A vaccine against AIDS can be found. This is perhaps the case.

   Perhaps, A vaccine against AIDS can be found. /
   A vaccine against AIDS can be perhaps found. /
   A Vaccine against AIDS can be found, perhaps.

7. The prime minister's position is wrong. It's clear.

Clearly, the prime minister's position is wrong. / The prime minister's position is clealy wrong. / The prime minister's position is wrong, clearly.

8. There's increasing opposition to people's owning SUVs. This is the actual situation.

Actually, there's increasing opposition to people's owning SUVs. / There is actually increasing opposition to people's owning SUVs. / There is increasing opposition to people's owning SUVs, Actually.

EXERCISE 3: Focus Adverbs

(Grammar Note 2)

Circle the letter of the choice with the correctly used focus adverb.

1. Bill believes that women should not fight. He feels _____ in noncombat roles.

   a. they should only serve b. only they should serve

2. Carrie thinks women can do most jobs men can do, but she feels _____ in combat.

   a. men should serve only b. only men should serve

3. Samantha is against gambling, but _____ the benefits of lotteries.

   a. even she can recognize b. she can even recognize

4. I'm in favor of higher taxes. _____ taxing food and medicine.

   a. Even I'm in favor of b. I'm even in favor of

5. My husband has some good reasons for supporting nuclear power. However, I _____ with his reasoning.

   a. don't just agree b. just don't agree

6. My father _____ the military draft; he's a military recruiter.

   a. doesn't just support b. just doesn't support

EXERCISE 4: Negative Adverbs

(Grammar Note 3)

Change one sentence in each pair. Use the negative adverb in parentheses.

1. I don't support the government's policy on taxation. My friends don't support the government's policy. (neither)

   I don't support the government's policy on taxation. Neither do my friends.

2. There are many women in the military worldwide. Women fight alongside men in combat. (rarely)

   There are many women in the military worldwide. Rarely do women fight alongside men in combat.

3. Some uninformed people oppose the military. Military service is useless. (in no way)

   Some uninformed people oppose the military. In no way is military service useless.

(continued on next page)

4. Violence won't ever be completely eliminated. Poverty won't be completely eliminated. (neither)

Violence won't ever be completely eliminated. Neither will poverty.

5. We need to stop global warming. We also need to find new energy sources. (not only)

We need to stop global warming. Not only need to we allow that, but we also need to find new energy sources.

6. I bought an SUV. It had occurred to me that SUVs could harm the environment, but I learned they could. (Never)

I bought an SUV. Never had it occurred to me that SUVs could harm the environment, but I learned they could.

EXERCISE 5: Negative / Focus Adverbs

(Grammar Notes 2–3)

Study the chart. Complete the sentences with the adverbs **even, just, only in,** *or* **not only . . . but also** *and a form of the verbs in parentheses.*

Country	Has a military	Has required military service	Allows women to serve in the military	Drafts women to serve in the military	Allows women to serve in combat
Brazil	X		X		X
Canada	X		X		X
China	X	X	X	X	
Costa Rica					
Israel	X	X	X	X	
Switzerland	X	X			
The United States	X		X		X
Venezuela	X		X		X

Facts about military service in eight countries:

1. Only in Costa Rica is there (there / be) no military.

2. Though officially neutral, __________ Switzerland __________ (have) a military.

3. __________ three countries __________ (have) required military service.

4. __________ do Brazil, Canada, the United States, and Venezuela allow women to serve in the military, __________ (they / allow) them to serve in combat.

5. __________ (men / require) to serve in combat in these four countries.

6. __________ Israel and China __________ (women / require) to do military service.

EXERCISE 6: Editing

There are seven mistakes in the use of adverbs in the letter. The first mistake is already corrected. Find and correct six more.

Dear Dad,

I'm waiting for the 5:25 train, so ~~just I~~ *I just* thought I'd drop you a note. I've been at the global warming conference. Actually, I almost didn't get to the conference because almost we didn't get our taxes done on time. Vicky and I stayed up late last night, though, and I mailed the forms this morning.

I hate income taxes! Only once in the last 10 years we have gotten a refund, and this time the form was so complicated that Vicky got even upset, and you know how calm she is. Maybe we should move to Antarctica or something. No taxes there.

Besides that, we've been having problems with Donna. It's probably nothing more serious than teenage rebellion, but whenever we try to lay down the law, she gets defensive. Rarely if ever she takes criticism well. The other night she and her friend stayed out until 1 A.M., and when we asked what they'd been doing she said, "We were just talking and listening to music at the Teen Club. Why can't you leave me alone?" Then she stomped out of the room. Fortunately, Sam and Toby have been behaving like angels—but they're not teenagers!

Meanwhile, Donna's school has started a new open-campus policy. Students can leave the campus whenever they don't have a class. Even they don't have to tell the school office where they're going or when they'll be back. No way do Vicky and I approve of that policy! School time, in our view, is for studying and learning, not for socializing. Little do those school officials realize how much trouble unsupervised teenagers can get into.

Well, Dad, here the train comes. I'll sign off now. Write soon.

Love,

Ken

STEP 4 COMMUNICATION PRACTICE

EXERCISE 7: Listening

A | *Listen to the next part of the radio call-in show. Where is the caller from?*

____

B | *Listen again and circle the letter of the correct answer.*

1. The caller listens to the radio show _____.
   a. every day
   (b.) once a week
   c. twice a week
   d. once every two weeks

2. The caller likes the program _____.
   a. a lot
   b. somewhat
   c. occasionally
   d. very little

3. The caller is basically closer to the viewpoint of _____.
   a. the man from Jamaica
   b. military leaders in her country
   c. the woman from Canada
   d. the U.N. secretary-general

4. The caller thinks military service should be _____.
   a. required
   b. abolished
   c. voluntary
   d. only one of many service options

5. The caller thinks fighting in combat _____ a woman is unfeminine.
   a. doesn't mean
   b. means
   c. can mean
   d. has always meant

6. The caller thinks combat isn't advisable for _____.
   a. any women
   b. college educated women
   c. women over 25
   d. mothers

7. The caller thinks pro-military people in her country _____ support the idea of women in combat.
   a. do
   b. don't
   c. might
   d. will eventually

8. The caller thinks national service is basically a _____ idea.
   a. foolish
   b. good
   c. complicated
   d. very expensive

EXERCISE 8: Pronunciation

A | *Read and listen to the Pronunciation Note.*

Pronunciation Note

In sentences with focus adverbs, the word following the focus adverb usually has the strongest stress in the sentence.

Examples: Even **I** like the cold weather. *(strongest stress on* I*)*
I even **like** the cold weather. *(strongest stress on* like*)*

B | *Listen to the sentences. Underline the stressed words.*

Examples: I love only you. (= You're the only one I love.)
Only I love you. (= I'm the only one who loves you.)

1. Bill can even understand this math.
2. Even Bill can understand this math.
3. I don't just agree with Nancy.
4. I just don't agree with Nancy.
5. We don't even understand you.
6. Even we don't understand you.
7. Only women can visit this club.
8. Women can only visit this club.

C | *Listen again and repeat the sentences.*

EXERCISE 9: Personal Inventory

A | *Complete each of the sentences with the indicated adverbs, drawing from your own experience.*

1. Basically, I . . .

____

2. Fortunately, I . . .

____

3. Even I . . .

____

(continued on next page)

4. I even . . .

____

5. Rarely do I . . .

____

6. I just don't . . .

____

7. I don't just . . .

____

8. Not only do I . . . but I also . . .

____

B | *PAIRS: Discuss your answers. Report interesting examples to the class.*

EXERCISE 10: Pros / Cons

A | *PAIRS: Choose a controversial topic that might be discussed on a TV or radio call-in show. You may select a topic from the box or choose one of your own.*

capital punishment	**the military draft**
cloning	**using hand-held cell phones while driving**
electric vs. gas-powered cars	**women in combat**

B | *Brainstorm and write down points supporting both sides of the issue.*

EXERCISE 11: Debate

CLASS: Choose a topic from Exercise 10. Have a debate on that subject. Follow the steps to prepare for the debate:

- Divide into two groups that will argue the opposing viewpoints.
- Brainstorm and write down points supporting your group's side of the issue.
- Do research outside of class, using the Internet if possible.
- To maximize your side's performance, make certain that you can predict and understand the arguments that the opposing side might present.

EXERCISE 12: Writing

A | *Write five paragraphs on a controversial topic. You may use one of the topics in Exercise 10 (including the subject debated) or select another topic of your own. Follow these steps:*

- Do research on your topic outside of class, using the Internet if possible.
- Be objective: Find specifics that support your viewpoint, but also touch on points opposite to your view.
- Try to use at least two sentence adverbs, two focus adverbs, and two negative adverbs in your composition.

Organize your composition in this way:

- Paragraph 1: Introduction. State your viewpoint. Mention the viewpoints on the other side of the issue.
- Paragraph 2: First reason for your viewpoint.
- Paragraph 3: Second reason for your viewpoint.
- Paragraph 4: Third reason for your viewpoint.
- Paragraph 5: Conclusion.

B | *Check your work. Use the Editing Checklist.*

Editing Checklist

Did you use . . . ?
☐ sentence adverbs correctly
☐ focus adverbs correctly
☐ negative adverbs correctly

UNIT 18 Review

Check your answers on page UR-3.

Do you need to review anything?

A | *Circle the word or phrase that correctly completes each sentence.*

1. Mom tries to get me to eat oatmeal, but I don't just / just don't like it.
2. Never had we / we had seen such a fine performance.
3. Bill is pro-military; he even thinks / even he thinks the draft should be renewed.
4. In our club members can only / only members can attend meetings.
5. I just don't / don't just love him; I want to marry him.
6. Pau is a terrible cook, but even he can / he can even boil eggs.
7. Rarely does Eva / Eva does arrive late at the office.
8. Here the train comes / comes the train.

B | *Correct the mistakes, including errors of punctuation, in the underlined words or phrases.*

1. Only in Australia kangaroos are found. ________________
2. Something has to change clearly. ________________
3. Not only should he hurry, but should he run. ________________
4. Seldom our team does lose. ________________
5. Members just can vote; non-members cannot. ________________
6. Here the money is that I owe you. ________________
7. Actually I did graduate from college. ________________
8. There the plane goes. ________________

C | *Circle the letter of the one underlined word or phrase in each sentence that is not correct.*

1. The author clearly (A) shows that rarely (B) the law is applied (C) fairly (D). **A B C D**
2. I actually (A) thought Ben wouldn't come at all (B), but (C) here comes he (D). **A B C D**
3. Rarely (A) will he accept (B) criticism, and (C) at times even he won't listen (D). **A B C D**
4. Never I have seen (A) as clearly (B) as I do now (C) how very (D) absurd that is. **A B C D**

UNIT 19 Adverb Clauses
SPORTS

STEP 1 GRAMMAR IN CONTEXT

Before You Read

PAIRS: Discuss the questions.

1. What is your view of sports? Is it basically positive, negative, or somewhere in between?
2. What are some benefits of sports? What are some negative aspects of them?

Read

Read the editorial about sports.

EDITORIAL
ARE SPORTS STILL SPORTING?

by Buck Jacobs

As I write this editorial, the World Cup is in full swing in South Africa. The competition seems a big success, with the world's major soccer teams playing in attractive venues. Similarly, the 2008 Summer Olympics in Beijing and the 2010 Winter Olympics in Vancouver were artistic triumphs. But **while sports may look good on the surface**, problems are lurking underneath. Partisanship is increasing; **because he penalized a player** in the 2008 European Championships, a British referee received death threats. **Since there are ever-increasing possibilities for product endorsement by athletes**, money is playing a larger role. Violence has certainly not diminished.

Throwing the Javelin

What is wrong? I've concluded that the whole sports scene is in need of repair and have identified three major excesses:

FIRST EXCESS: misplaced focus on fame. **When the Olympics began about 2,700 years ago in Greece,** the contests were related to war. The javelin throw, for example, paralleled the throwing of a spear in a battle. Running paralleled the physical exertion you might have to make **if an enemy was chasing you. When the**

(continued on next page)

EDITORIAL: **ARE SPORTS STILL SPORTING?**

modern Olympic games started in 1896, the philosophy had shifted to the promotion of peace. However, emphasis was still placed on demonstrating physical stamina and excellence in challenging contests.

How things have changed! **Although athletes still try to achieve their personal best**, the focus has shifted to the breaking of records and the achievement of fame. Can we really say that someone who finishes the 400-meter freestyle swim one-tenth of a second ahead of his or her nearest rival is a champion, **while that rival is an also-ran**?

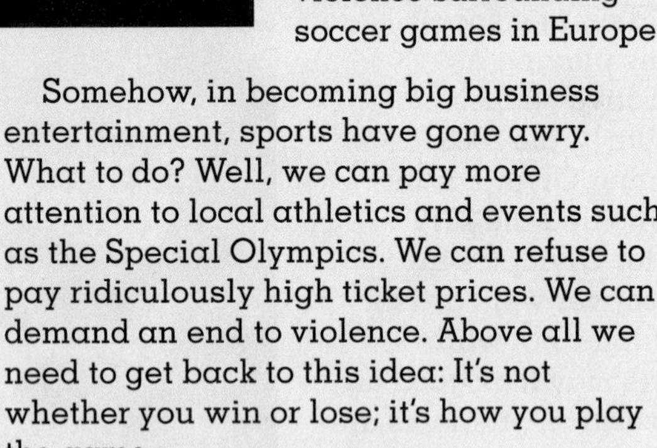

SECOND EXCESS: money. Consider the cost of attending a major athletic competition. In the United States, the average cost of a ticket to a National Football League game in 2010 is about $72. **If you add the cost of taking a family of four to a game**, the total is over $388. A ticket to an NBA basketball game is about $49. Baseball is cheaper, **though it's not really a bargain at an average ticket cost of $27**. I wondered why tickets are so expensive **until I remembered the key factor**: players' salaries. Basketball star Kobe Bryant earns over $23 million a year. Baseball player Alex Rodriguez makes at least $33 million yearly. Is anyone worth that much money? The president of the United States earns $400,000 a year, and U.S. public schoolteachers make a yearly average of about $50,000. Who is more valuable to society? What we pay people says a lot about what we value.

THIRD EXCESS: prevalence of violence. We see it **wherever we look**, and it's certainly not decreasing. Fights occur frequently in professional sports, with ice hockey one of the worst offenders. In the 2003–2004 season, for instance, player Steve Moore had to be hospitalized **because another player hit him in the head with his stick**. Unfortunately, there seems to be increasing acceptance of violence as "just part of the game." But **once we assume violence is inevitable**, it will be almost impossible to stop. This sort of thing doesn't just happen in North America, either. We've all heard about the well-publicized violence surrounding soccer games in Europe.

Somehow, in becoming big business entertainment, sports have gone awry. What to do? Well, we can pay more attention to local athletics and events such as the Special Olympics. We can refuse to pay ridiculously high ticket prices. We can demand an end to violence. Above all we need to get back to this idea: It's not whether you win or lose; it's how you play the game.

After You Read

A | Vocabulary: *Complete the definitions with the correct word from the box.*

also-ran	inevitable	partisanship	stamina
awry	lurking	prevalence	venues

1. ________________ are locations where events take place.
2. Something that is ________________ is considered impossible to avoid.
3. Something that is waiting in hiding is said to be ________________.
4. ________________ is defined as strength of body or mind to complete a task.
5. The common, general, or wide existence of something is termed ________________.
6. A loser in a competition is termed a(n) ________________.
7. ________________ is the condition of being devoted to or biased in support of a group or a cause.
8. Something that is away from the correct course is said to be ________________.

B | Comprehension: *Refer to the reading and complete each sentence with a single word.*

1. When the Olympics began, athletic contests were related to ________________.
2. The modern Olympic games were designed to promote ________________.
3. In both the ancient and the revived Olympic games, the original emphasis was on the pursuit of ________________ in physical contests.
4. According to the author of the editorial, the emphasis in today's Olympic games has shifted to the achievement of ________________.
5. The author states that, while a ticket to a baseball game is less expensive than one to a football or basketball game, it's still hardly a ________________.
6. The author says that the high cost of tickets today is most directly related to the need to pay the ________________ of players.
7. According to the author, there is an increasing acceptance of ________________ as being "just part of the game."
8. The author believes that we should support ________________ athletic contests and events such as the Special Olympics.

STEP 2 GRAMMAR PRESENTATION

ADVERB CLAUSES

Placement and Punctuation

Main Clause	Adverb Clause
We watched TV a lot	**when the Olympics were on**.
Tickets cost more	**because athletes earn so much**.

Adverb Clause	Main Clause
When the Olympics were on,	we watched TV a lot.
Because athletes earn so much,	tickets cost more.

Types

Adverb Clauses of Time	
Before I played basketball,	I was a soccer player.
The coach met with her players	**after the game was over**.
While the team was on the field,	the fans cheered continuously.

Adverb Clauses of Place	
I've seen children playing soccer	**everywhere I've been outside the United States**.
Anywhere you go,	sports stars are national heroes.
I work out at a gym	**wherever I travel**.

Adverb Clauses of Reason	
Since she plays well,	I want her on our team.
He was unable to play in the final game	**as he had hurt his ankle**.
Now that TV covers the games,	billions of people can see the Olympics.

Adverb Clauses of Condition	
Unless the tickets cost too much,	we'll go to the game next Saturday.
You'll be comfortable inside the dome	**even if it's cold and raining outside**.
Only if she wins the gold medal	will she get a professional contract.

Adverb Clauses of Contrast	
They won the game,	**though they didn't really deserve the victory**.
Although their team is talented,	they just didn't win.
Swimmers are rarely injured,	**whereas hockey players are often hurt**.

GRAMMAR NOTES

1

Remember that a **clause** is a group of words that contains at least one subject and a verb showing past, present, or future time. Clauses are either independent or dependent.

Independent clauses (also called main clauses) can stand alone as complete sentences.

- **You could win a medal.**
- **We'll go to the game.**

Dependent clauses (also called subordinate clauses) cannot stand alone. They need another clause to be fully understood.

INDEPENDENT CLAUSE / DEPENDENT CLAUSE

- You could win a medal **if you practice enough.**

Sentences containing both an independent clause and a dependent clause are called **complex sentences.** In a complex sentence, the main idea is normally in the independent clause.

DEP. CLAUSE / INDEP. CLAUSE (MAIN IDEA)

- **If we can get tickets**, we'll go to the game.

NOTE: In a complex sentence, the clauses can come in either order. If the dependent clause comes first, we place a comma after it.

- **Whenever I exercise**, I feel good.
- I feel good **whenever I exercise.**

2

Adverb clauses are dependent clauses that indicate **how**, **when**, **where**, **why**, or **under what conditions** things happen. Adverb clauses may also introduce a contrast.

- I went home **when the game was over**. *(when)*
- She dropped out of the race **because she was injured**. *(why)*
- They won the game, **although the score was very close**. *(contrast)*

Adverb clauses begin with **subordinating conjunctions** (also called subordinating adverbs), which can be either single words or phrases.

- It began to rain **while we were playing.**
- I have to practice a lot **now that I'm on the team.**

NOTE: Adverb clauses sometimes come inside independent clauses.

- Her ability **when she got to high school** was remarkable.

3

Adverb clauses of time indicate **when** something happens. They are introduced by *after, as, as soon as, before, by the time, once, since, until / till, when, whenever, while*, etc.

- The race will start **as soon as everyone is in place.**
- We always drink water **before we start a game.**

NOTE: *Once* means *starting from the moment something happens.*

- She'll earn a good salary **once she starts playing regularly**.

NOTE: *Until* and *till* have the same meaning. *Till* is informal and used more in conversation.

- I'll wait here **until / till they arrive.**

BE CAREFUL! In complex sentences, do not use *will* and *be going to* in the dependent clause to show future time.

- We'll leave **when they get here.**
  NOT: We'll leave when they ~~will~~ get here.

can use will & be going to in the independent clause.

(continued on next page)

4	**Adverb clauses of place** indicate **where** something happens. They are introduced by *anywhere, everywhere, where, wherever,* etc.	• Professional sports are played **where there are big stadiums**. • Major athletes are popular **wherever they go**.
5	**Adverb clauses of reason** indicate **why** something happens. They are introduced by *as, because, now that* (= because now), *since,* etc.	• She won the medal **because she had practiced tirelessly**. • **Since he didn't register in time**, he can't play.
	NOTE: *Since* is used both in adverb clauses of reason and of time.	• **Since Anna doesn't like sports**, she refused to go to the game. (*reason:* since = because) • Barry has played sports **since he entered high school**. (*time:* since = starting from that point)
	NOTE: *As* is used both in adverb clauses of reason and of time.	• **As he was badly hurt**, he had to drop out of the game. (*reason:* as = because) • He set a world record **as we were watching**. (*time:* as = while)
6	**Adverb clauses of condition** indicate **under what conditions** something happens. They are introduced by *even if, if, only if, unless, in case,* etc.	• You'll improve **if you practice daily**.
	Even if means that the condition does not matter; the result will be the same.	• **Even if he practices constantly**, he won't make the team.
	Only if means that only one condition will produce the result.	• Bi-Yun will make the team **only if another athlete drops out**.
	Unless means that something will happen or be true if another thing does not happen or is not true.	• **Unless you train a great deal**, you won't be a champion.
	In case means in order to be prepared for a possible future happening.	• We'd better take along some extra money **in case we run into difficulties**.
	NOTE: If the sentence begins with *only if,* the subject and verb of the main clause are inverted, and no comma is used.	• **Only if** another athlete drops out **will Bi-Yun** make the team.
	BE CAREFUL! Don't confuse *even if* or *even though* with *even*.	• **Even if** they win this game, they won't be the champions. • **Even** my mother understands the rules of baseball.

7	
Adverb clauses of contrast make a contrast with the idea expressed in the independent clause. They are introduced by *although*, *even though*, *though*, *whereas*, *while*, etc.	• He lost the race, **although he was favored**. • **Even though she is tall**, she doesn't score much.
We usually use *although*, *even though*, and *though* when we want to show an unexpected result.	• **Although / Even though / Though he is quite young**, he was selected for the team. *(comma after the clause)*
NOTE: We normally place a comma before or after a dependent clause of contrast.	• He was selected for the team, **though / although / even though he is quite young**. • **Though / Although / Even though he is quite young**, he was selected for the team.
To make a direct contrast, we use *while* or *whereas*.	• **While / Whereas downhill skiing is very expensive**, cross-country skiing is cheap.
USAGE NOTE: *Whereas* is used in formal written English and careful speech.	
NOTE: *While* is used to introduce both a clause of contrast and a clause of time.	• **While they lost the game**, they played their best. *(contrast)* • We ate **while we were watching the game**. *(time)*

REFERENCE NOTES

For a list of **subordinating conjunctions**, see Appendix 20 on page A-9.
For more practice on **future time clauses**, see Unit 3.

STEP 3 FOCUSED PRACTICE

EXERCISE 1: Discover the Grammar

In each of the sentences, underline the dependent clause once and the independent clause twice. Then write **contrast, place, time, reason,** *or* **condition** *above the dependent clauses.*

1. As I write this editorial, the World Cup is in full swing in South Africa.
2. While sports may look good on the surface, problems are lurking underneath.
3. Because he penalized a player in the 2008 European Championships, a British referee received death threats.
4. When the Olympic games started about 2,700 years ago in Greece, the contests held were basically those related to war.

(continued on next page)

5. Running paralleled the physical exertion you might have to make if an enemy was chasing you.
6. Although athletes still try to achieve their personal best, the emphasis has shifted away from the individual pursuit of excellence.
7. I wondered why tickets are so expensive until I remembered the key factor: players' salaries.
8. Baseball is cheaper, though it's not really a bargain at an average ticket cost of $27.
9. We see violence wherever we look.
10. Once we assume violence is inevitable, it will be almost impossible to stop.

EXERCISE 2: Word Order

(Grammar Notes 3, 5–7)

Rearrange the words to make sentences, each containing an adverb clause. Add necessary punctuation.

1. ticket / can / to / Before / lift / buy / a / you / you / have / start

   Before you can start, you have to buy a lift ticket.

2. player's / love / zero / If / score / the / one / forty / is / is / score

   ____

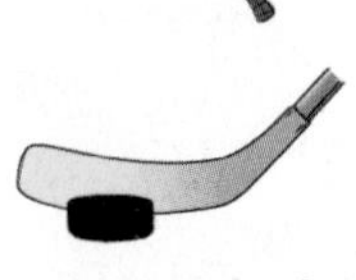

3. unless / can't / You / you / ice / have / game / skates / and / this / play

   ____

4. free-throw / line / You / after / you've / go / the / to / fouled / been

   ____

5. use / head / hands / Though / may / you / you / your / your / use / can't

   ____

6. miles / You've / you've / 26.2 / course / finished / run / the / when

   ____

7. bat / until / Your / team / team / can't / outs / three / makes / the / other

   ____

8. touchdown / scores / If / team / your / earns / points / a / it / six

   ____

EXERCISE 3: Combining Sentences

(Grammar Notes 3, 5–6)

Combine each pair of sentences into one sentence containing an adverb clause and a main clause. Keep the clauses in the same order. Add necessary punctuation.

1. There are similarities between the ancient and modern Olympics. There are also differences.

   Though / Although / While / Even though there are similarities between the ancient and modern Olympics, there are also differences.

2. Greek city-states were often at war with one another. Olympic contestants stopped fighting during the games.

   Although Greek city-states

3. The ancient Olympic games were outlawed by the Roman Emperor Theodosius I. They had been held for over 1,000 years.

4. He outlawed them in 393. Romans thought the Greeks wore too few clothes.

5. French educator Pierre de Coubertin revived the Olympics. He thought they would promote international peace.

6. Tug-of-war was dropped from the Olympics in 1920. American and British athletes disagreed about how it should be played.

7. New Olympic sports often first appear as demonstration events. They are adopted as medal sports.

8. Any sport can potentially become a medal event. It can be scored and fulfills certain criteria.

EXERCISE 4: Writing Adverb Clauses

(Grammar Notes 3, 5–7)

Look at the pictures. Complete the sentence describing each picture with an adverb clause. Use a different subordinating conjunction in each clause.

1. The Sharks will win the game ______________ **(condition)** If the player makes the basket ______________

2. The other team can't win ______________ **(condition)** ______________ ______________

3. ______________ **(contrast)** ______________ ______________, their fans still love them.

4. The players are doing their best ______________ **(contrast)** ______________ ______________

5. ______________ **(reason)** ______________ ______________, the competition was postponed.

6. The competition won't be held ______________ **(time)** ______________ ______________ improve.

EXERCISE 5: Editing

Read the student essay. There are eight mistakes in the use of adverb clauses, including incorrect subordinating conjunctions and incorrect verbs. The first mistake is already corrected. Find and correct seven more.

Why Sports?

by Jamal Jefferson

A lot of people are criticizing school sports these days. Some say there's too much emphasis on football and basketball ~~if~~ *while* there's not enough emphasis on education. Others say the idea of the scholar-athlete is a joke. Still others say sports provide a way of encouraging violence. I think they're all wrong. If anything, school sports help prevent violence, not encourage it. Why do I think sports are a positive force?

For one thing, sports are positive even though they give students opportunities to be involved in something. Every day on TV we hear that violence is increasing. I think a lot of people get involved in crime when they don't have enough to do to keep themselves busy. After you'll play two or three hours of basketball, baseball, or any other kind of sport, it's hard to commit a violent act even if you want to.

Second, sports teach people a lot of worthwhile things, especially at the high school level. If they play on a team, students learn to get along and work with others. Wherever their team wins, they learn how to be good winners; when their team will lose, they find out that they have to struggle to improve. They discover that winning a few and losing a few are part of the normal ups and downs of life. Also, there's no doubt that students improve their physical condition by participating in sports.

Finally, sports are positive although they allow students who do not have enough money to go to college to get sports scholarships and improve their chances for a successful life. Unless a young basketball player from a small village in Nigeria can get a scholarship to play for, say UCLA, he will have a chance to get an education and probably make his life better. If a young woman with little money is accepted on the University of Toronto swim team and gets a scholarship, she'll have the chance to earn a college degree and go on to a high-paying job. Because school sports programs have some deficiencies that need to be corrected, their benefits outweigh their disadvantages. I should know because I'm one of those students who got a sports scholarship. School sports must stay.

STEP 4 COMMUNICATION PRACTICE

EXERCISE 6: Listening

A | *Listen to the interview. What country is Lillian Swanson from?*

____

B | *Read the questions. Listen to the interview with a sports star. Then listen again and answer each question with a complete sentence containing an adverb clause.*

1. Why did Lillian Swanson become successful?

   Lillian Swanson became successful because her parents loved and supported her.

2. When did Lillian learn to swim?

   ____

3. Why does Lillian think she became a good swimmer?

   ____

4. Why did Lillian and her family spend a lot of time at the beach?

   ____

5. What did Lillian decide when she was 12?

   ____

6. Under what conditions did Lillian's parents agree to pay for lessons?

   ____

7. When did Lillian get discouraged?

   ____

8. Why can't Lillian imagine herself doing anything else?

   ____

9. What happened once Lillian started her lessons?

   ____

EXERCISE 7: Pronunciation

A | *Read and listen to the Pronunciation Note.*

Pronunciation Note

English speakers normally pause in a sentence in which a dependent adverb clause comes first in a complex sentence. They normally do not pause when a dependent clause comes second. However, a speaker normally pauses after or before an adverb clause that shows a contrast. The pause is indicated in writing with a comma.

EXAMPLES:

As soon as she graduates, she'll start her physical training. *(pause, comma)*

She'll start her physical training **as soon as she graduates**. *(no pause, no comma)*

Though he has a lot of talent, he doesn't work very hard at his sport. *(pause, comma)*

He doesn't work very hard at his sport**, though he has a lot of talent**. *(pause, comma)*

B | *Listen and repeat the sentences. Place a comma wherever you hear a pause.*

1. As soon as the game was over, we left the stadium.
2. Elena swam laps while I did my calisthenics.
3. Even though the team scored 10 runs they still didn't win.
4. In case you haven't heard the manager was fired.
5. I always manage to go to a gym whenever I'm traveling.
6. He makes a lot of money now that he's a major league player.
7. The coach was not popular with his players although he took them to the championship.
8. Tickets to the game were very expensive though I'd have to say the expense was justified.
9. She always warms up by swimming extra laps before she begins a competition.
10. After Daoud scored the winning goal he was mobbed by his teammates.
11. The team won't make the playoffs unless they win their next eight games.
12. Once he started wearing contact lenses he became a much more accurate player.

C | *PAIRS: Practice the sentences, making sure to pause when there is a comma.*

EXERCISE 8: Personal Inventory

A | *Write sentences with adverb clauses about your possible future, using the subordinating conjunctions in parentheses. Place the dependent clause first in half of the sentences and second in the other half.*

EXAMPLE: **When I'm rich,** I'll sleep on a soft pillow.

1. (when) ______________________________
____
2. (if) ______________________________
____
3. (unless) ______________________________
____
4. (in case) ______________________________
____
5. (because) ______________________________
____
6. (after) ______________________________
____
7. (as soon as) ______________________________
____
8. (once) ______________________________
____
9. (before) ______________________________
____
10. (although) ______________________________
____

B | *PAIRS: Discuss your answers. Report interesting answers to the class.*

EXERCISE 9: Picture Discussion

A | *GROUPS: Discuss what is happening in the picture. In your view, how does the picture reflect sports in the world today? Have sports everywhere become too violent, or is this sort of behavior just "part of the game"?*

B | *Discuss your conclusions with the class.*

EXERCISE 10: Writing

A | *Choose one of the topics and write three or four paragraphs about it. If possible, support your ideas with examples from your personal experience. Use adverb clauses in your composition.*

- Sports are valuable to society because they provide entertainment.
- Sports have become too violent.
- Sports provide opportunities to people who have few other opportunities.
- Sports stars earn ridiculously large salaries.

EXAMPLE: Though many people say that sports are overemphasized in our culture, my opinion is that the advantages of sports outweigh their disadvantages. In particular, I strongly believe that sports provide opportunities to people who don't have many other opportunities. Consider the inner-city boy, for example, whose parents can't afford to send him to college, even though he's a good student. One of my best friends falls into this category. He . . .

B | *Check your work. Use the Editing Checklist.*

Editing Checklist

Did you use . . . ?

☐ correct placement and punctuation of adverb clauses
☐ adverb clauses of reason correctly
☐ adverb clauses of condition correctly
☐ adverb clauses of contrast correctly

UNIT 19 Review

Check your answers on page UR-3.
Do you need to review anything?

A | *Circle the word or phrase that correctly completes each sentence.*

1. You won't be a champion if / unless you practice regularly.
2. Since / Even though the team is in the playoffs, I doubt they'll win the title.
3. We're taking along our racquets in case / although there's time to play.
4. Whenever / As Hai was running toward the goal line, he sprained his ankle.
5. Once / As Bahdoon gets used to his new position, he'll be a great help.
6. Nelson and Elena don't go dancing once / now that they have children.
7. Famous athletes are in demand wherever / whereas they go.
8. We'll be leaving as soon as / since she arrives.

B | *Correct the mistakes in the underlined words or phrases.*

1. I visit my cousin wherever I'm in town. ____________
2. Until she arrives, we'll be leaving. ____________
3. Only if I study for days, I'm not likely to earn an "A." ____________
4. Although she's seldom at home, I don't often stop to see her. ____________
5. Whereas he exercises will he lose weight. ____________
6. Because they played with great skill, they lost the game. ____________
7. Since flying costs a lot, bus travel is inexpensive. ____________
8. That check is going to bounce when we make a deposit. ____________

C | *Circle the letter of the one underlined word or phrase in each sentence that is not correct.*

1. We'll start when they will get here, as long as they get here soon. **A B C D**
   when (A) — will get (B) — as long as (C) — get (D)
2. Even you explain the game to Mom, she won't understand what's going on. **A B C D**
   Even (A) — explain (B) — won't (C) — what's going on (D)
3. As cars surely offer benefits, they unfortunately cause problems also. **A B C D**
   As (A) — surely (B) — unfortunately (C) — also (D)
4. We're angry because he's late, but I guess we'll wait until he'll arrive. **A B C D**
   because (A) — we'll (B) — until (C) — he'll arrive (D)

UNIT 20 Adverb and Adverbial Phrases
COMPASSION

STEP 1 GRAMMAR IN CONTEXT

Before You Read

PAIRS: Discuss the questions.

1. What is your definition of compassion?
2. How important a value is compassion in society?

Read

Read the article about compassion.

Compassion

It was the evening of September 29, 1994. **Having spent a wonderful day exploring the ruins at Paestum in southern Italy**, Reg and Maggie Green were driving south in the area of Italy known as the boot, **their children Nicholas and Eleanor sleeping peacefully in the back seat**. Suddenly an old, decrepit car pulled up alongside them, and an Italian with a bandanna over his face screamed at them, **signaling them to stop**. **Not knowing what to do**, Reg carefully weighed the options. If they stopped, they risked a potentially deadly confrontation with criminals; if they sped away, they might escape. **Guessing that their newer-model car could probably elude the old car the criminals were driving**, Reg floored the gas pedal. Shots rang out, **shattering both windows on the driver's side of the car**. The Greens' car took off, **easily outdistancing the bandits' car**. **Checking the children**, Reg and Maggie

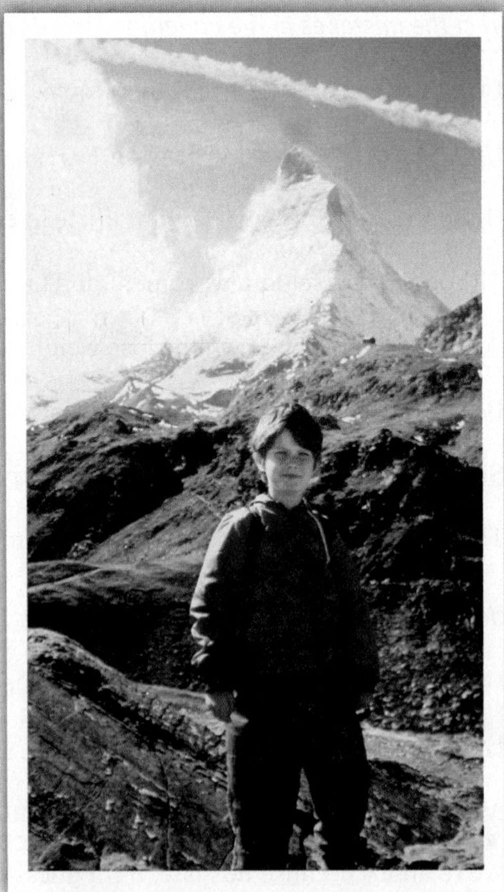

found them still **sleeping peacefully in the back seat**.

A bit farther down the road, Reg saw a police car parked on the shoulder and pulled over to alert the authorities. **Upon opening the door**, he saw blood oozing from the back of Nicholas's head. **After being rushed to a hospital**, Nicholas lay in a coma for two days. Then doctors declared him brain-dead.

This was not the end of the story, however. As Nicholas lay on his deathbed, Reg and Maggie decided that something good should come out of the situation. **Realizing that it would be far better to return good for evil than to seek revenge**, they offered Nicholas's organs for transplant. "Someone should have the future he lost," Reg said. **Profoundly moved by the gesture**, Italians poured out their emotions. Maurizio Costanzo, the host of a talk show, summed up the common feeling by saying, "You have given us a lesson in civility . . . shown us how to react in the face of pain and sorrow."

The great irony of this tragedy was that it was a mistake. Investigators later determined that Nicholas was killed by two petty criminals who thought the Greens were jewelers carrying precious stones. The criminals were placed on trial **after being turned over to the police**.

People all over Europe and North America reacted in sorrow. Headlines in Italian newspapers spoke of *La Nostra Vergogna* ("Our Shame"). Wherever the Greens went, they met Italians who begged their forgiveness. The Greens were given a medal, Italy's highest honor, by the prime minister.

Some good has indeed come out of Nicholas's death. Seven Italians received Nicholas's heart, liver, kidneys, islet cells (cells related to diabetes), and corneas. Perhaps more importantly, a blow was struck for organ donation. **Having heard Reg and Maggie speak on TV**, 40,000 French people pledged to donate their organs when they died. **On returning to the United States**, the Greens began to receive requests to tell their son's story and speak about organ donation. "It gradually dawned on us," said Reg, "that we'd been given a life's work."

Nicholas Green is gone, but others live on because of his parents' compassionate act. How many of us would do the same thing, **given the chance**?

After You Read

A | Vocabulary: *Match the blue words and phrases on the left with their meanings on the right.*

____ **1.** Suddenly an old, **decrepit** car pulled up alongside them.

____ **2.** An Italian with a **bandanna** over his face screamed at them.

____ **3.** Reg carefully **weighed** the options.

____ **4.** Reg thought his newer-model vehicle could probably **elude** the criminals' car.

____ **5.** Reg **floored** the gas pedal.

____ **6.** He saw blood **oozing** from Nicholas's head.

____ **7.** Nicholas was killed by two **petty** criminals.

____ **8.** Seven Italians received Nicholas's heart, liver, kidneys, islet cells, and **corneas**.

____ **9.** **A blow was struck** for organ donation.

____ **10.** It gradually **dawned on** us that we'd been given a life's work.

a. pushed to the maximum extent

b. flowing slowly

c. became apparent to

d. progress was made

e. large handkerchief

f. considered

g. broken-down

h. coverings on the outer surface of your eyes

i. unimportant

j. escape from

B | Comprehension: *Refer to the reading and complete each sentence with a single word.*

1. The Greens were traveling in the geographical area of Italy known as the ____________.

2. The Greens' car was newer than the ____________ car.

3. Shots shattered the windows on the ____________ side of the Greens' car.

4. After the shooting, Nicholas lay in a ____________ for two days.

5. The Greens offered Nicholas's organs for ____________.

6. Italians were profoundly ____________ by the Greens' donation of Nicholas's organs.

7. The ironic aspect of the Greens' tragedy was that it was a ____________.

8. The criminals were placed on ____________ after being turned over to the police.

STEP 2 GRAMMAR PRESENTATION

ADVERB AND ADVERBIAL PHRASES

Reducing Adverb Clauses of Time to Adverb Phrases

Adverb Clause		Adverb Phrase	
While they were in Italy,	they had trouble.	**While in Italy,**	they had trouble.
While I was in Italy,		Ø*	
When I am traveling,	I keep a journal.	**When traveling,**	I keep a journal.
When Sue is traveling,		Ø	

*Ø = no change possible

Changing Adverb Clauses of Time to Adverb Phrases

Adverb Clause		Adverb Phrase	
Before we left,	we visited Rome.	**Before leaving,**	we visited Rome.
Before Ann left,		Ø	
After they (had) investigated,	the police identified the killers.	**After investigating,**	the police identified the killers.
		After having investigated,	
When they heard Reg speak,	many Italians were moved.	**On / Upon hearing Reg speak,**	many Italians were moved.

Changing Adverb Clauses of Time to Adverbial Phrases

Adverb Clause		Adverbial Phrase	
While they waited at the hospital,	they were deeply troubled.	**Waiting at the hospital,**	they were deeply troubled.
When they heard the news,	they decided what to do.	**Hearing the news,**	they decided what to do.

Changing Adverb Clauses of Reason to Adverbial Phrases

Adverb Clause		Adverbial Phrase	
As he saw the guns,	he chose to flee.	**Seeing the guns,**	he chose to flee.
Because they were unable to catch him,	the pursuers fired several shots.	**Being unable to catch him,**	the pursuers fired several shots.
Because I've been to Bari,	I hope to return.	**Having been to Bari,**	I hope to return.
Because I'd been to Bari,	I hoped to return.		I hoped to return.
Since they were accused by the police,	they had to appear in court.	**Accused by the police,**	they had to appear in court.

GRAMMAR NOTES

1	Remember that a **clause** is a group of words with a subject and a verb that shows time. A **phrase** does not have both a subject and a verb showing time. It commonly has a present or past participle.	CLAUSE • **After he sped away**, he heard a shot. PHRASE • **After speeding away**, he heard a shot.
	Some **adverb clauses** can be shortened to **adverb phrases** in ways similar to the ways adjective clauses can be shortened: by **reducing** the clauses or by **changing** them.	ADVERB CLAUSE • We had a flat tire **while we were touring**. ADVERB PHRASE (REDUCED) • We had a flat tire **while touring**. ADVERB CLAUSE • **After we fixed the flat tire**, we were on our way again. ADVERB PHRASE (CHANGED) • **After fixing the flat tire**, we were on our way again.
	Negative adverb phrases contain the word *not* or *never* before the participle.	• After **not eating** all day, we were very hungry.
2	**Adverb clauses** can be **reduced to adverb phrases** when the clause has a form of *be*. To reduce an adverb clause to a phrase, omit the subject pronoun and the form of *be*. If the original sentence has commas, keep the commas in the reduced sentence.	ADVERB CLAUSE • **While they were driving**, they were attacked by bandits. ADVERB PHRASE • **While driving**, they were attacked by bandits.
	BE CAREFUL! You can reduce an adverb clause to an adverb phrase only if the subjects in both clauses of the sentence refer to the same person or thing.	• **Reg and Maggie** drove while **the children** were sleeping. NOT: Reg and Maggie drove ~~while sleeping~~.
	NOTE: An adverb phrase can come first or second in the sentence. When it comes first, we usually place a comma after it.	• **While driving**, they were attacked by bandits. • They were attacked by bandits **while driving**.
3	**Adverb clauses of time** beginning with *after*, *before*, *since*, and *while* can be **changed to adverb phrases** when the clause has no form of ***be***. To change an adverb clause to a phrase, omit the subject pronoun and change the verb to its *-ing* form. Keep the subordinating conjunction and the original punctuation.	ADVERB CLAUSE • **After they visited Paestum**, the Greens drove south. ADVERB PHRASE • **After visiting Paestum**, the Greens drove south.
	BE CAREFUL! You can change an adverb clause to a phrase only if the subjects in the two clauses of the sentence refer to the same person or thing.	• After **the bandits** saw the Greens' car, **the Greens** sped away. NOT: ~~After seeing the Greens' car~~, the Greens sped away.

4	A simple past or past perfect verb in an adverb clause changes to the *-ing* form or *having* + past participle in an adverb phrase.	• After they **(had) opened** the door, they saw the blood. • After **opening** the door, they saw the blood. OR • **Having opened** the door, they saw the blood.
5	***Upon*** or ***on*** + *-ing* in an adverb phrase usually has the same meaning as ***when*** in an adverb clause.	ADVERB PHRASE • **Upon / On realizing** what had happened, they pulled to the side of the road. ADVERB CLAUSE • **When they realized** what had happened, they pulled to the side of the road.
6	The **subordinating conjunction** is sometimes omitted in a phrase. A phrase without a subordinating conjunction is called an **adverbial phrase**.	ADVERB PHRASE • **While sitting on the porch**, I thought about my future. ADVERBIAL PHRASE • **Sitting on the porch**, I thought about my future.
	BE CAREFUL! Do not omit the subordinating conjunction in a passive construction.	• I worked for two years **before being accepted** at the university. NOT: I worked for two years ~~being accepted~~ at the university.
7	**Adverb clauses of reason** can be **changed to adverbial phrases**. The subordinating conjunctions *because*, *since*, or *as* at the beginning of a clause must be omitted in an adverbial phrase of reason.	ADVERB CLAUSE • **Because / Since / As the children were sleeping in the car**, they were not aware of what was happening. ADVERBIAL PHRASE • **Sleeping in the car**, the children were not aware of what was happening. NOT: ~~Because~~ sleeping in the car, the children were not aware of what was happening.
	Because / Since / As + a form of *be* can be changed to *being* in an adverbial phrase.	• **Because / Since / As** they **were** not satisfied, they decided to do something about the problem. • Not **being** satisfied, they decided to do something about the problem.
	A present perfect or past perfect verb in an adverb clause can be changed to *having* + past participle in an adverbial phrase.	• Because they **had been** moved by the situation, people became organ donors. • **Having been** moved by the situation, people became organ donors.

(continued on next page)

8

A **clause containing a passive verb** can be **changed** to an **adverbial phrase with just a past participle**. If the subordinating conjunction can be omitted without changing the meaning, delete the subject and any auxiliaries in the passive sentence.

- **Since I was given two options,** I chose the harder of the two.
- **Given two options,** I chose the harder of the two.

P.P pastparticiple

BE CAREFUL! If the subordinating conjunction cannot be omitted without changing the meaning, as in some clauses of time, form an adverb phrase by deleting the subject and changing the form of *be* to *being*.

- **Before I was told** the nature of the problem, I had no idea what to do.
- **Before being told** the nature of the problem, I had no idea what to do.

NOT: ~~Told the nature of the problem~~, I had no idea what to do.

REFERENCE NOTE

For **shortening adjective clauses to adjective phrases**, see Unit 13.

STEP 3 FOCUSED PRACTICE

EXERCISE 1: Discover the Grammar

A | *Underline the adverb phrase in each sentence. Circle the subordinating conjunction.*

1. Upon opening the door, he saw blood oozing from Nicholas's head.
2. Nicholas lay in a coma for two days after being rushed to a hospital.
3. On returning to the United States, Nicholas's parents received requests to tell their son's story.
4. The criminals were placed on trial after being turned over to the police.

B | *Read the sentences. Is the second sentence a correct rewriting of the first? Circle* **Y (Yes)** *or* **N (No).**

1. Having spent a wonderful day exploring the ruins at Paestum, Reg and Maggie Green were driving south.

   Y (N) Spending a wonderful day exploring the ruins at Paestum, Reg and Maggie Green were driving south.

2. An Italian with a bandanna over his face screamed at them, signaling them to stop.

   Y N An Italian with a bandanna over his face screamed at them while signaling them to stop.

3. Not knowing what to do, Reg carefully weighed the options.

   Y N Because he didn't know what to do, Reg carefully weighed the options.

4. Shots rang out, shattering both windows on the driver's side of the car.

   Y N Having shattered both windows on the driver's side of the car, shots rang out.

5. The Greens' car took off, easily outdistancing the bandits' car.

   Y N Having outdistanced the bandits' car, the Green's car took off.

6. Upon opening the door, Reg saw blood oozing from the back of Nicholas's head.

   Y N When he opened the door, Reg saw blood oozing from the back of Nicholas's head.

7. After being rushed to a hospital, Nicholas lay in a coma for two days.

   Y N After he was rushed to a hospital, Nicholas lay in a coma for two days.

8. How many of us would do the same thing, given the chance?

   Y N How many of us would do the same thing if we were given the chance?

EXERCISE 2: Adverb Clauses to Phrases

(Grammar Notes 1–3)

Read the sentences. Circle the subjects in both clauses and connect the circles. If the subjects refer to the same person or thing, shorten the sentence by reducing or changing the adverb clause to a phrase. If the subjects are different, write **cannot be shortened.**

1. When a broken-down car pulled alongside their car, an Italian with a bandanna over his face screamed at them.

   cannot be shortened

2. Reg carefully considered the options before he sped away.

   ____

3. Because the criminals were a deadly threat, Reg floored the gas pedal.

   ____

4. When Reg saw a police car parked on the shoulder, he pulled over to alert the authorities.

   ____

5. As Nicholas lay on his deathbed, Reg and Maggie decided that something good should come out of the situation.

   ____

6. Because the criminals thought the Greens had precious stones, they fired shots that killed Nicholas.

   ____

EXERCISE 3: Clauses / Phrases

(Grammar Notes 2–8)

A | *Read the article about an apparently grieving animal.*

A Caring Elephant That Died of Grief

By Sutapa Mukerjee, The Associated Press

LUCKNOW, INDIA. Distressed by a companion's death, Damini refused to move, to eat, to drink. For 24 days, zookeepers and veterinarians tried everything they could think of to save an elephant who seemed determined to die.

Despite all their efforts, Damini died yesterday in her enclosure. After she had suffered for so long, loose gray skin hung over her protruding bones, and bedsores covered much of her body.

Zoo officials said Damini was 72. She came to the zoo last year after she was taken from owners who were illegally transporting her. She was alone for five months until the arrival in September of a pregnant younger elephant named Champakali.

Champakali came from Dudhwa National Park, where she had worked carrying around tourists. When she became pregnant, park officials decided to send her to the zoo in Lucknow for a kind of maternity leave.

The two elephants "became inseparable in no time," said the zookeeper. Damini made herself available at all hours for Champakali, who seemed to love the attention.

"Elephants are very social animals. They can form very close bonds with others in their social group," said Pat Thomas, curator of mammals at the Bronx Zoo in New York City. "It's been pretty well documented that they do exhibit emotions that we would consider grieving" when a calf or other elephant dies.

However, he said, an age-related medical problem should not be discounted as well in the case of an elephant as old as Damini.

On April 11, giving birth to a stillborn calf, Champakali died. Damini seemed to shed tears, then showed little interest in food or anything else, according to zoo officials.

For days, Damini stood still in her enclosure, barely nibbling at the two tons of sugarcane, bananas, and grass heaped in front of her.

Her legs soon swelled up and eventually gave way. After that, Damini lay still on her side, head and ears drooping, trunk curled. Tears rolled from her eyes, and the 4-ton elephant rapidly lost weight.

A week ago, Damini completely stopped eating or drinking her usual daily quota of 40 gallons of water, despite the 116-degree heat.

Alarmed, veterinarians pumped more than 25 gallons of glucose, saline, and vitamins through a vein in her ear.

Yesterday, Damini died.

"It will take me some time to get over the death of my two loved ones," her keeper said.

B | *Refer to the article and follow the instructions.*

1. Rewrite the adverbial phrase in this sentence as an adverb clause.

   Distressed by a companion's death, Damini refused to move, to eat, to drink.

   Because Damini was distressed by a companion's death,

2. Read the original and revised sentences. Is the revised sentence correct?

   Original: After she had suffered for so long, loose gray skin hung over her protruding bones, and bedsores covered much of her body.

   Revised: After suffering for so long, loose gray skin hung over her protruding bones, and bedsores covered much of her body.

   _____ yes _____ no

3. Rewrite this sentence, changing the adverb clause to an adverb phrase.

   She came to the zoo last year after she was taken from owners.

   ____

4. Read the original and revised sentences. Is the revised sentence correct?

   Original: When she became pregnant, park officials decided to send her to the zoo in Lucknow.

   Revised: Becoming pregnant, park officials decided to send her to the zoo in Lucknow.

   _____ yes _____ no

5. Read the original and combined sentences. Is the combined sentence correct?

   Original: Elephants are very social animals. They can form very close bonds with others in their social group.

   Combined sentence: Being very social animals, elephants can form very close bonds with others in their social group.

   _____ yes _____ no

6. Rewrite the adverbial phrase as an adverb phrase by adding a subordinating conjunction.

   On April 11, Champakali died giving birth to a stillborn calf.

   ____

7. Rewrite the sentence as two independent clauses.

   Damini stood still in her enclosure, barely nibbling at the two tons of food in front of her.

   ____

EXERCISE 4: Adverb Phrases / Main Clauses

(Grammar Notes 3–8)

Look at the pictures, which are connected in a story. Write a sentence with an adverb or adverbial phrase and a main clause to describe each situation. Use the prompts.

1.

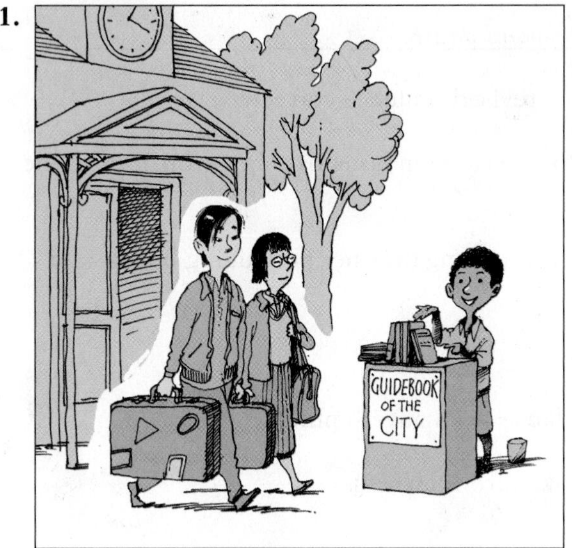

(present participle)

Coming out of the train station, the tourists saw a boy selling guidebooks.

2.

(present participle)

____

____

3.

(*not* + present participle)

____

____

4.

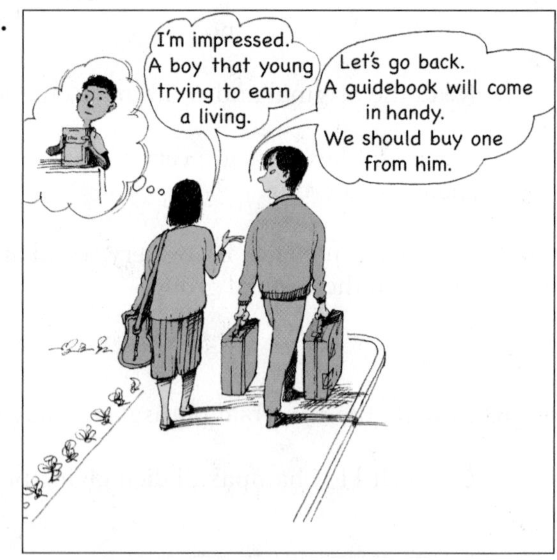

(past participle)

____

____

5.

(present participle)

6.

(*having* + past participle)

7.

(*after* + present participle)

8.

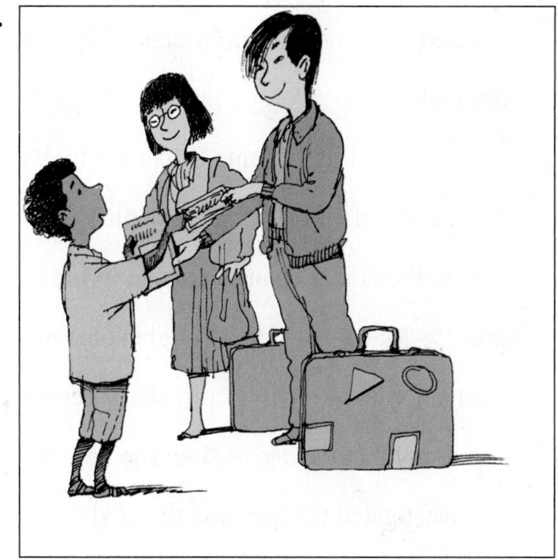

(*having* + present participle)

EXERCISE 5: Editing

Read the magazine article. There are seven mistakes involving the use of adverb and adverbial phrases. The first mistake is already corrected. Find and correct six more.

A Helping Hand

by Jim Lamoureaux

If you're at all like me, you tire of requests to help others. ~~Barraging~~ Barraged by seemingly constant appeals for money to support homeless shelters, the Special Olympics, or the like, I tend to tune out, my brain numbed. I don't think I'm selfish. But subjecting to so many requests, I only remember the flashy ones. By arguing that I don't have enough money to help others, I am able to ignore the requests. Or at least that was the way I saw the situation before sent by my magazine to South America to do a human interest story on homeless children. Having heard many TV requests asking viewers to sponsor a child overseas, I always said to myself, "I'll bet the money is pocketed by some local politician." My opinion changed when I saw the reality of the life of a poor child.

While landing in Santa Simona, I took a taxi to my hotel in the center of town, where I met Elena, a girl of 10 or 11. Sat on a dirty blanket on the sidewalk in front of the hotel, she caught my eye. Elena was trying to earn a living by selling mangoes. Smiling at me, she asked, "*Mangos, señor*? —Mangoes, sir?" I bought some mangoes and some other fruit, and we talked together. Elena's life had been difficult. Her parents were both dead, and she lived with an elderly aunt. Having polio at the age of five, she now walked with a limp. She and her aunt often went hungry.

Investigated the question the next day, I talked to several different authorities. Having become convinced that money from sponsors does in fact get to those who need it, I knew my attitude had to change. Learning that I could sponsor Elena for less than a dollar a day, I began to feel ashamed; after all, I spend more than that on my dogs. But what remains most vivid in my mind is my vision of Elena. She didn't beg or feel sorry for herself. Selling her mangoes, she earned a living, and her spirit shone through in the process. So I say to all of you reading this: The next time you hear an ad about sponsoring a child, pay attention.

STEP 4 COMMUNICATION PRACTICE

EXERCISE 6: Listening

A | *Listen to the news broadcast. Check (✓) the two subjects that are not mentioned.*

- ☐ political struggles in the nation of Franconia
- ☐ an oil spill in the Mediterranean
- ☐ a new vaccine for AIDS
- ☐ a new nation comes into existence
- ☐ World Cup news
- ☐ a rescue in a swimming pool

B | *Read the questions. Listen again to the news broadcast. Then answer each question in a complete sentence.*

1. When asked whether he would attend next week's peace conference, did rebel leader Amalde commit himself?

   No, he declined to commit himself.

2. According to Mr. Amalde, how could Mr. Tintor demonstrate good faith?

   ____

3. Did the president's aide speak on or off the record?

   ____

4. What did researchers from the Global Health Foundation acknowledge?

   ____

5. How is the new nation to be known?

   ____

6. What will it need in order to become a viable state?

   ____

7. Why had Michaels almost given up hope of being rescued?

   ____

8. How did Hutchinson save him?

   ____

EXERCISE 7: Pronunciation

A | *Read and listen to the Pronunciation Note.*

Pronunciation Note

Notice how the pronunciation of vowels in English changes when the stress shifts in words that are members of the same family:

EXAMPLES:

She has always been interested in **politics**.	(stress on the first syllable; the vowel in the second syllable has the schwa sound, /ə/)
She comes from a **political** family.	(stress on the second syllable; the vowel in this syllable assumes the pronunciation of a full vowel)

B | *Listen and repeat the sentences. In the boldfaced words, circle the syllables that have stress.*

1. The Greens were traveling in **Italy**.
2. They made a great impression on many **Italians**.
3. The Greens risked a deadly **confrontation** with the bandits.
4. The bandits **confronted** the Greens.
5. The **criminals** fired shots at the Greens' car.
6. These bandits engaged in **criminality**.
7. The great **irony** of this tragedy was that it was a mistake.
8. It was **ironic** that the bandits thought the Greens were jewelers.
9. The Greens **realized** they'd been given a life's work.
10. The **reality** of the situation was that Nicholas lost his life.

C | *PAIRS: Practice the sentences, taking turns so that each partner pronounces each sentence.*

EXERCISE 8: Personal Inventory

A | *Complete the sentences according to your personal experience.*

1. Having finished high school . . . , I . . . got a good jobs

2. Given the chance to . . . , I . . .

   Given the chance to learn English, I confident talk to

3. Not wanting to . . . , I . . .

4. Being unable to . . . , I . . .

5. While driving . . . , I . . .

6. After visiting . . . , I . . .

   After visting

B | *PAIRS: Discuss your answers. Report interesting examples to the class.*

EXERCISE 9: Group Discussion

A | *PAIRS: Review the article "A Caring Elephant That Died of Grief" on page 348. In small groups, discuss the questions.*

1. Compare animals and humans in regard to showing emotion. Do you think animals are capable of grief or any other kind of emotion?
2. Give a personal example of an animal showing grief or another emotion.

EXAMPLE: **A:** I don't think animals show emotion.
B: I disagree.
A: Why?
B: My aunt died last year. Her dog . . .

B | *Share your answers with the class.*

EXERCISE 10: Writing

A | *Write three or four paragraphs about an act you have witnessed that you believe qualifies as compassionate. Describe the situation fully. What made the act compassionate? Did the compassionate person have anything to gain from showing compassion? Use adverb and/or adverbial phrases in your composition.*

EXAMPLE: Perhaps the best example of compassion I have witnessed occurred about a year ago. Having attended an office party, I finally managed to leave about 10:00 P.M. Driving home on a major expressway, I suddenly felt the car slow down and heard a grinding noise. Realizing that I probably had a flat tire, I quickly pulled over to the side of the road. I looked for the jack to change the flat but couldn't find it. I thought about calling my brother but couldn't find my cell phone, either. Just then a group of teenagers slowed down and stopped . . .

B | *Check your work. Use the Editing Checklist.*

Editing Checklist

Did you use . . . ?

☐ adverb phrases of time correctly

☐ adverbial phrases of time correctly

☐ adverbial phrases of reason correctly

UNIT 20 Review

Check your answers on page UR-3.
Do you need to review anything?

A | *Circle the word or phrase that correctly completes each sentence.*

1. Not knowing / Because not knowing what to do, we called the service department.
2. Having caught cheating / Caught cheating, she failed the course.
3. Getting the tickets / Having gotten the tickets, we were able to leave.
4. Taksim turned off the lights before leaving / before left home.
5. On realizing / When realizing what had happened, we called the police.
6. During relaxing / Relaxing at home, I reminisced about the trip.
7. Having visited / Visiting Asia, I wanted to return some day.
8. We didn't know where to go before given / being given directions.

B | *Correct the mistakes in the underlined words or phrases.*

1. Heard a noise downstairs, Melinda called 911. ____________
2. Juan listens to music while does his homework. ____________
3. Having eating too fast, Bill got a bad case of indigestion. ____________
4. Upon finished the project, the crew celebrated. ____________
5. Being to France before, we skipped it on our last trip. ____________
6. Sam recovered after taking to the hospital. ____________
7. Having feared the weather, we took umbrellas. ____________
8. Having given the choice, I decided to walk to work. ____________

C | *Circle the letter of the one underlined word or phrase that is not correct.*

1. Believed (A) I clearly (B) had time, I narrowly (C) missed the plane I was taking (D). **A B C D**
2. I firmly (A) refused to give (B) money, to feel (C) that the pleas were only (D) frauds. **A B C D**
3. Being (A) new to the job, I didn't know what to do (B) before (C) told (D). **A B C D**
4. Upon (A) realize (B) we were right, they complied, not wanting (C) to anger (D) us. **A B C D**

UNIT 21 Connectors
MEMORY

STEP 1 GRAMMAR IN CONTEXT

Before You Read

PAIRS: Discuss the questions.

1. What is your earliest memory?
2. What are methods that help you to remember things?

Read

Read the article about memory.

TRY TO REMEMBER

by Helen Giuliani

Picture this: You're with a friend, **and** suddenly up walks somebody you've known for a long time. You want to introduce this person to your friend. **However**, just as you say, "Nancy, I'd like you to meet . . . ," your mind goes blank, and you don't remember the person's name. It's embarrassing and maybe a little worrisome. I wouldn't be too concerned, **though**, **for** it's also very common. As we get older, we tend to become more forgetful.

How does memory work, and what can we do to improve it? I was worried about memory loss on my part; **therefore**, I decided to do some research into the problem. Here's what I learned:

First: There are two types of memory, long-term and short-term. Long-term memory refers to things that we experienced some time ago and that form the core of our knowledge of ourselves. Short-term memory can be called "working" memory—the type we use in processing such things as phone numbers, names of new people we meet, and email addresses. As we grow older, our long-term memory holds up remarkably well. **Thus**, we are able to remember the vacation we took at the age of 10 to the Everglades and the alligators we saw there. **Meanwhile**, things have been happening to our short-term memory, which, **in contrast**, doesn't hold up as well as our long-term memory does. **Because** our short-term memory sometimes fails us, we may have difficulty remembering a name right after we meet someone or a phone number we've heard only twice.

TRY TO REMEMBER

Memory problems are generally short-term memory problems.

Second: Short-term memory operations occur in the frontal lobes of the brain. As we age, these lobes tend to lose mass, as much as 5 to 10 percent per decade. **However**, we can slow memory decline. Maintaining a steady supply of glucose can mitigate the problem of shrinking lobes. **Consequently**, elderly people would do well to eat several small meals each day rather than two or three big ones. There is evidence, **moreover**, that staying mentally active can help prevent memory deterioration.

Third: There are many materials on the market designed to help us remember things better. Do they work? Well, yes and no. All memory aids depend on the creation of a peg, or mental picture, on which to hang something we want to recollect. Suppose, **for example**, you have difficulty remembering names. Let's say you're at a party and are introduced to a woman named Sarah Baer. She has long, thick hair, rather like a bear's fur. Baer = Bear. **Furthermore**, the first syllable of "Sarah" rhymes with "bear." Sar and Baer. It might work. The point is to create a mental picture you can relate to the person, place, or thing you want to recall. The more vivid the association is, the greater is the chance that you'll remember it.

Most importantly, memory improvement takes work. The real problem in remembering something we learned is often the fact that we weren't paying enough attention when we learned it. Think about the last time you were introduced to someone whose name you immediately forgot. Were you really paying attention to the person's name, **or** were you focusing on the impression you might be making? Memory courses can work, of course, **but** they depend on techniques we can create and perform for ourselves. The real trick lies in our willingness to tap and use what's within us.

memory improvement takes work

After You Read

A | Vocabulary: *Match the **blue** words on the left with their meanings on the right.*

d **1.** Long-term memories form the **core** of our knowledge of ourselves.

h c **2.** Short-term memory operations occur in the frontal **lobes** of the brain.

f **3.** Maintaining a steady supply of **glucose** can mitigate the problem of shrinking lobes.

a b **4.** Maintaining a steady supply of glucose can **mitigate** the problem of shrinking lobes.

c a **5.** All memory aids depend on the creation of a **peg** on which to hang something.

d g **6.** We need a peg on which to hang something we wish to **recollect**.

e **7.** The more **vivid** the association is, the greater is the chance that you'll remember it.

g a **8.** The real trick lies in our willingness to **tap** and use what's within us.

a. lessen the seriousness of a harmful action

b. remember

c. something that can serve as a key organizing principle or example

d. most important or central part of something

e. sharp, clear, colorful

f. a natural form of sugar

g. use or draw from

h. rounded divisions of an organ, for example, the brain

B | **Comprehension:** *Circle* **T (True)** *or* **F (False)**. *Correct the false statements.*

1. Forgetting things such as another person's name is quite uncommon. **T** **F**
2. Long-term memory refers to things we experienced some time ago. **T** **F**
3. Short-term memory can be termed "working" memory. **T** **F**
4. Our short-term memory holds up better than our long-term memory. **T** **F**
5. Memory problems are generally short-term memory problems. **T** **F**
6. Elderly people would do better to eat several small meals daily instead of two or three big ones. **T** **F**
7. There is no evidence that staying mentally active can slow memory deterioration. **T** **F**
8. A key reason we forget things is that we often weren't paying enough attention when we learned something. **T** **F**

STEP 2 GRAMMAR PRESENTATION

CONNECTORS

Connectors: Placement and Punctuation	
Type of Connector	**Examples**
Coordinating Conjunction	I was worried, **so** I did some research.
Subordinating Conjunction	**Because** I was worried, I did some research.
	I did some research **because** I was worried.
Transition	I was worried. **Therefore**, I did some research.
	I was worried. I, **therefore**, did some research.
	I was worried. I did some research, **therefore**.

Connectors: Functions			
Function	**Coordinating Conjunctions**	**Subordinating Conjunctions**	**Transitions**
ADDITION	and, nor, or		besides, furthermore, indeed, in addition, moreover
CONDITION	or	if, even if, only if, unless	otherwise
CONTRAST	but, or, yet	although, though, even though, whereas, while	however, nevertheless, nonetheless, on the contrary, on the other hand
CAUSE / REASON	for	as, because, since	
EFFECT / RESULT	so		consequently, otherwise, therefore, thus
TIME		after, before, when, while	afterwards, meanwhile, next

Transitions: Connecting Sentences		
Functions	**Examples**	
ADDITION	She couldn't remember names.	**Furthermore**, she forgot addresses.
	Human brains lose mass.	**Indeed**, they may lose 10 percent a year.
CONDITION	Older people should eat several small meals a day.	**Otherwise**, their memory might deteriorate.
CONTRAST	I often have trouble with names.	**However**, I always remember faces.
	We all forget things.	**Nevertheless**, we shouldn't worry.
EFFECT / RESULT	I wasn't concentrating when we met.	**Consequently**, I couldn't recall her name.
	He wanted to improve his memory.	**Therefore**, he took a memory course.
TIME	He studied for his course.	**Meanwhile**, his wife read a book.
	She completed the book.	**Next**, she bought a memory video.

Transitions: Connecting Blocks of Text	
Functions	**Examples**
LISTING IDEAS IN ORDER OF TIME / IMPORTANCE	**First of all**, we need to distinguish between two types of memory.
GIVING EXAMPLES	**For example**, you need to stay mentally active.
SUMMARIZING	**To summarize**: Memory improvement requires work.
ADDING A CONCLUSION	**In conclusion**, we can prevent the deterioration of memory.

GRAMMAR NOTES

1	**Connectors** (often called discourse connectors) are words and phrases that connect ideas both within sentences and between sentences or larger blocks of text. Three types of connectors are **a. coordinating conjunctions** **b. subordinating conjunctions** **c. transitions**	 • I try hard, **but** I can never remember new people's names. • I can't remember her name, **although** I can remember her face. • I spent a lot on a memory improvement course. **However**, it was a waste of money.
2	**Coordinating conjunctions** join two independent clauses. Coordinating conjunctions come between clauses and are normally preceded by a comma. **Subordinating conjunctions** connect ideas within sentences. They come at the beginning of a subordinate (= dependent) clause. If the subordinate clause comes first in a sentence, it is followed by a comma. If the subordinate clause follows the independent clause, it is not usually preceded by a comma unless the clause sets up a contrast.	• I often forget things, **so** I write everything down. • I heard what you said, **but** what did you mean? • **Because** I often forget things, I write everything down. • I write everything down **because** I often forget things.
3	**Transitions** connect ideas between sentences or larger sections of text. Transitions that connect sentences can come at the beginning of a sentence, within it, or at the end. Common transitions include *besides*, *consequently*, *however*, *in addition*, *nevertheless*, *otherwise*, and *therefore*. At the beginning of a sentence, a transition is preceded by a period or semicolon and followed by a comma. In the middle of a sentence, it is preceded and followed by a comma. At the end of a sentence, it is preceded by a comma.	 • He said he would support the idea. **However**, I wouldn't count on him. • He said he would support the idea. I wouldn't, **however**, count on him. • He said he would support the idea. I wouldn't count on him, **however**.

4 There are five principal types of **transitions that connect sentences**:

a. Some transitions show **addition**. These include *additionally, besides, furthermore, in addition, likewise, moreover*, and *plus*.

- I remember her telephone number. **In addition**, I remember what street she lives on.
- I live too far away to visit you. **Besides**, I can never remember your address.

b. One transition of **condition**, *otherwise*, indicates that a result opposite to what is expected will happen if a certain action isn't taken.

- I need to write down your email address. **Otherwise**, I'll never remember it.

c. Some transitions show **contrast**. These include *however, in contrast, in spite of this, instead, nevertheless, nonetheless, still*, and *though*.

- Her speech was good; **nevertheless**, I can't support her ideas.
- Jim thinks I'm against his ideas. **On the contrary**, I'm one of his biggest supporters.

NOTE: *Though* is a contrast transition when it occurs at the end of an independent clause, when its meaning is equivalent to that of *however*. In other positions it is a subordinating conjunction.

- I carefully wrote down her name on a piece of paper. I lost the piece of paper, **though**. (*transition*)
- **Though** I've told him my name several times, he never remembers it. (*subordinating conjunction*)

d. Some transitions show **effect / result**. These include *accordingly, as a result, because of this, consequently, on account of this, otherwise, therefore*, and *thus*.

- I was not paying close attention when she was introduced. **Consequently**, her name escapes me.
- This new memory technique is helpful. **On account of this**, I recommend it to you.

e. Some transitions show **relationships** of actions, events, and ideas **in time**. These include *after that, afterwards, in the meantime, meanwhile, next*, and *then*.

- Bob spent three years in the military. **Meanwhile**, his brother was earning a college degree.
- I went to a memory workshop. **Afterwards**, I couldn't remember a single thing.

(continued on next page)

5	
Some **transitions connect blocks of text**. They usually come at the beginning of a sentence and are commonly followed by a comma. Such transitions have these uses:	
a. to **list ideas in order of time or importance**. These include *finally, first of all, most importantly, next, second, third,* etc.	• **First of all**, let's consider the question of short-term memory. • **Most importantly**, let's consider the question of memory improvement courses.
b. to **give examples**. These include *for example* and *for instance*.	• I can remember lots of things about people. **For example**, I always remember what they're wearing.
c. to **summarize**. These include *all in all, in summary, overall, to summarize*.	• **In summary**, these are the key points about memory loss.
d. to **add a conclusion**. These include *in conclusion* and *to conclude*.	• **To conclude**, let me just say that we can all improve our memory if we work at it.

REFERENCE NOTES

For more on **subordinating conjunctions**, see Unit 19.
For more complete lists of **transitions**, see Appendices 21 and 22 on pages A-9 and A-10.
For more practice on **connectors**, see **From Grammar to Writing** for Part VIII.

STEP 3 FOCUSED PRACTICE

EXERCISE 1: Discover the Grammar

A | *Identify the boldfaced words and phrases as coordinating conjunctions* (**C**), *subordinating conjunctions* (**S**), *or transitions* (**T**).

1. I wouldn't be too concerned, though, **for** it's also very common. C
2. I was worried about memory loss on my part; **therefore**, I decided to do some research into the problem. ~~S~~ T
3. **Meanwhile**, things have been happening to our short-term memory. T
4. **Because** our short-term memory sometimes fails us, we may have difficulty remembering a name right after we meet someone. S
5. Suppose, **for example**, you have difficulty remembering names. T
6. Were you really paying attention, **or** were you focusing on the impression you might be making? C

B | *Underline the transition in each sentence. Then identify it as a transition of addition* (**A**), *contrast* (**C**), *effect / result* (**R**), *time* (**T**), *or order of importance or presentation* (**O**).

1. However, just as you start to introduce your friend, your mind goes blank, and you don't remember the person's name. C
2. I was worried about memory loss on my part; therefore, I decided to do some research into the problem. R
3. First: There are two types of memory, long-term and short-term. O
4. Thus, we are able to remember the vacation we took at the age of 10 to the Everglades and the alligators we saw there. R
5. Meanwhile, things have been happening to our short-term memory. T
6. There is evidence, moreover, that staying mentally active can help prevent memory deterioration. A
7. Furthermore, the first syllable of "Sarah" rhymes with "bear." A
8. Most importantly, memory improvement takes work. ____

EXERCISE 2: Combining Sentences with Connectors

(Grammar Notes 2–5)

Combine each of the pairs of sentences into one sentence. Rewrite items 1–3 using a coordinating conjunction, a subordinating conjunction, and a transition. Rewrite item 4 with only a coordinating conjunction and a transition.

1. Jim is a wonderful man. I can't see myself married to him. (contrast)

   Jim is a wonderful man, but I can't see myself married to him.

   Although Jim is a wonderful man, I can't see myself married to him.

   Jim is a wonderful man; however, I can't see myself married to him.

2. He was having problems remembering his appointments. He bought a daily planner. (effect / result)

   He was having problems remembering his appointments so he bought ___.

   Consequently, he was having problems remembering his appointments

   ____

3. It's important for Nancy to take her medications. She forgot today. (contrast)

   ____

   ____

   ____

(continued on next page)

4. Jack remembers everyone's name. He never forgets a face. (addition)

____

____

EXERCISE 3: Completing Sentences with Connectors

(Grammar Notes 2–5)

Read a segment of a radio broadcast. Fill in the blanks with the connectors from the box. Use each connector once.

first	**in addition**	**meanwhile**	**otherwise**	**therefore**
however	**in fact**	~~**next**~~	**second**	

___Next___ (1.) we focus on the aftermath of the earthquake. Investigators have determined that it will cost approximately $8 billion to rebuild damaged highways. According to the governor, two actions have to be taken: ____________ (2.), the federal government will have to approve disaster funds to pay for reconstruction; ____________ (3.), insurance investigators will need to determine how much their companies will have to pay in the rebuilding effort. With luck, the governor says, some key highways could be rebuilt within six months. He cautioned, ____________ (4.), that the six-month figure is only an estimate. The process depends on timely allocation of funds, and certain insurance companies have been slow to approve such funds in the past. The rebuilding effort could, ____________ (5.), drag on for at least a year. ____________ (6.), bad weather could prevent the speedy completion of the project. ____________ (7.), it is taking some people as long as four hours to commute to work, and others haven't been able to get to work at all. Interviewed by our news team, one commuter who works in an office downtown said, "This has been ridiculous. It took me three hours to drive to work last Friday. I knew I'd have to find some other way of getting there; ____________ (8.), I'd never make it. Well, yesterday the train got me there in 50 minutes, and the trip was really pleasant. I even had the chance to read the morning paper. ____________ (9.), I'm going to switch permanently to the train."

EXERCISE 4: Writing Sentences with Conjunctions / Transitions

(Grammar Notes 2–4)

Look at the pictures. Write two sentences describing what happened to Hank in each picture. Use the prompts. Use commas to join clauses connected by coordinating conjunctions (and by the phrase in item 5). Use semicolons to join clauses connected by transitions.

1.

(and / in addition)

2.

(but / however)

3.

(so / consequently)

4.

(and / besides that)

5.

(while this was happening / meanwhile)

6.

(or / otherwise)

EXERCISE 5: Editing

There are seven mistakes involving connectors in this student composition. The first mistake is already corrected. Find and correct six more. You may add or eliminate words, but do not change word order or punctuation.

My Car Is Moving to the Suburbs

by Ed Snyder

October 12

Yesterday I drove my car to the downtown campus of the college. I usually have trouble finding a parking place, ~~however~~ but this time it was almost impossible. There were simply no parking places anywhere near the campus, so I had to park in the downtown mall, which is about a mile away. When I finished class, I walked back to the mall. Therefore, I couldn't remember where I'd parked my car! Believe it or not, it took me 45 minutes to find it, and I was about ready to panic when I finally did. That was the last straw. I've decided that I'm going to send my car to a new home in the suburbs.

I used to think that a car was the most wonderful thing in the world. I loved the freedom of being able to come and go to my part-time job or to the college whenever I wanted. A year ago I was in a carpool with four other people, nevertheless I hated having to wait around if my carpool members weren't ready to leave, so I started driving alone.

Although, I've changed my mind since then. Now it's clear to me that there are just too many disadvantages to having a car in town. For example, sitting stalled in your car in a traffic jam is stressful; besides, it's a phenomenal waste of time. In addition, it would cost me $200 a month to park my car in the city (which is why I don't do that); therefore, there's always the chance it will be vandalized.

Nonetheless, I've decided to leave it at my cousin Brent's house in the suburbs. Otherwise, I'll end up going broke paying for parking and a course in memory improvement. My car will have a good home, and I'll use it just for longer trips. When I'm in the city, though, I'll take the bus or the tram, otherwise I'll walk. Who knows? They say you can meet some interesting people on the bus. Maybe I'll find the love of my life. My only problem will be remembering which bus to take.

STEP 4 COMMUNICATION PRACTICE

EXERCISE 6: Listening

A | *Listen to the excerpt from a memory training workshop. Check (✓) the two things that are true.*

☐ The workshop visitor says he's from Hawaii.

☐ The visitor has a Hawaiian name.

☐ The visitor is wearing a tuxedo.

☐ The visitor is wearing brown shoes.

B | *Read the questions. Then listen again and answer the questions in complete sentences.*

1. What is the first point the workshop leader makes?

   It's important to get people's names in your short-term memory.

2. According to her, why is it important to remember clients' names?

   ____

3. What is the second point the leader makes?

   ____

4. What did the visitor tell the people in the workshop to do?

   ____

5. What are the two reasons one of the participants knows the visit was planned and not real?

   a. ______________________________

   b. ______________________________

(continued on next page)

6. Why were all the participants able to remember the last word the visitor said?

____

7. According to the workshop leader, what is the most important thing the participants in the workshop have to learn to do?

____

EXERCISE 7: Pronunciation

A | *Read and listen to the Pronunciation Note.*

Pronunciation Note

Notice the difference in pronunciation of clauses connected by coordinating conjunctions and those connected by transitions:

EXAMPLES: We visited Mexico on our trip, **and** we went to Costa Rica as well. (a small pause before the coordinating conjunction *and*; no pause after it)

We visited Mexico on our trip; **in addition**, we went to Costa Rica. (a major pause before the transition *in addition*, and a small pause after the transition)

A comma indicates a small pause; a semicolon indicates a major pause. Remember that a semicolon is equivalent to a period.

B | *Listen and repeat the sentences. Then insert semicolons and commas in the places where you hear major pauses and small pauses, respectively.*

1. Frank has an excellent memory; however, he doesn't use it to good advantage.
2. Frank has an excellent memory but he doesn't use it to good advantage.
3. Marta was having trouble remembering things so she signed up for a memory course.
4. Marta was having trouble remembering things consequently she signed up for a memory course.
5. You need to start writing things down otherwise you'll miss out on key appointments.
6. You need to start writing things down or you'll miss out on key appointments.
7. I have trouble remembering people's names yet I can always remember their faces.
8. I have trouble remembering people's names on the other hand I can always remember their faces.
9. You live awfully far away to visit besides you never come to see me.
10. You live awfully far away to visit and you never come to see me.

C | *PAIRS: Practice the sentences.*

EXERCISE 8: Game

Form two teams. Everyone writes a statement involving personal or general knowledge and containing a connector. One team makes its statements while the other team listens and takes notes. Teams take turns making statements. When all the statements have been made, teams attempt to reproduce the other team's statements. Score one point for each correctly remembered statement, and one point for a correct connector.

EXAMPLE: **Team A:** Washington, D.C., is the capital of the United States; however, it's not the largest city.
Team B: I have been to France three times, and I've been to Britain twice.

EXERCISE 9: Picture Discussion

PAIRS: Study the painting for two minutes. Then close your book. Write down as many details as you can remember. Then open your book again and check your memory. Which details were you able to remember best? Why?

EXAMPLE: I can remember ________________. I also remember ________________.
However, I can't remember ________________.

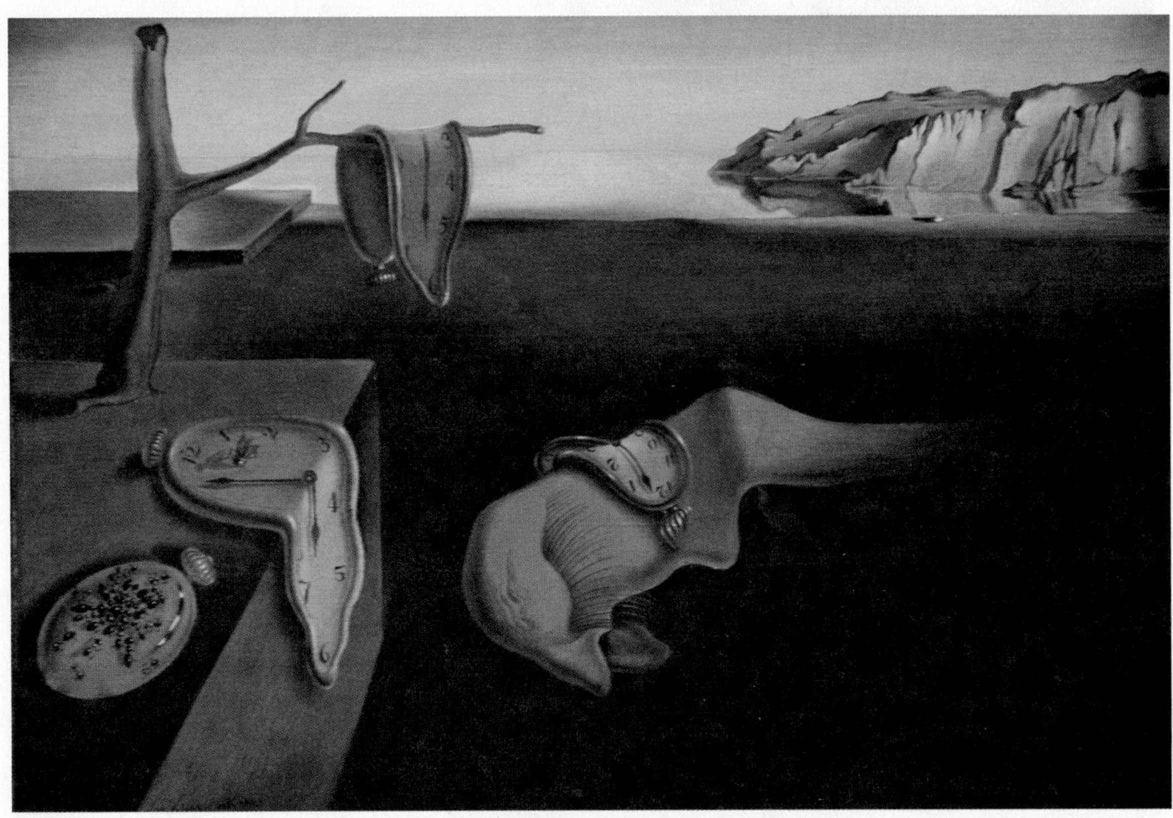

The Persistence of Memory
Salvador Dalí (Spanish, 1904–1989)

EXERCISE 10: Writing

A | *Write three or four paragraphs about a significant memory you have. Explain clearly why this memory is important to you, and speculate as to why you remember it well. Use specific details to support your ideas and statements. Include appropriate connectors in your composition.*

Example: One of my most significant, and most painful, memories is of my accordion recital when I was 13 years old. I had been taking accordion lessons for three years and was told by my teacher that I had made excellent progress. She scheduled me for a recital in which I was to play two easy songs and one difficult one. I looked forward to the recital and practiced hard. However, things didn't go at all as planned . . .

B | *Check your work. Use the Editing Checklist.*

Editing Checklist

Did you use . . . ?

☐ coordinating conjunctions correctly
☐ subordinating conjunctions correctly
☐ transitions correctly

UNIT 21 Review

Check your answers on page UR-3.
Do you need to review anything?

A | *Circle the word or phrase that correctly completes each sentence.*

1. I never forget a face; and / however, I have trouble remembering names.
2. I never forget a face, besides / though I have trouble remembering names.
3. Because / Besides Hari forgot to pay his utility bill, the city turned off his water.
4. Hari forgot to pay his utility bill; and / consequently, the city turned off his water.
5. The house is too expensive for us; otherwise / besides, I don't really like it.
6. The house is too expensive for us, and / though I don't really like it.
7. You'd better get up right now, or / because you'll miss the bus.
8. You'd better get up right now; however / otherwise, you'll miss the bus.

B | *Correct the mistakes in the underlined words or phrases.*

1. I was exhausted, but I went to bed at 8:00 P.M. ____________________
2. It's too early to get up; and I want to sleep in. ____________________
3. We need to get tickets, otherwise we won't get seats. ____________________
4. Nora didn't leave on time; so, she missed her flight. ____________________
5. However Bao has a degree, he has a very poor job. ____________________
6. Next the train arrived, I got a taxi to the hotel. ____________________
7. You're too young to have a car. Therefore, cars are expensive. ____________________
8. The café was cheap; furthermore, we decided to eat there. ____________________

C | *Circle the letter of the one underlined word or phrase that is not correct.*

1. Pets admittedly (A) cause problems; yet (B), they often (C) bring love also (D). **A B C D**
2. Indeed (A), Lee is highly (B) qualified. Example (C), she has an advanced (D) degree. **A B C D**
3. I got up late (A), and (B) I missed the bus, so (C) consequently (D) I got to work late. **A B C D**
4. First (A), study; or (B) second (C), attend class; otherwise (D), you'll fail. **A B C D**

From Grammar to Writing

USING TRANSITIONS

A key aspect of effective writing is the use of **transitions**: words and expressions that tie sentences and paragraphs together and give the reader an overall sense of where a piece of writing is going and where it has been.

There are two main types of transitions: (1) those that connect sentences and independent clauses; and (2) those that connect larger blocks of text.

Examples: Events in Geraldine's life had been going extremely well for years. **However**, just when she had come to feel secure, her fortunes changed dramatically.
(The transition ***however*** connects two sentences and introduces a contrast.)

There are several reasons why Andrew was not accepted at the university. **First**, his high school grades, while reasonably good, were not high enough. . . .
(The transition ***first*** is the type that connects larger blocks of text. It shows the reader that this is the initial reason the writer is giving to support the main idea. The reader will expect a similar transition—e.g., ***second*** or ***another reason***—to introduce the next reason.)

Refer to Unit 21 for more information on transitions. Also see Appendices 21 and 22 on pages A-9 and A-10.

1 | *Complete the paragraph with the transitions from the box.*

besides that **consequently** **first** **however** **most importantly** **second**

Recently the lives of Stella and Hank Wang have improved in several ways. ________________, they both secured new jobs that make them better off financially. Stella got a position as a proofreader and editor at a publishing company pioneering new workplace methods, and Hank was hired as a full-time consultant for an engineering firm. ________________, their new jobs have made their lives much less stressful. The difference between their new jobs and their old ones can be summed up in one word: flextime. Until they secured these new positions, Stella and Hank had a very difficult time raising their two small children. They were at the mercy of a nine-to-five schedule; ________________, they had to pay a lot for day care. In order to get to work on time, they had to have the children at the day care center by 7:30 every morning. Both of their new companies, ________________, offer a flextime schedule. As long as Stella and Hank both put in their 40 hours a week, they are free to work when it is convenient for them. __________________, they can take turns staying home with the children, and day care is just a memory. __________________, Stella and Hank feel that they are now doing a good job of parenting. The children are much happier because they are getting the attention they need.

2 | *Add appropriate transitions to the paragraph.*

There are a number of reasons why I prefer going out to movies to watching DVDs on TV. __________________, I often fall asleep when watching the TV screen, no matter how interesting the DVD is. The other night, __________________, I was watching *Gone with the Wind* on my flat screen TV. It was compelling for a while, but pretty soon my eyelids started getting heavy, and before I knew it I was in dreamland. __________________, watching movies is basically a social experience. There's a lot to be said for experiencing the group reaction to a film seen in a theater. When I watch movies on a TV screen, __________________, I'm often alone. I love my cat, but she doesn't make many perceptive comments about movies. __________________, the TV screen, no matter how large it is, diminishes the impact you get when watching a movie on the big screen. I have a 58-inch flat screen TV, and I love the programs I see on it. It's not the same as going out to a cinema, __________________. __________________, my recommendation is to find a friend who also likes movies and go out to the flicks.

3 | *Before you write . . .*

1. Most of us have clear opinions on a variety of topics. Think of an issue that concerns you and/or that you feel strongly about.
2. Describe your opinion / issue to a partner. Listen to your partner's description.
3. Ask and answer questions about your and your partner's issue. What are your reasons for thinking as you do? What are some reasons why people might disagree with you?

4 | *Write a draft of a composition in which you present your opinion. Follow the model. Remember to include information that your partner asked about. Use both types of transitions in your paragraph.*

Reasons why I think as I do:

____

____

____

____

Reasons why people might disagree with me:

____

____

____

____

5 | *Exchange compositions with a different partner. Complete the chart.*

1. The writer used both types of transitions. **Yes** ☐ **No** ☐

2. What I liked in the composition:

____

____

____

3. Questions I'd like the writer to answer about the composition:

Who ____________________________________?

What ___________________________________?

When ___________________________________?

Where __________________________________?

Why ____________________________________?

How ____________________________________?

(Your own question) __________________________?

6 | *Work with your partner. Discuss each other's chart from Exercise 5. Then rewrite your own composition and make any necessary changes.*

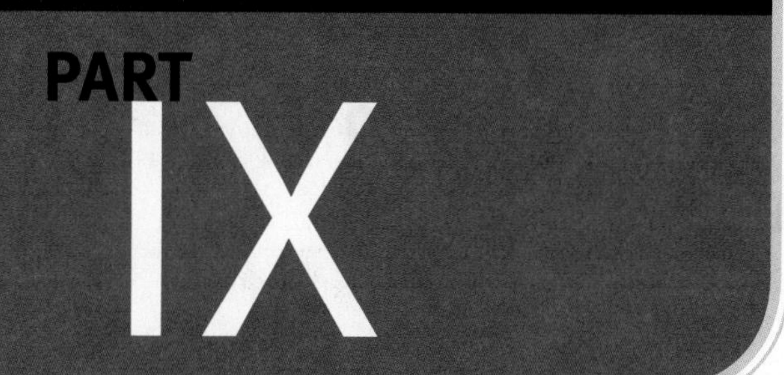

CONDITIONALS AND THE SUBJUNCTIVE

UNIT	GRAMMAR FOCUS	THEME
22	Conditionals; Other Ways to Express Unreality	Intuition
23	More Conditions; The Subjunctive	Advice

UNIT 22

Conditionals; Other Ways to Express Unreality

INTUITION

STEP 1 GRAMMAR IN CONTEXT

Before You Read

PAIRS: Discuss the questions.

1. What do you understand by "intuition"? Do you believe in intuition?
2. Have you had any experiences in which your or someone else's intuition proved correct?

Read

Read the story about trusting intuition.

Intuition

It was a sweltering day. Donna and Thain were driving down Maple Street, looking for a yard sale, when they spotted the old man hailing them.

"Nine-thirty in the morning, and it's already beastly hot. I **wish** I **had** an iced tea right now."

"Wow! Look at that old fellow, Donna. **I'd** sure **get** out of this heat **if** I **were** him... Pull over, will you? He**'s going to faint if** he **doesn't get** out of the sun."

"Thain, I **wish** you **would stop** taking pity on every weirdo you see. He**'ll** probably **kill** us and **steal** the car **if** we **pick** him **up**."

"I don't think so. He looks harmless to me."

"But, sweetie, we've got to get to the sale. There **won't be** anything worth buying **if** we **don't get** there soon. **If only** that bureau **would** still **be** there!"

"Well, it's just an inkling, but my male intuition is telling me we'd better stop."

"**If** I **had** a nickel for all the times we've done things because of your male intuition, **I'd be** rich. Aren't females supposed to have the intuition, anyway? OK, but I **hope** we **don't end up** in the headlines. I can see it all now: YOUNG MARRIED COUPLE MUTILATED BY SERIAL KILLER."

Intuition

They pulled up to the curb in front of the old man. "Need some help, sir?" Thain asked.

The old man smiled. "Yes, thanks. Could you take me to a pharmacy? I'm diabetic, and I've run out of medicine. I'm on a cross-country trip, but I keep forgetting to buy enough insulin. **If** I **don't take** my medicine regularly, I **go** into shock. **If only** I **weren't** so forgetful . . ."

They found a pharmacy and got the insulin. The old man said, "Now, **if** you **can** just **take** me to the bus station, I'**ll be** on my way."

Thain said, "Sure. We can do that."

At the bus station, they helped the old man out of the car. "Can you tell me your names and your address? When I get back home, I'll send you a token of my appreciation." They gave him their names and address, said good-bye, and proceeded to the yard sale.

As Donna had predicted, all of the good merchandise had been sold. "We'**d** probably **have** that bureau **if** we'**d gotten** here earlier, but I'm glad we helped the old guy. I'**ll be** surprised **if** we ever **hear** from him, though. You don't really believe he's taking a trip around the country, do you, Thain?"

In a few days they had forgotten about the incident. Three months later, on returning from a vacation, Donna was going through a pile of mail. She opened a long envelope with no return address.

"What in the world? Thain, come here and look at this!" There was a letter, neatly typed, which said,

Dear Thain and Donna,

I finished my trip around the country and had a marvelous time. I'm now back at home and expect I won't be traveling anymore. I met some wonderful people in my travels, the two of you among them.

Thank you for your kindness to a forgetful old man. **If** you **hadn't come** along when you did, I **might have died**. At the very least, I **would have become** quite ill **if** you **hadn't been** there to help. I **wish** there **had been** time for us to get to know one another. **If** I **had been** fortunate enough to have children of my own, I **couldn't have had** any nicer ones than you two. At any rate, I am enclosing a token of my gratitude.

My warmest regards,
Quentin Wilkerson

Something fluttered out of a second sheet of folded paper. It was a check for $100,000.

After You Read

A | Vocabulary: *Circle the letter of best meaning for the blue words from the reading.*

1. It was a **sweltering** day.
   - **a.** quite cool
   - **b.** rather warm
   - **c.** very hot
   - **d.** cold and windy

2. They spotted the old man **hailing** them.
   - **a.** waving at
   - **b.** shouting at
   - **c.** looking at
   - **d.** coming at

3. It's 9:30 A.M., and it's already **beastly** hot.
   - **a.** unfortunately
   - **b.** extremely
   - **c.** unpredictably
   - **d.** violently

4. I wish you would stop taking pity on every **weirdo** you see.
   - **a.** random person
   - **b.** old person
   - **c.** strange person
   - **d.** interesting person

5. If only that **bureau** would still be there!
   - **a.** dresser
   - **b.** sofa
   - **c.** bookcase
   - **d.** armchair

6. Well, it's just an **inkling**, but my male intuition is telling me we'd better stop.
   - **a.** conclusion
   - **b.** slight idea
   - **c.** strong belief
   - **d.** statement

7. I can see it all now: YOUNG MARRIED COUPLE **MUTILATED** BY SERIAL KILLER.
   - **a.** deliberately attacked
   - **b.** fatally shot
   - **c.** severely injured
   - **d.** robbed

8. I'll send you a **token** of my appreciation.
   - **a.** acknowledgment
   - **b.** official statement
   - **c.** testimony
   - **d.** small remembrance

9. Something **fluttered** out of a second sheet of folded paper.
   - **a.** dropped lightly
   - **b.** zoomed
   - **c.** appeared suddenly
   - **d.** fell heavily

B | Comprehension: *Refer to the reading and complete each sentence with a single word.*

1. At the beginning of the story, Donna and Thain are looking for a ____________ sale.
2. The old man may ____________ if he doesn't get out of the sun soon.
3. Donna is afraid that the old man might ____________ them if they pick him up.
4. Donna and Thain are a young ____________ couple.
5. The old man's medical problem is that he is ____________.
6. He needs to go to a pharmacy to get ____________.
7. When Donna and Thain got to the sale, all the good ____________ had been sold.
8. Judging from the gift he sent, we can assume the old man is ____________.

CONDITIONALS; OTHER WAYS TO EXPRESS UNREALITY

Present and Future Real Conditional

Present Conditionals	
***If* Clause**	**Result Clause**
If it **is** hot,	I **drink** iced tea.
If it **isn't** hot,	I **don't drink** iced tea.

Future Conditionals	
***If* Clause**	**Result Clause**
If it **rains**,	we **will close** the windows.
If it **doesn't rain**,	we **won't close** the windows.

Present Unreal Conditionals

Actual Situations	Conditionals	
	***If* Clause**	**Result Clause**
It **is** rarely hot in Antarctica.	If it **were** hot in Antarctica,	it **would be** unusual.
It **is** usually hot in Egypt.	If it **weren't** hot in Egypt,	
It rarely **rains** in the Sahara.	If it **rained** in the Sahara,	
It usually **rains** in the jungle.	If it **didn't rain** in the jungle,	

Past Unreal Conditionals

Actual Situations	Conditionals	
	***If* Clause**	**Result Clause**
They **stopped**, so they **were** late.	If they **hadn't stopped**,	they **wouldn't have been** late.
They **didn't stop**, so they **weren't** late.	If they **had stopped**,	they **would have been** late.
They **helped** the man, so he **sent** a gift.	If they **hadn't helped** the man,	he **wouldn't have sent** a gift.
They **didn't help** the man, so he **didn't send** a gift.	If they **had helped** the man,	he **would have sent** a gift.

"Mixed" Conditionals

Actual Situations	Conditionals	
	***If* Clause**	**Result Clause**
He **didn't have** children, so he **is** alone.	PAST If he **had had** children,	PRESENT he **wouldn't be** alone.
His memory **is not** good, so he **didn't buy** his medicine.	PRESENT If his memory **were** good,	PAST he **would have bought** his medicine.

Other Ways to Express Unreality

Actual Situations	*Wish / If only* Statement
She **will miss** the sale.	She **wishes** (that) she **wouldn't miss** the sale. **If only** she **wouldn't miss** the sale.
They **can't buy** the bureau.	They **wish** (that) they **could buy** the bureau. **If only** they **could buy** the bureau.
They **arrived** late.	They **wish** (that) they **hadn't arrived** late. **If only** they **hadn't arrived** late.

GRAMMAR NOTES

1

Conditional sentences describe situations that occur (or do not occur) because of certain conditions. They consist of two clauses, a **dependent condition clause** (also called the ***if* clause**) and an **independent result clause**. There are two types of conditional sentences: real and unreal.

Real (or factual) **conditionals** are sentences that describe situations that

a. occur regularly

- Water **boils** if it **reaches** 100° C. (RESULT: Water boils; CONDITION: if it reaches 100° C)

b. are likely or possible in the future

- If we **study**, we **will pass**. (CONDITION: If we study; RESULT: we will pass)

Unreal conditionals are sentences that describe situations that are untrue, unlikely, or impossible in the present or the past.

- If I **were** rich, I**'d buy** a car. (CONDITION: If I were rich; RESULT: I'd buy a car)
- I **would have helped** if you **had asked**. (RESULT: I would have helped; CONDITION: if you had asked)

NOTE: In conditional sentences, the clauses can come in either order. The meaning is the same. We place a comma after the *if* clause if it comes first. We don't generally place a comma after the result clause if it comes first. Either or both clauses can be negative.

- **If I don't finish my work early**, I won't be able to attend.

OR

- I won't be able to attend **if I don't finish my work early**.

2	We use **present real conditional** sentences to talk about general truths, scientific facts, or habits and repeated events. We use the simple present in both clauses. We can also use the present progressive in the *if* clause.	• Plants **die** if they **don't get** enough water. • People with diabetes **can control** their disease if they **take** insulin regularly. • If I**'m flying**, I always feel nervous.
	In **future-time situations**, we use the simple present or the present progressive in the *if* clause and the future with *will* or *be going to*, *may*, *might*, *can*, *could*, or *should* in the result clause.	• If Barry **passes** the final exam, he **might pass** the course. • Unless he **studies** hard, however, he **won't pass** the final exam.
	BE CAREFUL! Use the simple present in the *if* clause, even though the time referred to is future.	• I'll contact you as soon as I **hear** from her. NOT: I'll contact you as soon as ~~I'll hear~~ from her.
3	Use the **present unreal conditional** to talk about unreal, untrue, imagined, or impossible conditions and their results. Use the simple past form of the verb in the *if* clause. If the verb is *be*, use *were* for all persons. Use *could*, *might*, or *would* + the base form of the verb in the result clause.	• If I **loved** you, I**'d ask** you to marry me. • We **wouldn't stay up** so late if we **were** parents. • I **might watch** videos if I **had** the day off. • If I **were** you, I **wouldn't accept** the offer.
	BE CAREFUL! The simple past in the *if* clause is **past in form only**. It is not past in meaning.	
	BE CAREFUL! Don't use *would* in the *if* clause in present unreal conditional sentences.	• I'd buy a new car if **I had** the money. NOT: I'd buy a new car ~~if I would have~~ the money.
4	Use the **past unreal conditional** to talk about past unreal, untrue, imagined, or impossible conditions and their unreal results. Use the past perfect in the *if* clause. Use *could*, *might*, or *would* + *have* + past participle in the result clause.	• If I **had listened** to my inner voice, I **wouldn't have made** that mistake. • Mary **would have accepted** your proposal if you**'d asked** in time.
	We often use the past unreal conditional to express regret about a situation that actually happened in the past.	• I **would have lent** you money if I **had known** you were in financial difficulty.
	BE CAREFUL! Don't use *would have* in the *if* clause in past unreal conditional sentences.	NOT: I **would have lent** you money if I ~~would have~~ known you were in financial difficulty.

(continued on next page)

5	The times of the *if* clause and the result clause are sometimes different. Present unreal and past unreal conditional forms can be "**mixed**" in the same sentence.	PAST ACTION — PRESENT RESULT • If I **hadn't gone** to college, **I'd** still **be working** at the hardware store. *(I went to college. I'm not working at the hardware store.)* PRESENT ACTION — PAST RESULT • If Sam **were coming**, he **would have arrived** by now. *(Sam isn't coming. He hasn't arrived.)*
6	We often use **unreal conditionals** to express regret or sadness. In a similar way, we use ***wish*** + noun clause to express sadness or a desire for a different situation.	• I'd earn more **if I had a better job**. • I **wish** (that) **I had a better job**.
	a. Use *wish* + *could / would* + base form to express a wish about the future.	• I **wish** (that) you **would change** your mind about buying that house.
	b. Use *wish* + the simple past to express a wish about the present.	• My wife **wishes** (that) I **helped** her with the housework more.
	c. Use *wish* + the past perfect to express a wish about the past.	• My son **wishes** (that) he **hadn't taken** that job.
	BE CAREFUL! Don't confuse *wish* and *hope*. Use *wish* to express regrets about things that are unlikely or impossible to change. Use *hope* to express a desire about events that are possible or probable.	• I **wish** (that) she **would accept** my proposal. *(I don't think she will.)* • I **hope** (that) she **accepts / will accept** my proposal. *(It's possible or probable that she will.)*
7	***If only*** has a meaning similar to that of ***wish***. *If only* is followed by a noun clause without *that*.	• I **wish** (that) I were good at sports. • **If only** I were good at sports.
	Use the simple past after *if only* to express a wish about something that is contrary to fact at present.	• **If only we weren't** so busy.
	Use the past perfect after *if only* to express a wish that something had happened differently in the past.	• **If only I hadn't said** that.
	BE CAREFUL! Don't confuse *if only* with *only if*.	• **If only** Jerry studied more. *(= I wish he would study more.)* • **Only if** Jerry studied more would he have a chance of passing. *(= This would be the only way for him to pass.)*

STEP 3 FOCUSED PRACTICE

EXERCISE 1: Discover the Grammar

A | *Identify the sentences as real* (**R**) *or unreal* (**U**) *conditionals.*

1. I'd sure get out of the heat if I were him. ___U___
2. He's going to faint if he doesn't get out of the sun. ____
3. He'll probably kill us and steal the car if we stop and pick him up. ____
4. There won't be anything worth buying if we don't get there soon. ____
5. If I had a nickel for all the times we've done things because of your male intuition, I'd be rich. ____
6. If I don't take my medicine regularly, I go into shock. ____
7. We'd probably have the bureau if we'd gotten here earlier. ____
8. I'll be surprised if we ever hear from him, though. ____

B | *Identify the time of the conditional sentences as* ***past, present, future,*** *or* ***mixed.***

1. I wish I had an iced tea right now. ___present___
2. I'd sure get out of this heat if I were him. ________
3. I wish you'd stop taking pity on every weirdo you see. ________
4. If only that bureau would still be there. ________
5. If only I weren't so forgetful. ________
6. We'd probably have that bureau if we'd gotten here earlier. ________
7. If you hadn't come along when you did, I might have died. ________
8. I would have become quite ill if you hadn't been there to help. ________

EXERCISE 2: Present Real Conditionals

(Grammar Notes 1–2)

Arrange the words in the correct order to create present real conditional sentences. Use correct punctuation.

1. sometimes / below / Farmers / temperature / drops / crops / zero / springtime / the / their / if / lose

   Farmers sometimes lose their crops if the springtime temperature drops below zero.

2. their / If / go / into / don't / shock / take / diabetics / sometimes / insulin / they

   ____

(continued on next page)

3. out / sources / if / energy / run / will / We / develop / alternative / of / don't / fuel / we

____

4. continues / warming / If / icecaps / the / global / could / polar / melt

____

5. dies / Venus / it / A / doesn't / water / enough / flytrap / if / get

____

6. by / population / world / trends / will / If / billion / the / reach / 2060 / continue / present / nine

____

EXERCISE 3: Present / Future Conditionals

(Grammar Notes 2–3)

Use the phrases from the box to complete the story with present and future conditional forms.

how would you feel	**I'd want**	**I'll do**	**what would you do**
I'd call	**~~if I ask~~**	**it weren't**	**will you give**
I'd keep	**if I were**	**I will**	**you found**
I'd take	**if you really think**	**I wouldn't be**	**you were**

MARISA: Hello?

FABIO: Hi, Marisa. This is Fabio. Got a couple of minutes for your little brother?

MARISA: Always. What's up?

FABIO: ___If I ask___ (1.) you a question, ________ (2.) me an honest answer? Tell me what you really think, not what you think I want to hear?

MARISA: Of course ________ (3.). Shoot.

FABIO: ________ (4.) if ________ (5.) some money in a motel room?

MARISA: ________ (6.) it to the front desk. Why?

FABIO: Ana and I found $200 in our room at the motel we were staying at. She says we should keep it, but a little voice told me I should call and ask you. If ________ (7.) so much money, ________ (8.) concerned. ________ (9.) it. But $200 is quite a bit.

MARISA: You mean you think this all depends on the amount of money?

FABIO: Well, yes. Two hundred dollars is a significant amount, isn't it?

MARISA: I think it is. My take on this is that the previous occupants forgot it. ________________ (10.) if ________________ (11.) the one who left it?

FABIO: I guess ________________ (12.) someone to return it.

MARISA: Yeah. ________________ (13.) you, ________________ (14.) the front office and ask if anyone has inquired about it.

FABIO: OK, big sister. ________________ (15.) it ________________ (16.) it's the right thing.

MARISA: I do. But it's your choice, of course.

EXERCISE 4: *Wish / If Only* Sentences

(Grammar Notes 6–7)

A | *Look at the pictures. Write a sentence with* **wish** *for each.*

1.

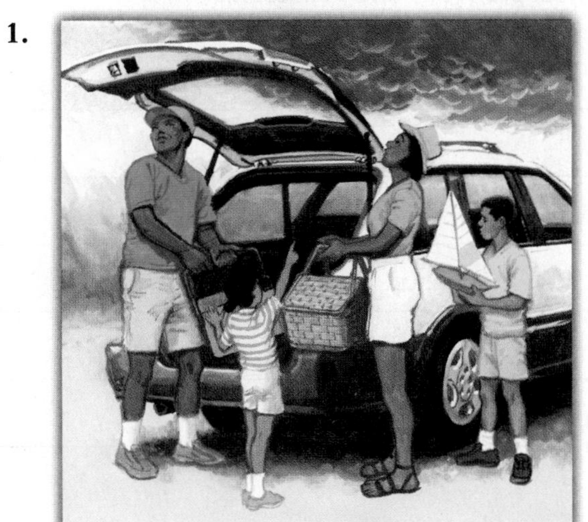

They wish the weather were better.

2.

____

3.

YES, OF COURSE.

____

4.

____

(continued on next page)

5. 

6. 

B | *Now rewrite each sentence with* **if only**. *Change subject pronouns and possessive adjectives where appropriate.*

1. *If only the weather were better.*
2.
3.
4.
5.
6.

EXERCISE 5: Mixed / Past Unreal Conditionals

(Grammar Notes 4–5)

Complete the story with mixed or past unreal conditional sentences.

Mai and Dinh were at the new racetrack one afternoon to meet their friends Kenny and Allison and then go to dinner. Time passed, and Kenny and Allison didn't show up, so Mai and Dinh began to grow impatient.

Dinh said, "Let's go. They ___would have arrived___ (1. arrive) by now if they ____________ (2. be / coming)." Now Mai and Dinh had never bet on a horse before and ____________ (3. not / do) so this time if Kenny and Allison ____________ (4. be) there. There's a first time for everything, however, and Mai said, "OK, but we might as well bet on a horse as long as we're here." They studied the racing form. Dinh wanted to bet on Magic Dancer, a horse that had won many times. Mai's intuition, however, was to go with Static, the horse that had won the fewest races. It's a good thing they followed Mai's intuition because things ____________ (5. turn out) quite differently if ____________ (6. they / not). They went to the stands to watch the race. At first it looked like Dinh's original idea had been right: Magic Dancer, the favored horse, was running in the lead. In the final seconds, though, Static moved up suddenly and finally passed Magic Dancer just before the finish line. Mai and Dinh couldn't believe their eyes. They'd won $10,000.

The next day they told Kenny and Allison about their adventure. "Sorry we didn't make it," Kenny said, "but we had a family emergency and couldn't call. I certainly ____________ (7. not pick) Static if ____________ (8. I / be / betting). Just think how much money ____________ (9. you / win) if ____________ (10. you / bet) $50 or $100 instead of $20! ____________ (11. you / be) rich now." Mai said, "It's too bad you had an emergency, but at least something good happened. We ____________ (12. not / be) $10,000 richer right now if ____________ (13. you / make it). So we have you guys to thank."

EXERCISE 6: Editing

There are six mistakes in the use of conditionals and related forms in the diary entry. The first mistake is already corrected. Find and correct five more.

June 4

had

This has been one of those days when I wish I ~~would have~~ stayed in bed. It started at 7:30 this morning when Trudy called me up and asked me for "a little favor." She's always asking me to do things for her and never wants to take any responsibility for herself. She acts as if the world owes her a living. I wish she doesn't think like that. Today she wanted me to take her to the mall because she had to get her mother a birthday present. At first I said I couldn't because I had to be downtown at 11 A.M. for a job interview. Trudy said she'd do the same for me if I would ask her. Then she said it wouldn't take long to drive to the mall, and I'd have plenty of time to get downtown from there. I gave in and agreed to take her, but something told me I shouldn't. If I had listened to my inner voice, I might have had a job right now. When we were on the freeway, there was a major accident, and traffic was tied up for over an hour. By the time we got to the mall, it was 11:30, so I missed the appointment. I think I probably would get the job if I had managed to make it to the interview because my qualifications are strong. If only I wouldn't have listened to Trudy! I just wish she doesn't ask me to do things like this. If she asks me again, I hope I can resist.

STEP 4 COMMUNICATION PRACTICE

EXERCISE 7: Listening

A | *Listen to the conversation. Check (✓) the three subjects that are not mentioned.*

- ☐ math class
- ☐ French class
- ☐ turning in a completed workbook
- ☐ turning in a completed term paper
- ☐ breaking up with a boyfriend
- ☐ finding a new boyfriend

B | *Listen again to the conversation. Answer the questions in complete sentences.*

1. What does April wish?

   April wishes she and Bob weren't going together.

2. What does Sally wish April hadn't done?

   ____

3. What did April think Bob would do if she refused?

   ____

4. What would Sally have done?

   ____

5. What will the teacher do if she finds out?

   ____

6. What would Sally do if she were April?

   ____

7. What does Sally think April should tell Bob?

   ____

8. What should April do if Bob gets mad and says he wants to break up?

   ____

EXERCISE 8: Pronunciation

A | *Read and listen to the Pronunciation Note.*

Pronunciation Note

In conversational or rapid speech, we often contract both ***would*** and ***had*** to /**d**/. Therefore, perceiving the pronunciation of the verb following these auxiliaries is important for understanding different sentences.

EXAMPLES: I wish **you'd try** my dessert. (= would try)
I wish **you'd tried** my dessert. (= had tried)

The key consideration is whether the verb after the auxiliary is a base form or a past participle.

B | *Listen to the sentences. Circle the verb phrase you hear.*

1. I wish you 'd stop / 'd stopped riding motorcycles.
2. I wish you 'd stop / 'd stopped riding motorcycles.
3. Mary wishes I 'd accept / 'd accepted the job.
4. Mary wishes I 'd accept / 'd accepted the job.
5. I sure wish she 'd call / 'd called me.
6. I sure wish she 'd call / 'd called me.
7. My dad wishes I 'd visit / 'd visited more often.
8. My dad wishes I 'd visit / 'd visited more often.
9. I wish it 'd rain / 'd rained more.
10. I wish it 'd rain / 'd rained more.

C | *PAIRS: Practice the sentences in random order, making sure to contract* **would** *and* **had**. *Your partner says which sentences he or she hears.*

EXERCISE 9: Conditional Game

Form two teams. Each team uses the prompts to construct eight conditional questions, four in the present and four in the past. Then each team creates two questions of its own, for a total of 10 questions. Take turns asking questions. The other team guesses what person or thing is being referred to. For answers, see page G-AK4.

Example: What / doing / if / spelunking
A: What would you be doing if you were spelunking?
B: We'd be exploring a cave.

Team A's Prompts

1. Where / be / if / in the capital of Honduras
2. How old / have to / be / if / the president of the United States
3. Where / traveling / if / the monetary unit / the won
4. Where / be / if / visiting Angkor Wat
5. Who / been / if / the emperor of France in 1804
6. Who / been / if / the first prime minister of India
7. What country / been from / if / Marco Polo
8. What mountain / climbed / if / with Edmund Hillary and Tenzing Norgay
9. ______________________________
10. ______________________________

Team B's Prompts

1. How old / be / if / an octogenarian
2. Where / be traveling / if / in Machu Picchu
3. What / be / if / the largest mammal
4. What country / be in / if / standing and looking at Angel Falls
5. Who / been / if / the inventor of the telephone
6. What kind of creature / been / if / a stegosaurus
7. What / been your occupation / if / Genghis Khan
8. Who / been / if / Siddartha Gautama
9. ______________________________
10. ______________________________

EXERCISE 10: Personal Inventory

A | *Complete the sentences according to your own experience.*

1. If I were ______________________________. (present)
2. I wish ______________________________. (present)
3. I wish ______________________________. (past)
4. If only I hadn't ______________________________. (past)
5. I wish ______________________________. (future)
6. I hope ______________________________. (future)
7. I would have ______________________________. (past)
8. I wouldn't have ______________________________. (past)

B | *PAIRS: Discuss your answers. Report interesting examples to the class.*

EXERCISE 11: Group Discussion

A | *GROUPS: Look again at the opening reading. How do you think the story ended? Would it have been ethical for Thain and Donna to cash the check Mr. Wilkerson sent them? Would it have been proper to keep the money? What would you have done if you had been in their situation?*

Example: **A:** If I'd been in their situation, I wouldn't have cashed the check.
B: Why not?

B | *Tell the class about what your group has decided. Discuss the issue further as a class.*

EXERCISE 12: Writing

A | *Write four or five paragraphs about a time when you ignored your intuition and inner voice and instead made a seemingly logical decision that turned out badly. Describe your original intuitive feelings, explain why you ignored them, and speculate on what would or might have happened if you had acted intuitively. Use conditional sentences and clauses with* **wish** *where appropriate.*

Example: A year ago I had an experience that taught me the advisability of going with my intuition. Looking back on the situation now, I wish I had paid attention to what my inner voice was telling me. Unfortunately, I didn't do that, and I had to suffer the consequences. I had saved up enough money for the down payment on a new car and was ready to close the deal. When a cousin heard of my plans, however, he offered to sell me his two-year-old car for half the price of the down payment. Something told me this was the wrong thing to do, but . . .

B | *Check your work. Use the Editing Checklist.*

Editing Checklist

Did you use . . . ?

☐ conditional sentences correctly

☐ clauses with ***wish*** correctly

☐ sentences with ***if only*** correctly

UNIT

22 Review

Check your answers on page UR-3.
Do you need to review anything?

A | *Circle the word or phrase that correctly completes each sentence.*

1. We won't be able to go on the picnic if it will rain / rains tomorrow.
2. I hope it doesn't / wouldn't rain tomorrow.
3. I'd like living here more if it rains / rained less.
4. If only it wouldn't / won't rain tomorrow!
5. I wouldn't be worried about tomorrow if it weren't / isn't raining now.
6. If it didn't rain / hadn't rained, we could have had the picnic last week.
7. If it weren't raining, I 'd / 'll be dry.
8. The sky would be darker if it would / were going to rain.

B | *Correct the mistakes in the underlined words or phrases in the story.*

1. Bao hopes he hadn't forgotten to change the oil in his car. ______________
2. If he had changed the oil, the engine won't have seized. ______________
3. If the engine will not have seized, the car wouldn't have stopped. ______________
4. He wouldn't have to pay a towing bill. ______________
5. He won't have had to replace the engine. ______________
6. He could have make it to the job interview. ______________
7. He probably will not be unemployed now. ______________
8. Bao wishes he listened to his inner voice. ______________

C | *Circle the letter of the one underlined word or phrase in each sentence that is not correct.*

1. If only (A) we would have (B) been able to (C) finish the job in the time we had (D). **A B C D**
2. If I was (A) you, I wouldn't (B) accept (C) the offer until I knew (D) more. **A B C D**
3. Toshi would have (A) arrived (B) by now if he would be (C) planning to come (D). **A B C D**
4. If (A) Omar had (B) had (C) children, he has (D) someone to care for him. **A B C D**

UNIT **23** **More Conditions; The Subjunctive**

ADVICE

STEP 1 GRAMMAR IN CONTEXT

Before You Read

PAIRS: Discuss the questions.

1. Do you ever read advice columns? Do you think they contain useful information?
2. What is a problem that you might potentially ask a columnist about?

Read

Read the letters to the advice columnist and her responses.

ASK ROSA

Dear Rosa,

Hank and I were best friends in high school, so when he **suggested we room** together in college I thought it was a great idea. Wrong! **Had I known** what a slob Hank really is, I never would have agreed. We have a small suite that has become a pigsty because Hank thinks it's beneath him to wash a dish and is convinced the floor is the place to keep clothes. Whenever I talk to Hank about it, he just says, "Hey, Jason, you need to lighten up. You're too solemn." I'm no neatnik, but I do prefer a semblance of order. I still like Hank and want to stay friends, but I'm feeling more like a doormat every day. What would you **recommend I do**?

Jason

Dear Jason,

No one should have to feel like a doormat. Unfortunately, there's no easy solution to your problem. I can suggest three potential remedies: First, Hank may be unaware there's actually a problem. **If so**, ask him if he really likes having dirty dishes and bugs all over the place. If he doesn't, he might lend his muscles and help with the cleaning. There's a chance this approach will work, but **if not**, remedy two is teaching him how to clean up—he just may not be used to it. You might **suggest he do** the dishes one day and you the next. **Should that not work**, remedy three is to remind him you both have a right to a reasonably clean and orderly living space, and you feel your rights are being violated. Sometimes an appeal to a person's sense of fairness can do the trick. Whatever you do, **it's important that Hank not feel** criticized. **Otherwise**, he'll probably become intransigent, so be moderate in your suggestions. Good luck.

Rosa

ASK ROSA

Dear Rosa,

Jim and I have been married for over four years now, and our marriage would be ideal **were it not** for the overbearing qualities of some of his extended family. I love Jim dearly, but there are times when I feel like I'm married to his family members as well. They often drop in without letting me know they're coming, and at this point I'm spending more time with them than with Jim. Besides that, his sister Hannah constantly bombards me with requests that I do favors for her. For example, she **insists I take** her grocery shopping every week, even though she has her own car and is perfectly capable of doing this on her own. Even worse, his cousin Helen often **requests I lend** her money. At this point, Helen owes me about $750, but if I mention it she just says, "Carla, you know I'm good for it. I just need to get some bills paid off, and then I can pay you back." Rosa, I feel like I'm being taken advantage of. I know how important Jim's extended family is to him, but I'm at the end of my rope. What would you **suggest that I do**?

Carla

Dear Carla,

You're experiencing one of the most common problems faced by young marrieds, so don't feel you're alone. The problem sounds quite fixable. My guess is that your husband probably doesn't know what's going on and doesn't realize the depth of your frustration. Here's my advice: have a heart-to-heart talk with Jim. First tell him you appreciate his extended family but also feel you and he need more time alone together, that **without** it, your relationship can't develop as it should. **Suggest they** only **come over** at designated times. Also tell him you want to be helpful but feel his sister and cousin are asking too much of you. I'll bet he'll be willing to speak to them privately. When you're telling Jim about this, of course, **it's essential that you not criticize** his family members. That will probably cause resentment. Just give an honest statement of your feelings. **With** a little bit of extra communication with Jim, you can right the ship and make your marriage stronger. Good luck, and hang in there!

Rosa

After You Read

A | Vocabulary: *Match the blue words and phrases on the left with their meanings on the right.*

____ **1.** Had I known what a **slob** Hank is, I never would have agreed.

____ **2.** We have a small suite that has become a **pigsty**.

____ **3.** Jason, you need to **lighten up**.

____ **4.** I'm no **neatnik**, but I do prefer a semblance of order.

____ **5.** I'm no neatnik, but I do prefer a **semblance** of order.

____ **6.** I'm feeling more like a **doormat** every day.

____ **7.** Otherwise, he'll probably become **intransigent**.

____ **8.** Our marriage would be ideal were it not for the **overbearing** qualities of some of his extended family.

____ **9.** I'm **at the end of my rope**.

____ **10.** With a little bit of extra communication, you can **right the ship**.

a. outward appearance

b. stubbornly resistant

c. almost desperate

d. tending to order other people around

e. fix the situation

f. very dirty room or house

g. person excessively concerned about cleanliness and order

h. lazy, dirty, or messy person

i. one who allows others to dominate him or her

j. stop taking things so seriously

B | Comprehension: *Refer to the reading and complete each sentence with a single word.*

1. It was Hank's suggestion that he and Jason ________________ together in college.

2. Hank is not a ________________ person.

3. Jason is not a compulsively neat person, but he likes a certain amount of ________________.

4. Rosa says Hank may just not be ________________ to cleaning up.

5. Rosa suggests that appealing to Hank's sense of ________________ may help the situation.

6. Carla is bothered by the fact that some of her husband's extended family ________________ in without letting her know they're coming.

7. Rosa says intrusiveness on the part of in-laws is a common problem faced by young ________________.

8. Rosa says Carla should suggest to Jim that his family members come over only at ________________ times.

9. Rosa says it's essential that Carla not ________________ Jim's family.

STEP 2 GRAMMAR PRESENTATION

MORE CONDITIONS; THE SUBJUNCTIVE

Implied Conditions

Nonstandard Condition	(= Implied Condition)	Result Clause
With a bit of luck,	(If we have a bit of luck,)	we can fix the problem.
Without your help,	(If you hadn't helped,)	I wouldn't have succeeded.
But for his investments,	(If he didn't have investments,)	he'd have no income.
She might be lucky; **if so**,	(If she is lucky,)	she'll meet some new friends.
He might get the chance; **if not**,	(If he doesn't get the chance,)	he won't take the job.
She is lonely; **otherwise**,	(If she weren't lonely,)	she wouldn't need company.

Inverted Conditions

Inverted Condition	(= Standard Condition)	Result Clause
Were he in love,	(If he **were** in love,)	he would get married.
Were he **not** in love,	(If he **weren't** in love,)	he wouldn't get married.
Had I **seen** her,	(If I **had seen** her,)	I would have called you.
Should we **do** it,	(If we **should do** it,)	we will celebrate.

The Subjunctive in Noun Clauses

Verbs of Advice, Necessity, and Urgency + Subjunctive	
Main Clause	**Noun Clause**
Frank's teacher **suggested**	(that) he **take** an additional class.
The boss **demanded**	(that) Rosa **arrive** at work by 9:00.
The fireman **insisted**	(that) she **leave** the burning building immediately.

Adjectives of Advice, Necessity, and Urgency + Subjunctive	
Main Clause	**Noun Clause**
It is **advisable**	(that) he **arrive** one-half hour before the appointment.
It is **mandatory**	(that) no one **enter** the building without a permit.
It is **urgent**	(that) she **call** home at once.

GRAMMAR NOTES

1	**Conditions in conditional sentences** are sometimes implied rather than stated directly in an *if* clause.	
	Conditions may be implied by using *but for*, *if not*, *if so*, *otherwise*, *with*, *without*, etc.	• Your brother may be lonely. **If so**, he should join a singles group. *(= If he is lonely . . .)*
	In a sentence with an implied condition, there is no change in the result clause.	• Mary needs to be part of the decision. Otherwise, **she'll never be happy**. *(= If she isn't part of the decision, she'll never be happy.)*
	As with other conditional sentences, the condition may precede or follow the result clause.	• **With a little extra communication**, you can fix the problem. • You can fix the problem **with a little extra communication**.
2	**Unreal conditions** with *had* (past perfect), *should*, and *were* are sometimes expressed by deleting *if* and **inverting** the subject and the verb.	• **If I had known** he was lazy, I wouldn't have roomed with him. • **Had I known** he was lazy, I wouldn't have roomed with him.
	If there is an inverted condition, there is no change in the result clause.	• If I were to accept the job, **I would insist on benefits**. • Were I to accept the job, **I would insist on benefits**.
	As with other conditional sentences, the inverted condition clause can precede or follow the result clause.	• **If I were to move,** I'd have to get a new roommate. • I'd have to get a new roommate **if I were to move**.
	NOTE: Inverted conditional sentences with *should* imply that an action or event is unlikely to happen. The meaning of *should* in this type of sentence is much different from its usual meaning.	• **Should something go wrong**, we need to have a backup plan. *(= It is unlikely that something will go wrong, but we need to be prepared.)*
	BE CAREFUL! Negative inversion is formed by adding *not* after the inverted verb and the subject. Don't contract *not* and the verb.	• **Had I not received** the phone call, I wouldn't have been able to help. NOT: ~~Hadn't I~~ received the phone call, I wouldn't have been able to help.
	USAGE NOTE: Sentences with inverted condition clauses have the same meaning as conditionals with *if* but are more formal.	

3	The **subjunctive** is somewhat uncommon in English. However, one common example is the use of *were* in unreal conditions.	• If I **were** you, I'd visit my parents more often. • We could go on a picnic if it **weren't** raining.
	BE CAREFUL! This use of *were* occurs only in present unreal conditions. It is not used for past situations.	• If I **were** there, I would help her. NOT: ~~If I were there~~, I would have helped her.
4	Another form of the **subjunctive** uses the **base form** of a verb in noun clauses.	MAIN CLAUSE NOUN CLAUSE • We recommend (that) he **see** a lawyer.
	BE CAREFUL! The main verb in a noun clause can be past, present, or future. However, the subjunctive verb is the base form.	• We recommended (that) he **sell** his house. NOT: We recommended (that) he ~~sold~~ his house.
	Form the negative of a subjunctive verb by placing *not* before the base form.	• My aunt and uncle insisted (that) we **not come** to visit them today.
	To form a passive subjunctive, use *be* + the past participle.	• The doctor recommends (that) Uncle John **be hospitalized**.
	NOTE: In noun clauses with subjunctive constructions, we can usually omit the word *that*.	
5	The **subjunctive** with the base form of the verb is used in noun clauses following **verbs of advice**, **necessity**, and **urgency**, such as *demand*, *insist*, *propose*, *recommend*, and *suggest*.	• I **propose** (that) we **ask** Mom and Dad about their wishes. • My parents **insisted** (that) I **come** to visit them often.
	BE CAREFUL! We do not use infinitives after these verbs.	• He **suggested** (that) we **talk**. NOT: He suggested (that) we ~~to talk~~.
	Note that *insist (on)*, *propose*, *recommend*, and *suggest* can also be followed by a gerund phrase. The meaning of this structure is similar to the meaning of a sentence with a subjunctive in a noun clause.	• We **insist on / propose / recommend / suggest getting** another bid for the job.
	Note that the verbs *ask*, *order*, *require*, *urge*, etc., may also occur in the pattern verb + object + infinitive. When they are used in subjunctive constructions, the word *that* is usually not omitted.	• I **asked** that my brothers and sisters **be** present. OR • I **asked** my brothers and sisters **to be** present.

(continued on next page)

6	The **subjunctive** is also used after **adjectives of advice**, **necessity**, and **urgency**, such as *advisable, crucial, desirable, essential, important, mandatory, necessary*, and *urgent*. Subjunctive verbs after adjectives of urgency, necessity, and advice occur in the pattern *It* + *be* + adjective + *that* clause. We do not usually omit the word *that* in this type of clause.	• It is **essential** that elderly people **be treated** with dignity. • It's **important** that she **understand** her options. • It was **necessary** that my brother **see** a lawyer.
	NOTE: The pattern shown above can be replaced with *It* + *be* + adjective + *for* + noun or object pronoun + infinitive, which is more informal.	• It's **important for her to understand** her options. • It was **necessary for my brother to see** a lawyer.

REFERENCE NOTE

For a list of **verbs and phrases followed by the subjunctive**, see Appendix 24 on page A-10.

STEP 3 FOCUSED PRACTICE

EXERCISE 1: Discover the Grammar

A | *Read the sentences. Do the underlined words and phrases show implied conditionals* (**IM**), *inverted conditionals* (**IV**), *or subjunctive verb* (**S**) *constructions?*

1. Hank <u>suggested we room</u> together in college. S
2. <u>Had I known</u> what a slob Hank really is, I never would have agreed. ____
3. What would you <u>recommend I do</u>? ____
4. This may work, but <u>if not</u>, try teaching him how to clean up. ____
5. <u>Should that not work</u>, remedy three is to appeal to his sense of fairness. ____
6. Our marriage would be ideal <u>were it not</u> for the overbearing qualities of some of his extended family. ____
7. Be moderate in your suggestions; <u>otherwise</u>, he may become intransigent. ____
8. It's <u>essential that you not criticize</u> his family. ____
9. <u>With</u> a little bit of extra communication, you can right the ship. ____

B | *Read the pairs of sentences. Is the second sentence a correct rewriting of the first? Circle* **Y (Yes)** *or* **N (No).**

1. I would have recommended she sell it a long time ago.

   (Y) N I would have recommended her selling it a long time ago.

2. She's always said it's important for her to keep her independence.

   Y N She's always said it's important that she keep her independence.

3. I propose you make a new offer on the house.

   Y N I propose you to make a new offer on the house.

4. I'd recommend you look into joining a singles group.

   Y N I'd recommend you to join a singles group.

5. It's essential that you understand what your job responsibilities would be.

   Y N It's essential for you to understand what your job responsibilities would be.

6. Our marriage would be ideal were it not for the overbearing qualities of some of his extended family.

   Y N If it weren't for the overbearing qualities of some of his extended family, our marriage would be ideal.

EXERCISE 2: Implied Conditionals

(Grammar Note 1)

Read the conversation between a man and his doctor. There are six conditional sentences. The first sentence is underlined. Underline five more sentences. Rewrite the sentences by replacing the **if** *clauses with these nonstandard conditions:* **if so, if not, otherwise, with, without.** *One will be used twice.*

DOCTOR: Bob, you've got to improve your diet. <u>If you don't, you're going to get sick.</u> Too much fast food is not good for you.

BOB: There isn't time to go to a decent restaurant. I'm working 12 hours a day.

DOCTOR: Maybe your boss will let you have an extra half hour for lunch. If he will, that would solve your problem.

BOB: And if he won't, what can I do? He's a task master.

DOCTOR: Then I'd suggest you pack yourself a lunch every day. But now here's another thing: You need to stop smoking.

(continued on next page)

Bob: Impossible. If I don't have cigarettes, I can't make it through the day.

Doctor: There must be a way. You can do it if you find a buddy who has the same problem. You have friends at work, don't you?

Bob: I sure do. I'd hate my job if I didn't have my friends. Maybe there's someone else who's trying to stop smoking.

Doctor: Hopefully there is. Anyway, promise me you'll try to quit.

Bob: OK. I can promise to try.

1. Otherwise, you're going to get sick.
2. ______________________________
3. ______________________________
4. ______________________________
5. ______________________________
6. ______________________________

EXERCISE 3: Inverted / Implied Conditionals

(Grammar Notes 1–2)

A | *Fill in the blanks in the story with the items from the box.*

had she known	**if so**	~~**were she to stay**~~
if not	**otherwise**	**with**

Doris Allen had just moved to St. Louis from Russellville, the small city where she had grown up and attended college. For some time, Doris had felt it was necessary for her to leave Russellville. Were she to stay (1.) there, she felt, she would just fall into a rut she would never escape from, so she decided to go to the big city and start a new life. At the age of 23, however, she needed to work. ______________ (2.) how difficult it would be to find employment, she might have stayed in her hometown. She loved the big city, though, and she had been looking hard for a job. The only problem was that Doris needed to find a job fairly soon; ______________ (3.), she wouldn't be able to afford her apartment. A good deal of her savings were already gone. There was another problem: Having spent the last five years in college, Doris had worked only in the summers and was unaccustomed to job hunting. One day she was wandering around downtown, feeling that ______________ (4.) a bit of luck she might find something. She saw a pleasant-looking florist's shop. Maybe they were hiring; ______________ (5.), she might get a job. ______________ (6.), she wouldn't lose anything by going in and asking. Without even thinking further, she walked in."I'm Doris Allen, and I was wondering whether you were doing any hiring. I was a botany major in college, and I have a lot of experience with flowers and gardening."

The manager said, "Actually, we're expanding and do need someone to work part-time. The position could become full-time eventually. I was just going to put up a sign in the window. Tell me more about your experience."

Doris got the job.

B | *Rewrite each word or phrase from Part A with an* **if** *clause that restates the condition.*

1. *If she were to stay* ______________
2. ______________
3. ______________
4. ______________
5. ______________
6. ______________

EXERCISE 4: Verbs of Urgency and Subjunctives

(Grammar Notes 4–5)

Describe the action of each picture by completing each sentence on the next page. Use subjunctive verb forms and appropriate subjects.

1.

2.

3.

4.

5.

6.

1. The police officer is suggesting the woman call a towing company.

2. The workers are demanding ______.

3. The wife is insisting ______.

4. The woman is proposing ______.

5. The real estate agent is recommending ______.

6. The travel agent is suggesting ______.

EXERCISE 5: Adjectives of Urgency and Subjunctives

(Grammar Note 6)

A | *What do young people need for a good start to adult life? Complete each sentence with the adjective in parentheses and a verb from the box.*

communicate	find	~~have~~	make	stay	take

1. It is desirable that they have (desirable) good self-esteem.

2. It is ______ (necessary) responsibility for their own actions.

3. It is ______ (important) satisfying employment.

4. It is ______ (essential) most of their own decisions.

5. If they are married, it is ______ (crucial) with each other.

6. It is ______ (advisable) in touch with family and close friends.

B | *Now rewrite each sentence in Part A using* **for** *+ noun or object pronoun + infinitive.*

1. It is desirable for them to have good self-esteem.

2. ______

3. ______

4. ______

5. ______

6. ______

EXERCISE 6: Editing

Read the letter. It has seven mistakes in verb constructions. The first mistake is already corrected. Find and correct six more.

December 10

Dear Hei-Rim,

It's time I wrote and filled you in on what's been happening since I left Russellville. I finally got a job! Remember when you suggested I just ~~went~~ go walking around, getting a sense of what St. Louis was like? A few weeks ago I was getting rather worried since I had spent most of the money I had saved to get me through the job-hunting period. It's not all that easy for someone fresh out of college to find a job, you know. I had gotten to the point where it was absolutely essential that I found something or come back to Russellville. So I decided to follow your advice. I had known how easy this would be, I would have tried it the first week I was here. I started walking around in the downtown area, and before I knew it, I saw a beautiful little florist's shop. I walked right in, unafraid, and asked if they needed anyone. Can you believe that they did?

I was really happy in my job until my boss hired a new assistant manager who has been making my life miserable. Among other things, he demands me to make coffee for him. He also insists that I'm doing other things that aren't in my job description. I took this job to work with plants, not to serve him coffee. I think I need to tell him where I stand. It's important that he stops treating me as his personal assistant. I have a few days off for the holidays. Do you have some time off? If so, how about coming down here for a visit? Wouldn't that be fun? I have a spare bedroom in my apartment. If you can come, I suggest you to drive, as it isn't far. Please write or email and let me know.

Love,

Doris

STEP 4 COMMUNICATION PRACTICE

EXERCISE 7: Listening

A | *Listen to the conversation. Why is the daughter working so much?*

____

B | *Read the questions. Listen again to the telephone conversation and answer the questions in complete sentences.*

1. What did the daughter ask her mother to do?

   The daughter asked her mother to babysit.

2. What did the daughter almost do when the mother said no?

   ____

3. Had the mother known who was calling, what would she have done?

   ____

4. What did the mother have to do the last time this happened?

   ____

5. According to her mother, what is it important that the daughter do?

   ____

6. What does the mother's friend suggest she do?

   ____

EXERCISE 8: Pronunciation

A | *Read and listen to the Pronunciation Note.*

Pronunciation Note

English has "silent" consonants that are not pronounced in many words but are pronounced in other words in the same family.

Examples: You're too **solemn**. ("n" is not pronounced)
There are times when **solemnity** is a good thing. ("n" is pronounced)

B | *Listen to the sentences. Cross out silent consonants that are not pronounced. Circle the same consonants in words where they are pronounced.*

1. **a.** Your marriage is already strong.

   b. You can make it stronger.

2. **a.** Too much exercise can give you muscular aches.

   b. Maybe he'll lend his muscles and help with the cleaning.

3. **a.** I love autumn more than any other season.

   b. The autumnal equinox occurs around September 21 in the Northern Hemisphere.

4. **a.** Ask them to come over at designated times.

   b. We've designed our new house and are going to have it built.

5. **a.** There are plenty of people who want to ban the bomb.

   b. We're bombarded with attention.

6. **a.** There are crumbs all over the floor.

   b. Their relationship has crumbled.

C | *PAIRS: Practice the sentences.*

EXERCISE 9: Personal Inventory

A | *Complete each of the sentences, drawing from your own experience or opinions. Use subjunctive verb forms where appropriate.*

1. My parents suggested ____________________
2. My parents insisted ____________________
3. It's essential that I ____________________
4. It's important for me ____________________
5. It's essential that a person ____________________
6. Had I known ____________________
7. Were I ____________________
8. Should I ____________________

B | *PAIRS: Discuss your answers. Report interesting examples to the class.*

EXERCISE 10: Group Discussion

A | *Read the statements. Write* **A (Agree), D (Disagree),** *or* **IB (In Between),** *according to your personal beliefs.*

_____ **1.** It's desirable that young people work for a year or two before going to college.

_____ **2.** It is advisable that young people not be allowed to drive until they are at least 18.

_____ **3.** It is essential that national governments pay for the health care of the citizens.

_____ **4.** It is reasonable that national governments provide low-cost loans to students who want to attend college.

_____ **5.** It is important that young people participate in some form of national service.

B | *SMALL GROUPS: Discuss your answers. Share your group's opinions with the rest of the class.*

EXAMPLE: **A:** I think it is desirable that young people work for a year or two before going to college.
B: Why?
A: They need a break from at least 12 years of school.

EXERCISE 11: Picture Discussion

GROUPS: Discuss one of the pictures. The daughter or son of a friend is going to make a visit to one of these countries and has asked for your input. Give advice, using subjunctive verb constructions with **suggest, recommend,** *and* **it is essential that** *plus any others that are appropriate. Include a negative sentence.*

EXAMPLES: If the person is visiting the United Kingdom, I suggest he / she stay in bed and breakfasts.
I recommend he / she pack a raincoat and a sweater.
It's essential that he / she visit Stonehenge.
It's crucial that he / she not forget to take his / her passport.

China

France

Egypt

Brazil

EXERCISE 12: Writing

A | *Write four or five paragraphs about a time when you took some good advice or a time when you took some bad advice. Explain the situation fully and show why the advice was good or bad. In your composition use subjunctive verb constructions (such as* **suggest, recommend, necessary that,** *etc.) and at least one implied conditional.*

EXAMPLE: One of the worst pieces of advice I've ever taken was to go out for the football team in high school. My friend Mark had suggested I try to make the team and had assured me I would make it if I did. I've never been very good at football, and I knew that in the back of my mind, but for the sake of popularity and togetherness I took Mark's suggestion. Had I known how badly the situation would turn out, I never would have done it. Here's what happened . . .

B | *Check your work. Use the Editing Checklist.*

Editing Checklist

Did you use . . . ?

- ☐ subjunctives with verbs of advice correctly
- ☐ subjunctives with adverbs of necessity correctly
- ☐ implied conditionals correctly
- ☐ inverted conditionals correctly

UNIT 23 Review

Check your answers on page UR-3.
Do you need to review anything?

A | *Circle the word or phrase that correctly completes each sentence.*

1. You need to get some job retraining. With / Without it, you risk being laid off.
2. Juan may or may not go to college. If so / If not, he'll be working for his father.
3. I think something is wrong with the car. If so / If not, we'd better have it fixed.
4. You have to take notes; if not / otherwise, you'll forget.
5. Our house is on the market. If so / With a bit of luck, the sale will go through.
6. I may not pass the class; if not / if so, I'll have to take it over.
7. Ana has a daughter; without / if not her daughter, she'd be all alone.
8. The traffic is heavy, but with / if a bit of luck, we'll be on time.

B | *Correct the mistakes in the underlined words or phrases.*

1. Give me a call; but for that, I may forget the meeting. ____________
2. Hadn't I reminded Jiro of the party, he would have forgotten. ____________
3. Hana suggested that I called the airline, but I didn't. ____________
4. I might be late. That should happen, go without me. ____________
5. But her pension, she would never be able to survive financially. ____________
6. It's crucial that Linh understands the gravity of his situation. ____________
7. Jae-Yong may be coming; if not, you can ride back with him. ____________
8. It is surprising that Jane like to scuba dive. ____________

C | *Circle the letter of the one underlined word or phrase in each sentence that is not correct.*

1. I had known (A) how you would act (B), I wouldn't have suggested (C) you come (D). **A B C D**
2. I suggest (A) Aki to attend (B) class. She'll be (C) more likely to pass if she does (D). **A B C D**
3. Dev would ask (A) Frida to marry (B) him he were (C) in love, but he isn't (D). **A B C D**
4. I'm glad you suggested (A) I followed (B) my intuition. I did (C), and it worked (D). **A B C D**

From Grammar to Writing

AVOIDING RUN-ON SENTENCES AND COMMA SPLICES

To strengthen your writing and make it effective, you should avoid two common types of errors: the **run-on sentence** and the **comma splice**. A run-on sentence is a group of words containing at least two independent clauses without any punctuation separating them. A comma splice is the joining of two independent clauses with only a comma.

EXAMPLES: The old man felt ill he needed to get out of the sun quickly.
(run-on sentence—No punctuation separates the two independent clauses.)

The old man felt ill, he needed to get out of the sun quickly.
(comma splice—A comma separates the two clauses, but a comma is not adequate punctuation.)

Correct run-on sentences and comma splices in the following ways:

1. Insert a period between the independent clauses.
   The old man felt ill**. He** needed to get out of the sun quickly.

2. Insert a semicolon between the independent clauses: (Don't capitalize the word after the semicolon unless it is a proper noun or *I*.)
   The old man felt ill**;** he needed to get out of the sun quickly.

3. Join the two independent clauses with a comma and a coordinating conjunction:
   The old man felt ill**, so** he needed to get out of the sun quickly.

4. Make one of the independent clauses dependent by adding a subordinating conjunction, and separate the two clauses with a comma if the dependent clause comes first:
   Because the old man felt ill**,** he needed to get out of the sun quickly.

5. Convert one of the two clauses into an adverbial phrase if the subjects of the two clauses are the same:
   Feeling ill, the old man had to get out of the sun quickly.

1 | *Correct the run-on sentences and comma splices by using the method given in parentheses.*

1. Nancy says she wants to do something worthwhile if so, she should consider volunteer work. *(period)*

2. I need to get a bank loan, otherwise, I'll have to file for bankruptcy. *(semicolon)*

3. Donna didn't want to stop for the old man Thain persuaded her it was a necessity. *(comma and coordinating conjunction)*

4. I was learning to be assertive I learned many things about myself. *(subordinating conjunction and comma)*

5. Nancy felt dominated by her mother-in-law, she needed to take assertive action. *(Make the first clause an adverbial phrase.)*

2 | *Read the passage. Correct the nine mistakes consisting of run-on sentences and comma splices. Capitalize where necessary.*

Call it either intuition or good vibrations. Whatever you want to call it, it works. Last summer I was on a committee to hire a new head nurse at the nursing home where I work, we interviewed two candidates as finalists, a man named Bob and a woman named Sarah on paper, Bob was better qualified he had a master's degree while Sarah had only a bachelor's degree, however, Sarah was the one who really impressed us she answered all of the questions straightforwardly and simply, Bob, on the other hand, evaded some of our questions while simultaneously trying to make us think he knew everything and could do everything all of us on the committee just liked Sarah better in fact, she got the job because she was the person we all felt we wanted to work with. Our intuition wasn't wrong, she's turned out to be a wonderful nurse.

3 | *Before you write . . .*

1. We are sometimes encouraged to act according to our intuition. Think of a time when you or a friend acted according to intuitive feelings, and those feelings turned out to be correct.
2. Describe your experience to a partner. Listen to your partner's description.
3. Ask and answer questions about your and your partner's topic. Why do you think following intuition worked successfully? Does this mean we should always act intuitively?

4 | *Write a draft of a composition about your (or a friend's) intuitive experience. Follow the model. Remember to include information that your partner asked about. Read your draft aloud and correct any run-on sentences or comma splices.*

Details about my (or my friend's) intuitive experience:

____

____

____

____

(continued on next page)

My explanation of why I think it worked to act on the basis of intuition:

____

____

____

____

Reasons why I think we should / should not always follow our intuition:

____

____

____

____

5 | *Exchange compositions with a different partner. Complete the chart.*

1. The writer's composition is free of run-on sentences and comma splices. **Yes** ☐ **No** ☐
2. What I liked in the composition:

   ____

   ____

   ____

3. Questions I'd like the writer to answer about the composition:

   Who ____?

   What ____?

   When ____?

   Where ____?

   Why ____?

   How ____?

   (Your own question) ____?

6 | *Work with your partner. Discuss each other's chart from Exercise 5. Then rewrite your own composition and make any necessary changes.*

Appendices

1 Irregular Verbs

Base Form	Simple Past	Past Participle
arise	arose	arisen
awake	awoke	awoken
be	was/were	been
bear	bore	born/borne
beat	beat	beaten/beat
become	became	become
begin	began	begun
bend	bent	bent
bet	bet	bet
bite	bit	bitten
bleed	bled	bled
blow	blew	blown
break	broke	broken
bring	brought	brought
broadcast	broadcast/broadcasted	broadcast/broadcasted
build	built	built
burn	burned/burnt	burned/burnt
burst	burst	burst
buy	bought	bought
cast	cast	cast
catch	caught	caught
choose	chose	chosen
cling	clung	clung
come	came	come
cost	cost	cost
creep	crept	crept
cut	cut	cut
deal	dealt	dealt
dig	dug	dug
dive	dived/dove	dived
do	did	done
draw	drew	drawn
dream	dreamed/dreamt	dreamed/dreamt
drink	drank	drunk
drive	drove	driven
eat	ate	eaten
fall	fell	fallen
feed	fed	fed
feel	felt	felt
fight	fought	fought
find	found	found
fit	fitted/fit	fitted/fit
flee	fled	fled
fling	flung	flung
fly	flew	flown
forbid	forbade/forbid	forbidden
forget	forgot	forgotten
forgive	forgave	forgiven

Base Form	Simple Past	Past Participle
forgo	forwent	forgone
forsake	forsook	forsaken
freeze	froze	frozen
get	got	gotten/got
give	gave	given
go	went	gone
grind	ground	ground
grow	grew	grown
hang	hung*/hanged**	hung*/hanged**
have	had	had
hear	heard	heard
hide	hid	hidden
hit	hit	hit
hold	held	held
hurt	hurt	hurt
keep	kept	kept
kneel	knelt/kneeled	knelt/kneeled
knit	knit/knitted	knit/knitted
know	knew	known
lay	laid	laid
lead	led	led
leap	leaped/leapt	leaped/leapt
learn	learned/learnt	learned/learnt
leave	left	left
lend	lent	lent
let	let	let
lie *(down)*	lay	lain
light	lit/lighted	lit/lighted
lose	lost	lost
make	made	made
mean	meant	meant
meet	met	met
pay	paid	paid
plead	pleaded/pled	pleaded/pled
prove	proved	proved/proven
put	put	put
quit	quit	quit
read	read	read
rid	rid	rid
ride	rode	ridden
ring	rang	rung
rise	rose	risen
run	ran	run
saw	sawed	sawed/sawn
say	said	said

* hung = hung an object
** hanged = executed by hanging

(continued on next page)

Base Form	Simple Past	Past Participle
see	saw	seen
seek	sought	sought
sell	sold	sold
send	sent	sent
set	set	set
sew	sewed	sewn/sewed
shake	shook	shaken
shave	shaved	shaved/shaven
shear	sheared	sheared/shorn
shine	shone*/shined**	shone*/shined**
shoot	shot	shot
show	showed	shown
shrink	shrank/shrunk	shrunk/shrunken
shut	shut	shut
sing	sang	sung
sink	sank/sunk	sunk
sit	sat	sat
slay	slew/slayed	slain/slayed
sleep	slept	slept
slide	slid	slid
sneak	sneaked/snuck	sneaked/snuck
speak	spoke	spoken
speed	sped/speeded	sped/speeded
spend	spent	spent
spill	spilled/spilt	spilled/spilt
spin	spun	spun
spit	spat/spit	spat
split	split	split
spread	spread	spread
spring	sprang	sprung
stand	stood	stood
steal	stole	stolen
stick	stuck	stuck
sting	stung	stung
stink	stank/stunk	stunk
strike	struck	struck/stricken
swear	swore	sworn
sweep	swept	swept
swim	swam	swum
swing	swung	swung
take	took	taken
teach	taught	taught
tear	tore	torn
tell	told	told
think	thought	thought
throw	threw	thrown
understand	understood	understood
upset	upset	upset
wake	woke	woken
wear	wore	worn
weave	wove/weaved	woven/weaved
weep	wept	wept
win	won	won
wind	wound	wound
withdraw	withdrew	withdrawn
wring	wrung	wrung
write	wrote	written

* shone = intransitive: *The sun shone brightly.*
** shined = transitive: *He shined his shoes.*

2 Non-Action Verbs

Examples: She **seems** happy in her new job.
I **have** a terrible headache.
The food **smells** good.
Mary **owes** me money.

Appearances
appear
be
concern
indicate
look
mean (= signify)
parallel
represent
resemble
seem
signify (= mean)

Emotions
abhor
admire
adore
appreciate
care
desire
detest
dislike
doubt
empathize
envy
fear
hate
hope
like
love
regret
respect
sympathize
trust

Mental States
agree
amaze
amuse
annoy
assume
astonish
believe
bore
care
consider
deem
deny
disagree
disbelieve
entertain (= amuse)
estimate
expect
fancy
favor
feel (= believe)
figure (= assume)
find (= believe)
guess
hesitate
hope
imagine
imply
impress
infer
know
mean
mind
presume
realize
recognize
recollect
remember
revere
see (= understand)
suit
suppose
suspect
think (= believe)
tire
understand
wonder

Senses and Perception
ache
feel
hear
hurt
notice
observe
perceive
see
sense
smart
smell
sound
taste

Possession
belong
have
own
pertain
possess

Wants and Preferences
desire
need
prefer
want
wish

Other
cost
include
lack
matter
owe
refuse
suffice
weigh

3 Non-Action Verbs Sometimes Used in the Progressive

Examples: The students **are being** silly today.
We**'re having** dinner right now. Can I call you back?
Mary **is smelling** the roses.
The cook **is tasting** the soup.

ache	bore	expect	hear	include	perceive	sense
admire	consider	favor	hesitate	indicate	presume	smell
agree	deny	feel	hope	lack	realize	sympathize
amuse	disagree	figure	hurt	look	refuse	taste
annoy	doubt	find	imagine	notice	represent	think
assume	empathize	guess	imply	observe	see	wonder
be	entertain	have	impress			

4 Irregular Noun Plurals

Singular Form	Plural Form	Singular Form	Plural Form	Singular Form	Plural Form
alumna	alumnae	elf	elves	paramecium	paramecia
alumnus	alumni	fish	fish/fishes*	people***	peoples
amoeba	amoebas/amoebae	foot	feet	person	people
analysis	analyses	genus	genera	phenomenon	phenomena
antenna	antennae/antennas	goose	geese	—	police
appendix	appendixes/appendices	half	halves	policeman	policemen
axis	axes	index	indexes/indices	policewoman	policewomen
basis	bases	knife	knives	protozoan	protozoa/protozoans
businessman	businessmen	leaf	leaves	radius	radii
businesswoman	businesswomen	life	lives	series	series
cactus	cacti/cactuses	loaf	loaves	sheaf	sheaves
calf	calves	louse	lice	sheep	sheep
—	cattle	man	men	shelf	shelves
child	children	millennium	millennia/millenniums	species	species
crisis	crises	money	moneys/monies**	thesis	theses
criterion	criteria	moose	moose	tooth	teeth
datum	data	mouse	mice	vertebra	vertebrae/vertebras
deer	deer	octopus	octopuses/octopi	wife	wives
dwarf	dwarfs/dwarves	ox	oxen	woman	women

* fishes = different species of fish
** monies/moneys = separate amounts or sources of money
*** a people = an ethnic group

5 Non-Count Nouns

Abstractions
advice
anarchy
behavior
chance
decay
democracy
energy
entertainment
evil
freedom
fun
good
happiness
hate
hatred
honesty
inertia
integrity
love
luck
momentum
oppression
peace
pollution
responsibility
slavery
socialism
spontaneity
stupidity
time
totalitarianism
truth
violence

Activities
badminton
baseball
basketball
biking
billiards
bowling
boxing
canoeing
cards
conversation
cycling
dancing
football
golf
hiking
hockey
judo
karate
reading
sailing
singing
skating
soccer
surfing
taekwon do
talking
tennis
volleyball
wrestling

Diseases
AIDS
appendicitis
bronchitis
cancer
chickenpox
cholera
diabetes
diphtheria
flu (influenza)
heart disease
malaria
measles
mumps
pneumonia
polio
smallpox
strep throat
tuberculosis (TB)

Foods
barley
beef
bread
broccoli
cake
candy
chicken
corn
fish
meat
oats
pie
rice
wheat

Gases
carbon dioxide
helium
hydrogen
neon
nitrogen
oxygen

Liquids
coffee
gasoline
juice
milk
oil
soda
tea
water

Natural Phenomena
air
cold
electricity
fog
hail
heat
ice
lightning
mist
rain
sleet
slush
smog
smoke
snow
steam
thunder
warmth
wind

Occupations
banking
computer technology
construction
dentistry
engineering
farming
fishing
law
manufacturing
medicine
nursing
retail
sales
teaching
writing
work

Particles
dust
gravel
pepper
salt
sand
spice
sugar

Solid Elements
aluminum
calcium
carbon
copper
gold
iron
lead
magnesium
platinum
plutonium
radium
silver
sodium
tin
titanium
uranium

Subjects
accounting
art
astronomy
biology
business
chemistry
civics
computer science
economics
geography
history
linguistics
literature
mathematics
music
physics
psychology
science
sociology
speech
writing

Other
clothing
equipment
film
furniture
news

6 Ways of Making Non-Count Nouns Countable

Abstractions
a piece of advice
a matter of choice
a unit of energy
a type/form of entertainment
a piece/bit of luck

Activities
a game of badminton/baseball/basketball/cards/football/golf/soccer/tennis, etc.
a badminton game/a baseball game, etc.

Foods
a grain of barley
a cut/piece/slice of beef
a loaf of bread
a piece of cake
a piece/wedge of pie
a grain of rice
a portion/serving of . . .

Liquids
a cup of coffee, tea, cocoa
a gallon/liter of gasoline
a can of oil
a glass of milk, water, juice
a can/glass of soda

Natural Phenomena
a bolt/current of electricity
a bolt/flash of lightning
a drop of rain
a clap of thunder

Particles
a speck of dust
a grain of pepper, salt, sand, sugar

Subjects
a branch of accounting/art/astronomy/biology/chemistry/economics/geography/linguistics/literature/mathematics/music/physics/psychology/sociology, etc.

Other
an article of clothing
a piece of equipment
a piece/article of furniture
a piece of news/a news item/an item of news
a period of time

7 Nouns Often Used with the Definite Article

the air
the atmosphere
the authorities
the Bhagavad Gita
the Bible
the cosmos
the Creator
the earth
the economy
the Empire State Building
the environment
the European Union
the flu
the gross national product (GNP)
the Internet
the Koran
the measles
the Milky Way (galaxy)
the moon
the movies
the mumps
the ocean
the police
the *Queen Mary*
the radio
the sky
the solar system
the stock market
the stratosphere
the sun
the Taj Mahal
the *Titanic*
the United Nations
the universe
the Vatican
the world

8 Countries Whose Names Contain the Definite Article

the Bahamas
the Cayman Islands
the Central African Republic
the Channel Islands
the Comoros
the Czech Republic
the Dominican Republic
the Falkland Islands
the Gambia
the Isle of Man
the Ivory Coast
the Leeward Islands
the Maldives (the Maldive Islands)
the Marshall Islands
the Netherlands
the Netherlands Antilles
the Philippines
the Solomon Islands
the Turks and Caicos Islands
the United Arab Emirates
the United Kingdom (of Great Britain and Northern Ireland)
the United States (of America)
the Virgin Islands

9 Selected Geographical Features Whose Names Contain the Definite Article

Gulfs, Oceans, Seas, and Straits

the Adriatic Sea
the Aegean Sea
the Arabian Sea
the Arctic Ocean
the Atlantic (Ocean)
the Baltic (Sea)
the Black Sea
the Caribbean (Sea)
the Caspian (Sea)
the Coral Sea
the Gulf of Aden
the Gulf of Mexico
the Gulf of Oman
the Indian Ocean
the Mediterranean (Sea)
the North Sea
the Pacific (Ocean)
the Persian Gulf
the Philippine Sea
the Red Sea
the Sea of Japan
the South China Sea
the Strait of Gibraltar
the Strait of Magellan
the Yellow Sea

Mountain Ranges

the Alps
the Andes
the Appalachians
the Atlas Mountains
the Caucasus
the Himalayas
the Pyrenees
the Rockies (the Rocky Mountains)
the Urals

Rivers

(all of the following can contain the word *River*)

the Amazon
the Colorado
the Columbia
the Danube
the Don
the Euphrates
the Ganges
the Huang
the Hudson
the Indus
the Jordan
the Lena
the Mackenzie
the Mekong
the Mississippi
the Missouri
the Niger
the Nile
the Ob
the Ohio
the Orinoco
the Po
the Rhine
the Rhone
the Rio Grande
the St. Lawrence
the Seine
the Tagus
the Thames
the Tiber
the Tigris
the Volga
the Yangtze

Other Features

the Arctic Circle
the Antarctic Circle
the equator
the Far East
the Gobi (Desert)
the Kalahari (Desert)
the Middle East
the Near East
the North Pole
the Occident
the Orient
the Panama Canal
the Sahara (Desert)
the South Pole
the Suez Canal
the Tropic of Cancer
the Tropic of Capricorn

10 Verbs Used in the Passive Followed by a *That* Clause

Example: It **is alleged that** he committed the crime.

allege
assume
believe
claim
fear
feel
hold
postulate
predict
say
theorize
think

11 Stative Passive Verbs + Prepositions

Example: The island of Hispaniola **is divided into** two separate nations.

be bordered by
be composed of
be comprised of
be connected to/with/by
be covered by/with
be divided into/by
be filled with
be found in/on, etc.
be intended
be joined to
be known as
be listed in/as
be located in/on, etc.
be made (out) of
be made up of
be measured by
be placed near/in
be positioned near/in
be related to
be surrounded by

12 Verbs Followed by the Gerund

Example: Jane **enjoys playing** tennis and **gardening**.

abhor
acknowledge
admit
advise
allow
anticipate
appreciate
avoid
be worth
can't help
celebrate
confess
consider
defend
delay
deny
detest
discontinue
discuss
dislike
dispute
dread
endure
enjoy
escape
evade
explain
fancy
fear
feel like
feign
finish
forgive
give up (= stop)
imagine
keep (= continue)
keep on
mention
mind (= object to)
miss
necessitate
omit
permit
picture
postpone
practice
prevent
put off
recall
recollect
recommend
report
resent
resist
resume
risk
shirk
shun
suggest
support
tolerate
understand
urge
warrant

13 Verbs Followed by the Infinitive

Example: The Baxters **decided to sell** their house.

agree
appear
arrange
ask
attempt
beg
can/cannot afford
can/cannot wait
care
chance
choose
claim
come
consent
dare
decide
demand
deserve
determine
elect
endeavor
expect
fail
get
grow (up)
guarantee
hesitate
hope
hurry
incline
learn
manage
mean (= intend)
need
neglect
offer
pay
plan
prepare
pretend
profess
promise
prove
refuse
remain
request
resolve
say
seek
seem
shudder
strive
struggle
swear
tend
threaten
turn out
venture
volunteer
wait
want
wish
would like
yearn

14 Verbs Followed by the Gerund or Infinitive without a Significant Change in Meaning

Examples: Martha **hates to go** to bed early.
Martha **hates going** to bed early.

begin
can't bear
can't stand
continue
hate
like
love
prefer
propose
start

15 Verbs Followed by the Gerund or the Infinitive with a Significant Change in Meaning

forget
I've almost **forgotten meeting** him. (= At present, I can hardly remember.)
I almost **forgot to meet** him. (= I almost didn't remember to meet him.)

go on
Jack **went on writing** novels. (= Jack continued to write novels.)
Carrie **went on to write** novels. (= Carrie ended some other activity and began to write novels.)

quit
Ella **quit working** at Sloan's. (= She isn't working there anymore.)
Frank **quit to work** at Sloan's. (= He quit another job in order to work at Sloan's.)

regret
I **regret telling** you I'm taking the job. (= I'm sorry that I said I would take it.)
I **regret to tell** you I'm taking the job. (= I'm telling you now that I'm taking the job, and I'm sorry I'm taking it.)

remember
Velma **remembered writing** to Bill. (= Velma remembered the previous activity of writing to Bill.)
Melissa **remembered to write** to Bill. (= Melissa didn't forget to write to Bill. She wrote to him.)

stop
Hank **stopped eating**. (= He stopped the activity of eating.)
Bruce **stopped to eat**. (= He stopped doing something else in order to eat.)

try
Martin **tried skiing**. (= Martin sampled the activity of skiing.)
Helen **tried to ski**. (= Helen attempted to ski but didn't succeed.)

16 Adjective + Preposition Combinations

These phrases are followed by nouns, pronouns, or gerunds.

Examples: I'm not **familiar with** that writer.
I'm **amazed at** her.
We're **excited about** going.

accustomed to
afraid of
amazed at/by
angry at/with
ashamed of
astonished at/by
aware of
awful at
bad at
bored with/by
capable of
careful of
concerned with/about
content with
curious about
different from
excellent at
excited about
familiar with
famous for
fascinated with/by
fed up with
fond of
furious with/at
glad about
good at
good with
guilty of
happy about
incapable of
intent on
interested in
intrigued by/at
mad at (=angry at/with)
nervous about
obsessed with/about
opposed to
pleased about/with
poor at
ready for
responsible for
sad about
safe from
satisfied with
shocked at/by
sick of
slow at
sorry for/about
suited to
surprised at/about/by
terrible at
tired from
tired of
used to
weary of
worried about

17 Verbs Followed by Noun / Pronoun + Infinitive

Example: **I asked Sally to lend** me her car.

advise
allow
ask*
cause
choose*
convince
encourage
expect*
forbid
force
get*
hire
invite
need*
order
pay*
permit
persuade
remind
require
teach
tell
urge
want*
warn
would like*

*These verbs can also be followed by the infinitive without an object.

Examples: **I want Jerry to go.**
I want to go.

18 Adjectives Followed by the Infinitive

Example: I was **glad to hear** about that.

advisable*
afraid
alarmed
amazed
angry
anxious
ashamed
astonished
careful
crucial*
curious
delighted
depressed
desirable*
determined*
difficult
disappointed
distressed
disturbed
eager
easy
ecstatic
embarrassed
encouraged
essential*
excited
fascinated
fortunate
frightened
furious
glad
good
happy
hard
hesitant
important*
impossible
interested
intrigued
likely
lucky
mandatory*
necessary*
nice
obligatory*
pleased
possible
prepared
proud
ready
relieved
reluctant
right
sad
scared
shocked
sorry
surprised
touched
unlikely
unnecessary*
upset
willing
wrong

* These adjectives can also be followed with a noun clause containing a subjunctive verb form.

Examples: It's **essential to communicate.**
It's **essential that she communicate with her parents.**

19 Sentence Adverbs

Examples: **Clearly**, this is the best course of action.
This is **clearly** the best course of action.
This is the best course of action, **clearly**.

actually	certainly	evidently	happily	mainly	perhaps	significantly	thankfully
amazingly	clearly	fortunately	honestly	maybe	possibly	surely	understandably
apparently	definitely	frankly	hopefully	mercifully	probably	surprisingly	unfortunately
basically	essentially	generally	importantly	overall			

20 Words That Begin Dependent Clauses

Subordinating Conjunctions (to introduce adverb clauses)

after
although
anywhere
as
as if
as long as
as many as
as much as
as soon as
as though
because
because of the fact that
before
despite the fact that
due to the fact that
even if
even though
even when
everywhere
if
if only
inasmuch as
in case
in spite of the fact that
no matter if
no matter whether
now that
on account of the fact that
once
only if
plus the fact that
provided (that)
providing (that)
since
so that
so . . . that (= in order to)
such . . . that
though
till
unless
until
when
whenever
where
whereas
wherever
whether (or not)
while

Relative Pronouns (to introduce adjective clauses)

that
when
where
which
who
whom
whose

Others (to introduce noun clauses)

how
how far
how long
how many
how much
however (= the way in which)
if
that
the fact that
what
what color
whatever
what time
when
where
whether (or not)
whichever (one)
whoever
whomever
why

21 Transitions: Sentence Connectors

To Show Addition

additionally
along with this/that
also
alternatively
as a matter of fact
besides
furthermore
in addition
indeed
in fact
in other words
in the same way
likewise
moreover
plus

To Show a Contrast

actually
anyhow
anyway
as a matter of fact
at any rate
despite this/that
even so
however
in any case
in contrast
in either case
in fact
in spite of this/that
instead (of this/that)
nevertheless
nonetheless
on the contrary
on the other hand
rather
still
though

To Show an Effect / Result

accordingly
as a result
because of this/that
consequently
for this/that reason
hence
in consequence
on account of this/that
otherwise
then
therefore
this/that being so
thus
to this end

To Show Time and Sequence

after this/that
afterwards
an hour later (several hours later, etc.)
at last
at this moment
before this/that
from now on
henceforth
hitherto
in the meantime
just then
meanwhile
next
on another occasion
previously
then
under the circumstances
until then
up to now

22 Transitions: Blocks of Text

all in all
another reason/point, etc.
finally
first(ly)
in conclusion
in short
in sum
in summary
last(ly)
most importantly
second(ly)
the most important reason/factor, etc.
third(ly) (fourth[ly], etc.)
to conclude
to resume
to return to the point
to summarize

23 Reporting Verbs

Example: "This is the best course of action," Jack **added**.

add
allege
allow
ask
claim
comment
confess
exclaim
maintain
murmur
note
observe
point out
query
report
respond
say
shout
tell
wonder
yell

24 Verbs and Expressions Followed by the Subjunctive (Base Form)

Examples: We **demand (that)** he **do** it.
It is **essential (that)** he **do** it.
The professor **suggested (that)** we **buy** his book.

After Single Verbs
ask*
demand
insist
move (= formally propose something in a meeting)
order*
prefer*
propose
recommend
request*
require*
suggest
urge*

After *It* + Adjective + Noun Clause
it is advisable that
it is crucial that
it is desirable that
it is essential that
it is important that
it is mandatory that
it is necessary that
it is obligatory that
it is reasonable that
it is required that
it is unnecessary that
it is unreasonable that

* These verbs also take the form verb + object pronoun + infinitive.

Examples: We **asked that** she **be** present.
We **asked her to be** present.

25 Pronunciation Table

These are the pronunciation symbols used in this text. Listen to the pronunciation of the key words.

VOWELS

Symbol	Key Word	Symbol	Key Word
i	beat, feed	ə	banana, among
ɪ	bit, did	ɚ	shirt, murder
eɪ	date, paid	aɪ	bite, cry, buy, eye
ɛ	bet, bed	aʊ	about, how
æ	bat, bad	ɔɪ	voice, boy
ɑ	box, odd, father	ɪr	beer
ɔ	bought, dog	ɛr	bare
oʊ	boat, road	ɑr	bar
ʊ	book, good	ɔr	door
u	boot, food, student	ʊr	tour
ʌ	but, mud, mother		

CONSONANTS

Symbol	Key Word	Symbol	Key Word
p	pack, happy	ʃ	ship, machine, station, special, discussion
b	back, rubber		
t	tie	ʒ	measure, vision
d	die	h	hot, who
k	came, key, quick	m	men
g	game, guest	n	sun, know, pneumonia
tʃ	church, nature, watch	ŋ	sung, ringing
dʒ	judge, general, major	w	wet, white
f	fan, photograph	l	light, long
v	van	r	right, wrong
θ	thing, breath	y	yes, use, music
ð	then, breathe	t̬	butter, bottle
s	sip, city, psychology		
z	zip, please, goes		

Glossary of Grammar Terms

action verb A verb that describes an action.

- *James* ***telecommutes*** *three days a week.*

active sentence A sentence in which the subject acts upon the object.

- ***William Shakespeare*** *wrote* ***Hamlet****.*

adjective A part of speech modifying a noun or pronoun.

- *The* ***blue*** *sofa is* ***beautiful****, but it's also* ***expensive****.*

adjective clause A clause that identifies or gives additional information about a noun.

- *The man* ***who directed the film*** *won an Oscar.*

adjective phrase A phrase that identifies or gives additional information about a noun.

- *In that movie, the actress* ***playing the heroine*** *is Penélope Cruz.*

adverb A part of speech modifying a verb, an adjective, another adverb, or an entire sentence.

- *Ben drives his* ***incredibly*** *valuable car* ***very carefully****.*

adverb clause A dependent clause that indicates how, when, where, why, or under what conditions things happen; or which establishes a contrast. An adverb clause begins with a subordinating conjunction and modifies an independent clause.

- *We're going to leave for the airport* ***as soon as Jack gets home****.*

adverb / adverbial phrase A phrase that indicates how, when, where, why, or under what conditions things happen. An adverb phrase modifies an independent clause.

- *We learned a great deal of Spanish* ***while traveling in Mexico****.*

An adverbial phrase performs the same functions as an adverb phrase but does not contain a subordinating conjunction.

- ***Having had the professor for a previous class****, I knew what to expect.*

auxiliary (helping) verb A verb that occurs with and "helps" a main verb.

- ***Did*** *Mary contact you? No. She* ***should have*** *called at least.*

base form The form of a verb listed in a dictionary. It has no endings (*-s*, *-ed*, etc.).

- *It is mandatory that Sally* ***be*** *there and* ***participate*** *in the discussion.*

causative A verb construction showing that someone arranges for or causes something to happen. ***Get*** and ***have*** are the two most common causative verbs.

- *We* ***got*** *Martha to help us when we* ***had*** *the house remodeled.*

clause A group of words with a subject and a verb that shows time. An **independent clause** can stand by itself. A **dependent clause** needs to be attached to an independent clause to be understood fully.

INDEPENDENT — DEPENDENT

- *We'll go out for dinner when Mom gets back from the bank.*

comma splice An error resulting from joining two independent clauses with only a comma.

- *I understand the point he made, however, I don't agree with it.* (comma splice)
- *I understand the point he made; however, I don't agree with it.* (correction)

common noun A noun that does not name a particular thing or individual.

- *We bought a* ***turkey****, cranberry* ***sauce****, mashed* ***potatoes****, and* ***rolls*** *for the special* ***dinner****.*

complement A noun or adjective (phrase) that describes or explains a subject or direct object.

- *Hal is* ***a man with unusual tastes****. He painted his house* ***orange****.*

compound modifier A modifier of a noun that is composed of more than one word. A compound modifier is usually hyphenated when it precedes a noun.

- *My* ***five-year-old*** *daughter can already read.*

conditional sentence A sentence containing a dependent clause showing a condition and an independent clause showing a result. The condition may or may not be fulfilled.

CONDITION — RESULT

- *If I had enough time, I would visit Morocco.*

coordinating conjunction A word connecting independent clauses or items in a series. The seven coordinating conjunctions are ***and***, ***but***, ***for***, ***nor***, ***or***, ***so***, and ***yet***.

- *Mom had forgotten to buy groceries, **so** we had a supper of cold pizza, salad, **and** water.*

count noun A noun that can be counted in its basic sense. Count nouns have plural forms.

- *The **students** in my **class** all have at least one **sibling**.*

definite article The article ***the***; it indicates that the person or thing being talked about is unique or is known or identified to the speaker and listener.

- *China is **the** most populous nation in **the** world.*

definite past The simple past form; it shows an action, state, or event at a particular time or period in the past.

- *I **lived** in Spain in the '90s and **visited** there again last year.*

dependent clause A dependent clause is a group of words that cannot stand alone as a sentence: It requires a main (independent) clause for its meaning.

MAIN CLAUSE DEPENDENT CLAUSE

- *They saw the bandit, who was wearing a bandanna.*

direct object A noun or pronoun that receives the action of a verb.

- *Martin discovered an autographed **copy** of the novel.*

direct (quoted) speech The exact words (or thoughts) of a speaker, which are enclosed in quotation marks.

- ***"Barry,"*** *Phyllis said,* ***"I want you to tell me the truth."***

embedded question A question that is inside another sentence.

- *He didn't know **what he should buy for his mother**.*

focus adverb An adverb that focuses attention on a word or phrase. Focus adverbs come before the word or phrase they focus on.

- ***Even*** *I don't support that idea. It's too radical.*

fragment A group of words that is not a complete sentence. It is often considered an error.

- *Because he doesn't know what to do about the situation.* (fragment)
- *He's asking for our help because he doesn't know what to do about the situation.* (correction)

future in the past A verb construction showing a state, action, or event now past but future from some point of time in the past.

- *We **were going to help** Tim move but couldn't. Sam said he **would help** instead.*

generic Referred to in general; including all the members of the class to which something belongs.

- ***The computer*** *has become essential in today's world.*
- ***Whales*** *are endangered.*
- ***An orangutan*** *is a primate living in Borneo and Sumatra.*

gerund A verbal noun made by adding ***-ing*** to a verb.

- *Dad loves **cooking**, and we love **eating** what he cooks.*

identifying (essential) clauses and phrases Clauses and phrases that distinguish one person or thing from others. They are not enclosed in commas.

- *The student **who is sitting at the end of the second row** is my niece.*
- *The film **starring Johnny Depp** is the one I want to see.*

if **clause** The clause in a conditional sentence that states the condition.

- ***If it rains***, *they will cancel the picnic.*

implied condition A condition that is suggested or implied but not stated fully. Implied conditional sentences use expressions such as *if so*, *if not*, *otherwise*, *with*, and *without*.

- *You may be able to get the item for half price. **If so**, please buy one for me as well. (= if you are able to get the item for half price)*

indefinite article The articles ***a*** and ***an***; they occur with count nouns and indicate that what is referred to is not a particular or identified person or thing.

- *In the last year I have bought **an** old **house** and **a** new **car**.*

indefinite past The present perfect; it shows a past action, event, or state not occurring at any particular or identified time.

- *We **have seen** that movie several times.*

indirect object A noun or pronoun that shows the person or thing that receives something as a result of the action of the verb.

- *Martin gave **Priscilla** an autographed copy of his new novel. He also gave **her** a DVD.*

indirect (reported) speech A report of the words of a speaker. Indirect speech does not include all of a speaker's exact words and is not enclosed in quotation marks.

- *Phyllis told Barry* ***that she wanted him to tell her the truth***.

infinitive ***To*** + the base form of a verb.

- *Frank Jones is said* ***to be*** *the author of that article.*

inverted condition The condition of a conditional sentence, stated without the word *if*. Inverted conditions occur with the verbs *had*, *were*, and *should*, which come first in the sentence and are followed by the subject.

- ***Had I*** *known that would happen, I never would have agreed.*

main (independent) clause A clause that can stand alone as a sentence.

MAIN CLAUSE DEPENDENT CLAUSE

- *They saw the bandit, who was wearing a bandanna.*

mixed conditional A conditional sentence that shows the hypothetical present result of a past unreal situation or the hypothetical past result of a present unreal situation.

- *If I had taken that job, I would be living in Bucharest now.*
- *Sam would have arrived by now if he were planning to come.*

modal (auxiliary) A type of helping verb. ***Can***, ***could***, ***had better***, ***may***, ***might***, ***must***, ***ought to***, ***shall***, ***should***, ***will***, and ***would*** are modals. They each have one form and no endings.

- *You certainly* ***can*** *do that; the question is whether you* ***should*** *do it.*

modal-like expression An expression with a meaning similar to that of a modal. Modal-like expressions have endings and show time.

- *Russell* ***has to*** *find a new job.*

non-action (stative) verb A verb that in its basic sense does not show action.

- *It* ***seems*** *to me that Joe* ***has*** *a problem.*

non-count noun A noun that in its basic sense cannot be counted.

- ***Smoke*** *from the* ***fire*** *filled the* ***air***.

nonidentifying (nonessential) clauses and phrases Clauses and phrases that add extra information but do not distinguish one person or thing from others. They are enclosed in commas.

- *Henry,* ***who is a member of the hockey team,*** *is also a star basketball player.*

noun clause A dependent clause that performs the same function as a noun. Noun clauses function as subjects, objects, objects of prepositions, and complements.

- ***What I want to do*** *is spend a week relaxing on the beach.*

noun modifier A noun that modifies another noun.

- *What did you buy,* ***milk*** *chocolate or* ***chocolate*** *milk?*

parallelism (parallel structure) The placing of items in a series in the same grammatical form.

- *Marie loves* ***hiking***, ***riding*** *horses, and* ***collecting*** *artifacts.*

participial adjective An adjective formed from present and past participial forms of verbs.

- *The* ***bored*** *students were not paying attention to the* ***boring*** *speaker.*

passive causative A verb structure formed with ***have*** or ***get*** + **object** + **past participle**. It is used to talk about services that you arrange for someone to do for you.

- *I usually* ***have my dresses made*** *by Chantal.*

passive sentence A sentence that shows the subject being acted upon by the object.

- **Hamlet** *was written by* **William Shakespeare**.

perfect forms Verb constructions formed with the auxiliary verbs ***had***, ***has***, and ***have*** and a past participle. They include the **past perfect**, **present perfect**, and **future perfect**.

- *I* ***had*** *never* ***been*** *to Brazil before 1990. Since then* ***I've been*** *there eight times. By this time next year,* ***I'll have been*** *there ten times.*

phrase A group of related words without a subject or a verb showing time.

- ***Relaxing in the hammock***, *I pondered my future.*

proper noun The name of a particular individual or thing. Proper nouns are capitalized.

- ***Stella*** *and I both think that* ***Rio de Janeiro*** *and* ***Paris*** *are the world's two most beautiful cities.*

quantifier A word or phrase showing the amount or number of something.

- *Ken earned* ***a lot of*** *money selling books. I bought* ***a few of*** *them myself.*

relative pronoun A pronoun used to form adjective clauses. ***That***, ***when***, ***where***, ***which***, ***who***, ***whom***, and ***whose*** are relative pronouns.

- *The fairy tale* ***that*** *always scared me when I was a child was "Rumpelstiltskin."*

reporting verb A verb such as ***said***, ***told***, or ***asked***, which introduces both direct and indirect speech. It can also come after the quotation in direct speech.

- *The mayor* ***said****, "I've read the report."* OR *"I've read the report," the mayor* ***said****.*

result clause The clause in a conditional sentence that indicates what happens if the condition occurs.

- *If it rains,* ***they'll cancel the picnic****.*

run-on sentence An error resulting from the joining of two independent clauses with no punctuation.

- *I think therefore, I am.* (run-on sentence)
- *I think; therefore, I am.* (correction)

sentence adverb An adverb that modifies an entire sentence. It can occur at the beginning, in the middle, or at the end of a sentence.

- ***Fortunately,*** *Sarah was not hurt badly in the accident.*

stative passive A passive form used to describe situations or states.

- *North and South America* ***are connected by*** *the Isthmus of Panama.*

subjunctive A verb form using the base form of a verb and normally following a verb or expression showing advice, necessity, or urgency. The verb *be* has the special subjunctive form *were*, which is used for all persons.

- *We always* ***insist*** *that our daughter* ***do*** *her homework before watching TV.*
- *If I* ***were*** *you, I would pay off my mortgage as soon as possible.*

subordinating conjunction A connecting word used to begin an adverb clause.

- *We were relieved* ***when*** *Jack finally called at 1 A.M.*

tag question A statement + tag. The **tag** is a short question that follows the statement. Tag questions are used to check information or comment on a situation.

- *She's an actor,* ***isn't she?***

topic sentence A general sentence that indicates the content of a paragraph.

- *There are several things to keep in mind when you visit a Japanese home.*

transition A word or phrase showing a connection between sentences or between larger blocks of text.

- *Climate change is a serious problem.* ***However,*** *it is not as serious as the problem of poverty.*

unreal conditional sentence A sentence that talks about untrue, imagined, or impossible conditions and their results.

- *If I were you, I would study a lot harder.*

zero article The absence of a definite or indefinite article. The zero article occurs before unidentified plurals or non-count nouns.

- ***Whales*** *are endangered.*
- ***Water*** *is necessary for survival.*

Unit Review Answer Key

Note: In this answer key, where the contracted verb form is given, it is the preferred form, though the full form is also acceptable. Where the full verb form is given, it is the preferred form, though the contracted form is also acceptable.

UNIT 1

A **1.** are doing **2.** loves **3.** takes **4.** 'm getting **5.** seem **6.** attends **7.** is playing **8.** like

B **1.** have lived **2.** has directed **3.** has been working **4.** have owned **5.** have been remodeling **6.** has been running

C **1.** B **2.** C **3.** D **4.** B **5.** A **6.** D

UNIT 2

A **1.** got **2.** have done **3.** have been **4.** have visited **5.** was **6.** went **7.** wanted **8.** have never known

B **1.** met **2.** attended **3.** had invited **4.** was **5.** had known **6.** proposed

C **1.** D **2.** B **3.** A **4.** D **5.** C **6.** D

UNIT 3

A **1.** have to **2.** 'll be **3.** 'll call **4.** lets **5.** 'll stop by **6.** get

B **1.** taking **2.** leaves OR is leaving **3.** get **4.** 'll have been flying OR will have flown **5.** 'll be **6.** 're spending OR 'll spend OR 're going to spend **7.** 'll send **8.** 're

C **1.** C **2.** B **3.** C **4.** A **5.** C **6.** D

UNIT 4

A **1.** weren't supposed to **2.** didn't have to **3.** shouldn't have **4.** could **5.** 'd better not **6.** must have **7.** 's got to **8.** aren't allowed to **9.** could have **10.** Hadn't we better

B **1.** must OR have got to **2.** should **3.** can't OR must not **4.** must (simply) OR has to (simply) **5.** should you

C **1.** A **2.** A **3.** C **4.** B **5.** C

UNIT 5

A **1.** must **2.** might **3.** might **4.** couldn't **5.** should **6.** ought not to **7.** had to **8.** 's got to be **9.** must have been **10.** must

B *Possible answers*
1. Jeremy may have had to work late.
2. Mari must have missed her flight.
3. They can't have heard the news.
4. We should know the answer soon.
5. You could have gotten a scholarship.

C **1.** C **2.** C **3.** C **4.** A **5.** B

UNIT 6

A **1.** C **2.** NC **3.** NC **4.** C **5.** NC **6.** C **7.** NC

B **1. a.** any **b.** a drop of
2. a. some **b.** some pieces of
3. a. any **b.** a grain of
4. a. some **b.** a game of

C **1.** C **2.** D **3.** C **4.** B **5.** A

UNIT 7

A **1.** G **2.** N **3.** D **4.** G **5.** G **6.** D **7.** N **8.** N

B **1.** The **2.** a **3.** the **4.** an **5.** The **6.** — **7.** —

C **1.** B **2.** C **3.** A **4.** B **5.** D

UNIT 8

A **1.** Most **2.** amount of **3.** any **4.** a lot of **5.** a couple of **6.** The number of **7.** many **8.** little **9.** plenty of **10.** no

B *Possible answers*
1. many **2.** much **3.** a lot of **4.** a few **5.** a lot of **6.** Every

C **1.** B **2.** C **3.** D **4.** A

UNIT 9

A 1. sweltering humid summer
2. chilly late winter
3. new pink silk
4. handsome young European
5. beautiful new brick
6. dirty little old

B 1. an eleven-year-old son
2. a 900-page novel
3. a short-haired bandit
4. six 55-minute periods
5. a voter-initiated proposal
6. strange-looking people
7. Chinese ivory statue
8. a gray short-haired cat

C 1. A 2. C 3. D 4. C 5. C

UNIT 10

A 1. what the punch line of the joke was
2. why he always tells that joke
3. what time the meeting starts
4. what *hyperbole* means
5. whether Samira liked the party
6. what Mary does for a living
7. how long she's been a writer
8. whether or not

B 1. what Mary meant
2. whether or not Bob
3. Whatever you want
4. That Alison loves Kahlil
5. what we should give Russell
6. the fact that Ben helped us
7. that she was

C 1. D 2. B 3. A 4. C

UNIT 11

A 1. it was
2. had finished
3. if she was
4. to be sure
5. not to
6. if he would
7. she would come by
8. could

B 1. if he would
2. told
3. she didn't feel well OR, "I don't . . ."
4. needed
5. if he had ever
6. have seen
7. not to
8. "We didn't."

C 1. D 2. A 3. C 4. A 5. C

UNIT 12

A 1. who 2. where 3. whom 4. whose 5. which 6. when 7. sees 8. who

B 1. who lives next door
2. The book that Sara bought OR The book Sara bought
3. whose dog is barking
4. whom we met
5. where I was born
6. when we spoke
7. ,who is a student,
8. whose parents work here

C 1. A 2. A 3. D 4. D

UNIT 13

A 1. which
2. whose
3. whom
4. which
5. whom
6. interested
7. which was
8. starring

B 1. which 2. which 3. whom 4. which 5. whom 6. who 7. who 8. which

C 1. C 2. C 3. C 4. D

UNIT 14

A 1. is being constructed
2. had his car serviced
3. were caught
4. died
5. been
6. being
7. been
8. the job done by noon

B 1. is reported
2. is being reported
3. has been reported
4. was reported
5. was being reported
6. had been reported
7. will be reported
8. will have been reported

C 1. B 2. A 3. B 4. D

UNIT 15

A 1. is bordered by
2. as
3. is claimed
4. is believed to be
5. by
6. is located in
7. is thought to
8. are alleged

B 1. by
2. is said
3. is surrounded
4. are alleged
5. are believed
6. is claimed
7. of
8. is regarded

C 1. C 2. B 3. A 4. D

UNIT 16

A **1.** not smoking
2. shopping
3. Emiko's
4. Not giving
5. to having
6. seeing
7. being awakened
8. not having been invited

B **1.** finishing
2. Having missed
3. coming
4. driving
5. being told
6. seeing
7. having taken
8. mentioning

C **1.** B **2.** A **3.** C **4.** D

UNIT 17

A **1.** to do
2. to accept
3. to give up
4. smoking
5. to lock
6. locked
7. to confront
8. to be criticized

B **1.** strong enough
2. warned you
3. to postpone
4. be typed
5. to have had
6. not to get
7. to have forgotten
8. to finish

C **1.** D **2.** B **3.** A **4.** C

UNIT 18

A **1.** just don't
2. had we
3. he even thinks
4. only members
5. don't just
6. even he can
7. does Eva
8. comes the train

B **1.** are kangaroos
2. ,clearly
3. but he should
4. does our team lose
5. Just members
6. is the money
7. Actually,
8. goes the plane

C **1.** C **2.** D **3.** D **4.** A

UNIT 19

A **1.** unless
2. Even though
3. in case
4. As
5. Once
6. now that
7. wherever
8. as soon as

B **1.** whenever
2. As soon as
3. Even if
4. Because
5. Only if
6. Although
7. Whereas
8. unless

C **1.** B **2.** A **3.** A **4.** D

UNIT 20

A **1.** Not knowing
2. Caught cheating
3. Having gotten the tickets
4. before leaving
5. On realizing
6. Relaxing
7. Having visited
8. being given

B **1.** Having heard
2. while doing
3. Having eaten
4. finishing
5. Having been
6. being taken
7. Fearing
8. Given

C **1.** A **2.** C **3.** D **4.** B

UNIT 21

A **1.** however
2. though
3. Because
4. consequently
5. besides
6. and
7. or
8. otherwise

B *Possible answers*
1. so
2. besides
3. or
4. consequently
5. Although
6. After
7. Besides
8. consequently

C **1.** B **2.** C **3.** D **4.** B

UNIT 22

A **1.** rains
2. doesn't
3. rained
4. wouldn't
5. weren't
6. hadn't rained
7. 'd
8. were going to

B **1.** wishes
2. wouldn't
3. hadn't
4. have had to
5. wouldn't
6. made
7. wouldn't
8. had listened

C **1.** B **2.** A **3.** C **4.** D

UNIT 23

A **1.** Without
2. If not
3. If so
4. otherwise
5. With
6. if not
7. without
8. with

B *Possible answers*
1. otherwise
2. If I hadn't
3. call
4. Should that happen
5. But for
6. understand
7. if so
8. likes

C **1.** A **2.** B **3.** C **4.** B

Games Answer Key

UNIT 7

9. Game

Answers				
The type of tree that used to grow on Easter Island What is the (Chilean) wine palm?	The ship that sank in the Atlantic in 1912 on its first voyage What is the *Titanic*?	The place in a city or town where one keeps one's money What is a / the bank?	The home country of the first European to see Easter Island What is Holland / the Netherlands?	The name of the people who settled Easter Island Who are the Polynesians?
The animals that have been reintroduced in national parks What are wolves?	The circular object that was not used in moving the Easter Island statues What is the wheel?	The outer covering of a tree What is bark?	The body of water in which Easter Island is located What is the Pacific (Ocean)?	The people in a particular circumstance who have a great deal of money Who are the rich / wealthy?
The material from which the Easter Island statues are made What is stone?	A form of precipitation that is necessary for crops to grow What is rain?	A form of energy that involves the use of radioactive material What is nuclear power?	The device invented by Easter Islanders to move their statues What is the / a canoe rail?	A liquid substance used to produce gasoline What is petroleum / oil?
The place in a city or town where one can mail letters What is a / the post office?	A type of natural phenomenon that devastated the country of Haiti in 2010 What is an earthquake?	The part of the human body that is the seat of intelligence What is the brain?	The nation over which Hurricane Katrina formed What is the Bahamas?	The electronic device invented in 1944 by Farnsworth and Zorinsky What is the computer?
A type of animal killed by wolves in Yellowstone National Park What is the / an elk?	A woodwind instrument that uses a reed and was invented about 1700 What is a / the clarinet?	The people in a particular circumstance who are badly off economically Who are the poor?	A polluting material in the ocean that birds and fish mistake for food What is plastic?	In the Arctic and subarctic region, the part of the soil that doesn't thaw in the summer What is (the) permafrost?

8. Game

Team A

1. **A:** Which country has fewer people, Canada or Mexico?
   B: Canada has fewer people.

2. **A:** Which country has more land area, Canada or the United States?
   B: Canada has more land area.

3. **A:** Which country produces less oil, Venezuela or Mexico?
   B: Venezuela produces less oil.

4. **A:** Which country has no snowfall, Somalia or Tanzania?
   B: Somalia has no snowfall.

5. **A:** Which country has fewer rivers, Libya or Nigeria?
   B: Libya has fewer rivers.

6. **A:** Which country has a smaller number of people, Monaco or Cyprus?
   B: Monaco has a smaller number of people.

7. **A:** Which country produces a large amount of gold, Nigeria or South Africa?
   B: South Africa produces a large amount of gold.

8. **A:** Which city has less rainfall, Aswan, Egypt, or Athens, Greece?
   B: Aswan, Egypt, has less rainfall.

Team B

1. **A:** Which country has fewer people, Great Britain or Spain?
   B: Spain has fewer people.

2. **A:** Which country has more land area, Australia or Brazil?
   B: Brazil has more land area.

3. **A:** Which country produces less oil, the United States or Saudi Arabia?
   B: The United States produces less oil.

4. **A:** Which country has no military, Colombia or Costa Rica?
   B: Costa Rica has no military.

5. **A:** Which country has fewer rivers, Yemen or Turkey?
   B: Yemen has fewer rivers.

6. **A:** Which country has a smaller number of people, San Marino or Kuwait?
   B: San Marino has a smaller number of people.

7. **A:** Which country uses a larger amount of nuclear energy, the Netherlands or France?
   B: France uses a larger amount of nuclear energy.

8. **A:** Which city has less rainfall, Antofagasta, Chile, or Nairobi, Kenya?
   B: Antofagasta, Chile, has less rainfall.

8. Game

Team A

1. **A:** Which island is composed of the nations of Haiti and the Dominican Republic?
   B: Hispaniola is composed of the nations of Haiti and the Dominican Republic.

2. **A:** Which Central American country is bordered by Panama and Nicaragua?
   B: Costa Rica is bordered by Panama and Nicaragua.

3. **A:** Which people are considered by some to be the descendants of Atlanteans?
   B: The Basque people are considered by some to be the descendants of Atlanteans.

4. **A:** Which legendary creature is thought to live in the Himalayas?
   B: The yeti is thought to live in the Himalayas.

5. **A:** Which individual is claimed to have been the assassin of U.S. President John F. Kennedy?
   B: Lee Harvey Oswald is claimed to have been the assassin of U.S. President John F. Kennedy.

6. **A:** Which individuals are regarded as great humanitarians?
   B: Albert Schweitzer and Mother Teresa are regarded as great humanitarians.

Team B

1. **A:** Which Caribbean nation is composed of many islands?
   B: The Bahamas is composed of many islands.

2. **A:** Which Caribbean nation is located about 90 miles south of Florida?
   B: Cuba is located about 90 miles south of Florida.

3. **A:** Which forest creature is said to live in the Pacific Northwest?
   B: Bigfoot is said to live in the Pacific Northwest.

4. **A:** Which lost continent is thought to have been located in the Atlantic Ocean?
   B: Atlantis is thought to have been located in the Atlantic Ocean.

5. **A:** Which planet was thought to be the center of the universe before Copernicus?
   B: Earth was thought to be the center of the universe before Copernicus.

6. **A:** Which presidents are regarded by many as the greatest American presidents?
   B: George Washington and Abraham Lincoln are regarded by many as the greatest American presidents.

9. Conditional Game

Team A

1. **A:** Where would you be if you were in the capital of Honduras?
   B: You would be in Tegucigalpa if you were in the capital of Honduras.

2. **A:** How old would you have to be if you were the president of the United States?
   B: You would have to be at least 35 years old if you were the president of the United States.

3. **A:** Where would you be traveling if the monetary unit were the won?
   B: You would be traveling in North or South Korea if the monetary unit were the won.

4. **A:** Where would you be if you were visiting Angkor Wat?
   B: You would be in Cambodia if you were visiting Angkor Wat.

5. **A:** Who would you have been if you had been the emperor of France in 1804?
   B: You would have been Napoleon if you had been the emperor of France in 1804.

6. **A:** Who would you have been if you had been the first prime minister of India?
   B: You would have been Jawaharlal Nehru if you had been the first prime minister of India.

7. **A:** What country would you have been from if you were Marco Polo?
   B: You would have been from Italy if you had been Marco Polo.

8. **A:** What mountain would you have climbed if you had been with Edmund Hillary and Tenzing Norgay?
   B: You would have climbed Mt. Everest if you had been with Edmund Hillary and Tenzing Norgay.

Team B

1. **A:** How old would you be if you were an octogenarian?
   B: You would be between 80 and 89 if you were an octogenarian.

2. **A:** Where would you be traveling if you were in Machu Picchu?
   B: You would be traveling in Peru if you were in Machu Picchu.

3. **A:** What would you be if you were the largest mammal?
   B: You would be a blue whale if you were the largest mammal.

4. **A:** What country would you be in if you were standing and looking at Angel Falls?
   B: You would be in Venezuela if you were standing and looking at Angel Falls.

5. **A:** Who would you have been if you had been the inventor of the telephone?
   B: You would have been Alexander Graham Bell if you had been the inventor of the telephone.

6. **A:** What kind of creature would you have been if you had been a stegosaurus?
   B: You would have been a dinosaur if you had been a stegosaurus.

7. **A:** What would your occupation have been if you had been Genghis Khan?
   B: You would have been an emperor if you had been Genghis Khan.

8. **A:** Who would you have been if you had been Siddartha Gautama?
   B: You would have been the founder of Buddhism if you had been Siddartha Gautama.

CREDITS

PHOTO CREDITS:

Page 1 (left) Shutterstock.com, (right) AP Images/Scott Cohen; **p. 2** Shutterstock.com; **p. 15** AP Images/Scott Cohen; **p. 23** David Howells; **p. 28** Printed by permission of the Norman Rockwell Family Agency. Copyright © 1930 the Norman Rockwell Family Entities; **p. 34** Shutterstock.com; **p. 49** (left) Stock Montage/Getty Images, (right) Shutterstock.com; **p. 57** Bruce Stephens/Impact Photos/Imagestate; **p. 69** Stock Montage/Getty Images; **p. 70** Steve Wood/Getty Images; **p. 77** Shutterstock.com; **p. 89** (left) Shutterstock.com, (right) Bettmann/Corbis; **p. 105** Arte Wolfe/Getty Images; **p. 115** (left) Shutterstock.com, (right) Shutterstock.com; **p. 116** Shutterstock.com; **p. 127** iStockphoto.com; **p. 135** AP Images/Petr David Josek; **p. 147** Bettmann/Corbis; **p. 173** Copyright © 2011 photolibrary.com; **p. 195** (left) Shutterstock.com, (right) Warner Bros./Photofest; **p. 196** Shutterstock.com; **p. 197** Danita Delimont/Alamy; **p. 211** Warner Bros./Photofest; **p. 212** (top) Moviestore collection Ltd/Alamy, (bottom) AF archive/Alamy; **p. 233** (left) Dale O'Dell/SuperStock, (right) Classic Image/Alamy; **p. 244** AP Images/The Columbian/Dave Olson; **p. 247** (left) Dale O'Dell/SuperStock, (right) AP Images/Eric Draper; **p. 263** (top left) Eric Schaal/Getty Images, (top right) Eye Ubiquitous/Alamy, (bottom left) Classic Image/Alamy, (bottom right) Gianni Dagli Orti/Corbis; **p. 269** (left) Pictorial Press Ltd/Alamy, (right) Julian Hirshowitz/Corbis; **p. 285** Pictorial Press Ltd/Alamy; **p. 300** Julian Hirshowitz/Corbis; **p. 307** (left) AP Images/Lou Requena, (right) Digital Vision/Getty Images; **p. 308** Pearson Education; **p. 318** Pearson Education; **p. 323** Shutterstock.com; **p. 324** Tom & Dee Ann McCarthy/Corbis; **p. 337** AP Images/Lou Requena; **p. 340** AP Images/FILES; **p. 358** Digital Vision/Getty Images; **p. 371** M.Flynn/Alamy; **p. 372** Bonnie Kamin/PhotoEdit; **p. 377** (left) Corbis RF/Alamy, (right) Shutterstock.com; **p. 378** Corbis RF/Alamy; **p. 396** Shutterstock.com; **p. 411** (top left) Shutterstock.com, (top right) Shutterstock.com, (bottom left) Shutterstock.com, (bottom right) Shutterstock.com.

TEXT CREDITS:

Pages 15–16: "A Match Made in the Mall" Used with permission of The Associated Press Copyright © 2010. All rights reserved.

Page 23: "From *The Washington Post,* © (2/12/2001) The Washington Post. All rights reserved. Used by permission and protected by the Copyright laws of the United States. The printing, copying, redistribution, or retransmission of the Material without express written permission is prohibited."

Pages 50–51: Based on information in Rex Shelley, *Culture Shock: Japan* (Portland, OR: Graphic Arts Publishing, 1993).

Pages 69–70: Based on information in "St. Brendan's Isle. www.castletownpress.net/brendan.htm and "Who the Heck Did 'Discover' the New World?" by Donald Dale Jackson. *Smithsonian,* September 1991, pp. 76–85. Reprinted with permission.

Page 79: "Why We Itch" from *Imponderables* ©1986, 1987, a book by David Feldman.

Pages 105–106: Based on Jared Diamond, "Twilight at Easter," *The New York Review of Books.*

Page 112: EARTHWEEK by Steve Newman © *Earth Environment Service.* Dist. By UNIVERSAL UCLICK. Reprinted with permission. All rights reserved.

Page 128: *The World Almanac and Book of Facts,* 2004 (New York: World Almanac Education Group, Inc., 2004) and *The World Almanac and Book of Facts,* 2010 (New York: World Almanac Education Group, Inc., 2010).

Page 146: Adapted from the introduction to *Appointment in Samarra* by John O'Hara. New York: Harcourt, Brace, and Company, 1934. Story originally written by W. Somerset Maugham in his play *Sheppey.*

Pages 156–157: Author unknown. The story is adapted from one that has been circulating on the Internet for a number of years.

Page 165: Includes material adapted from "Humor," *The World Book Encyclopedia,* Volume H. (Chicago: World Book, 1998), pp. 435–436; and "Humour and Wit," *Encyclopedia Britannica,* Macropaedia (Chicago: Encyclopedia, 1998), p. 686.

Page 170: David Field, "They *Do* Have a Sense of Humor, " *USA Today,* September 22, 1998. Reprinted with permission.

Pages 173–174: Based on information in online article "Leadership and Communication for Business Professionals." August 12, 2008.

Pages 196–197: Bryce, Tim. *Morphing into the Real World: The Handbook for Entering the Work Force.* MBA Press. Copyright 2007 Tim Bryce. Palm Harbor, FL.

Pages 223, 227: "A Beautiful Mind", from LEONARD MALTIN'S MOVIE AND VIDEO GUIDE 2003 by Leonard Maltin, copyright ©1991–1999, 2000–2004 by Leonard Maltin. Used by permission of Dutton Signet, a division of Penguin Group (USA) Inc.
Pages 234–235: Based on information in Mark McGwire, "15 Minutes of Fame," *Biography Magazine,* September 1998; and Richard Severn, " D.B. Cooper: Perfect Crime or Perfect Folly?" *Seattle Times,* November 17, 1996.
Pages 250–251: Based on the article "Body Ritual Among the Nacirema" by Horace Minor (found in *American Anthropologist,* Vol. 58. Vol. 1 156 pp.18–21).
Pages 270–271: Based on Judith Viorst's essay "Friends, Good Friends, and Such Good Friends" in Alfred Rosa and Paul Eschholz, eds., *Models for Writers: Short Essays for Composition,* 3rd Ed. New York: St. Martin's Press, 1989.
Pages 323–324: Includes material based on Simon Haydon's "The Only Foul He Saw Was on the U.S." The Associated Press, June 19, 2010.
Pages 340–341: Based on information in Brad Darrach's "Journey: A Brave Family Changes Horror into Healing after a Child Dies," *Life,* October 1, 1995, pp. 42+
Page 348: Sutapa Mukerjee, "A Caring Elephant That Died of Grief," *The Seattle Post-Intelligencer*, May 6, 1999, Copyright: The Associated Press.
Pages 358–359: "How Quickly We Forget" *U.S. News and World Report,* October 13, 1997, p. 52. Reprinted by permission.
Pages 396–397: Based on information in: "How to Survive a Messy Roommate." http://wikihow.com/Survive-a-Messy-Roommate.

ILLUSTRATION CREDITS:

Steve Attoe: pp. 32, 167, 251, 406; **Burmar Technical Corporation:** p. 257; **A.J. Garces:** p. 235; **Chris Gash:** pp. 80, 260; **ElectraGraphics, Inc./Gene Gonzales:** pp. 8, 59, 90, 330, 396; **David Klug:** p. 336; **Jock MacRae:** p. 332; **Andy Myer:** p. 367; **Thomas Newsom:** pp. 188, 387, 388; **Dusan Petricic:** pp. 25, 65, 66, 120, 350, 351; **Susan Scott:** pp. 225, 369; **Meryl Treatner:** p. 51

INDEX

This index is for the full and split editions. All entries are in the full book. Entries for Volume A of the split edition are in black. Entries for Volume B are in red.